SWIFT AT MOOR PARK

when He was in Italy, was called Wottoni, therefore, He should be called so in England; And I advise Him, that it should be Wottoni in His next Edition.

But 'tis worth considering what kind of Person our Reflecter has thought proper for such a Cavil: One brought up and long conversant with Persons of the greatest Quality at home and abroad; In Courts, in Parliaments, in privy Councils, in Foreign Embassys, in the Mediations And the great Assemblyes met upon those Occasions of generall Peace in Christendom; And yet perhaps more ~~distinguisht~~ knowne by his Writings than by the great Employments He has had or refused; And this is the Person Mr Wotton pursues so insolently with a pitifull Grammaticall Criticism, and a mistaken one too.

One would wonder who this great man should be, that ups both Antients and Moderns with such an Arrogance; Why, 'tis a young Scholar that confesses He owes all the Comforts

of

Sir William Temple on himself,
as copied by his secretary Swift.

From Temple's "Hints: written at the Desire of D^r. F. and of His Friend" (Rothschild Collection no. 2253), ca. 1697, later reworked and expanded into the essay *Some Thoughts Upon Reviewing the Essay of Antient and Modern Learning*. Reproduced by permission of the Master and Fellows of Trinity College, Cambridge. In his own hand, Temple has modestly crossed out the word "distinguisht" and replaced it with "knowne."

SWIFT
AT MOOR PARK

*Problems in
Biography and Criticism*

A. C. ELIAS, JR.

THE UNIVERSITY OF PENNSYLVANIA PRESS
Philadelphia
1982

Library of Congress Cataloging in Publication Data

Elias, A.C.
    Swift at Moor Park.

    Includes bibliographical references and index.
    1. Swift, Jonathan, 1667–1745. 2. Temple,
William, Sir, 1628–1699. 3. Moor Park (Surrey)
4. Authors, Irish—18th century—Biography.
5. Statesmen—Great Britain—Biography.
I. Title.
PR3726.E4   828'.509 [B]   81–14830
ISBN 0–8122–7822–4   AACR2

Printed in the United States of America

In Memoriam
JAMES MARSHALL OSBORN

Contents

Foreword

This is a study involving many minor, often complicated matters, which together raise major questions about Swift's life and art. My subject is the first decade of Swift's career, a period which has more often inspired broad assertion than thorough investigation. Of the fragmentary evidence which survives, much has gone unevaluated and some ignored. Redressing the balance may require further work, but the study which follows offers a foundation for it.

Few of us delight in proving our expectations wrong at every turn, and we enjoy it even less if we conclude our search with fewer certainties than we felt in beginning it. I started work with full confidence that I would soon find confirmation for my beliefs, a compound of all the usual assumptions and conclusions about Swift and his work in the 1690s. One by one I have had to abandon them, and with them the clear if somewhat two-dimensional mental image of Swift which they conveyed. In their place I can find nothing half so neat, or simple, or comforting—only the sense of a peculiar consistency in the evidence I have dealt with, and an even stronger feeling that it shows the imprint of an intelligence which is both very different from, and a good deal more powerful than, what we usually like to imagine in Swift as a young man. The same holds true in a way for his work of the period, from the most laughable ode to *A Tale of a Tub*. The face and personality which lie behind them—Swift's precise convictions, motivations, and intentions at Moor Park—I am somewhat less ready to answer for in a positive sense, beyond the impression that he enjoyed his mischief and guarded his privacy. Further research should help to narrow the possibilities, supply more details, and advance the work of reassessing his satiric gift, not just in the 1690s but in the decades which followed. At Moor Park, I believe, lie the figures which allow a more accurate reckoning of Swift's peculiar greatness. The skills which he sharpened there he never forgot, and the impulse which prompted his Moor Park satires served him well long afterwards.

If my findings were unexpected, so too was the route I eventually followed to them—largely determined by the fragmentary nature of the record for Swift's career in the 1690s. I began by inspecting his work in editing Temple's *Letters* (under Temple's supervision) and ended, not as I had hoped, with lessons I could apply to Swift's treatment of his own correspondence thirty-odd years later but with matters of far broader literary implications. In between, I investigated Swift's translations from Temple's French (again for the *Letters*), other duties which Temple assigned his secretaries in the 1690s (most easily traceable for Thomas Swift, Swift's cousin and temporary replacement at Moor Park), Temple's Moor Park estate papers (1698–99), Swift's debatable references to Temple in the 1690s and later (including the early odes), the traditions of Swift biography which have discouraged fresh research on the Moor Park period, and some of the many Temple echoes and analogues in *A Tale of a Tub*.

Along the way I have come to question much of the literary criticism dealing with Swift's writings, more for its method than its findings. Of all major authors in English, Swift is probably the hardest for modern critics to cope with—not only because he habitually mocks all that we academics hold dear but also because he affects us in ways which our training leaves us handicapped in dealing with. When we teach ourselves to read and analyze literature with professorial dispassion, we find ourselves hamstrung when dealing with an author skilled at playing tricks with his readers—provoking their laughter in unsettling ways, stirring them up obscurely, making fools of them. Before we can analyze the literary ways and means of Swift's satire, we may find that we need to confess how badly we've been stung by it—an awkward position at best, and for intellectuals a well-nigh intolerable one. For most of us concerned with Swift, self-esteem is at stake too strongly, too obscurely, in too many ways. We cannot quite trust ourselves. It is little wonder that Swift criticism has demonstrated such bewildering variety and vehemence over the years, even apart from the predictable effects of changing critical fashions.

We need to do better. Beginning with the documentary record—studying it thoroughly, analyzing it, where possible extending it, and seeing where it leads before we try to apply it—offers a less capricious basis for literary criticism than the more traditional approach of reading a text a few times and then consulting the secondary literature about it. There is a better chance that the available evidence will help determine our findings, instead of the other way around. By narrowing the range of options open to us, the inglorious business of appraising transcripts and autographs, unsorting variant editions, and tracing through biographical minutiae Swift's circumstances, likely purposes, and intended readerships at the time of composition should help point the way towards less subjective critical solutions. If we manage to go astray even so, it at least gives others a means of tracing and profiting from our mistakes. Meanwhile it should also help us avoid the pitfalls of the quasi-scholarly history-of-ideas approach to criticism, which allows the critic to seize upon some cultural or intellectual trend of Swift's time (a time nearly as diverse and bewildering as our own) to help him work out his reactions to Swift. Though otherwise a critic in the traditional mold, John Traugott may have a point when he grumbles about "the pseudo-scientific determinism in scholarship that explains [away] a refractory writer by a system of ideas which were, we are told, his heritage and environment." As a result, he notes, we are presented with a Swift who not only fits neatly into standard categories but also bears a frequent resemblance to the critic himself—a Swift who "comes to seem much like a university lecturer." We know Swift's work to be the product of his life and personality, but his contemporaries found that personality no easy matter to sort out. As much today as in his own time, there are no safe short-cuts.

For more than the usual reasons, then, what matters most in the following study is its documentary evidence, duly weighed, collated, and analyzed. Here I have usually aimed at fullness in what I treat, though it may make for slower reading than a more generalized discussion would, especially in the troublesome but essential business of establishing the texts which shed light on Swift's secretarial duties. For the same reason I have allowed myself a good deal of latitude in my notes, both in frequency and length. Many are endnotes, or even short appendices, rather than footnotes in the usual sense. A reader should be able to move through the text without needing to turn to the end to consult them. Instead they chiefly address themselves to the student or working scholar who wishes to pursue a particular point in greater detail. Besides citing my sources, they may provide contexts governing interpretation, list additional pertinent sources, evaluate the sources' reliability, suggest areas for further research, or develop points which may prove useful for the student to know but which would only introduce needless interruptions or digressions in the text itself.

Behind nearly every published research piece stand many librarians, colleagues, correspondents, and friends who have helped it on its way, even when they themselves remained ignorant of its scope or findings. For especially generous aid or encouragement, at one stage or another in my work, I thank Shirley F. Corke, Frank H. Ellis, Philip Gaskell, Robert D. Hume, Stephen R. Parks, Elizabeth G. Riely, Grace A. Savage, Annick Scouten-Rouet, and David Woolley. An even greater debt of gratitude, if possible, is owing to Arthur H. Scouten, who continued his support and encouragement even after wading through two successive drafts of the piece. In addition I am grateful to Hugh Amory, Andrea M. Bassett, Suzanne Bolan, Lord Brabourne and the Trustees of the Broadlands Archive, J. K. Bridcut, A. P. Burton, Carl P. Daw, W. A. N. Figgis, P. J. Gautrey, the late Arthur Halcrow, Nancy P. Homans, Theodore Hofmann, Trevor Kaye, D. F. Lamb, Louis A. Landa, the Very Rev. Henry A. Lillie, George P. Mayhew, Colin L. McKelvie, G. C. R. Morris, Lady Osborn, Lyman Riley, Marte E. Shaw, Edwin Wolf 2nd, James Woolley, and many others including staff members at the several libraries I have consulted, especially the Beinecke at Yale, the Public Record Office in London, the Haverford and Bryn Mawr college libraries, the Library Company of Philadelphia, and the Van Pelt Library at the University of Pennsylvania. Special thanks are due to my uncomplaining proofreader and arbiter of style, Susan H. Elias. For permission to inspect and quote manuscript materials, I have made specific acknowledgments in the endnotes. In the case of two especially useful collections—the Osborn Collection at Yale and the Rothschild Collection at Trinity College, Cambridge—an additional acknowledgment seems in order, to the late James M. Osborn on the one hand, and on the other to Lord Rothschild and the Master and Fellows of Trinity. On a variety of heads, Dr. Osborn also provided shrewd counsel and unfailing encouragement, from the first stages of my project in 1969 until shortly before his death in 1976. It seems only right that this book be inscribed to his memory.

A. C. E.

Philadelphia

SWIFT AT MOOR PARK

CHAPTER ONE

Swift as Secretary:

The Downton Transcript and Swift's Translations from Temple's French Letters

In his first major publishing venture, Jonathan Swift appeared before the world not as an author in his own right but as the loyal secretary, amanuensis, and translator of Sir William Temple, the diplomat who had negotiated the popular but ineffectual Triple Alliance of 1668 and who later retired to compose, publish, or ready for the press the memoirs and other writings on which his fame as a statesman and a thinker was largely to rest. Late in 1699, not long after Temple died at the age of seventy, Swift brought out his two-volume *Letters*.[1] Though often overlooked by Swiftians, they bear witness to one of the most important yet problematic periods in his life—the years between 1689 and 1699, which he largely spent working for Temple. Except for two attempts at pursuing his career in Ireland, in 1690–91 and again between 1694 and 1696, Swift passed the decade at Moor Park, Temple's country house near Farnham in Surrey.

To all appearances, Swift's talents must have developed tremendously during his years with Temple. He first arrived at Moor Park as a 21-year-old Irish student with little to recommend him beyond his uncles' business connections with the Temple family. (Temple's father had been Master of the Rolls in Ireland, and although he operated through proxies, Temple himself had succeeded to the office.) For nearly seven years Swift had studied at Trinity College, Dublin, but by the time that the Irish political upheaval drove him away in early 1689, just short of his M.A., he had achieved few formal distinctions beyond a slightly substandard bachelor's degree and a somewhat above-average record for getting into disciplinary scrapes.[2] By the time he left Moor

Park for good, ten years later, Swift had become a writer of mature and extensive power. It was at Moor Park, apparently, that he composed much of his first true masterwork, *A Tale of a Tub*.

As the formative period in Swift's literary career, the Moor Park years figure centrally in the competing views of Swift advanced by critics and biographers, both apologists and antagonists, stretching back to the 1750s. Because relatively little evidence survives about Swift at Moor Park, it has had to bear a disproportionately heavy weight of generalization. At the same time, much of that little has gone unevaluated, though cited and counter-cited with impressive regularity over the years. Some archival materials have in turn received short shrift from scholars; others have not been consulted at all. Theory has a way of dictating the kinds of evidence to be sought in its support, and when major questions are at issue the tendency is often to limit documentary research to areas which promise relatively prompt and unequivocal answers. What were Swift's true feelings about Temple? How did Temple really feel about Swift? On what personal footing did the two live at Moor Park, and how did the experience help to shape Swift's mind and art? Here the surviving evidence offers relatively little in the way of prompt, direct and unequivocal answers, and even less which holds up to close examination. What it allows instead is an unexpectedly helpful response to a pair of lesser questions, seldom raised and never before investigated in any depth. Whatever the personal relationship between the two men, Temple employed Swift for years as his secretary and amanuensis. What exactly did Temple expect from Swift and the other secretaries he employed at various times? What exactly did Swift do in his work? If laborious to trace, the answers here at least are fairly straightforward, and in turn they provide a fresh approach to the more central issues concerning Swift in the 1690s.

It is in this way that the *Letters* which Swift published for Temple in 1699 allow a new opening for investigating the nature of Swift's relationship with Temple and the degree of influence which Temple exerted on his thought and literary style. Indirectly the *Letters* also help provide the foundation for a new assessment of Swift's aims, methods, and projected readership in his Moor Park writings—the early odes, the *Tale*, and *The Battle of the Books*. His work with Temple's correspondence accordingly deserves close attention, especially in the one area for which Swift claimed major literary responsibility.

To most of his Continental correspondents Temple wrote in French, and as printed in 1699, these letters appear with English translations in facing columns. Swift admitted responsibility for "the greater Part" of the translations,[3] and they have attracted occasional comment. To all appearances, Swift took liberties with Temple's text. On the right side of a page appears an elegant and somewhat elaborate text in French—dull reading, perhaps, but an apparent tribute to Temple's fluency—and on the left a concise, idiomatic, and sometimes colloquial version in English. The Huguenot refugee Abel Boyer, a Whig journalist with little reason to praise Swift, grumbled in 1714 about "the *Faults* in the *Translation,* which, indeed, are many, and some of them very gross," but noted somewhat condescendingly that "it would be ungenerous to bear too hard upon him upon that score."[4] More recent critics have hailed the translations as something of a milestone in Swift's development as a prose stylist. Archibald E. Irwin, who made a careful study, finds in them "Swift's triumphant revelation both of the sense of the originals and of his own mind and art at this early date," and asserts that "Swift's conciseness and his instinctive sense of balance have never been earlier demonstrated."[5] Irvin Ehrenpreis praises Swift for "a freshness of speech which Temple rarely affords" and notes that "the prose style of the English ranks in idiomatic refinement with the elegance of Swift's original letters."[6] But if Swift's translations shed light on his development as a writer— or, as Boyer implies, on his competence as a translator—they do so in unexpected ways. Plainly stated, the French text printed in 1699 is *not* the text which Swift had translated but rather a gallicized and prettified revision of it. Far from taking liberties with Temple's French, Swift seems to have translated it with unusual restraint, practically word for word. If the results sometimes sound Swiftian, the reasons lie more in the nature of Temple's original French than in his secretary's supposed initiative as a translator.

By the same token, tracing the letters' advance towards publication provides important new evidence about the working relationship between the two men in the 1690s, during Swift's third and final sojourn with Temple, when he enjoyed more of the master's confidence than ever before. The results suggest the need for rethinking the interpretation now current—marshalled in Ehrenpreis's biography and echoed in Irwin's article, among many others—of a modified father-son relationship, profound in its effects on Swift's mind and pen, and marked on his side by an almost excessive respect, admiration, and affection for Temple.[7] For evidence, such theories largely rest upon Swift's Moor Park writings and his surviving references to Temple, usually highly flattering or deferential. These too deserve fresh evaluation, within the contexts which Swift framed for them. On the face of it, Swift's Pindaric *Ode to the Honble Sir William Temple* has as little in common with his French translations as they in turn have with the Digression on

Madness in *A Tale of a Tub*. Yet all three, in their different ways, are products of Swift's experience at Moor Park. What illuminates the one raises questions about the others, and the answers, when obtainable, carry more important implications yet, implications about the vaguely unsettling, peculiarly "Swiftian" quality of Swift's greatest work, not just in the *Tale* but in his later writings as well. Certainly in later years Swift exhibited a highly developed sense of the various readerships that he addressed and a unique talent for playing humorous games with them, by enlisting their laughter against easy targets and insensibly shifting it into less comfortable lines of advance. Against all expectations, it is now beginning to look as if he developed and quietly perfected these skills at Moor Park, with Temple's small circle serving both as critics and as guinea pigs.

But this is to anticipate conclusions much too far in advance. With a figure as problematic as Swift, a scholar does better to advance with caution, carefully accumulating evidence until a pattern of some sort can emerge. First we must examine the unglamorous and often petty business of Swift's secretarial work at Moor Park, beginning with the *Letters* which Temple had him prepare for publication.

The Downton Transcript of Temple's Letters

Until he died, Swift preserved a working transcript of Temple's *Letters,* and it is the transcript, not the printed text, which sheds light on Temple's French and Swift's work in translating it. Though available to scholars for many years, the transcript has received no scholarly attention apart from a few early attempts to identify the different autographs that it contains. Acquired at Swift's death by Lord Chesterfield, it eventually passed into Lord Rothschild's collection and is now at Trinity College, Cambridge.[8] It is a patchwork of many hands—eight by my count, including Temple's—and dates in its earliest parts from the period 1670–72, when Temple's secretary Thomas Downton copied the bulk of the letters of the period 1665–70. In its latest parts, the transcript seems to date from the period 1696–98, when Swift copied in six late additions to the letters, had young Esther Johnson (later celebrated as Stella) copy a seventh, and elsewhere entered corrections under Temple's direction (Appendix A). Ten years after the *Letters* appeared in print, Swift wrote Temple's sister and companion, Lady Giffard, to explain the statesman's general practice in preparing copy for the press. "Nothing of his ever printed in my Time was from the Originall," Swift pointed out:

the first Memoirs was from my Copy; so were the Second Miscellanea: so was the Introduction to the English History: so was every Volume of Letters, They were all copied from the Originals by Sr Wm Temples direction, and corrected all along by his Orders. . . .[9]

Later in the letter, Swift elaborates on Temple's usual habits of correction. "The Corrections were all his own," he explains, "ordering me to correct in my Copy as I rec^d it, as he allways did."[10] Here Swift confirms privately what he had earlier stated publicly, in the preface to the 1699 *Letters*. Apart from his work with the foreign-language letters, he explains, "I pretend no other Part, than the Care, that Mr. Downton's Book should be correctly transcribed, and the Letters placed, in the Order they were writ."[11] Swift adds that Temple "was pleased to be at the Pains of reviewing, and to give me his Directions for digesting them into Order" (I, sig. A3^v).

Textually as well as chronologically, the Downton transcript represents something of an intermediate state. Most of Temple's letters were official dispatches of the period 1665–70, and the originals had gone to his correspondents without much chance of retrieval later on. Even so, he had ample manpower for having copies made before posting the originals. During his embassy at the Hague he employed half a dozen clerks,[12] and probably could count on nearly as many in his earlier post at Brussels. In the preface to the third volume of *Letters*, published in 1703, Swift not only speaks of working from a transcript which Temple oversaw, but states that the letters were originally "Selected by [Temple] himself from great Numbers yet lying among his Papers."[13]

No doubt the situation had been similar for the earlier volumes of letters, largely selected before Swift entered Temple's service. The Osborn Collection at Yale, for instance, preserves four loose copies of letters from the earlier period, and two of them seem to provide the text followed in the Downton transcript.[14] With a full range of such letters, in loose copies, Temple could make his selections and, when necessary, enter minor corrections. (On some occasions, as we shall see, he could also radically expand a letter written years before or could even rewrite a letter almost from scratch, to change its implications and endow himself with greater foresight than he possessed at the time.) Downton or another scribe could then copy them into the Downton volume, for further correction or revision. These done, Temple would have needed a fresh transcript, for making the remaining textual changes which are embodied in the printed text, and finally, perhaps, an additional fair copy for Swift to send to the printer. Unfortunately, neither has survived.

Except with Temple's French, the final stages involved no major textual changes. In Temple's English, Spanish, and Latin letters, the transcript stands fairly close textually to the printed version. The exception stands out. Set side by side, Temple's French letters show signs of pervasive revision between transcript and printed text. When Temple writes to a new governor of Spanish Flanders, for instance, the transcript has him say that "Je seray fort aise de lier le commerce ou J'ay desja lié l'amitié" (T, p. 344), applying the verb *lier* in its occasional sense of *entering into* (cf. *lier conversation avec quelqu'un*). By contrast, the printed text gives the idea in a prosier but more proper French—that "je seray fort aise d'avoir une liaison d'affaires avec celuy avec qui j'ay deja des liaisons d'amitié. . ." (II, 230–31). When Temple condoles with a German envoy over poor accommodations in England, he calls them "v[ot]re mauvais vin et logement à Oxford" in the transcript (T, p. 147), while the printed text refers more elaborately to the "mauvais giste d'Oxford, & [le] mechant Vin que vous y avez bû" (I, 16). In the same letter, Temple jokes affectionately about the envoy's master, the warlike Bishop of Munster, who leads his soldiers a merry life. In the transcript, Temple writes that the bishop "se leve à quatre heures du matin, leur donne la benediction et les envoye au Diable . . . ," but the printed text drops all mention of the bishop's early rising. It states only that he "leur donne sa Benediction, & les Envoye au diable . . ." (I, 20).

In evaluating Swift's translations, both Irwin and Ehrenpreis compare the *printed* French with the translation appearing opposite, and find reasons to praise Swift's stylishness and daring. In most cases, though, a comparison with the earlier transcript French shows Swift translating from it almost verbatim. In the compliments to the new Spanish governor, for instance, Swift translates Temple saying "I shall be very glad to enter into Business where I have already entred into Friendship" (II, 230–31), an exact rendering of the transcript's "Je seray fort aise de lier le commerce ou J'ay desja lié l'amitié." If Irwin finds a characteristically Swiftian sharpness in the verbal parallels in English, the credit lies with Temple's original rather than with any liberties taken in translation. For the German envoy's poor accommodations, Swift renders the transcript's plain phrase, "v[ot]re mauvais vin et logement à Oxford," with the plain but literal "your bad Wine and Lodging at Oxford" (I, 16). Any credit for presenting the fundamental sense so directly belongs to Temple's original French, not to Swift's freedom in translating. Irwin also praises Swift's command of the letters' historical background—apparently astonishing in its scope —in being able to supply the Bishop of Munster's habitual hour of rising in 1665.[15] The printed French makes no mention of it, after all. Undoubtedly Swift absorbed a certain amount of historical background during his years working for Temple, but where the translation states that the bishop "rises at four a Clock, gives them [his soldiers] his Benediction, and then sends them to the D——" (I, 20), the transcript in fact reports that the bishop "se leve à quatre heures du matin, leur donne la benediction et les envoye au Diable. . . ." If Swift takes any liberty in translating, it seems merely in omitting the redundant "du matin" ("rises at four a Clock"), in translating "la" by "his" (in "his Benediction"), and in adding "then" to emphasize the antithesis in the final phrase, "and then sends them to the D——" ("et les envoye au Diable").

By the same token, Ehrenpreis praises Swift's translations for their epigrammatic bite, especially in parallels or antitheses which seem mild in the printed French.[16] He cites Temple's comment to the Dutch statesman De Witt, that:

in this Age there is so little Honour in being a good Man, that none are suspected to employ their Vanity about it, any more than their Pursuits. (II, 300)	au reste, dans un siecle comme le nôtre, il y a trop peu de gloire á etre homme de bien, pour s'attirer le soupçon d'avoir tourné ses veues á ce coté lá, & borné sa vanité á si peu de chose. (II, 300)

Not only does Swift seem to sharpen the parallel but also to change its terms. In the French, literally translated, Temple says there is little glory for a man "to incur the suspicion of having turned his views in that direction" (being thought virtuous), and completes the parallel with "and limited his vanity to so small a thing." The emphasis falls on the world's contempt for that trifle, virtue ("si peu de chose"). While retaining the same basic idea—the lack of glory in being "a good Man"—Swift's English makes a fresh distinction between employing one's "Vanity" and employing one's "Pursuits." The French speaks only of one's "veues," or 'views.' Although Ehrenpreis does not raise the point, nothing could sound more Swiftian than the resulting implication: that men will more readily imagine themselves famous for virtue, than try to earn such fame through their actions. Compared to the printed French, Swift's English indeed arrives at what Ehrenpreis calls a new "freshness of speech." Compared to the transcript French, on the other hand, the translation reveals practically no change or improvement:

. . . because in this Age there is so little Honour in being a good Man, that none are suspected to employ their Vanity about it, any more than their Pursuits.	. . . puisque dans ce Siecle il y a si peu de gloire d'estre homme de bien, et qu'on sera guere soupconné d'y employer sa vanité nonplus que ses poursuittes.
(II, 300)	(T, p. 346)

If the translation differs at all from the transcript French, it is in the trifling matter of translating "gloire" as "Honour" (in its sense of reputation), changing 'one will hardly be' ("on sera guere") to the plainer "none are," and dispensing with the construction "et que," which replaces the preceding conjunction "puisque," to coordinate the two clauses ("Puisque . . . et que . . ."). For the rest, Swift translates word for word, even in the very English-sounding ellipsis "any more than their Pursuits" ("nonplus que ses poursuittes"). If his translation reflects a peculiarly Swiftian bite, the transcript's French text deserves most of the credit.

A broad sampling of Temple's French letters confirms the impression.[17] In every instance the transcript reveals variant readings, usually a considerable number, and in a great majority Swift's translations follow them almost literally. Even when the transcript text received relatively few corrections before publication, it is easy to see which version Swift followed. When Temple begins a late letter to Abraham de Wicquefort, for instance, Swift's translation appears to follow the French text printed opposite:

If by the Course of Publick Affairs it were permitted me to cultivate any Correspondence in the Country where you are. . . .	Si les conjonctures & les situations des affaires publiques, m'avoient permis d'entretenir quelque correspondence au païs ou vous etes. . . .
(II, 313)	(II, 313)

The differences seem trifling at best: "les conjonctures & les situations" instead of the plainer English "the Course," an active rather than a passive verb, and "entretenir" for "to cultivate." Even so, the transcript text is closer yet, and removes each difference—although the passive verb is awkward enough in French. "Si par le train des affaires publiques," it reads, "il m'auroit êté permis de cultiver aucune correspondence au païs ou vous êtes . . ." (T, p. 359). "Si par le train" translates quite literally as "If by the Course," the verb is in the conditional passive, and "cultiver" produces its cognate in English, "to cultivate." Swift is translating the transcript text—and translating it as literally as possible, even to the extent of choosing English cognates. Later in the same letter the process is even clearer, when Temple complains about changes in Charles II's policies, which have negated Temple's work with the Triple Alliance:

For since his Majesty has thought fit to change the Course of his Councils, in the pursuit whereof I was so long and so sincerely engaged. . . .	Car depuis que sa Majesté a trouvé bon de changer la face de son conseil, auquel j'ay eté si long temps & si sincerement devoué. . . .
(II, 314)	(II, 314)

Although Irwin pins a good deal of significance on them,[18] the disparities again seem minor: "the Course" for "la face," the plural rather than the singular in "Councils," the added phrase "in the pursuit," "was" for 'have been' ("j'ay eté"), and "engaged" for "devoué" ('devoted'). Again the transcript text makes good the disparities and reveals how closely Swift translated:

For since his Majesty has thought fit to change *the Course of his Councils, in the pursuit whereof I was* so long and so sincerely *engaged*. . . .	Car depuis que Sa Majesté a trouvé bon de changer *le train de ses conseils, á la poursuite dequels j'etois* si longtems et si sincerement *engagé*. . . .
(II, 314, my emphases)	(T, p. 359, my emphases)

In practically every instance Swift favors the French words' cognates in English: "changer"/ "to change," "ses conseils"/ "his Councils," "poursuite"/ "pursuit," "longtems"/ "long," "sincerement"/ "sincerely," "engagé"/ "engaged."

In other letters the situation is much the same. At one point Temple talks of "l'equité de la cause" in the printed text (II, 173), but the transcript reads "la justice de l'affaire" (T, p. 338) and the translation, "the Justice of the Affair." The French armies will draw upon themselves "toutes nos forces sur les bras," according to the printed text somewhat earlier (I, 290), but the transcript threatens them with "la fforce de Nos Armes" (T, p. 162). Swift accordingly translates it "the Force of our Arms." At another point, the printed text reads "tous les Pais bas etoient comme en desespoir" (II, 87), but the transcript says "le Pais Bas estoit desesperé" (T, p. 330). Swift follows suit: "Flanders was desperate." "Dans ma premiere audience je l'avois si fort pressé," Temple begins elsewhere in the printed text (I, 285), but the transcript transposes the words' order—"Je l'avois a ma premiere audience si fort pressé" (T, p. 162). So does Swift: "I had at my first Audience prest him so closely. . . ." "J'ay trouvé à propos, afin de le satisfaire pleinement," Temple begins a little later in the same letter, as printed (I, 287–88), but

the transcript reads "j'ay trouvé bon pour son entiere satisfaction."
Again Swift translates verbatim, with "I thought fit for his entire satisfaction . . ." (I, 287). The list could go on almost indefinitely.

The surprising thing is that Swift's English reads so well. As a rule,
literal translations tend to sound stilted, almost foreign. In the family
of languages, French may stand closer to English than Greek or Rus-
sian, but there are still substantial differences in idiom, grammar, and
syntax. Supplying exact English equivalents for each word in a French
sentence will seldom produce a good English sentence. It does not
sound quite right, for instance, to declare with La Rochefoucauld that
"the refusal of praises is a desire to be praised two times," or to say that
"what makes for us the vanity of others insupportable, it's that it
wounds our own"—although in his native French La Rochefoucauld
reads smoothly enough, "Le refus des louanges est un désir d'être loué
deux fois," and "Ce qui nous rend la vanité des autres insupportable,
c'est qu'elle blesse la nôtre."[19] That Swift could translate Temple's
French so closely, and still produce English so idiomatic, may stem in
part from Swift's native skill, but a great deal of credit must go to the
kind of French which Temple wrote. It is a language French in its
vocabulary but frequently English in its syntax and idiom. There is
something not quite French in Temple's phrase "pour son entiere satisfaction," although "for his entire satisfaction" sounds English enough,
and "la fforce de Nos Armes" has a similarly English ring (the French
word *armes* serving less readily for synecdoche than does *arms* in English). It may sound well enough to say, with another of Swift's translations, that "For all that, he would not be satisfied . . ." (I, 290), but in the
transcript French the phrase "for all that" does not sit well: "Pour tout
cela il ne voulut pas se contenter . . ." (T, p. 162). The corrections in the
printed text produce a version much easier on the ear: "Tout cela ne le
satisfait pas, & il . . ." (I, 290). A page earlier, Swift's translation mentions
an article in a treaty and wonders if its terms "were strong enough" (I,
289), a phrase which follows the transcript's "estoient forts assez" (T, p.
162). The printed version quietly restores the adverb to its proper place,
"etoient assez forts" (I, 289).

Anglicized idiom makes up only one aspect of Temple's original
French. Both Irwin and Ehrenpreis rightly emphasize the translations'
surprising crispness in parallel and antithesis, and the transcript reveals
that, as a translator, Swift merely brings out Temple's original bent. A
good crisp parallel often requires ellipsis—a weeding out of dispensable
but grammatically justified verbiage—to bring the parallel elements
closer together. In this, modern French is often less amenable than
English, in which (for instance) a single subject can without strain take

a series of elaborate compound verbs (each with its full complement of objects and qualifiers) with the same subject understood but not repeated. At one point in the transcript, Temple follows English practice when he lists Charles II's many services to his Spanish allies. When Swift translates, the result sounds perfectly idiomatic in English. The King, says Temple, has been the first to respond to the problems in Spanish Flanders,

a contracté ses Alliances l'hyver passé, mis une flotte en mer l'esté suivante, envoyé ses Ambassadeurs à Aix la Chapelle, fondé la Triple Alliance, & sollicité encore d'autres Princes pour s'y joindre. (T, p. 330)	contracted his Alliances last Winter, set a Fleet to Sea the Summer following, sent Ambassadors to Aix la Chapelle, founded the Triple Alliance, and sollicited other Princes to join in it. (II, 88)

In French, however, the long string of participial constructions ("contracté . . . mis . . . envoyé . . . fondé . . . & sollicité . . .) sounds something less than the Parisian spoken in the 1690s and after.[20] The printed text largely solves the problem, and weakens the parallels, by breaking the sentence into independent clauses. Charles has been the first to respond to the problem of Flanders,

tout l'hyver dernier sa Majesté a employé á faire traiter ses Alliances, et á faire equiper une flote qui a paru en mer; L'eté suivante il a envoyé ses Ambassadeurs à Aix la Chapelle, il a cementé la Triple Alliance, & fait solliciter divers Princes de s'y joindre en plus grand nombre. (II, 88)

If the printed text can weaken Temple's antitheses or parallels, occasionally it makes them more explicit, though not more concise. In one passage Irwin praises Swift's translation for cutting through to the "fundamental sense" even at the expense of damaging a parallelism:[21]

I have received much Satisfaction as well as Honour by yours of the 25th, and am very glad to observe the same Conformity of Sentiments between us. . . . (I, 284)	J'ay eprouvé beaucoup de Satisfaction, & reçeu beaucoup d'Honneur par vôtre Lettre du 25 de ce mois; & je suis fort aise de remarquer une aussi grande Conformité de Sentimens entre nous. . . . (I, 284)

While the translation omits the repetitious parallelism, "eprouvé beaucoup de Satisfaction & reçeu beaucoup d'Honneur," it merely follows

Temple's French in the transcript: "J'ay reçeu beaucoup de satisfaction aussi bien que de l'honneur par la vostre du 25 et suis fort aise de remarquer cette conformité des Sentiments entre Nous . . ." (T, p. 162). Again there are as many weaknesses in the French as strengths in the English which results from it. To begin a coordinating clause with "and am" may be standard in English letter-writing, but in modern French "et suis" may grate on the ear. There is something unsatisfactory in the opening clause, too. To receive "much Satisfaction as well as Honour" sounds crisp in English, but the French original seems wordy and awkward, in part thanks to "beaucoup de" for "much": "J'ay reçeu beaucoup de satisfaction aussi bien que de l'honneur." For that matter, in French, the verb *recevoir* does not suit with the noun *satisfaction*, which is more a feeling to experience ("éprouver") than an object to receive.

Sometimes the transcript's French is as hard to read as its literal translation is easy. Because of its compression and its occasional use of legalisms like "le party contractant," one of Temple's comments on a treaty may require rereading in French, while Swift's close translation (with the help of judicious punctuation) makes sense the first time around:

Si tels mots n'y sont pas le party contractant ne peut pas les faire entrer par quelque sienne interpretation sans consentement de l'autre parti, ny sentence de quelque arbitre.	If these Words are not there, the Party contracting cannot bring them in by any Interpretation of his own, without Consent of t'other Party, or Sentence of some Arbitrator.
(T, p. 330)	(II, 86)

Here as elsewhere Temple generally seems to be thinking in English, although he clothes his thoughts in French. The printed text gives a French which is not only more graceful, but easier to follow:

Si pareils mots n'y sont pas, un des partis contractans ne peut pas les y faire entrer par une interpretation de sa façon, á moins que le consentement de l'autre parti intervienne, ou que de part & d'autre on convienne de s'en rapporter á la decision d'un arbitre. (II, 86)

In the process, of course, Temple's original conciseness has been lost.

In an essay written in the period 1688–90, Temple left other signs that he felt somewhat uncomfortable with French—or at least that he preferred a sturdier, more archaic version which was closer in syntax to English. Although he lists the sixteenth-century authors Montaigne and Rabelais as the two "great Wits among the moderns" in France, he grudgingly concedes that it is his near-contemporaries—La Rochefoucauld, Bussy-Rabutin, and Voiture, "with several other little Relations or Memoirs that have run this Age"—who "seem to have Refined the French Language to a degree, that cannot be well exceeded." Even so, Temple remains doubtful about such refinements. He suspects that

> it may have happened there, as it does in all Works, that the more they are filed and polished, the less they have of weight and of strength; and as that Language has much more fineness and smoothness at this time, so I take it to have had much more force, spirit, and compass, in Montaigne's Age.[22]

More than forty years before, in the early 1650s, Temple had in fact written English essays modelled on Montaigne's, and to judge by the French in the Downton transcript, his study of Montaigne had at least as much influence on his French usage as any actual experience in speaking the language. The freer syntax standard in Montaigne's time, for instance, would have permitted Temple's string of elaborate compound verbs on Charles II's helpfulness in Spanish Flanders. By the same token, some expressions at odds with modern French—like "quelque sienne interpretation," with *sienne* used adjectivally—prove correct enough in a sixteenth-century context. The archaic touch is most immediately evident, perhaps, in Temple's French spelling. Despite the diversity of copyists working on the Downton transcript, it is fairly consistent in retaining the supernumary *s*'s usually dropped by the 1690s or replaced by accents on the preceding vowels—"tousjours" for "toujours," "mesme" for "même," "estoit" for "étoit" (modern "était"), "esmouvoir" for "émouvoir," "la vostre" for "la vôtre." In a sense, the final revisions of Temple's French correct not only his anglicisms but his archaisms as well, and the "force, spirit, and compass" of a dialect modelled on Montaigne's is suppressed to produce the "fineness and smoothness" of the French of a later and more elegant age.

Although examples of irregular, old-fashioned, or awkward French abound in the transcript, it would be unfair to exaggerate Temple's weakness in the language. Given his location and his needs as a diplomat, he was surely fluent enough, with a sufficient vocabulary and a readiness in using it. French was the preferred second language of the better classes in Holland, and when Temple sat down privately with the Grand Pensionary De Witt in 1668, in discussions which resulted in the Triple Alliance, it was doubtless in French that the two men spoke. Formally, as a diplomat, Temple would have had to deal in French during the greatest part of his embassies abroad—about a decade in all (1665–70, 1674–78).[23] It would have mattered little how English and outmoded his style or accent appeared, so long as he made himself clearly understood. For that matter, Temple had no particular need of elegant or idiomatic French, and enjoyed only limited exposure to it. He never served in French territory and, as an exponent of an anti-French foreign policy, seldom dealt long or closely with Frenchmen, except exiled Huguenots or mavericks like J. H. Gourville. He addresses almost all his printed French letters to people for whom French was also a second language—Dutchmen like De Witt or De Wicquefort, Spaniards like Castel-Rodrigo, Germans like the Elector of Mainz, and even an Italian, Cosimo de' Medici, Grand Duke of Tuscany. To Temple the diplomat, a Parisian grace in French would have been a dispensable luxury during negotiations over the wording of treaties or dispositions of alliances. No matter how inelegant, the French of his transcript letters is usually serviceable enough.

Publishing it for all the world to see would have been another matter. However many his virtues, Temple possessed a lively sense of his own importance, especially in his retirement years after 1681. The last eighteen or nineteen years of his life he chiefly devoted to writing, editing, and publishing his own works. Whatever other purposes they served,[24] they project (with remarkable doggedness and consistency) a highly flattering public image of himself as the incorruptible statesman and compleat gentleman, a bulwark against French absolutism and a paragon of honesty in a scheming court, who gave unstintingly of his services and then retired, with no reward but the consciousness of his own virtue, to a blameless life in the country where, without pedantry or unbecoming levity, he exhibited his gentility and virtuosity in an impressive range of subjects applicable to the public good, from the cure of gout to the state of popular education in English history, and from his success in introducing new strains of grapes into Surrey to the merits of the estimable (but unfortunately bogus) classic author Phalaris.[25]

Temple set great store on such virtues, and on greatness generally. In his six-part essay *Of Heroick Virtue*, the longest he ever wrote, he celebrates human greatness in the most fervid and romantic terms, urges his contemporaries to emulate the examples of the past, and spurs them forward with the hope of success. By definition, heroic virtue springs "from some great and native Excellency of Temper or Genius transcending the common race of Mankind, in Wisdom, Goodness and Fortitude," he explains, and in practice a great man is one who originates just institutions of government, who introduces or fosters learning, the arts, and agriculture, and who patriotically establishes or preserves his people in mighty kingdoms and empires.[26] His heroes include Confucius, Alaric, Pericles, Odin ("the first and great Hero of the Western Scythians"), William the Silent of Holland, Saturn and Jupiter (early kings of Crete), Scanderbeg, Manco Capac (the Sun's son, who became the first Inca), Almansur of Cordoba, Osiris (the mighty Egyptian king), Tamerlane, Moses, and Henri IV of France. Temple concludes the fifth section with a call to arms. "Who-ever has a mind to trace the Paths of Heroick Virtue, which lead to the Temple of True Honour and Fame," he writes,

> need seek them no further, than in the Stories and Examples of those Illustrious Persons here assembled. And so I leave this Crown of never fading Lawrel, in full view of such great and noble Spirits, as shall deserve it, in this or in succeeding Ages. Let them win it and wear it.[27]

The conclusion to the sixth and final section is more stirring yet. After celebrating military genius, Temple points out that it confessedly ranks second to the arts of peace, especially wise and patriotic statecraft. Wars cause destruction, but good government's effects "are preserving and encreasing the Lives and Generations of Men, securing their Possessions, encouraging their Endeavours, and by Peace and Riches, improving and adorning the several Scenes of the world." He concludes with the heady observation that, "if among the Ancients, some men have been esteemed Heroes, by the brave Atchievements of great Conquests and Victories; It has been, by the wise Institutions of Laws and Governments, that others have been honoured and adored as Gods."[28]

Temple's ideals of heroic virtue help to illuminate the public image which he meant to project, and at least to some extent they may illuminate the more flattering contemporary tributes based on that image. Temple's first biographer, Abel Boyer, takes a fairly cautious approach. Although he stops short of endowing Temple with heroic virtue in its more divine aspects, he makes the most of the great man's public image. Boyer wished to "represent and record his *publick*, not his *private Life*," and accordingly declined to draw a "*formal Character*" of him. Even so, Boyer observes, "Any intelligent Reader will, from the Account of his *Life* and *Writings*, readily form to himself the *Idea* of an *accomplish'd Gentleman*, a *sound Politician*, a *Patriot*, and a *great Scholar*. . . ."[29] In 1714, Boyer's duty was to make the most of Temple's merits, to enforce the lesson of Temple's Protestant policies. Despite the need for puffery, Boyer can only carry matters so far. Temple's vanity is something that he cannot quite evade. He concludes his summation by admitting that, "if this great *Idea* should, perchance, be shaded by some Touches of *Vanity* and *Spleen*," the intelligent reader "will be so candid as to consider, that the greatest, the wisest, and the best of Men have still some Failings and Imperfections, which are inseparable from human Nature."[30]

In an eulogy written shortly after Temple's death, Swift dispenses with mortal failings altogether. His evaluation comes even closer to Temple's ideal of heroic virtue—and with it, to the image which the great man meant to project:

> He was a Person of the greatest Wisdom, Justice, Liberality, Politeness, Eloquence, of his age or Nation; the truest Lover of his Country, and one that deserved more from it by his eminent publick services, than any Man before or since: Besides his great deserving from the Commonwealth of Learning; having been universally esteemed the most accomplisht writer of his time.[31]

Swift emphasizes the patriotism and public service which lie at the heart of heroic virtue, and his tribute reads like a gloss on the heroic temperament defined by Temple—the "great and native Excellency of Temper or Genius transcending the common race of Mankind, in Wisdom, Goodness, and Fortitude."

Such praise may sound odd coming from a man who not long before, in *A Tale of a Tub*, was composing ironic instructions for writing panegyric—that a needy poet should "get by heart a List of the Cardinal Virtues, and deal them with the utmost Liberality to his Hero or his Patron. . . ."[32] Even so, its burden suggests something about Temple's reasoning as he edited his French letters. It would hardly have suited with greatness—and with so accomplished and elegant a writer, the veteran of so many years on the Continent—to appear in print speaking an outmoded and anglicized French. Even if few English readers might notice his French usage, increasing numbers of Huguenots were living in England after Louis XIV revoked the Edict of Nantes in 1685. Temple's Continental audience also deserved consideration. Each of his books before 1699 had appeared in French translation, usually within a year of its English publication, and in fact the *Letters* themselves came out in French in 1700.[33] With his English letters translated into standard French, both contemporary and idiomatic, his French letters would stand out noticeably. Temple had every reason to wish them fully revised for publication.

The Revising of Temple's French Letters

Even from its earliest stages, the Downton transcript shows more textual correction and revision for its French letters than for the others. Revisions appear in Temple's hand as well as Swift's. To credit Swift's report of "correct[ing] in my copy as I rec^d it" from Temple, their autograph interlineations probably represent at least two stages of correction—the first before Swift's time, when Temple entered his own corrections, and the second somewhat later, when Swift read Temple the text and marked down any further corrections from Temple.[34] Of the five letters which the transcript preserves in duplicate copies, both copied and recopied in the transcript, three are by Temple in French and show the second scribe entering the occasional minor adjustments added in the first copy, to provide a fair copy for further minor adjustments.[35]

All in all the transcript conveys an impression of editorial fussing in the French letters. As for the final, full-scale revisions which produced the printed French text, Temple almost certainly would have maintained an active interest, assuming that his health permitted. Probably it did. In at least one instance, the printed text introduces new material present in neither the transcript nor in Swift's translation— material which Temple alone could have supplied. Late in February 1667/8, on the eve of the French truce with the Spaniards in Flanders, Temple voices his hopes for a general suspension of arms. In the printed text alone, Temple adds that the suspension is one "qui selon toutes les apparences ne sera pas long tems differée" (I, 292). Within three or four months the suspension actually took place, but in February the appearances could not have been so promising, except perhaps to an unusually penetrating mind. Differences still existed between England and Holland, Sweden had not yet ratified the Triple Alliance, Spain was proving recalcitrant about making peace with France, and money remained a problem. The allies had no men in the field, but the French were threatening Brussels while Marshal Turenne pressed for an easy and total victory.[36] Supplied by hindsight, Temple's prediction of peace endows him with greater foresight than he probably possessed. As we shall see, some of the revisions which Temple made in his English letters work towards the same end. Similarly, when Temple makes a jovial reference (in an earlier letter) to the Baron Wreden's "little mistress here"—a close translation of the transcript's "petite Maitresse en decá" (T, p. 147)—the printed version specifies her nationality: "vôtre petite maitresse Brabançonne" (I, 18). Only Temple would have known that his friend from Munster, to the northeast of Holland, kept a mistress from Brabant, to the south. The addition of so petty a detail suggests that Temple closely supervised whoever was rewriting his French for him.

Probably Temple had a Frenchman do the job. In the mid-1690s, after more than a decade of living in the English countryside, Temple's command of the language would have been weaker, not stronger, than when he had served Charles II in Holland. Conceivably, but less plausibly, Swift might have done the work for him. After all, Swift occasionally wrote in French himself,[37] his library contained an extremely large selection of French titles,[38] and in his preface to the *Letters* he claimed to have corrected Temple's French. "I have also made some literal amendments," he informs the reader, "especially in the Latin, French, and Spanish," before having the texts translated (I, sig. A2ᵛ). Even so, there is something rather odd in the claim. Granting, for the moment, that Swift knew enough French for the task, how could he have amended Temple's Spanish? There is no evidence that he knew Spanish beyond whatever vague comprehension he derived from his knowledge of French and Latin. In later years he owned the *Book of Common Prayer* in Spanish (London, 1707) and a Spanish-French-Italian dictionary (Cologne, 1671), but his beloved Cervantes he owned only in English translations.[39]

For that matter, Swift could not have chosen a more awkward place to pretend proficiency or superiority in Spanish. At the bottom of the same paragraph, he makes a bow in the direction of Temple's sister, Lady Giffard. After taking the blame for most faults in the translations, he adds that "I speak only of the French and Latin; for the few Spanish Translations, I believe, need no Apology."[40] Besides Temple, it was Lady Giffard, not Swift, who was the competent Spanish-speaker in the Temple household, or at least fancied herself such. Poor Swift had in fact been employed at least once to enter her corrections and then copy out her translations from the Spanish.[41]

As for Latin, Temple set up for something of an expert. Not ten pages after Swift's claim, in the letters themselves, appears Temple's condescending remark that the Bishop of Munster "speaks the only good Latin that I have yet met with in Germany," as if Temple were an acknowledged judge of good spoken Latin. As the author of the essay *Upon Ancient and Modern Learning* (1690), he had already staked a public claim of proficiency in the classics. While Swift no doubt knew Latin at least as well as the great man himself—Temple had left Cambridge without taking his degree, after devoting his two years there mainly to tennis and other entertainments[42]—his claim of making "literal amendments" in Temple's Latin seems somewhat impolitic at first glance. Indeed, almost no such changes seem to have entered the Latin text, in the Downton transcript or afterwards. If only by association, then, Swift's claim of amending the French seems somewhat dubious, unless Swift uses the phrase "literal amendments" literally (and somewhat misleadingly) to refer to the letters of the alphabet. "Literal amendments" could then mean the amendment of an occasional letter in a word, to correct scribal error, to regularize spelling, or (especially in Latin) to correct case, tense, or gender.

Even this reading of the phrase fails to solve the problem of the final revisions in Temple's French. To judge from his own French letters, written years later, Swift probably lacked the fluency to produce the sort of French printed in Temple's *Letters*. In 1690 Temple had credited Swift with knowing "latine and greeke"—but only "some French."[43] In his later letter to the Grand Duke of Tuscany's secretary, for example, Swift sometimes employs idioms which can pass in French but ring even truer in English: "après tout, Monsieur, c'n'est que juste que . . ." ('after all, sir, it's only fair that . . .'), or "une demy douzaine de tetes" ('half a dozen heads'). Literal translation turns the text into idiomatic English. At one point, after reporting the fall of the Harley-Bolingbroke ministry which he supported, Swift explains that

Je me retirè à la campagne en Berkshire, d'ou apres ce triste evenement, Je venois en Yrlande, ou je demeure en mon Doyennè et attens avec le Resignation d'un bon Chretien la Ruine de notre Cause et de mes amis, menacès tous les jours par la Faction Domin[ante].[44]	I retired to the country in Berkshire, whence after this unhappy event I came to Ireland, where I live in my deanery and await with the resignation of a good Christian the ruin of our cause and of my friends, threatened daily by the dominant faction.

Even if "le Resignation" is an innocent slip of the pen for "la Resignation," or "Je me retirè" for "Je me suis retiré" (or "Je me retirai"), there is something less than Parisian about "Je venois en Yrlande," with its verb in the imperfect (instead of a correct form, "je viens," "je vins," or "je suis venu en Irlande"). Swift's French, in sum, is barely the equal of Temple's.

The last and best reason why Swift could not have recast Temple's French—or why Temple himself could not, either—is that the printed text works counter to the spirit of the originals, which Swift's translations reflect so faithfully. In his preface, Swift praises Temple's stylistic virtuosity in the letters, "wherein the Style appears so very different, according to the difference of the Persons, to whom they were address'd . . . ." Indeed, Swift remarks, "one may discover, the Characters of most of those Persons, he writes to, from the Stile of his Letters" (1,sig. A3ʳ). Swift's evaluation undoubtedly reflects Temple's view of the matter. Long before Swift ever entered his employ, Temple had already chosen the great majority of letters for the collection. A number contribute little to the narrative beyond a sense of the recipient's character

—and of Temple's divergent styles in writing them. A good example is
Temple's hearty note to the Munster envoy, Baron Wreden, which
appears in the transcript in Downton's autograph (T, p. 147; I, 16–21). In
contents, the letter has little to say beyond a few sketchy rumors about
the Bishop of Munster's movements on the Dutch frontier. Temple
gives equal play to teasing Wreden about his journey in England, advis-
ing him how to flirt with English girls, and sounding generally hail-
fellow-well-met. Unless Temple meant the letter to demonstrate his
command of a jolly and informal style, and to characterize Wreden as
a *bon vivant* (or himself as a man who could hold his own with one), its
presence in the collection makes little sense. By translating the earlier
text, Swift captures the same style and tone in English, but whoever cast
Temple's French into its final form seems to have missed much of the
point. "V[ot]re mauvais vin et logement à Oxford" may be awkward
French, but as we have seen, it sounds plainer and heartier than the
revised version, "au mauvais giste d'Oxford, & au mechant Vin que vous
y avez bû." With the first sentence, plain and hearty in the transcript,
the printed version starts off on the wrong foot:

J'ay recù la votre, & je me rejouis de votre arrivée á la Cour; je n'ay jamais douté qu'un aussi honette homme que vous, & qui a l'honneur d'etre Envoyé par un Prince aussi distingué, n'y trouvâit toute sorte de bon acceuïl.	J'ay receu la vostre, et me rejouis de votre arrivée à la Cour ou Je n'ay jamais douté la bonne reception d'un si honneste homme venant de la part d'un si brave prince.
(I, 16)	(T, p. 147)

Though more correct (despite the odd accenting), the printed version
weakens Temple's effect by introducing flowery phrases like "qui a
l'honneur d'etre Envoyé" (replacing the plainer "venant de la part de")
and by winding up with an elaborate subjunctive verb, complete with
its pleonastic *ne*, in "qu'un aussi honette homme . . . n'y trouvâit
. . . ." By staying closer to the original, Swift's translation preserves
Temple's tone much better: "I received yours, and am glad of your
Arrival at Court, where I never doubted the good Reception so honest
a Gentleman would find, who came from so brave a Prince" (I, 16).

As someone who knew Temple's intentions, and translated the
earlier text, Swift would not have recast Temple's French in such
flowery terms, especially since it makes the translation appear to take
liberties when printed in the facing column. The revised French text
leaves Swift open to charges of sloppy translating—like Boyer's com-

ment in 1714—and may well have dictated Swift's half-apologetic tone in the preface, about "whatever faults there may be in the Translation." Although Temple himself would probably have preferred a revision more faithful to his original tone, he could not have objected too strenuously to what reached print. For the majority of readers, reading only the English text, Swift's translation would preserve the flavor of the originals, while anyone inspecting the French column opposite would find a French that flatters Temple's mastery of the tongue.

If neither Swift nor Temple personally made the final revisions, and if Temple had reason to approve them when Swift did not, the solution must lie in a third party whom Temple brought in for the purpose. Thanks to intolerance in France, Huguenot refugees were common enough in England in the 1690s—and often poor enough to hire out as French masters. Boyer himself had to scramble to make a living earlier in the decade: he too worked as a French master, but eventually fared better than most.[45] No French names appear in the list of employees drawn up at Temple's death and now preserved in the Osborn Collection at Yale University, but the job would not necessarily have justified a continuing place on the payroll. For that matter, Temple had a Huguenot for a daughter-in-law, although she apparently lived away from Moor Park and remained unpopular with the family.[46]

Amusingly enough, in light of his later strictures on Swift's translation, the leading candidate is Boyer himself. At least in 1714, as we shall see, Boyer seems to have had ties with Temple's sister Lady Giffard. In the strikingly Modern preface to his *Royal Dictionary* of French and English, which appeared in the year of Temple's death, he flatters Temple in a way which only Temple or one of Temple's intimates would easily have recognized. Other lexicographers, says Boyer, have missed "the greatest *Beauties* and *Delicacies* of the *English Tongue,* which are scatterd up and down the Writings of the great Masters of that Language, such as Archbishop Tillotson, Bishop Sprat, Sir Roger l'Estrange, Mr. Dryden, Sir William Temple, and some few others. . . ." So far Boyer's tribute is public and impersonal, but he continues with a private *hommage* echoing Temple himself. Out of Temple and the other "great Masters" of the English language "might be composed a full and perfect Dictionary, if gather'd with industrious Care and Labour, and digested into good Order, for the *Architect* is only wanting, and not the *Materials* for such a Building." In the last phrases with their metaphor suitably pointed with italics (one of the "common Privileges of a Writer," Swift said about this time, is that "whatever word or Sentence is Printed in a different Character, shall be judged to contain something extraordinary either of *Wit* or of *Sublime"*) Boyer echoes Temple's prescription for a general history of England, in the preface to the *Introduction to the History of England.* By joining together the work of the most esteemed historical authors, says Temple, a public-spirited editor might frame a full body of English history, "if collected with Pains and Care, and digested with good Order; *for the Architect is only wanting, and not the Materials for such a Building.*"⁴⁷ Elsewhere in his own preface, Boyer acknowledges the help of "my Worthy and ingenious Friend Mr. Savage, who, with no small pains, has encreased my Collections with above a thousand Words of his own Gathering." Here is the probable link to Temple. The "Worthy and ingenious" Mr. Savage is the translator and miscellaneous writer John Savage, whom Sir Harold Williams supposes the Mr. Savage who travelled to Farnham, next door to Moor Park, to preach the eulogy at Temple's funeral or memorial service. (We do not know his prior connections with Moor Park, but clearly a stranger would not have been summoned for such a task.) To get the best "Delicacies" of the English tongue, Boyer also acknowledges "the Advice of several Ingenious and Learned English Gentlemen, to direct him [Boyer] in his Undertaking." If Temple had called on Boyer, through Savage, to help polish his French letters, it is not improbable that he honored the Huguenot with a little advice in return.⁴⁸

In the end, the reviser's identity matters relatively little, so long as Swift's and Temple's roles begin to emerge. Between Swift's later testimony to Lady Giffard, and the autograph evidence in the Downton transcript itself, it is clear that Temple remained in close control of the editing while the transcript was in use, from about 1670 until some point in the late 1690s. The final French revisions further suggest that Temple retained his control in the last stages as well. Swift would have had special reason to translate faithfully if Temple were still in the picture, and the Downton transcript illustrates how closely and literally he did the job. Whenever the printed French text shows a noticeable variation from the translation, in matters of fact or of phrasing, a reader can feel fairly certain that Swift is merely following copy. In three cases out of four, the transcript will reveal a French so close to the translation that it is sometimes possible to predict its exact wording in advance.

Swift's Translations: The Question of Texts

In the remaining instances, oddly enough, the transcript French stands no closer to Swift's translation than does the printed French. In the letter to De Witt of 17 April 1668, for instance, occurs a passage in which the printed and transcript French texts resemble each other more closely than they do the translation:

<table>
<tr>
<td>

Car Je n'ay pas encore remarqué
aucune chose dans le cours de
cette affaire dont je n'auray pas
venu a bout avec vous sans le
moindre chagrin ou chaleur mais
de bonne grace mesme. . . .

(T, p. 168)

</td>
<td>

Je n'ay encore rien remarqué dans
le cours de cette affaire dont je ne
fusse venu á bout avec vous sans
le moindre chagrin, mais même
agrement. . . .

(i, 352–53)

</td>
</tr>
</table>

Although somewhat closer to the transcript than to the printed French,[49] Swift's translation omits two elements which both French texts agree on: the qualifying idea of "encore" ('I have not *yet* observed') and the final positive phrase, "mais de bonne grace mesme" or "mais même agrement." "For I have not observed one thing in the course of this Affair," it reads, "which you and I could not have compassed without the least Heat or Discontent . . ." (i, 352–53). Similarly, in a later letter to De Witt, the translation uncharacteristically phrases an idea in the passive voice, when both French versions agree on the active. In the transcript text, Temple tells De Witt that "vostre domestique vous a tousjours relasché des fatigues que le publique vous a donné" (T, p. 186), and the printed text reads similarly if more elaborately, "votre domestique vous a toujours servi d'unique relachement dans les fatigues que vous causent les affaires publiques . . ." (i, 398). Swift could easily have kept the clause active by using the verbs "lessened" or "eased," but instead he inverts the order and chooses the passive verb "were eas'd": "your Fatigues for the Publick were eas'd by your Domestick Entertainments . . ." (i, 398). In the process, he fails to translate the French texts' qualifier "tou[s]jours," in "Fatigues for the Publick were [always] eas'd," and he shortens the relative clause around "les fatigues que . . ." to make it a short prepositional phrase, "your Fatigues for the Publick."

In another passage (in a different letter), he even seems to omit one of Temple's illustrative details. Writing to his Dutch friend De Wicquefort after hostilities had broken out between Holland and England in 1672, Temple dwells on his wish to repay De Wicquefort's past kindnesses. He alludes to the laws which govern private commerce between belligerent nations. "Since Publick Edicts do not forbid any Commerce that is only used for withdrawing Effects in either Country," reads the translation, "I am by that means allowed to acquit my self of the Acknowledgments I ow you . . ." (ii, 313–14). According to the English text, the laws permit commerce which "only" involves withdrawing effects from the other nation. Both French texts add a second, related legal provision, the right to adjust accounts in either country (which would involve deposits as well as withdrawals). Oddly enough, the transcript French is in all else extremely close to the translation, as if Swift had translated literally in every other respect:

. . . comme les edits publiques ne defendent pas le commerce qui se fait sur l'occasion de retirer les effets, ou adjuster ses contes dans l'un ou l'autre pais. . . .	. . . comme les Declarations des Princes ne deffendent pas cette sorte de commerce, qui n'a pour but que de retirer les effets & de souder ses comptes de part & d'autre. . . .
(T, p. 359)	(ii, 313)

Such departures from the transcript text are fairly insignificant in themselves, but compared to Swift's standard practice they seem downright reckless. What can account for a translation which suddenly takes liberties with Temple's text after following it so slavishly elsewhere? Perhaps Swift was inconsistent as a translator—faithful most of the time but on occasion somewhat daring, perhaps to tighten up Temple's tendency towards diffuseness. In all three of the passages just quoted, Swift's translation gives the most concise text—and thus the most Swiftian, as Ehrenpreis and Irwin would point out. Certainly there is something easy and attractive in such a hypothesis, which would grant Swift a modest fraction of the credit for the English text's virtues. Since Temple apparently oversaw the final rewriting of his French text (and felt the work necessary, to begin with), he probably took a similar interest when his secretary was busy translating some time earlier. After all, nine out of ten English readers would read Temple in the English version, not the French. But perhaps he did not check Swift's translations closely, or regularly. He had gout (or diseases which he diagnosed as such) and occasionally suffered bad spells in the 1690s.[50] His secretary might have felt freer, at such times, to risk an occasional departure from literal translation. Or possibly Swift received special permission for the departures. Most of them tend to cluster in a few letters, although the same letters contain many other passages which Swift appears to translate literally from the Downton text.

Curiously, these letters are usually ones which Temple had special reason to single out for editorial attention. When he wrote about De Witt's "Domestick Entertainments" helping ease his public responsibilities, for instance, Temple was composing a letter of condolence— an especially ticklish genre in which, to judge from the number he published, Temple particularly prided himself. De Witt's wife had just died, and Temple writes him a delicate and polished missive praising his close family feeling and urging him not to grieve too hard (I, 398–401). The letter adds little to Temple's narrative except to demonstrate the depth of the author's friendship, his delicacy, and his grace in a difficult task. This was hardly the first time that Temple chose to publish a private letter of condolence. In his first volume of *Miscellanea* (1679), he had printed one addressed to the Countess of Essex, offering condolences on her daughter's death and urging her not to grieve too much,[51] and in the *Letters* themselves there are at least three others besides the one to De Witt—most notably the letter "To Mon^r —— upon the Death of his Daughter" (II, 270–71), which provides more graceful words of sympathy and philosophic advice against grieving too much.[52] Similarly, Temple had reason to pay special attention to the late letter to De Wicquefort (II, 313–16), with its elaborate conceit about withdrawing effects from belligerent nations. In the transcript it appears as a late addition, copied in Swift's hand and (as we shall see) very likely composed or written not long before. Its studied portrait of Temple idling in an innocent country retirement (which as Woodbridge shows, was actually a busy time of writing tracts which urged a pro-Dutch foreign policy[53]) seems aimed more at public readers than at De Wicquefort personally. In print it appears as the last of the letters by Temple, and functions as a sort of coda. So too with the 1668 De Witt letter about the diplomatic difficulties which he and Temple could so easily compass if left to themselves: the letter deserved Temple's special attention, although for different reasons. On 17 April, when Temple originally wrote, he had just recently completed the Triple Alliance, moved to Flanders to negotiate Spanish cooperation, and was rushing to conclude matters in Brussels before travelling to Aix to negotiate the final peace treaty with France, Spain, Holland, and the German powers. It was one of the most exhausting periods of Temple's career, and by the time he reached Aix eleven days later, he fell ill enough to take to bed and have his secretary Downton assume some of his letter-writing duties (I, 354, 356, 365). Not surprisingly, the letter to De Witt shows Temple's French at its worst—muddy, headlong, and sometimes garbled.[54] The text required, and received, more revision than most of the other French letters.

The same letter to De Witt helps provide the explanation for Swift's patches of relatively free translation. The explanation is an unexpected one. Not only does the letter show Swift translating literally from the transcript French in places—and departing from it in others—but a few passages also show Swift translating literally from the *printed text* in turn. It is almost as if, while translating, Swift guessed some of the French revisions which the future would bring, missed fire on a few others, and otherwise confined himself to the uncorrected French of the Downton transcript. In the first few clauses of the letter (1, 347; T, p. 168), the transcript and printed French texts resemble each other fairly closely, but the few variations reveal that Swift follows the transcript here. For the transcript's talk of recent dispatches "lesquelles Nous font accroire," he gives the literal equivalent, "which make us believe," while the printed text reads "qui nous donnent lieu de croire" ('which give us occasion to believe'), and for the transcript's "Je ne voy pas la moindre difficulté" he translates literally with "I do not see the least Difficulty," while the printed text reads "je ne vois point de diffi- culté" ('I see no difficulty'). At the end of the page, when the two French texts diverge again, Swift starts to follow the printed French instead:

And for Spain, I never had the least scrupule upon their Conduct; And I still believe, as I ever did, that unless we drive them to Despair. . . .	A l'egard d'Espagne, je n'ay jamais eu le moindre scrupule sur sa conduite; et je croy encore, comme je l'ay toujours crû, qu'à moins que nous ne la reduisions au desespoir. . . .
	(1, 347)

Except for "A l'egard d'Espagne," which is not quite the same as "And for Spain," the translation is literal enough.[55] By contrast, the transcript text begins "et pour l'Espagne," which is closer to Swift's translation, but then rapidly parts company: "et pour l'Espagne Je n'ay jamais eu le moindre scrupule n'y n'en auray pas si nous ne la jettons pas à la fin dans les derniers desespoirs." Not only is the phrasing different after "le moindre scrupule," but the transcript provides an extra idea—that Temple "n'y n'en aura pas" ('nor [ever] will have [any such scruple]').[56]

Three pages later, it is even possible to see both the printed and the transcript texts contributing to a single sentence which Swift translates. In the general order of details (numbered 1 through 3 below) and in a few phrases (here emphasized), the translation follows the printed text:

So that by this Project, he sees *clearly*, [1] he must be confined *within Brussels as in a Prison*, [2] shut up by French Garrisons, [3] within seven Leagues of him on one side, and eight on the other. . . .	De sorte qu'il voit tres *clairement*, que par ce projet [1] il sera *dans Brusselles comme en prison*, [2] ou en ôtage á l'egard de la France, ses garnisons [3] d'un coté n'en etant qu'á huit lieues, et de l'autre qu'á sept. . . .
(1, 350)	(1, 350)

The order of details is much the same, but except for "clairement" and "dans Brusselles comme en prison," the phrasing is more elaborate in the printed French. By contrast, the transcript French omits any mention of seeing "clearly" and any comparison to prisons. It lists the details out of the order in which Swift translates them—the one participle "enfencé" ('sunk' or 'crammed') doing double duty, along the way, for both "confined" and "shut up"—but still preserves most of the phrasings which Swift uses:

So that by this Project, he sees clearly, [1] he must be confined within Brussels as in a Prison, [2] shut up by French Garrisons, [3] within seven Leagues of him on one side, and eight on the other. . . . (I, 350)	desorte que par ce projet il voit [1a] qu'il sera obligé de se voir enfencé [3] à sept lieues d'un costé et à huit de l'autre [1b] de Brusselles [2] par les Guarnisons de ffrance. . . . (T, p. 168)

Practically without exception, the transcript phrases appear closely translated somewhere in the English text: "par les Guarnisons de ffrance" by "by French Garrisons," "il sera obligé de se voir enfencé" by "he must be confined" (although 'see himself' would be closer than "be"), and "à sept lieues d'un costé et à huit de l'autre" by "within seven Leagues . . . on one side, and eight on the other" (compare with the printed French, which gives eight leagues first, then seven). As usual, Swift seems to translate so closely, whether in the transcript phrases or in the printed text's phrase, "dans Brusselles comme en prison," that it is hard to believe that his translation either took liberties with the syntax of the transcript French, if he was translating the transcript, or that it took liberties with the vocabulary of the printed French, if he somehow had secured the final revision to translate.

Instead, Swift seems to be working from an intermediate text—a text which preserves most of the transcript vocabulary but improves the syntax and adds a couple of new ideas. Alternate explanations are conceivable but much less likely. Perhaps, on occasion, Swift translated freely from the transcript, and Temple (charmed by the prison simile and his secretary's talents generally) told the French master, or whomever, to incorporate Swift's changes into the final French text. Unfortunately, the reverse is just as often the case. As we have seen, the printed French sometimes agrees more with the transcript than with Swift's translation—and not always to its best advantage stylistically. For that matter, incorporating elements from the translation would introduce complications in the reviser's work, involving a constant comparison back and forth between the transcript French and the translation. It would also reduce the likelihood of altering a letter's tone. Consulting Swift's translation, for instance, should have reminded Monsieur that Temple meant the Baron Wreden letter to sound jolly and informal, but we have noticed that the revisions still miss the point. Another possible hypothesis would involve a translation from both texts at once—Downton's transcript and the printed French—but here the difficulties multiply even more. Why stick so closely to a superseded text, in three places out of four, especially when the resulting translation risks charges like Boyer's, of faulty translation? Why reject Temple's late additions or corrections of fact, like those involving the Spanish truce or Baron Wreden's mistress? And most of all, if Swift had the freedom to choose which reading to translate, why does he cramp his style by translating so literally so much of the time? A final hypothesis might have Swift and the Frenchman working at the same time, translating and revising Temple's French piecemeal, so that for any French letter Swift might hope to find an occasional sentence ready-revised but surrounded by uncorrected ones. Here the absurdities are even more self-evident. Who would set about overhauling a text by first settling, bee-like, on a few isolated phrases and sentences, when he knew that he must revise the surrounding ones as well? And even if he began revising this way, why would Swift insist on elbowing him aside to translate a partly revised text, instead of waiting for the final product?

A much more realistic hypothesis involves an intermediate French text, partway between the Downton transcript and the text printed in the *Letters*. Before calling in outside help, for the final revisions, Temple would have been wholly in character to try once more to shore up his French, especially in the more sensitive or awkwardly-phrased letters. In Swift he had a secretary who could make a fair copy from the Downton transcript, in which to enter the new corrections. As already noted, the Downton transcript itself shows evidence of recopying for revision, but was growing too full to accommodate new transcriptions of Temple's thirty French letters. After receiving its revisions and corrections (rather minor ones compared to the professional rewriting yet to come) this second transcript would be ready for Swift to translate. Afterwards it must have received its final French revisions. With the second transcript in hand, complete with its early readings (taken from the Downton transcript) and the revisions newly added, the man responsible for the final rewriting could then opt to restore occasional Downton readings which had been altered in the second transcript. This would explain the occasional passages in which Swift's translation seems to introduce material absent in both the Downton transcript and the printed text.[57] The occasional passages with translations which mirror the printed French text would represent alterations added first in the intermediate transcript and then carried verbatim into the final rewriting. The great bulk of Swift's English, which reflects the Downton transcript, would represent Downton readings carried over without further alteration into the new transcript. The occasional spots of translation which seem intermediate between the Downton and the printed texts would represent second-transcript alterations which Monsieur carried a little further. This category would include the passages which seem an amalgam of both, like the one about the Spaniards being "shut up by French Garrisons" within Brussels. Temple's original past participle, "enfencé" ('sunk,' 'crammed,' or 'forced') seems to develop into two separate participles in the version which Swift translates (the French equivalents of "confined" and "shut up"), while the printed text develops the idea of "confined" and "shut up" even further, into "[être] dans Brusselles comme en prison" and "[être] en ôtage." Similarly, in an early letter to the French adventurer Gourville, a new element develops in one passage. In the Downton transcript, Temple reports that De Witt is extremely pleased with him for his sincerity and openness, and that "moy avec toute la raison du monde Je me loüe infiniment de Luy et de la Sienne" (T, p. 157; 'am infinitely pleased with him and his'). In the translation, Swift alters the final element ("et de la Sienne") to tighten and complete the parallel, with Temple saying that "I with all the Reason in the World am infinitely pleased with him *upon the same Score*" (1, 180, my italics). In the printed French, the order is changed and the final phrase, "upon the same Score," develops into a clause of its own: "moy, je me loue infiniment de luy; j'en ay toutes les raisons du monde, & je dois á toute sa conduite les eloges qu'il donne á la mienne."

In theory, of course, there can be no absolute certainty of an intermediate French text, at least until its transcript turns up. Either Swift was fairly consistent in translating closely, or he was quite inconsistent. If his translations reflect a basically consistent practice, then their noteworthy anomalies in phrasing, syntax, or subject matter must reflect textual variants present in Swift's French copy-text. If Swift were inconsistent as a translator—and unpredictably so—the alternate hypotheses come into play, with all their awkward and implausible ramifications. Comparing the Downton transcript, the translation, and the printed French has produced ample evidence that Swift aimed at word-for-word translation, even to seeking English cognates for Temple's French vocabulary. Swift seems to translate literally in the many passages which mirror the Downton French (the great bulk of the translated material), and he seems to translate literally in the occasional passages which mirror the printed French. What is more, his translations can even mirror both texts within a single paragraph or sentence. In pragmatic terms, an intermediate French text provides the only viable explanation of the anomalies in the translation.

The Intermediate French Revisions and the Question of Authority

Who then made the intermediate textual changes which the translation reflects? Whoever it was, he usually retained the Downton transcript's expressions when changing its structure—even when the wording is too elliptical for the best French usage, as in "et pour" rather than
"à l'égard de" or "enfencé à sept lieues d'un costé et à huit de l'autre par
. . ." rather than "ses garnisons d'un coté n'en etant qu'á huit lieues, et
de l'autre qu'a sept." In the great majority of the translations, of course,
the reviser retains almost everything intact from the Downton transcript. Clearly he was not the native speaker who undertook the final
rewriting. More likely, it was Temple himself. The letter to De Witt of
27 May 1668, for instance, shows a change in ideas between the Downton
transcript and the version which Swift translated. It is a subtle change
which only Temple would have introduced. Now that the treaty of Aix
is final, writes Temple, England and Holland must work towards put-
ting Spain in a better posture for defending her Flemish territories.
After conquering enough of Spanish Flanders to leave the rest almost
defenseless, Louis XIV had offered Spain the alternative of yielding
France either the conquered Flemish territory or Spain's territory of
Franche-Comté, in Burgundy (I, 327–29). Surprisingly, Spain chose to
retain the Franche-Comté. Meanwhile Louis had overrun most of it and
had levelled the Spanish fortifications there (I, 350). Therefore, writes
Temple in the Downton version, the best occasion of entering into
further negotiations would be "la restitution de la Bourgogne dans un
estat si peu convenable a la promesse du Roy tres Chretien" (T, p. 171).
Once the Spanish receive the Franche-Comté back, with its defenses
destroyed, the allies can demand further satisfaction, because the
French king's alternative had mentioned the territory in its original,
undamaged state, before France had invaded it. By the time Swift translated the passage, the emphasis had changed. Now the occasion for
entering into further negotiations will be *"to represent that* the Restitution of Burgundy in the Condition it is in at present, is *an offer* not
agreeable to the Promises of the Most Christian King" (I, 397, my italics).[58] In other words, Spain should not accept the territory back and
then complain, as the Downton version suggests, but should rather
consider it "an offer" subject to further negotiation before any restitution takes place. To a layman the distinction may seem minor, since in
both cases the allies' bargaining position would depend on Louis's will-
ingness to keep his early promises. Even so, an experienced diplomat
like Temple would have appreciated the differences in application, since
the French could argue that, by receiving the territory back, Spain

would imply its acceptance of the bargain—damage or no damage to the territory involved. And since Temple's letter only discusses vague future contingencies, rather than negotiations actually under way, only Temple would have cared enough to alter his suggestions to make them seem cannier than they actually were. As it turned out, the question was wholly academic. Spain received the territory back, apparently without demur,[59] and Temple never alludes to the subject again. No matter how immersed in the Downton transcript, Swift could not have known enough to change the text himself.

If Temple supervised the intermediate textual revisions (as was the case at all other stages), and if Temple originated at least some of them himself, there is still a good chance that he allowed his secretary to propose a few for consideration. At least in Temple's French, this might account for Swift's odd claim of responsibility for making "literal amendments." Swift's later letter to Temple's sister at least furnishes a precedent for textual alterations proposed by Swift and accepted by Temple. In an early draft of Temple's *Memoirs, Part III*, which Temple prepared for the press in the 1690s and which Swift brought out in 1709, there appeared a passage criticizing the good faith of the Earl of Sunderland. In April 1697, Sunderland briefly entered office as Lord Chamberlain. Through December Swift apparently entertained hopes of advancement through him, presumably on the strength of Temple's recommendation.[60] Speaking of Temple in 1709, Swift concedes that "that passage about my Ld Sunderland was left out by his Consent; thô to say the Truth at my Intreaty; and I would fain have prevailed to have left out another."[61] If Swift could make suggestions about the *Memoirs, Part III* in 1697, and hope that Temple might accept them, there is every reason to suspect that he enjoyed the same privilege, during the same general period, with the *Letters*. Indeed, the Downton transcript preserves one long passage lacking in the printed text, and it is just the sort of thing which Swift might have counselled Temple to remove. In his letter of 2 November 1669, Temple sends Sir Orlando Bridgeman, then Lord Keeper, a list of suggestions for increasing Charles II's revenues. As printed, the letter furnishes six particular schemes (II, 52–55), none affecting the clergy. In the Downton transcript he adds another (appearing in fifth place, T, p. 231). "I cannot imagine," writes Temple, "but ye Bishops and Clergy may be disposed to give the King freely in consideration of his present wants a tenth at least of all their temporall, and spirituall Revenue . . ." and then proceeds to supply details and legal precedents for the proposal. The proposal would have been repugnant to Swift in later years, and probably would have upset him in the period immediately following his ordination in 1694. On the other hand, Tem-

ple had equally good reasons to wish the passage removed. In a publication meant to glorify his opposition to France, the fountainhead of
absolutism, it little suited to show himself suggesting ways for Charles
to stretch the royal prerogative—especially by reviving old and dubious
precedents, an unpopular proceeding in which Charles, his father, and
his brother James had all indulged. Printing a suggestion aimed against
the clergy would have been even more dangerous for Temple's reputation. His praise of Dutch religious toleration, in the *Observations upon the
United Provinces of the Netherlands* (1672/3), had already raised doubts
about the depth of his religious belief, and in later years his contemporary, Bishop Burnet, accused him of irreligion.[62] To Bridgeman, Temple urged the King's ecclesiastical prerogative "by ye Papall power
being invested in him by Act of Parliament," and suggested that the
King might extort the money by threatening the Church with "the
frequent tenths that were payd upon severall occasions of old to the
Pope"—or, if necessary, remind it "what advantages the King might at
any time make by yielding to a generall temper of the Nation to the
prejudice of their great Revenues in lands aswell as other powers." In
one breath Temple cynically invokes the precedent of the Pope, the
bugbear of Restoration England, and in the other he as cynically suggests the disestablishment of the Church, a reminder of the Crom-
well era. Not only would the passage have damaged Temple's public
image, as the sole prop of public virtue and honesty in Charles's time,
but its extreme naiveté would have hurt his reputation for political
sagacity, to which even Burnet subscribed.[63] Not surprisingly, the
passage appears in the Downton transcript with a large X drawn
through it.

If there is no firm evidence, in the end, that Swift proposed some
of the changes adopted in the intermediate French text which he translated, the temptation to think so remains strong. Often his translations
reflect a slightly more concise text than what the Downton transcript
provides. In the final letter to De Wicquefort, for instance, with all its
marks of revision for the intermediate transcript, Temple speaks most
plainly in the translation: "In the mean time, I thank you for the Favour
of your last . . ." (II, 314). In the Downton transcript, the final phrase had
appeared as a pair of relative clauses: "Je vous rend grace en même tems
de la faveur que j'ay recû par la vôtre qui m'a êté dernierement rendüe"
(T, p. 359). The printed text returns to the same syntax.[64] Unfortunately,
stylistic evidence is often unreliable, and when it involves minor points
of conciseness, in writing a foreign language, it is chancier yet. For a
secretary to propose emendations would be the most natural thing in
the world, especially when he sees his master ill at ease in a language,

and fretful about it. Even so, it seems impossible to identify any one such emendation with reasonable hope of certainty.

Swift and Temple's English Letters

If the Downton transcript reveals that Swift witnessed a good deal with Temple's French letters but enjoyed little initiative, other evidence suggests that the same pattern holds true even more strongly for Temple's letters in English. Between the time of Swift's final entries in the Downton transcript and the appearance of the *Letters* in print, Temple apparently authorized few if any substantive changes in the English texts. On the other hand, at least three of the letters which Swift and young Esther Johnson copied into the transcript represent texts on which Temple had been working in the late 1690s, either to rewrite substantially or to compose from scratch. He meant the *Letters* to serve as something more than a miscellaneous collection of historical documents, and here he needed to improve upon the record. In both the prefaces to the *Letters* and to the *Memoirs, Part III* (1709), Swift reports Temple's oft-expressed design to have the published *Letters* serve in place of the first part of his memoirs, covering his embassies abroad between 1665 and 1670. These memoirs Temple had burned, Swift suggests, because they contained too much praise for Temple's early patron Lord Arlington, then the chief architect of England's foreign policy.[65] Although Temple had long idolized the man, Arlington proved a good deal less staunch in his pro-Dutch and anti-French principles than Temple had wanted to believe. At a time when Temple thought that he was serving Arlington by trying to maintain the Triple Alliance, Arlington had been helping to arrange the antithetical secret Treaty of Dover (1670), by which Charles II became a pensioner of the French king. Despite considerable tacking about, Arlington eventually lost most of his power at Court and became an open figure of fun. After Temple returned to the diplomatic service in 1674 under a new patron (his wife's cousin Danby), Arlington even made a hurried trip to Holland to meddle in business which Temple considered his own prerogative there.

By substituting a collection of letters for his memoirs, and by choosing the letters carefully, Temple could partly disguise the extent of his early admiration for Arlington. At the same time Temple needed to give the collection narrative shape and present himself in the most favorable light that circumstances allowed. On the face of it, the policies he had followed so enthusiastically abroad between 1665 and 1670 had produced embarrassing results. The anti-Dutch alliance with the Bishop of Munster, which he had pursued in 1665–66, backfired painfully when the much-admired Bishop pocketed most of his English subsidies and made a separate peace with Holland. Temple's pro-Dutch Triple Alliance of 1668 had laid the groundwork for his friend De Witt's downfall and the Anglo-French war which devastated Holland in 1672. Since the Triple Alliance proved as lastingly popular in England as it had been ephemeral in its operation, the *Letters* celebrate it at great length, with a disproportionate amount of space devoted to letters paying tribute to Temple's greatness and despatch in the negotiations. Although the historian Keith Feiling has found in Temple "a wild and sanguine ardour, carried away by any imaginable combination of the moment, and bearing the successive imprint of stronger personalities,"[66] the *Letters* instead celebrate his steadiness, his sagacity, and his impressive foresight as to the course of future events.

From the surviving evidence, we may judge that Temple succeeded in finding a large number of letters which he could publish with little or nothing in the way of alteration. Of the fifteen English letters for which I have found originals or official copies, thirteen show no alterations beyond occasional stylistic improvements or deletions of trivia.[67] On the other hand he can be seen making large-scale revisions or additions in a few especially sensitive letters, some of them traceable only through intermediate copies. As early as the 1670s, for instance, Thomas Downton copied into the transcript the important letter to Arlington dated July 1669 and printed in *Letters*, II, 72–79. The printed text reads much as the transcript version does (T, pp. 241–45), but the A.L.s. in the Public Record Office is markedly different.[68] For the transcript version, Temple dropped much of the original. After the first two sentences, he expanded and completely rewrote what remained of the opening paragraphs, which discussed the English bargaining position for a projected marine treaty covering the rights of the Dutch and English East India Companies. The revised text endows Temple with unexpected foresight as to the influences secretly working at Court to destroy the Triple Alliance and to come to terms with the hated French. In the original Temple seems unaware of them. The impression is unwittingly confirmed by his sister, Lady Giffard, who had been with him at the Hague during this time. Writing in 1690, she recalled that Temple "had observed a disposition before to complain of the Dutch upon small occasions," but that he still "suspected nothing till my Lord Arlington the September after [i.e. in 1670] hurried him over [to England] in soe much hast. . . ."[69] The printed *Letters* remedy this defect. Of course letters carry a greater air of authenticity than memoirs do, even when they are self-collected and self-edited: Temple's perspicacious and unusually early premonitions about the French drift at Court have accordingly found their way into the history books.[70]

Because Temple almost certainly retained the loose copies from which the transcript had been worked up, Swift would have had opportunities to ascertain the revisions made before his time. Others he saw more directly. Before Temple had him enter the late additions in the Downton transcript, Swift drew up an index of its contents then extant, including Temple's important letter to his father of 10 May 1666. The letter sums up and gives narrative shape to the section of the *Letters* dealing with Temple's Munster negotiations. Although the pages in question have since been cut out of the transcript, the letter began on p. 34 and according to Swift's index took up no more than six pages originally. Working under Swift's supervision, young Stella then copied the same letter into a blank section of the transcript (T, pp. 194–204). Although her hand is at least as compact as those of the earlier copyists employed on the volume, the recopied text fills a good ten pages this time. While we do not know how the earlier text read, Temple had clearly taken the opportunity to expand it extensively.[71] Just as clearly, Swift would have known what was going on. As revised and published (I, 52–66), the letter recounts Temple's heroic dash to and from Munster shortly before the Bishop deserted the English, and it documents his perspicacity in guessing the Bishop's true intentions just in time to hold up the last installment of his subsidy. To judge from the 1669 letter to Arlington, we may suspect that Temple took the opportunity to endow himself with a little extra foresight or sagacity, or at least to sharpen the drama.

After Stella copied the expanded letter to Temple's father, Swift himself transcribed six new letters not listed in his earlier index. As a group they serve a useful narrative purpose by summarizing and commenting upon the actions traced piecemeal in the other letters. For two of the six, the discovery of loose drafts dating from the 1690s suggests that Temple composed or at least heavily reworked them then to help supplement the original letters in the transcript. Now in the Harold Williams bequest at Cambridge, the first is Temple's autograph draft of his letter to his brother Sir John, dated 23 May 1672 and eventually printed in the *Letters*, II, 309–12. Rather sloppily penned, the draft contains half a dozen revisions in Temple's hand, mainly stylistic. Collation suggests that it served as Swift's copy text for the finished version entered in the transcript (T, pp. 318–19). Certainly the letter served a useful purpose in the collection. With a keen and judicious analysis, it summarizes developments in foreign affairs since the next earliest letter in the collection, dated a full eight months before. Indeed the neat chronological fit itself suggests that Temple composed the letter years after its ostensible date, to help round out the collection.[72] Now in the British Museum (though not in the Longe Deposit of Temple's diplomatic papers), the other loose draft gives the early text of Temple's letter to his friend Orlando Bridgeman dated 23 Mar. 1668, eventually printed in the *Letters*, I, 327–34. Again in Temple's hand, the document is even more a working draft than the first. Frequent corrections and alterations are entered in Temple's and a second hand. By size and watermark, the paper is the same used in the other draft and in several documents known to have been drawn up at Moor Park in the period 1697–99. Once again, the letter reads as if Temple had the benefit of hindsight. He gives an impressive analysis of the complex 'Alternative' question concerning France, Spain, and the Franche-Comté in 1668, including an exposition of the Spanish viceroy's "inmost Thoughts upon this Subject."[73]

Neither of the loose copies contains any sign of Swift's autograph, as if Temple used him for nothing more important than making fair copies in the Downton transcript (and supplying notes, as he did, about the proposed location of each added letter in the order already established). By the same token, it is difficult to believe that Swift did not have some inkling of what the letters represented. We may likewise wonder about the authenticity of the four other useful letters which he copied at this time: Temple to his brother, 10 Oct. 1667 (printed in *Letters*, I, 119–28); to Bridgeman again, 24 Apr. 1669 (II, 64–70); to his father again, 14 Sept. 1671 (II, 302–8); and to Abraham de Wicquefort, 10 Oct. 1672 (II, 313–16). Many of Temple's loose papers of this period have been scattered, and the miscellaneous provenance of the two suspicious drafts suggests that some of the others may one day surface somewhere else. With the two drafts so far traced, we are meanwhile left with the impression that Temple did not exactly avail himself of his secretary's talents for English composition.

Swift's Work with the Letters: *Implications and Conclusions*

Do the *Letters* hold anything else for which Swift can receive credit for exercising some initiative? The question has important implications. In any normal working relationship, a halfway capable secretary soon earns a certain latitude in his work, and in Swift Temple could count on an employee of more than usual intelligence and linguistic facility. In the late 1690s, when Swift seemingly worked on the Downton transcript, he was also busy with *A Tale of a Tub*—a book which, if nothing else, shows a fair share of intelligence and skill.[74] To judge from the surviving textual evidence, which supports Swift's claims in his prefaces and his letter to Lady Giffard, he exercised more initiative in the 1699 *Letters* project than for any of the six other titles which Temple employed him in readying for the press. In the bulky companion volume of *Letters* (1703), which contains no French translations, Swift claims to omit "several Letters Addressed to Persons with whom this Author Corresponded without any particular Confidence, farther than upon account of their Posts"[75]; for the *Memoirs, Part III* (1709) he privately admitted asking Temple to delete the two unflattering references to Lord Sunderland. For these and the four other titles—*Miscellanea, The Second Part* (1690), *Memoirs of What Past in Christendom* (1691), *An Introduction to the History of England* (1694), and *Miscellanea, The Third Part* (1701) —I can find nothing else to show that Swift ever deviated from Temple's implicit and explicit instructions, except perhaps in timing publication of the posthumous works. The *Memoirs, Part III*, for instance, embarrassed Lady Giffard by appearing during the life of a widowed friend of whose husband the book spoke harshly.[76] Before conceding his part in timing the publication, and in agitating for the Sunderland deletions, Swift tells her that "By particular Commands, one thing is understood, and by generall ones another. And I might insist upon it, that I had particular Commands for every Thing I did, though more particular for some than for others." He then outlines his work for Temple (making fresh copies and correcting "all along by his Orders") and defends Temple's choice of him as literary executor:

> Madam; I pretend not to have had the least Share in Sr Wm Temples Confidence above his Relations, or his commonest Friends; (I have but too good Reason to think otherwise). But this was a thing in my way; and it was no more than to prefer the Advice of a lawyer or even of a Tradesman before that of his Friends, in Things that related to their Callings. Nobody else had conversed so much with his Manuscripts as I, and since I was not wholly illiterate, I cannot imagine whom else he could leave the Care of his Writings to.[77]

In his choice of imagery—the comparison to a lawyer or "even" a tradesman furnishing advice "in Things that related to their Callings" —Swift seems to suggest that he sometimes proffered professional advice as Temple's secretary. The description also hints at resentment or wounded pride. He discounts any personal confidence with the great man above "his commonest Friends," claims to "have but too good Reason to think otherwise," and half implies that Temple could deal with him as with a mere tradesman. Anger with Lady Giffard must account for much of Swift's tone, but not necessarily for all of it.[78] Since he was also anxious to emphasize his obedience to Temple's wishes, the letter may exaggerate this as well. Accordingly the *Letters* of 1699 take on special importance as a test of Swift's claims. Because of his translations (and the possibility of his "literal amendments" in Temple's French), they show Swift carrying more responsibility than elsewhere. They seem to date from Swift's last sojourn at Moor Park, when he should have enjoyed Temple's confidence more than before, and because the Downton transcript survives, they permit an intimate glance at Swift's work for Temple.

By rights, then, the *Letters* ought to reveal Swift working enthusiastically for Temple, receiving special confidence and exercising a correspondingly broad initiative in making emendations, deletions, and most of all, translations. Irwin searches the translations for evidence of a "close personal relationship with Sir William Temple," and finds passages which (compared to the printed French) make Swift appear warmly filial, in "functioning to shield Sir William from himself" or to "protect Sir William's published image."[79] In more general terms, Ehrenpreis maintains that "to the lonely refugee, who had never known his own father, and whose nearest substitute for one (Uncle Godwin) was dying or dead, the role of a son must have been all too easy to imagine" in 1689, and that despite diffidence on Swift's part and reserve on Temple's, the "relationship probably developed the more painlessly. . . ." Ten years later, with Swift as far to seek as ever in his career, Ehrenpreis sees Swift still "pretending to believe that Sir William would act as the father Swift would have liked to have had" and diverting any natural resentment towards surrogate figures instead. Of Swift's work for Temple after 1696, Ehrenpreis accordingly asserts that "Swift functioned less as a clerk than as a companion and literary aide."[80]

The Downton transcript fails to substantiate the impression. At each step, it seems to confirm Swift's testimony and suggest that Temple kept his secretary on a short leash—that Swift did little beyond copy, read aloud, and enter Temple's corrections. He may also have offered an occasional emendation of Temple's French for the master's approval, but direct textual confirmation is lacking. As a translator, he stayed so close to his text that he would seem even more like a clerk, plodding mechanically on, did not Temple's anglicized French lend itself so well to literal translation. In matters of vocabulary, perhaps, Swift may have exercised a modest and occasional license, but the evidence is uncertain. Especially in the Baron Wreden letter, with its jocular familiarity, the translation may reflect a muted freedom with vocabulary. Some phrases which Irwin finds "stronger, tougher, and more concrete" in the translation[81] seem almost equally superior when the translation is compared to the Downton text: "great Belly" (I, 20) for "gros ventre" in the Downton transcript (T, p. 147) as well as the printed French; "half a dozen Glasses" for "six verres" in both French versions (I, 16); "over Bogs and Marshes" for Downton's "à travers de marois" and the printed text's "a travers de Marais impracticables" (I, 20). If the intermediate transcript survived to confirm the impression, there would be no difficulty in assigning Swift some credit here. Unfortunately, the Baron Wreden letter belongs to the number which show definite signs of alteration in the intermediate text,[82] and it is equally possible that Swift merely translates intermediate revisions which the later reviser rejected. The phrase "great Belly," for instance, may render a slangier intermediate reading, "grosse panse," changed back to the original "gros ventre" in the printed text. "Bogs and Marshes" may render something like "bourbiers et marois," intermediate between the Downton "marois" and the printed "marais impracticables," and "half a dozen" may translate "une demi douzaine de," changed from "six" and later changed back to it.[83] In each particular instance, certainty is impossible, but probably at least a few of them represent his own quiet initiative as translator. Swift must have sensed the tone which Temple meant to take with Wreden. The seeming liberties of Swift's translation, however minor in themselves, reflect the colloquial bonhomie for which the transcript French strives.

If Swift receives every benefit of the doubt, as a translator and possible reviser of Temple's French, any Swiftian qualities in his translations still depend overwhelmingly on the nature of the French which his patron wrote. Ehrenpreis rightly observes that they exhibit "a freshness of speech which Temple rarely affords"—in English, at least.[84] Temple's English letters usually sound more ponderous and studied. For most of a decade, Swift had to immerse himself in Temple's English style as he copied, read, entered corrections for, and otherwise helped Temple ready some seven separate titles filling more than 3,000 octavo pages as published, all but the 1699 *Letters* almost exclusively in English. To judge by the *Letters*, however, Temple's French style seems to have influenced Swift more than his English, if indeed the stylistic similarities noted by Irwin and Ehrenpreis actually stem from Temple's influence. How could Swift be influenced more by Temple's French than by his English, or to phrase the question more realistically, why should Temple sound more Swiftian when writing in a language less familiar to him than English?

The answer lies in the nature of Temple's French, which shows him essentially thinking in English, employing English syntax, and clothing the result in a suit of French vocabulary. When a man feels thoroughly at home in his own language, and then seeks to frame his thoughts in a less familiar tongue, the first casualty is rhetorical polish. He falls back on the simpler and more natural constructions which he grew up with, thinks in, and at least on everyday occasions, still tends to speak in. So it sometimes seems with Temple. In his English letters, conciseness often gives way to digressive fluency. He usually writes with an air of dignity and offhand eloquence, though never too elaborate or ostentatious to suit with the character of gentlemanly candor. As clause succeeds clause, at a moderate but regular pace, they tone down potential sharpness or dazzle in his antitheses and parallels. Even when he confides in an old friend like Bridgeman—Temple's closest friend in government and, at the time of writing, one of the few at Whitehall who still endorsed Temple's pro-Dutch policies—Temple comes across as a man of eloquence, tact, and offhand dignity:

> I am glad to receive your Lordship's Opinion concerning the Continuance of our Measures abroad, because I see not at present where we can take better: And I the more need some such Encouragements as your Opinion gives me; because, to say the Truth, I should not be very apt to concur with you in it from the Observation I can make from hence of several other Circumstances: However, nothing ought to discourage such publick Hearts as your Lordship from contributing all they can to the Firmness of such Counsels, as they esteem most Just and Safe at least, if we are not in Condition to think so far as Glorious:

> *Multa dies variusq; Labor mutabilis Aevi*
> *Detulit in melius*————   (II, 256–57)

In substance, Temple's comments are harsh: his pro-Dutch policies are being supplanted by worse ones; he feels little hope, but still wants Bridgeman to continue his support as long as he safely can. In manner, Temple betrays no trace of harshness or even crispness beyond the elliptical phrase "I see not at present where we can take better." Instead he sounds perfectly composed. Alternating clauses of cause and effect set up an unhurried rhythm ("I am glad . . . because . . . : And I the more need some Encouragements . . . because . . ."). When he turns from fears to hopes ("However, nothing ought to discourage . . .") nothing disrupts either the rhythm or the sense of poise behind it. The final antithesis, between "Just and Safe" courses of action and "Glorious" ones, loses its potential edge through wordy qualification, and concludes with an apt tag from Vergil which, if nothing else, shows Temple's easy self-command.[85] Temple sounds candid enough in acknowledging his feelings, open gratitude for "such Encouragements as your Opinion gives me," but he never stoops to awkwardness or informality. Bridgeman remains "your Lordship" (by virtue of being Charles's Lord Keeper) and is invoked gracefully if somewhat condescendingly in the third person ("nothing ought to discourage such publick Hearts as your Lordship from contributing all they can . . ."). A few pages later, Temple cannot even thank his own father for a gift of money, without a certain dignity in his periods and a graceful negligence in his tone:

> I must make you my humble Acknowledgments for so great a Present, as you have been pleased to send me towards that Expence I have resolved to make at Sheen: And assure you, no part of it shall either go any other way, or lessen what I had intended of my own. . . . (II, 288)

All told, Temple's English style suits "a Person of the greatest Wisdom, Justice, Liberality, Politeness, Eloquence," as Swift later phrased it. Temple probably worked hard to achieve it. In her *Life* of Temple, Lady Giffard distinguishes between his natural manner as reflected in his unpublished early essays, which she praises with typical hyperbole, and the more restrained manner which he adopted in pieces meant for publication. "Such a spirit & range of fancy & imagination, I beleeve, has seldom bin seen," she confides, "wch he us'd to say cost him afterwards so much pains to suppress in all he writt and made publick, & wch perhaps might keep them from passing so well with niser people, as they did with me."[86] Writing in a less familiar language, Temple is generally less successful in his efforts at suppression. Tight, natural phrasing often replaces his gentlemanly periods, and the usual impression of poise gives way to more direct expressions of human feeling. Not long after writing to Bridgeman, he writes to De Witt, a friend almost as close as Bridgeman, to convey similar sentiments. Temple's policies have failed, but De Witt has just sent him some testimonies of his high opinion of him. Temple begins gracefully enough, by attributing De Witt's praise to De Witt's generosity and good nature, but before long a note of uncharacteristic harshness creeps in:

> . . . mais schachant que l'opinion que Vous tesmoignez de Moy n'est fondée que sur celle de mes bonnes intentions, Je ne veux plus me defendre puisque dans ce Siecle il y a si peu de gloire d'estre homme de bien, et qu'on sera guere soupçonné d'y employer sa vanité nonplus que ses poursuittes. (T, p. 346)

Until he reaches "ce Siecle" and its sense of priorities, he maintains something like his usual dignified pace, but afterwards he slips into uncharacteristic conciseness. Instead of muffling, it emphasizes the final antithesis and the bitterness of mind behind it. As we have already seen, Swift's 'Swiftian' translation does justice both to the phrasing and the tone: ". . . in this Age, there is so little Honour in being a good Man, that none are suspected to employ their Vanity about it, any more than their Pursuits" (II, 300). In other, more everyday letters, Temple sounds equally natural if somewhat less emotional. Writing to De Witt on business in late February 1668, for instance, Temple begins with his usual attempt at graceful stateliness, somewhat hobbled by his French:

> J'ay receu beaucoup de satisfaction aussi bien que de l'honneur par la vostre du 25 et suis fort aise de remarquer cette conformité des Sentiments entre Nous depuis que Nous sommes separez qu'il y avoit tousjours durant mon Sejour à la Haye. Je vous ecriray asture [à cette heure] de mon encre l'ayant fait auparavant de celle du Marquis qui ne voulut pas se contenter sans que Je vous fisse cette despesche là. . . . (T, p. 162)

Instead of providing Temple's usual march of full clauses, measured but distinct, the first sentence comes out somewhat jumbled, with its slightly confusing succession of prepositional phrases and short relative clauses ("entre . . . depuis que . . . que . . . durant . . ."). With the second sentence, Temple falls back even more on ellipsis which sharpens his antithesis, "ecriray asture de mon encre l'ayant fait auparavant de celle du Marquis." As Swift translates the text—or a practically identical intermediate version, which corrects "mon encre" to "mon propre encre"—Temple sounds like a plain-speaking businessman trying for an initial flourish but soon abandoning the attempt:

> I have received much Satisfaction as well as Honour by yours of the 25th, and am very glad to observe the same Conformity of Sentiments between us since we parted, that there ever was while I resided at the Hague. I shall write to you now with *my own Ink;* having already done it with that of the *Marquess,* who would not be satisfied, 'till I sent you that Dispatch. . . . (I, 284; Swift's emphases)

In both instances Temple's French makes for livelier English in the translation and fulfills, along the way, Temple's wish to exhibit his versatility of style. His English letters may also vary a little in tone and style, but in them the public Temple is almost always audible—graceful, dignified, seemingly candid but always poised, as a gentleman should be. His French letters, by contrast, cover a wider range of tone and style, and often sound as if a man were actually speaking them, rather than an author exercising his quill to achieve a more graceful and stylized approximation of speech. By lacking the special command of French which would enable him to project his preferred image of himself, Temple falls into a style closer to Swift's.[87]

The question of influence is harder to establish. Even Ehrenpreis, who takes it for granted that "Swift derived his literary style immediately from Temple," still warns that the two men's "common traits often seem more innate than acquired; and even when a trait does appear to have been taught or learned, it is often the effect either of general fashion or of common masters."[88] Swift's translations compound the difficulty. Conceivably, as Swift translated, the syntax and vocabulary of Temple's original French achieved a lasting impression on the young secretary—much more, at least, than Temple's English letters did. A likelier source of influence would be Temple's everyday speech, which his French seems to reflect. On and off for a decade, Swift enjoyed ample opportunity to hear the great man talk, and Temple's everyday vocabulary and speech patterns must have become thoroughly familiar to him. How far they may have affected Swift's writing style is another question, far too indeterminate to answer. It is hard enough to define Swift's style to begin with, except to note its variousness. The most traditional definitions cite his conciseness, his preference for concrete diction, and his sharpness of parallel and antithesis,[89] but even at his most characteristic, Swift can sound windy, fuzzy in diction, and muddy in his periods.[90] If anything can comprehend Swift's style, it is probably his penchant for speaking in voices other than his own, and in shifting them frequently, without warning. As Ehrenpreis observes of Swift's letters to Stella, an observer can continually "observe his art springing from its deepest source, his games with identity, and with human speech as the most precise register of personality."[91] If Swift's prose generally imitates actual speech (more than literary models, at least), then Temple's natural accents probably exerted more influence on Swift than his standard written rhetoric. Temple's French letters may then provide a vague sort of model. As Irwin points out, Temple's tone can shift from letter to letter, whether hearty to Baron Wreden, businesslike to De Witt, or sympathetic on the death of De Witt's daughter.[92] But this is true of any sort of personal correspondence. Whether in the 1660s or the 1980s, the average letter-writer automatically addresses a favorite nephew in terms noticeably different from those in which he addresses his bank manager. If Temple differs from the norm, it is chiefly in being conscious of the fact and by counting it a stylistic virtue (at least to judge from Swift's comment in the preface to the *Letters*).

In more important respects, Temple's use of tone contrasts strongly with Swift's. Within any one letter, whether French or English, Temple's voice remains largely the same, except for the occasions in French when linguistic difficulties produce an uncharacteristic crispness or plainness. In French or English, Temple almost always strives to present himself seriously, in generally flattering terms. Swift's best letters show different impulses at work. In a single letter to Stella, for example, Swift can play with four or five different voices, each undercutting the other.[93] There and elsewhere in his personal letters, Swift will sometimes wrap himself in the mantle of dignity, but most often only to mock himself in it. Some years later, for instance, in an informal letter to his friend John Gay, he pauses for a message to the Duchess of Queensberry. It is in exaggeratedly dignified terms. Gay had amused her with tales of Swift's table manners at Pope's villa at Twickenham, where the forks had two prongs instead of the more elegant three. "I desire you will tell her Grace," Swift replies,

> that the ill management of forks is not to be helpt when they are only bidential, which happens in all poor houses, especially those of Poets, upon which account a knife was obsolutly necessary at Mr Pope's, where it was morally impossible with a bidential fork to convey a morsel of beef with the incumberance of mustard & turnips into your mouth at once.[94]

Swift and Gay well knew that Pope's house was far from "poor," and in purpose and effect, Swift's burlesque show of superiority could not differ more from Temple's show of gentility. If, as Ehrenpreis maintains, Temple's literary style and aesthetic judgment must represent "either models or points of departure for Swift's own,"[95] the two men's letters suggest that here, at least, Swift found in his employer a point of departure in the most radical sense.

In only a few instances, chiefly in the 1690s, does Swift seem to model his epistolary style on Temple's. Usually it happens when he means to impress a naive correspondent, or put distance between himself and an importunate one. In Swift's earliest extant letter to Jane Waring—ostensibly written to second his proposal of marriage but, as Ehrenpreis suggests, more probably composed with full confidence that she would continue to demur[96]—Swift begins by hinting his romantic impatience in a series of crisp philosophical parallels and antitheses much in the manner of Temple's French:

> Impatience is the most inseparable quality of a lover, and indeed of every person who is in pursuit of a design whereon he conceives his greatest happiness or misery to depend. It is the same thing in war, in courts, and in common business. Every one who hunts after pleasure, or fame, or fortune, is still restless and uneasy till he has hunted down his game: and all this is not only very natural, but something reasonable too; for a violent

desire is little better than a distemper, and therefore men are not to blame in looking after a cure.

Swift continues by reporting himself "hugely infected" with this malady and "vain enough" to think he has reasons, on Jane's account. Meanwhile the damage has already been done. Few maidens are likely to credit impatience in a man who pauses to philosophize so neatly about it, much less to value it in a man who calls it "little better than a distemper" and who seeks after "a cure," which (after all) might include its suppression as much as its gratification.

Temple's more grandiloquent and genteel English style appears in an earlier letter to Swift's young cousin Deane Swift, written as Jonathan prepared to leave England and take holy orders in Ireland in 1694. Then nineteen or twenty, the cousin was working in Portugal with a prosperous stepbrother, the eldest surviving son of Swift's beneficent Uncle Godwin and now an influential merchant in Lisbon's English community. To qualify for the priesthood, Swift needed to produce some promise of a church living ready to accommodate him. Accordingly, without mentioning the requirement, and after lavishing compliments on the influential stepbrother, Swift broadly hints that "I wish it may ever lye in my Cosin's way or Yours to have Interest to bring me in Chaplain of the Factory" in Lisbon.[97] Before proceeding to business, though, Swift flatters the young cousin with an elaborate show of interest in him and his letters describing Portugal. (Indeed, there is nothing else among Swift's surviving letters and works to suggest that Swift took much interest in the young man at any other point in their lives.[98]) Between the easy but dignified periods, the tendency towards digressiveness, and the affable yet condescending tone, the style is vintage Temple, as reflected in his English letters:

> I received your kind Letter to day from your Sister, and am very glad to find you will spare time from Business so far as to write a long Letter to one you have none at all with but Friendship, which, as the World passes, is perhaps one of the idlest Things in it. 'Tis a pleasure to me to see You sally out of your Road, and take Notice of Curiosityes, of which I am very glad to have Part, and desire You to set by some idle minutes for a Commerce which shall ever be dear to Me, and from so good an Observer as you may easily be, cannot fail of being useful. . . .[99]

To a callow youth, far from the center of power in England and even farther from the life of a country gentleman, such blandishments from a famous gentleman's intimate associate must have been gratifying.[100] Not only does Swift profess pleasure that the cousin "will spare time from your Business so far as to write," as if the cousin were conferring the benefit, but he also dwells gracefully on the pleasure of more such benefits and their undoubted salubriousness ("from so good an Observer . . . cannot fail of being useful"). The cousin would hardly notice any oddity in the easy touch of world-weariness (". . . Friendship, which as the World passes, is perhaps one of the idlest Things in it"), because Jonathan, at the ripe old age of twenty-six, had undoubtedly seen a great deal of the world in England. The tone is so pervasively affable and genteel that the cousin would scarcely have noticed, much less resented, the equally pervasive condescension, culminating in " 'Tis a pleasure to see You sally out of your Road," as if the cousin's road normally precluded noticing anything of interest, or as if his *raison d'être* were Swift's amusement.[101]

When at last Swift reaches the time to begin talking business (after much on the cousin's description of Portugal, and on Swift's gratitude to the influential stepbrother), he introduces it with an off-hand negligence which again sounds like Temple:

> I forgot to tell You I left Sir William Temple a month ago, just as I foretold it to You, and every thing happened thereupon exactly as I guest. He was extream angry I left Him, and yet would not oblige Himself any further than upon my good Behaviour, nor would promise any thing firmly to Me at all; so that every Body judged I did best to leave Him. . . .[102]

To Swift, whose career was hanging fire in 1694, the rupture would have loomed large, but to his distant cousin he implies that the event was too minor to remember at first: "I forgot to tell You. . . ." Although Swift's style is more concise than earlier in the letter, the tone remains Temple's. The emphasis sits squarely on Swift's prescience and good judgment. He has left Moor Park *"just as I foretold it,"* and everything has happened *"exactly as I guest . . .* so that *every Body judged I did best* to leave Him."* It is Temple, not his erstwhile associate, who is the loser. Swift describes the great man as "extream angry," while affecting indifference himself. To the transcriber of Temple's memoirs and letters, with their emphasis on Temple's prescience and good judgment, a suitable model would not have been hard to find. It would be only natural for a hero-worshipping secretary to ape his master's style or stance. To employ it so deftly and so knowingly argues something more. If Swift echoes Temple to Jane Waring and to his young cousin Deane, while maintaining a more natural style with his relatively sophisticated correspondents, it would almost seem that the secretary had subjected Temple's style to a long, hard scrutiny, and found even better uses for it than his master had.

In the final analysis, Swift's work with the Temple letters strongly suggests that master and secretary maintained an association more complex and less poignant than currently believed. As a document of a modified father-son relationship, and as a test of Temple's confidence in Swift in their last years together, the Downton transcript is a decided disappointment. It reveals Swift working more as a secretary or glorified clerk than the "companion and literary aide" that Ehrenpreis describes. That Temple entrusted his veteran secretary with making the French and Latin translations may argue some degree of confidence, but by translating so closely and doggedly, Swift exercises an almost minimal initiative. To judge by the Downton transcript and Swift's later testimony, Temple maintained a close control and scrutiny at every step from the original copying in the 1670s to the final revising in the 1690s, almost certainly including the work of translation. Copying, reading aloud, entering Temple's corrections, then copying or arranging for a fresh transcript, reading aloud, and entering more corrections—session after session, day after day—Swift would have sensed more strongly than any casual reader what Temple meant the letters to show the world of himself. More pertinently, in the French letters, the secretary would have enjoyed a ringside seat for witnessing the spectacle of the great statesman Temple, the veteran of ten years' diplomacy on the Continent and the repository of the "greatest Wisdom, Justice, Liberality, Politeness, Eloquence, of his Age and Nation," fussing repeatedly over his irreducibly anglicized and outmoded French, and finally sending it out for professional treatment. If Swift was busy writing *A Tale of a Tub* during the same period, as seems most probable, he must have possessed a certain strength of mind, not to mention a certain habit of irony. To guess his reactions would probably be presumptuous, given the lack of direct documentary evidence, but it would be even more presumptuous to assume that the experience had no effect on his filial hero-worship, assuming he ever indulged in any. On other occasions when Temple failed to embody one of Swift's presumed ideals, or actively disobliged him, Ehrenpreis theorizes that Swift sought his ideal elsewhere, scourged himself for his master's failing, or blamed it on a convenient third party.[103] With the *Letters,* Swift's experience would have made such excuses difficult. He spent too much time with the transcripts and the translations to ignore Temple's practice in favor of some mistily-imagined ideal, especially since Temple's decision to supersede the French text which he translated struck so close to home, by exposing Swift to sneers like Boyer's. After following Temple's "particular Commands" at each step, even a past master of self-deception would find no occasion to blame himself or others for his employer's lack of dignity. Between 1696 and 1698, to judge from his *Tale*'s Digression on Madness, Swift's penchant ran more towards unmasking or satirizing self-deception.

CHAPTER TWO

Further Secretarial Duties:

Swift, Thomas Swift, and Temple's Campaigns Against Dunton and DuCros

As we have seen, the Downton transcript suggests the need for reopening the question of Swift's experience at Moor Park and his attitudes towards Temple, with all their implications about Temple's influence on Swift's mind and art. Judging by what the transcript reveals, Swift's feelings were almost certainly more complex and ambivalent than currently believed, and probably less naive as well. Any safe conclusions must follow thorough inspection and evaluation of all the surviving evidence, both Swift's recorded references to Temple and contemporary records of Swift's life in the 1690s. Even then, a full understanding may prove impossible. For one thing, too little survives from the time, less than for any other period in Swift's life except possibly for the five years following the fall of the Harley-Bolingbroke ministry in 1714 and the four or five years preceding Swift's mental dissolution in 1741–42. For another, Swift is a notoriously dangerous man to quote out of context, and all too often his contexts are highly complicated and ambiguous. Practically everyone who has ever theorized about Gulliver's *Travels*, for instance, has at least considered seeking support from Swift's famous letters to Pope on the subject, dated 29 September and 26 November 1725, with their assertions that "principally I hate and detest that animal called man, although I hartily love John, Peter, Thomas and so forth," that "I have got Materials Towards a Treatis proving the falsity of that Definition *animal rationale,* and to show it should be only *rationis capax,*" that "I am not content with despising it [the world], but I would anger it if I could with safety," and that "after all I do not hate Mankind, it is vous autres who hate them because you would have them reasonable Animals. . . ."[1] Out of context, parts of the letters provide almost limitless possibilities. In context, the possibilities narrow and grow tentative, not only from Swift's shifts in tone, which leave nothing wholly serious, but from his apparent purpose, which involved teasing yet encouraging Pope for expressing a wish to appear as Swift's partner in writing benevolent satire. In the end the two letters function less to reveal Swift's private thoughts on the *Travels*, whatever they were, than to show Swift probing tentatively towards some sort of literary alliance or partnership with Pope, whose views of acceptable public images and intended readerships differed from Swift's even when their satiric inclinations ran parallel.[2]

The 'Penitential' Letter and Thomas Swift's Preferment

Even in his earliest writings, it is risky to quote Swift out of context. From his letter to his young cousin in Lisbon, for instance, it is clear that Swift and Temple had a parting of the ways in 1694, when Swift left Moor Park for Ireland and ordination. How deep the rift was is another question. Taken out of context, Swift's statement suggests that Temple was in fact "extream angry" at losing Swift, as if he found him indispensable.[3] The context suggests otherwise. Swift writes to impress an unsophisticated youth and shows definite signs of exaggerating the dramatic elements in the letter, along with his own central position, by contrasting Temple's extreme ire with his own implied (and highly dubious) nonchalance. Four months later Swift found that he needed Temple's voucher for his good behavior at Moor Park. He wrote to request it and received it almost immediately.[4] Out of context, Swift's statement seems to mean that Temple, being "extream angry," must have drawn on large reserves of forbearance or affection in providing the testimonial so promptly. In context, though, the claim of Temple's anger may only mean that he felt a mild and transitory annoyance, and accordingly supplied the testimonial without consulting any feelings deeper than an ordinary employer's. If anyone was angry, it was probably Swift himself, despite his show of indifference. After all, Temple had declined to provide him with firm assurances of advancement in England. When Swift wrote to request the testimonial, he began the letter with the unexpected greeting, "May it please Your Honor"—the only such superscription to be found among the many hundreds of his surviving letters. A servant seeking reinstatement might have used such a formula, and as Swift well knew, it likewise resembled the proper formula for addressing royalty ('May it please Your Majesty,' 'May it please Your Highness'). The letter's physical format also follows a practice used in letters to royalty. After entering the greeting at the top of the first page, Swift left a great blank space before beginning his message, humbly at the bottom—much as he did many years later, in flattering jest, with the Duchess of Queensberry ("My beginning thus low is meant as a Mark of respect, like receiving your Grace at the bottom of the Stairs").[5] While Temple's self-esteem should have blinded him to such anomalies, coming from so young and inexperienced a correspondent, the formula remains suspicious to a less partial eye, as if Swift wrote in suppressed anger or sarcasm.

The letter's tone gives a similar impression. A little forelock-tugging is one thing, but Swift overdoes it. In the letter's superscription Temple was "Your Honor," and so he generally remains in the body of the letter. Swift rings the changes with the phrase: "The Sense I am in, how low I am fallen in Your Honor's Thoughts . . . I intreat Your Honor to understand . . . I intreat that Your Honor will consider this . . . the Reasons of quitting your Honor's Family . . . all entirely left to Your Honor's Mercy . . . all I dare beg at present from Your Honor . . . the Health and Felicity of Your Honor and Family . . ." and so on. Is it Sir William Temple whom Swift addresses or the honor which Temple felt his due? A disgraced butler might have written in such terms and meant them. With Swift it is hard to avoid a sense of something angrier and more complicated going on.

A reconstruction of events at Moor Park strengthens the impression that Swift had much to be angry about and Temple comparatively little. When Swift wrote to his young cousin Deane Swift on 3 June 1694, he said that he had left Temple's service "a month ago, just as I foretold it to You," or about May 1 after a period of dissatisfaction long enough to allow forewarning a correspondent in Portugal who has since replied to his note. Very possibly Swift's departure took place before all was settled with Temple's *Introduction to the History of England*, which was to appear in the fall. The inconvenience to Temple should not have been too great. By May Temple had a replacement secretary waiting in the wings, if not already ensconced at Moor Park. To make matters worse, Temple had been arranging preferments for the man during Swift's last few months in office. They were preferments of the sort which Temple had so conspicuously failed to provide for Swift, despite the greater claims which Swift had.

Swift's replacement was his own cousin Thomas, who had been his schoolmate at Kilkenny, at Trinity College, Dublin, and most recently at Oxford, from which both received their M.A.s in July 1692.[6] Both contemplated careers in the Church, but the ecclesiastical constitutions

and canons (no. 33) required a candidate to arrange for a church appointment before being admitted to holy orders. Since 1692 Temple had been
promising Jonathan a good living, a prebend in the King's gift. By
November of that year, Jonathan was complaining to his uncle William
Swift that Temple, "tho' he promises me the certainty of it, yet is less
forward than I would wish. . . ."[7] After another year of working and
waiting at Moor Park, Jonathan finally saw Temple bestirring himself
—not for Jonathan but for his cousin Thomas, then staying in London.
Under the circumstances it would be the most natural thing in the
world to react as Jonathan did, by quitting Moor Park and seeking
ordination on his own in Ireland.

In many instances the details are lacking, but the general outline
of Thomas Swift's progress can now be reconstructed from the diocesan
Subscription Book in Winchester and from parish registers preserved
in the Guildford Muniment Room.[8] Manning and Bray, the historians
of Surrey, record that Thomas was instituted rector of Puttenham,
Surrey, on 15 January 1693/4.[9] The living was in the King's gift. In one
instance, though, Manning and Bray have mistaken the facts. A bishop
will only institute a new incumbent when the living is vacant. The
Puttenham parish registers reveal that another man, not known to
them, was rector there until his death the following December. Five
days after his burial, Thomas Swift arrived at Puttenham to take possession and to make the appropriate entry in the register ("Successit Ec-
clesiae Parochiali de Puttenham Thomas Swift Oxon: A: M: Dec.ʳ 25.
1694"). A Crown living like Puttenham could not normally be filled in
five days or a week. Someone would have to contact the government to
nominate the candidate, the Crown would have to present him to the
bishop, the bishop would then have him instituted in Winchester and
finally arrange for the archdeacon or some other local clergyman to
manage his induction at Puttenham. Instead it seems that Thomas had
only gained the presentation or right of succession to the living in
January 1693/4. This was common enough practice for the times, and
the clerical forms appended to the 1695 *Valor Beneficiorum* include two
specimen Grants of Presentation on the next avoidance, for aspiring
candidates to copy out for their patrons' signature.[10]

Because Thomas could not succeed at Puttenham until the incum-
bent died, he received something else for the interim. The diocesan
Subscription Book reveals that he was licensed curate for East Clandon,
Surrey, on 5 March 1693/4, less than two months after the date of the
Puttenham business.

The names and places suggest the rest of the story. The rector of
Puttenham when Thomas received his grant of presentation was Simon

Geree, the brother of the successful pluralist John Geree (sometimes spelled Gery) who had long been Vicar of Farnham, next door to Moor Park, and nonresident Rector of East Clandon, fourteen miles down the road beyond Guildford. In death as in life, Simon Geree seems to have depended upon his brother: the year after John Geree buried him at Puttenham, John was named guardian of his three sons.[11] Simon had succeeded to the Puttenham living fairly late in life—in 1692, when his brother was sixty-three—and he apparently installed himself there even more expeditiously than Thomas Swift was to do two years later. The previous rector had died on 11 November 1692, and the entry for his burial three days later is recorded in the hand safely assignable to Simon Geree.[12] Almost certainly he had received the reversion of the living some time before, during the decline of his predecessor (first appointed in 1636 and, from the evidence of the parish registers, inactive after 1690).

Dependent as he was on his brother, Simon Geree had no known contacts at Court, the fount of patronage for Crown livings like Puttenham, just as Thomas Swift had no known leverage in Surrey except through Moor Park and his family's connection with Temple, himself fairly new to that part of the county. On the other hand, Temple had acquaintance enough at Court, beginning with the King and Queen.[13] John Geree's influence seems to have been purely local. His two livings were not in the King's gift, the patrons of East Clandon being a local family named Heath and that of Farnham being the Archdeacon of Surrey, titular Rector of Farnham. Geree had kin in the vicinity and seems himself to have been related (most probably as a son or nephew) to the Stephen Geree who had been Rector of Abinger, Surrey, until his death in 1665, four years before John received his living at Farnham.[14] Temple had a family friend and potential helper to provide for, just as John Geree had a dependent brother with family. The evidence points towards mutual accommodation, Temple using his influence at Court to provide for Geree's elderly brother and then, when it became useful to have Thomas Swift in the neighborhood, calling upon Geree to furnish a sinecure for Thomas until the living at Puttenham should again fall vacant. The succession of traded favors probably goes back even further. Temple, for instance, had a poor young cousin named William Dingley (probably a brother of Rebecca Dingley, his sister's attendant at Moor Park and Stella's lifelong friend) whom he seems in some respects to have treated as a dependent.[15] Through his own family and through Temple's, Dingley had no hereditary connections with Corpus Christi College, Oxford, but it was there he matriculated in May 1691, six months after Geree's son John enrolled at the same college. (As students and fellows the two were to remain together there for sixteen years, receiving their B.A.s in 1694/5, their M.A.s in 1697/8, and their B.D.s in 1707.) Quite probably the senior Geree had something to do with the arrangements made for Dingley.[16]

Thomas Swift's clerical activities (or lack of them) bear out the impression of traded favors. It is questionable how much benefit, if any, John Geree derived from his new curate for East Clandon. Thomas Swift's name and handwriting do not appear in the parish registers there, and in the book of churchwardens' accounts, which the rector or his representative was supposed to sign each year, Thomas's signature is lacking.[17] (On 15 April 1694, more than a month after Thomas was licensed curate and signed the Subscription Book in Winchester, it was Geree himself who signed the churchwardens' accounts in East Clandon. The following April there are no signatures at all but for one of the outgoing wardens.) For at least part of Thomas's tenure as curate, we know that he was working at Moor Park as secretary, and it is entirely possible that he was there as early as March or April 1694, a month or so before his cousin Jonathan finally departed. Thomas's elevation to the rectory of Puttenham the following December seemingly made little difference to his sense of priorities. At least for the first few months, Temple continued to take precedence. Although Puttenham is only four miles from Moor Park, Thomas's autograph does not appear at all in the parish registers there between the time of his induction at Christmas 1694 and the following June (a single burial entry). He did not take over for good until July or early August, when he began new registers.

Despite Ehrenpreis's supposition that Jonathan may have recommended Thomas to Temple as his replacement, a surviving letter of Jonathan's betrays a certain sourness about the prospects open to Thomas. While Puttenham was not a rich living (perhaps £60 or £70 a year[18]) it was still better than anything Jonathan had received.[19] More important, it allowed Thomas to take holy orders in England—something which Thomas seemingly wasted little time in doing, to judge from his obtaining a curate's license in March.[20] Jonathan writes on 6 December 1693, about a month before Thomas's grant to Puttenham came through. At the time Thomas was staying in London with his uncle Charles Davenant, the political writer, former commissioner of the excise, and once and future M.P. (Jonathan, by contrast, had no near kin in England with half Davenant's influence and contacts.) Thomas had written to Jonathan reporting a choice of positions open to him (at least two fairly certain, another much less so) but still had managed to complain of some area of unhappiness. "Y^r Letter speaks of so many

Choices of Employment," Jonathan replies, "that one would think you to[o] busy to be very unhappy. . . ." The tone softens as the paragraph continues, but when he later asks Thomas to help him with minor business in town, the tartness creeps back. "Tho You are so crammd with business," Jonathan begins, "I must needs desire yr assistance in. . . ." In closing he gives Thomas a brief report on a poem in progress but declines to send him a copy. He has completed 250 lines, he says, "and if I could tell what is become of Mr Thomas Swift whom I formerly knew I would send them to Him for his Judgment, but for yr self, it is Ominous and so I'll Conclude. . . ." The tone is jocular but the implications not altogether comfortable: Thomas has changed so much that Jonathan must consider withdrawing his trust.

Most significantly, perhaps, Thomas had asked his cousin for advice on one of the career choices offered to him. This Jonathan had declined to give: "For the rest, I think the advise of a Friend is very far from being disinterested, and to avoyd that was the very reason I forebore it." He also declines to advise him upon the least certain of Thomas's career options. "I cannot at this distance give a judgment near enough upon yr other hopes," he continues rather obscurely, "but if they be not certain, I think there is no avoyding the Choice of what is; This I told you, or something like it before." Certainly Jonathan "cannot much Pity yr present Circumstances," which at the very least "keep yr mind and yr body in Motion. . . ."[21] There is not much in the way of warmth or congratulation here. Jonathan had declined giving his advice before, and he now declines it again. We do not know how he figured in Temple's plans for Thomas, if he figured at all, but from the tone of his letter we may guess that he felt himself left out or passed over in some way. It is conceivable that Temple had once offered him the same option which Thomas eventually accepted, and that Jonathan unwisely turned it down in the hope that Temple would make good on the more impressive prebendal appointment promised in 1692. Whatever the case, Jonathan still found himself becalmed when his cousin's sails were at last beginning to fill.

This was in December. By May Thomas had accepted the grant to Puttenham, taken holy orders, received his curate's sinecure for East Clandon, and was waiting in the wings to replace his cousin. Jonathan's bargaining position, if any, would have deteriorated even further. We may doubt that he left Moor Park in any charitable frame of mind, or that he felt any calmer the following October, when he found he had to beg a testimonial from Temple which would allow him to take holy orders in Ireland and secure an even more remote and unattractive benefice than Puttenham.

Temple's Project for a General History of England

Though a loser in one sense, Swift spared himself an unedifying spectacle, and a demeaning task, by leaving England when he did in 1694. Some of the details remain uncertain, but the general tenor is clear enough. Temple had been preparing his *Introduction to the History of England* for the press, and Swift's stand-in, Thomas, took over the secretarial duties. Although he ostensibly conceived it as an introduction for an approved general history of England—he treats only the earliest historical periods himself—Temple decided on publishing the book separately. Its title page carries the date 1695, but it appeared during the autumn of 1694, the publishers being Richard and Ralph Simpson. By 7 November it was being reviewed in a servile essay, full of the usual paraphrase and unacknowledged liftings, in the journal *Miscellaneous Letters, Giving an Account of the Works of the Learned*.[22] About the same time Temple received an equally flattering request from the eccentric Grub Street bookseller John Dunton, whose *Athenian Mercury* Temple greatly admired. Some months before, as Temple understood from Dunton, Dunton had supposedly undertaken a general history of England—just the sort of thing for which Temple said he had originally designed the *Introduction*. Would Temple furnish (as Thomas later paraphrased it) some "Directions & Instructions in ye Management of such a work"? In a letter of 9 November, the autograph copy of which survives in the Osborn Collection at Yale, Temple had Thomas answer Dunton, encourage the scheme, and hint that the *Introduction* could be incorporated into it. Through Thomas he proposed a patchwork history drawn from the work of the finest and best-esteemed authors already in print, a scheme already proposed in his preface to the *Introduction*, and he made specific suggestions for the sections to follow his own, which had only carried through to the death of William the Conqueror.[23]

Temple's plan was doomed from the start. Too many different publishers, including the Simpsons, owned the copyrights involved. More correspondence followed—Dunton afterwards mentioned "the Letters" which Temple sent him—but nothing came of the scheme besides some useful advertising points for Dunton. Their first announcements of the project came in the *London Gazette* for 8 November (the day before Temple answered Dunton's first letter) and in Dunton's *Athenian Mercury* for 13 November. There Dunton and his partners advertised the approaching publication of proposals for "a *General History of England*, pursuant to the Model and Directions laid down by Sir William Temple, in his late Introduction to the *History of England*."[24] At first promised "speedily" and "in a few days," the *Proposals for Printing a General History of England* duly appeared on 21 November. Temple's name figures prominently in the main body of the *Proposals,* but the undertakers no longer claim that the history will follow Temple's proposed model and directions. Instead they merely state that "The *Books* which we intend to consult for this *Great Work,* are those mentioned by Sir William Temple in his *Introduction,* and the Letters which he was pleased to send us. . . ." The history is not to be a composite work, after all, but rather a new composition by the minor historian James Tyrrell, several of whose dialogues on the English constitution, collectively known as *Bibliotheca Politica,* had appeared between 1692 and 1694. Even so, the main body of the *Proposals* keeps the spotlight squarely on Temple. At the start Dunton cites "The Complaint made by Sir William Temple in his late Introduction to the *History of England,* that we have not hitherto any good and approved *General History of England."* He justifies the present project by quoting "Sir William Temple's judicious Reflection" in the *Introduction,* about the need for such a work. Mentioning Temple's letters to him lends strength to a later claim, of "the Helps we promise our selves from the Correspondence that we have settled with divers Learned Men." Dunton concludes that "the great Authority of Sir William Temple" should be "sufficient to convince any Man of the *Great Usefulness* of such an *Undertaking.* . . ."[25]

To do Dunton justice, there is no reason to doubt his good faith in approaching Temple. Taken together, his earlier advertisements and the *Proposals* themselves suggest that he changed course after his negotiations with Temple fell through. Dunton's early advertisements of 8 and 13 November imply a composite history assembled from existing materials, rather than a new-written history by a single author, and instead of naming Tyrrell they speak only of "a learned Gentleman" or "that *Learned Gentleman* who has actually undertaken this *Province"* of incorporating some new manuscript materials being sent in. Writing to his old friend John Locke only three weeks before, Tyrrell himself says nothing about undertaking a history of England. He has just finished his thirteenth dialogue of *Bibliotheca Politica,* he tells Locke, and is now ready to begin a series of dialogues upon religion.[26] In the *Proposals* themselves, the text of the main section features Temple prominently enough but never even mentions Tyrrell. It treats the projected history so vaguely that, if printed under a different title, it could do double duty for a composite history of the sort that Temple had in mind. No author is mentioned, only a kind of editor. Much as in the earlier advertisements, Dunton invites patriotic readers to submit "any *Manuscripts, Memoirs, or Corrections* which they have made in the *Histories of England* already publish'd," and assures them "that they shall be carefully perus'd, and made use off for the Improvement of the Work," by the unnamed "Learned Gentleman who has undertaken this *Province.*" The same man will "take care that all *Defects* of former Authors be supplied. . . ."

Following the main section of proposals, and contrasting strongly with it, comes a section set in different type under the heading "Additional Proposals." Here Dunton gives a very different impression. The proposed history is decidedly not a composite affair, but rather a work to be composed by Tyrrell alone, whose high qualifications Dunton sets forth without once mentioning Temple's name. If Temple enters at all, it is through an indirect reference which suggests that Dunton's feelings towards him had undergone sudden alteration. Temple's *Introduction to the History of England,* just published, had given what Temple considered proper attention to important developments in early English history up to the end of William the Conqueror's reign. Treading close on its heels, the *Proposals* for Tyrrell's history announce that the first volume should be ready by July 1695, and that it should contain a full and proper treatment of important developments in England *"from the Flood to William the Conqueror"*—chronologically the bulk of the period just treated by Temple, although Temple had in fact slighted the Saxon and earlier periods in favor of the Conqueror's reign. Dunton follows his outline of the volume's contents and use of proper sources (a point on which Temple was especially offhand[27]) with a summation pointedly set in italics: *"A Work that never yet hath been performed by any other."*[28]

Even before he read Dunton's *Proposals,* Temple had cause for anger. Without waiting for Temple's reply to his first letter—indeed, it seems, without first making sure of the copyright situation—Dunton had capitalized on Temple's name to drum up interest in the forthcoming proposals. Even worse, Temple got nowhere with his plan for a composite history assembled from the work of "Persons of great Worth and Learning, much honoured or esteemed in their Times," as he puts it in his preface to the *Introduction.* Instead of seeing his *Introduction* reprinted at the head of a collection of "approved & esteemed Authours" only—"authours of name or estimation," to use Thomas's phrases in the surviving letter to Dunton—Temple found his book passed over and his name involved with a much less appropriate cast of characters. James Tyrrell was no Lord Herbert of Cherbury, no Sir Francis Bacon or Sir Thomas More, to name three of the "approved & esteemed Authours" whom Temple associated with himself in the proposed collection. Neither a celebrated statesman nor an acclaimed genius, Tyrrell was a mere private gentleman, a pedestrian and somewhat pedantic writer who, despite his Willia-

mite politics and his knowledge of historical sources, brought neither
fame nor a background in public affairs to his task. (The unnamed
"Learned Gentleman" in Dunton's advertisements would have
sounded even worse.)

Admittedly Temple had published his *Introduction* "to invite and
encourage some worthy Spirit, and true Lover of our Country" to
produce a "good or approved general History of England," but Tyrrell
could hardly have qualified for the task. In his preface to the *Introduction*,
Temple had expressed contempt for scholars of Tyrrell's sort, the tedious, painstaking kind of historian who is deficient in taste and personally undistinguished. Other nations have produced good general histories, he says, "but ours have been written by such mean and vulgar
Authors, so tedious in their Relations, or rather Collections, so injudi-
cious in the Choice of what was fit to be told or to be let alone, with so
little Order, and in so wretched a Style," that their works are hardly
worth troubling with. Despite Temple's patriotic call for "some abler
Hand" to carry on his historical work, now that he has taken care of the
most difficult periods of English history, it is doubtful that Temple
would have approved any prospective author at all. He implies that the
few acceptable candidates have already declined the task. For the honor
of his nation, Temple himself had once thought of producing an
abridged history of England like Mezeray's of France, but as he modestly notes, reminding his readers of his famous public career, "those
Thoughts were soon diverted by other Imployments, wherein I had the
Hopes, as well as the Intentions of doing some greater Services to my
Country." Since then he has likewise "endeavoured to engage some of
my Friends in the same Design, whom I thought capable of atchieving
it, but [I] have not prevailed; some pretending Modesty, and others too
much valuing Ease."[29] Instead of a new history, it seems, the only
realistic hope in the mid-1690s lies with a composite work, which a man
of lesser talents could assemble: "for the Architect is only wanting, and
not the Materials for such a Building." Since England apparently cannot produce an "abler Hand" than Temple's in 1694, Temple responded
to Dunton's letter not by suggesting possible authors for a new work,
but by laying down directions for a composite history drawn from the
old. To find Dunton proceeding with a new work, after all, would have
irritated Temple nearly as much as the use which Dunton made of
Temple's name, in the *Proposals* themselves.

By rights Temple should have expected even worse treatment from
a Grub Street eccentric like Dunton, whose rather dubious *Athenian
Mercury* was at this time carrying frequent advertisements for his own
"Elixir Stomachium" (or "Elixir Stomachicum," as Dunton alterna-

tively spells it), a distinguished palliative for ailments of that organ. Betrayal of a misplaced confidence, all the same, can gall worse than betrayal of a more reasonable one. Events make clear how strongly Temple responded to Dunton's proceedings. More than most journal publishers of the day, Dunton had mastered the art of using his journal to advertise his other chief wares (the stomach elixir being only a side-line). Week after week, the *Athenian Mercury* carried a full complement of house advertisements for the current crop of Dunton's books and pamphlets. Its editorial columns often served to puff the same wares. For a major endeavor like Tyrrell's *General History of England,* a multi-volume project depending upon advance sale of subscriptions, a reader would reasonably expect a great deal of play. With his advertisements of 13 and 20 November, Dunton began in typical fashion, but thereafter the advertisements ceased. Since Dunton retained his share in the *History* until Volume I appeared in 1696, it was not as if he had suddenly lost his financial interest in the book's success.[30] At irregular intervals brief advertisements for the project appeared in *The Present State of Europe,* a more restrained journal published by two of Dunton's three partners in the history, but the *Athenian Mercury* maintained an uncharacteristic silence. Possibly Dunton shared Temple's enthusiasm for the composite history and lost the feeling when he had to substitute the Tyrrell project. All the same, Dunton was not a man to neglect something in which he had a financial stake. More probably he received some sort of communication by which Temple made his displeasure known. (The Dunton-Temple correspondence was more extensive than the one surviving letter by Thomas Swift and the original inquiry which occasioned it: we recall Dunton's reference to the "Letters" he had received from Temple, and we shall soon see Thomas mentioning the "letters" which Dunton had sent to Temple.) Whatever happened, if it did not actually shame or scare Dunton from the usual publicity campaign, was enough to inspire the hostile note in the "Additional Proposals" section which Dunton printed with the *Proposals.*

Thomas Swift and Temple's Campaign Against the Dunton Project

Although some details remain obscure, Temple's next step is more easily determined. Again it involved negotiations conducted through his secretary. This time Temple used Thomas to sneak behind Dunton's back and encourage a project designed to drive Dunton's off the market. Communicating through Thomas at Moor Park in February 1694/95, Temple made the same old proposals for a general history, now in direct

competition with Dunton's, to the bookseller Richard Bentley (no relation to Temple's later foe, the classicist of the same name).[31] Thomas has
long been eager to present Temple's case, it seems. Indirectly and then
directly, on his last two London visits, he has tried contacting Bentley
and associates. Thomas pretends to write Bentley on his own account,
but Temple's anger and bruised pride show through all too clearly.
Pretending that Temple had not even deigned to read Dunton's letters
—presumably Thomas had read them to him aloud—Thomas complains
that the Dunton party "made a noise with my patron's name, whilst
they took a way clear contrary to his directions [for the history], and yet
pretended that he writ, when it was I writ to them, for he did not so
much as read their letters." Thomas has taken it on himself to ask the
Simpsons, owners of the *Introduction*'s copyright, to join Bentley's
group and together undertake the rival history. To speed the process
along, some of Bentley's colleagues having balked at including the
Simpsons, Thomas has likewise taken it on himself to visit Bentley's
shop "once or twice" (without finding Bentley there), and now he takes
it on himself to divulge Temple's valuable directions for the history,
"since you seem desirous of these directions." Thomas can make assurances with a boldness surprising in so obscure a young parson: "I will
engage to get you subscriptions by my own acquaintance in these parts,
and Sir William Temple's directions, and the goodness of the method,
will get you more." Otherwise Bentley is asked to say nothing of the
business and (a matter of recurrent concern) "not to make use of Sir
William Temple's name."

Mostly it is eagerness and optimism which prevail, though seldom
unmixed with the twin preoccupations of glorifying Temple's name
and thwarting the rascal Dunton. Temple's *Introduction* will stand at the
head of an unsurpassable history drawn from "so many great authors"
who, in a phrase reminiscent of Temple, "were some of the wisest, the
greatest, or the best acquainted with affairs of any in their own time."
(Elsewhere in the letter, as in the earlier letter to Dunton, Thomas calls
for "approved and esteemed authors" and "authors of name and estimation.") In such a collection, works by anonymous writers pose a problem, it seems, because they are "published without a name." It is not
enough that the anonymous history of Richard II which Temple recommends be good in itself. Though unnamed, its author must also be a man
of standing, or so Temple implies by distinguishing between what is
"written well" and what is "by a good hand." The life of Richard which
Temple thinks he once saw was "written well, and by a good hand, as
he was then informed, though published without a name." Temple
could judge the book's merits for himself, but learning the author's

identity—and so determining how great his name, how 'good' his 'hand' —would depend on outside information.[32]

With its assemblage of distinguished histories by distinguished public figures, Temple's plan offers a publisher tremendous advantages, not the least of them the chance to ruin Dunton's rival project. Thomas assures Bentley that "no man will pretend to equal you"—here a glance at Dunton—if Bentley embraces Temple's proposals. By commissioning a new history instead of assembling a good composite one, the Dunton group has lost a great advantage. Should Bentley follow suit, Thomas predicts dire consequences. "But if you pretend to make most of your history *de novo*," he tells Bentley, "it will either take up many years doing, or will prove but a second edition of Sir Richard Baker," whose rather credulous *Chronicle of the Kings of England* (1643) suffered from a reputation which Addison and Fielding were to make good comic use of *(Dictionary of National Biography)*. "Some hand of note will take up the method which you slight," Thomas continues in melodramatic style, "and then a mercenary pen will never bear a second impression." But as Thomas well knew, the Bentley associates had no intention of slighting the composite history plan. They had apparently committed themselves to the idea well before the Simpsons tried to have Temple's *Introduction* included in the book: the Simpsons discovered that Bentley's associates had "made proceedings already another way." Thomas's threat is no threat at all, but rather an encouragement. It is the Dunton group which has slighted Temple's methods. In the angry prediction that "a mercenary pen will never bear a second impression" is a promise of triumph for Bentley, as Thomas's next words make clear. He knows the course which Bentley has taken. "You will find, by the event, that I guess well," he says: "I wish you a great deal of success. . . ." The "mercenary pen" is Tyrrell's, in a word. When Bentley enters the fray, it is the Dunton history which will never reach a second impression—a most desirable end, for which Bentley's success will seemingly provide the means.

Thomas makes one other point in passing, meant to demonstrate the value of Temple's specific directions for the history. He implies that even Dunton realizes their great worth and fears lest Bentley find them out. To get a copy of the directions, Thomas indicates, Thomas had to go back to Dunton, to whom he had originally sent the directions in November. Dunton would not yield them up unless Thomas promised *not* to do precisely what he does in the letter—give them to Bentley:

> . . . Dunton's society, when they could not take them [Temple's directions for the history], because they had not those authors in their own

power to print, yet when I was in town, would by no means let me have a copy, unless I would promise never to communicate them to your party. I wish you may make that advantage of them which the others are afraid of, by following their directions.[33]

Here Thomas demonstrates more loyalty towards Temple's cause than thoughtfulness about the action which his statement implies. In so glorious an undertaking, it seems, even a clergyman need not scruple breaking his word to a rascal like Dunton.

But can Thomas be trusted here? To act as he acted with Dunton suggests that Temple's directions for the history are a great secret, worth their weight in gold, as he implies throughout the letter. In fact, Temple's basic idea and half of his specific suggestions had been public property since November, when Temple announced them in the preface to his *Introduction*. To all appearances Bentley and his associates had long since taken the hint, and by the time Thomas wrote, their project was well advanced, as the publication of their proposals would prove. Thomas claims that he sends Temple's directions because "you seem desirous" of them, but the Simpsons' visit to Bentley and his own two bootless visits do not suggest much burning enthusiasm on Bentley's part. With its precious cargo of directions, Thomas's letter looks like an attempt to place Bentley under obligations to Temple, when Temple had less to give than to ask. That Temple managed to influence the outcome a little even so, the Bentley group's printed proposals would make clear. Meanwhile there is more than a touch of disingenousness in Thomas's letter for him. Possibly Thomas did not actually need to break his word for Temple's sake, and instead is merely exaggerating a half-truth or spreading a lie for him here.

That the question should even arise attests to the false position which Thomas so readily adopts in the letter. In his dubious dealings with Dunton (to give him the benefit of the doubt) he may actually have acted on his own initiative, but in all else it is impossible to credit his claims for himself. Instead it appears that he worked under close and attentive supervision. Of themselves, obscure country clerics do not pretend to issue authorizations for major publishing projects, especially when the project involves the use of a famous living author's published writings. The Simpsons would hardly have done Thomas's bidding in approaching Bentley unless they knew that they were obliging Thomas's master as well. Indeed the attitudes, moods, and preoccupations of Thomas's letter—often even the phrasing—point back to his employer. For that matter, three minor corrections in Temple's autograph appear on Thomas's surviving draft of the Dunton letter. This is almost certainly a copy used in drafting the letter to Bentley, if not the actual copy which Thomas implied that he made at Dunton's shop. With one exception, the outline for a composite history which Thomas sent Bentley reproduces, practically word for word, the outline composed for Dunton, and where Temple corrects in the Dunton copy, the letter to Bentley follows the altered reading (Appendix B). Temple's autograph corrections emphasize how fully he must take responsibility for his secretary's effusions.

If Thomas's letter to Bentley documents a course of action as questionable, in its way, as Dunton's behavior towards Temple, it also allows Temple the pretense of standing innocently on the sidelines while his secretary sees to the details and dirty work. Officially, at least, Thomas's doings have nothing to do with the great gentleman who so obviously authorized them. Bentley cannot make public claims, as Dunton did, that Temple had approached him. And even if his course of action had been more gentlemanly, Temple could hardly have acknowledged any interest in it at such a time. Thomas wrote to Bentley on 14 February 1694/5, only seven days after Temple's wife Dorothy—the Dorothy Osborne of the famous love letters to Temple forty years before—had been buried in Westminster Abbey.[34] Under such circumstances a gentleman could hardly be expected to concern himself with publishing projects, much less with thwarting a rascally bookseller or placing his own name among "so many great authors" who "were some of the wisest, the greatest, or the best acquainted with affairs of any in their own time." The decencies of mourning presumably kept Temple from consulting his notes and furnishing anew the historical directions which Thomas had to solicit from Dunton and then recopy (with Temple's minor alterations) into the letter to Bentley. In that letter Thomas gives no hint of the tragedy which Temple has suffered, but if nothing else the letter indicates that Temple was not so overwhelmed, seven days after burying his wife, as to forget the importance of his campaign for an English history collected from the greatest authors extant. To judge from the use made of Swift himself on Temple's death five years later, when the family needed someone to help with funeral arrangements in London (chapter 3), Thomas may well have carried a double commission on the second of the two London visits that he mentions. On the one hand he checked with the Simpsons and visited Bentley's shop, but when he found Bentley absent, he claims, "my own business called me away, and so put a stop to this." It is likely that "my own business" was actually Temple's as well, but of a different nature.

It is interesting to note that Temple's efforts, and Thomas's, bore some fruit. After wishing Bentley success, Thomas concludes his letter by reporting himself "willing to see your proposals, if you send any abroad." This was on 14 February. Sometime before 6 March Bentley, Richard Chiswell, and five other publishers issued *Proposals for Printing a Compleat History of England: Or, The Lives of all the Kings To His Present Majesty.* On one count the *Compleat History* proposals must have been disappointing, though not unexpectedly so. When the Simpsons had tried to include Temple's *Introduction* in the project, they found that Bentley's group had "made proceedings already another way." Sure enough, for the period down to the Norman Conquest, the *Compleat History* proposals list Milton's *History of Britain,* a far more scholarly and professional work than Temple's *Introduction.* Otherwise the proposals reflect Temple's ideas, Temple's sense of priorities, and very likely, Temple's influence as well. Not only do they announce a composite history of the sort that he wanted, but wherever practicable they also follow his specific recommendations about which authors to use, as laid down in Thomas's letter to Bentley and in Temple's preface to the *Introduction.*[35]

Most gratifying of all, perhaps, the proposals attack Dunton's project much more vigorously than they puff their own. First and last, the *Compleat History* proposals have a dog-in-the-manger air. With a circumspection surprising among publishers seeking subscribers, Bentley and his group make no great claims for their own proposed history. A composite effort, they concede, "may come short of the Perfection [which] might be wished for," but it "is certainly practicable, and seems the most accurate that can be reasonably expected. Such as it is, we freely submit it to the Judgment of the Learned. . . ." To the question of Dunton's proposed history, they devote much more attention. Like Temple, they imply that no one currently available is able to write an acceptable history of England. They even make an apparent bow in Temple's direction. As Temple records it, Temple once meant to serve England by writing an approved abridged history like Mezeray's of France, until great state occasions called him away, and he presents his *Introduction* not as a discrete work but as a difficult preliminary effort paving the way for a continuation by some future public-spirited worthy. On both counts, the Bentley proposals pay due homage to men like Temple, who prove that no one man can suddenly sit down and dash off a complete English history. "What would be the great Ornament of our History, if once finish'd," they observe in general terms,

> has been the main Discouragement from attempting it. We have not wanted Persons of the greatest Abilities, who, out of a Concern for the Publick, have set about it with the utmost Resolution; but have been either

surpriz'd by Death, or diverted by Business, or frighted by the growing Difficulties from undertaking the whole, and confin'd themselves to some particular part.[36]

As Thomas had reported to Bentley not long before, Temple believed that writing a new history "would perhaps be a greater undertaking than any man believes, before he engages in such an attempt." In their attack upon the Dunton-Tyrrell project, the Bentley associates chiefly rely upon this point, and although the rival project is never actually named, the attack is no less direct. The Dunton *Proposals* had called for a general history of England "From the Flood" down to the reign of William and Mary; the first volume, containing the period *"from the Flood to William the Conqueror,"* was promised "within Six Months from January next ensuing," that is from January 1694/95. In the November 1694 *Present State of Europe,* the Dunton group had gone even further, with an advertisement promising the entire work "To be finish'd about next Michaelmas Term."[37] Bentley and his partners now insinuate that the task is impossible, and that Dunton is trying to trick the public. Writing a complete history of England involves so much work, they observe, that it represents "full Employment for the Age of any one Man, let him begin as early as he pleases and set out with all the Advantages imaginable"—not too far from Temple's words to Bentley, "a greater undertaking than any man believes, before he engages in such an attempt." To drive home their application, the Bentley proposals next resort to italics: *"Such is the Wisdom of those Undertakers, who would perswade the World they are in earnest, when they promise to run through all the Changes,* from the Flood *to this very Day, in the Compass of one poor Year."*[38]

Thus threatened in their campaign for subscribers, Dunton and his partners promptly brought out a broadside countering the Bentley group's charges. Here they disparage the composite history that Bentley proposes, proclaim the superiority of their own wares, and (interestingly enough) conclude with reflections against "the *Great* Undertakers of this *pretended Compleat History,"* who, they suppose, will take the subscription money and run. "We could make many more *Animadversions* on their Design," Dunton warns in closing, "but think these sufficient at present."[39] The italicized *"Great"* looks like a hit at Temple, whose ambitions to enthrone himself with More and Bacon Dunton knew all too well—and whose part in the Bentley proposals, it would seem, Dunton here hints his knowledge of. The only "great" man specifically named in Bentley's proposals had been the historian Camden, long dead, and the undertakers had taken a modest enough line for themselves. Sad to say, Dunton's rejoinder seems to have carried the day. The first volume of Tyrrell's *General History of England* duly appeared in 1696, after some delays in composition, but the Bentley group's composite history was tabled and not revived until 1701 or so.[40]

Swift and Temple's Campaign Against DuCros

While Thomas and Temple were busy maneuvring, to be sure, Swift himself was otherwise occupied in Ireland. It is debatable how much he eventually learned about the alarums and excursions involving Thomas, the *Introduction,* and Temple's dealings with Dunton and Bentley. Certainly circumstances favored his finding something out after he returned to Moor Park in 1696, the same year the first volume of the Dunton history finally appeared. His curious *Abstract of the History of England,* worked up from Temple's *Introduction* about this time, suggests that Temple's secretary was developing a gratifying consciousness of what mattered in English history (Appendix C). The copy of at least one of Thomas's letters for Temple survived among the Moor Park manuscripts with which Swift worked so intensively. In addition, Swift may well have resumed some ties with Thomas, who continued as rector of Puttenham, four miles east of Moor Park in Surrey. That Swift learned something, at least, about Temple's dealings with the booksellers seems apparent from the Introduction to *A Tale of a Tub.* Here Dunton is pilloried suitably enough (perhaps a little *too* suitably, considering Temple's parallel ambitions) for announcing plans to publish "a faithful and painful Collection" of criminals' last dying speeches, which Swift considers "the choicest Treasury of our British Eloquence"—in sum, "A Work highly useful and curious, and altogether worthy of such a Hand."[41]

More important, perhaps, Thomas's two letters for Temple provide a rare glimpse of working conditions at Moor Park. Like the Downton transcript and one or two other surviving documents, Thomas's letters illustrate in detail the sort of work which Temple expected a secretary to perform, and at the same time they illustrate the sort of master for whom the secretary worked. As much as the Downton transcript does, they paint a picture not easily reconciled with the modern vision of Swift at Moor Park—the naive and high-minded hero worshipper, daily confronted with his model for greatness. At least in Thomas's time (sandwiched between Swift's second and last sojourns with Temple) the model seems to have been less concerned with the substance than the appearance of greatness—shining greatly, that is, through his published writings, while quietly taking pains to punish those who crossed him in his quest. On both counts, it was for the secretary to carry out instructions about ways and means to which so great a master could not stoop.

Possibly Dunton's behavior brought out the worst in Temple; possibly the grief of losing Lady Temple exacerbated it. All the same, Temple's literary career had been his chief business in Swift's time as much as in Thomas's. In Swift's autobiographical fragment, written more than thirty years later, Swift drily remarked that he had been "often trusted with matters of great Importance" by Temple. He cites a single example, a bootless errand he had run for Temple at Court, as Temple's messenger and emissary to plead for the bill for triennial Parliaments.[42] But Temple generally kept aloof from politics through the 1690s, and most of the "matters of great Importance" would more plausibly have involved his papers and the decisions he took about publishing or defending them. In 1692–93, for instance, Temple became embroiled in some way in an undignified pamphlet war with an obscure Frenchman named DuCros, and it appears that his secretary Swift played a substantial role of some sort. DuCros had helped to dupe Temple and the English at the congress of Nimeguen, in 1678. In his *Memoirs of What Past in Christendom* (1691) Temple recounted his side of the story, complete with a brief but supercilious character of DuCros. In late 1692 or early 1693, possibly after trying to blackmail Temple, DuCros published a pamphlet commenting sharply on Temple's "intolerable and ridiculous Vain-glory," complaining about Temple's treatment of him, controverting Temple's account of affairs at Nimeguen, and lodging assorted angry charges against Temple.[43]

Within the first few months of 1693 two anonymous pamphlets answered DuCros—the first a partly supercilious, partly sarcastic effort entitled *An Answer to a Scurrilous Pamphlet, Lately Printed, Intituled, A Letter from Monsieur de Cros, to the Lord ———* (London: for Randal Taylor, 1693), the second an equally curious but more even-tempered piece called *Reflections upon Two Pamphlets Lately Published . . .* (London: for Richard Balding, 1693—imprimatur dated 21 April). Contemporaries supposed the *Answer* to be Temple's. By it Temple "hath much more injured his fame than the coxcomb Le Cross could ever have done," one reader observed. More recently it has been fathered on Temple together with Swift, working under Temple's direction, or even on Swift alone, writing without Temple's knowledge. *Reflections upon Two Pamphlets* also attacks DuCros but argues that the *Answer* is a forgery, written by a third hand in imitation of Temple, while Temple's biographer Woodbridge argues that the *Reflections* itself is the work of a third hand, perhaps writing under Temple's directions.[44] The best account of the matter now available is Woodbridge's, and in some instances Woodbridge is clearly wrong. Temple could not possibly have written the *Answer*, he reasons, because Temple never referred to himself in the third person and because (here echoing an argument in the *Reflections*) Temple disapproved of ridicule and never stooped to heavy-handed colloquial sarcasms of the sort common in the *Answer*. But as we shall see, Temple soon afterwards composed some "Hints," meant to be incorporated and published in another man's work, in which Temple generously praised himself in the third person and directed inelegant, heavy-handed sarcasms at the head of a young opponent whom he considered too far beneath him to answer openly.[45] (Interestingly enough, the *Answer* not only echoes Temple's distaste for having to deal with opponents far beneath him, but also echoes his phrasing rather precisely, in advance. In 1698, probably referring to his own "Hints," Temple wrote to a friend that he once diverted an attack on an opponent because he had "no mind to Enter the List, with such a Mean, Dull, Unmannerly PEDANT," while in 1693 the author of the *Answer* had observed that "to be forced to enter the Lists with a feeble, inglorious and despicable Adversary, is somewhat afflicting."[46]) That Temple could write in such a vein need not mean that he wrote the *Answer*, to be sure, but it suggests that the whole DuCros question deserves a closer look. This it has reportedly received in an unpublished study by George Mayhew. A fresh approach must wait until Mayhew's material can reach print in one form or another.[47]

Meanwhile Thomas's work in 1694–95 provides a useful index to the ways in which Temple may have employed Swift two years before and to the freedom of initiative, if any, which Swift may have enjoyed. Like Dunton in 1694, DuCros was hardly a figure with whom a gentleman of name and estimation could easily bandy words in public, but even more than Dunton, he had given Temple provocation enough. In one way or another, a secretary should have come usefully to hand.

CHAPTER THREE

Swift's References to Temple

Autobiographical Fragment, Prefaces to Late Temple Works, the Ode to the Honble Sir William Temple *and Other Early Verse, the* Journal to Stella *and Marginalia in Burnet's History, the* Journal d'Estat de M^r T———, *Inscriptions in Books Received from Temple*

Like the Downton transcript and Swift's 'penitential' letter to Temple before ordination, the two Thomas Swift letters suggest the need for examining the available evidence more closely than has been the rule, with attention to the practical contexts which so often inform it. Considerations of intended readerships and motivations in writing, for instance, permit a more realistic evaluation of the various references which Swift made to Temple over the years. Most are strongly positive —often ludicrously so, when Swift writes for public consumption or for Temple himself. Under the circumstances this is entirely natural, no matter what the state of Swift's actual feelings. Even in his middle twenties and early thirties, Swift was neither unambitious nor simple-minded. Thanks in part to Temple's literary efforts since the 1670s (greatly intensifying after the time Temple brought Swift to Moor Park) Swift's employer had largely succeeded in impressing his public image on English readers.[1] By associating himself with a man of such notable virtue, politeness, patriotism, and general greatness, Swift could only have enhanced himself. If he felt anything besides respect and veneration, he would have risked hurting himself by admitting it, even in letters to his acquaintance. By the 1690s Temple's reputation had reached its zenith, while his secretary remained poor, obscure, and without influence elsewhere. Then and in the years immediately following, negative comment could only have reflected against him. Potential patrons do not, as a rule, smile on applicants known to speak slightingly of past employers. Shows of loyalty or deep respect build confidence instead.

Even if Swift could expect people to believe and sympathize with any unflattering account of Temple, he had little reason to venture one. For most of a decade, as Temple's secretary and clerk, he had worked on projects meant to raise and strengthen the master's public image. Temple himself had failed to speed Swift's career, and the secretary left Moor Park with nothing to show for his work beyond Temple's £100 bequest and literary executorship—itself a kind of commitment towards maintaining the great man's image, at least until he sold the last of the posthumous pieces.[2] Why tear down what he had worked so long to build up, when he could only hurt his career in the process?

After Swift achieved a measure of fame and security, with the Harley-Bolingbroke ministry and later in his Dublin deanery, he had less occasion to speak of Temple but little reason to change his tenor when he did. As a clergyman Swift was tainted with satire. Some of his friendships added a suspicion of Jacobite leanings, especially after Bolingbroke and Bishop Atterbury joined the Pretender in France. It could not have hurt, when necessary, to mention an association with an Old Whig famed for virtue and rectitude. On the other hand, to validate the association in the eyes of others, Swift could claim few marks of Temple's special favor. Swift's autobiographical fragment, a sometimes distorted piece which probably dates from the period 1727 to 1729, necessarily treats his Moor Park years and Temple with them. The treatment is rather cursory. As far as he goes, Swift emphasizes Temple's trust in him even more than his own admiration for Temple. After explaining his first absence from Moor Park, for instance, Swift reports that "he soon went back to Sr Wm Temple; with whom growing into some confidence, he was often trusted with matters of great Importance." Swift then draws attention to Temple's closeness to King William, and explains the "matters of great Importance"—one occasion in 1693 when Swift carried some written advice to Court and "gave the King a short account of the Matter, but a more large one to the Earl of Portland. . . ." Not once does Swift mention his years of secretarial work. His manuscript account concludes with Swift continuing "in Sr W Temple's house till the Death of that great Man, who besides a Legacy [of a 100 ll *erased*] left him the care and trust and Advantage of publishing his posthumous Writings." The sentence shows a becoming admiration for "that great Man" and more exaggeration of the great man's favor, because the erasure of £100 makes "Legacy" sound more substantial.[3] Under the circumstances, it is hardly surprising that, here or elsewhere, Swift can exaggerate Temple's reliance on him or sound uncritical in his admiration. The true surprise is that he did not strike the note more often. In his surviving letters, at least, he seldom invokes Temple's name gratuitously. Except in an occasional letter to Temple's relatives, he seldom mentions Temple at all after his lean years ended in 1713.[4]

Swift's Prefaces to Temple's Posthumous Publications

Each of Swift's references to Temple operates within a specific as well as a general practical context. Examples abound in Swift's prefaces for the four posthumous works: the *Letters* of 1699, *Letters to the King* (1703), the *Miscellanea, The Third Part* (1701), and the *Memoirs, Part III* (1709).[5] Whether he loyally defends Temple from criticism, as he does in the *Memoirs* preface, or asserts that "It is generally believed, that this Author, has advanced our English Tongue, to as great a Perfection as it can well bear," as he does in the 1699 *Letters* preface, Swift addresses the public as Temple's literary executor. In tone and substance he demonstrates respect, modesty, loyalty, and obedience to his master's "particular Commands," as he phrases it in the preface to the 1703 *Letters*. As he notes in the next paragraph there, it is an office "without the least Pretension to Merit or to Praise"—except of course as the executor graces it through his modesty, respect, loyalty, and obedience to the decedent's wishes. In the process, though, Swift begins to lose his independence as a commentator. Did Swift actually think that Temple deserved a reputation for perfecting the English tongue, as the first *Letters* preface implies, or does the literary executor merely conform to Temple's thinking here as elsewhere? The praise itself seems to echo Temple's ambivalent compliment to his contemporary French memoirists who, having sacrificed stylistic force and spirit, "seem to have Refined the French Language to a degree, that cannot be well exceeded."[6] For that matter, Swift justifies his praise through a claim almost certainly Temple's—that the letters vary admirably in style with the people addressed, as in the hearty letter to Baron Wreden discussed in the preceding chapter:

> that this Author, has advanced our English Tongue, to as great a Perfection as it can well bear; and yet, how great a Master he was of it, has I think, never appeared so much, as it will in the following Letters; wherein the Style appears so very different, according to the difference of the Persons, to whom they were address'd. . . . (I, sig. A2^v–A3^r)

For all their blind praise and partiality, the prefaces speak doubtfully for Swift's genuine feelings. The Downton transcript bears out only their lesser claims, about obeying Temple's "particular Commands" and accordingly forfeiting "the least Pretension to Merit or to Praise."

In the end, Swift's various prefaces make the best sense as reflections of the practicalities which faced him at the time of writing. In 1699, for instance, Swift was less secure in his career than in 1701, 1703, or 1709.[7] It is no coincidence, surely, that the 1699 preface shows him fullest of the praise and admiration so becoming in the recipient of a patron's favors. More than the others, it breathes an air of high-minded naïveté which has misled more than one reader. Before the preface proper, Swift inserted a dignified and equally high-minded dedication to William III. Ehrenpreis taxes Swift for lacking the shrewdness to dedicate more realistically, to a lesser political light like the speaker of the English House of Commons.[8] Had the *Letters* appeared in March or April 1699, when Swift was pushing his fortunes in London, the charge would carry weight. Instead, all the evidence suggests that Swift composed both dedication and preface sometime between May and October, after he had given up hope and committed himself to following the Earl of Berkeley to Ireland as secretary and domestic chaplain.[9] Canny English dedications would have helped Swift relatively little in Ireland, where he could not pursue them through personal attendance in London. By the same token, dedicating to an Irish politician would have been foolish until Swift had been there long enough to test the wind and choose his man—no easy task itself, in 1699.[10] Dedicating to the King was far more useful, although in a different sense. Accepting the post with Lord Berkeley signalled an end to Swift's immediate hopes for an English living through the King, whom he had apparently petitioned after leaving Moor Park in February or early March on the basis of a vague promise which he believed Temple had once won from William.[11] Promises to dead men have a way of fading fast: if Swift could achieve nothing with Temple still fresh in people's memories, his further prospects were worthless. In a strictly pragmatic sense, the dedication was useless after May or June—if not worse than useless, because both its timing and the *Letters'* contents should have made it less than welcome reading for the King, then embarked on a temporary policy of accommodation with France.[12]

The usefulness of the dedication came not in its doubtful appeal to William himself (who probably never saw it) but its likely effect on the general reading public, including people whom Swift might find useful the next time he sought favors or patronage in England. Just as Swift's preface makes much of his dutiful and admiring relationship with the great man Temple, the dedication should also have reminded the public of Temple's close relationship with the King himself, whose marriage he had helped to negotiate. Since Temple had steered clear of active involvement in party politics, and since current opinion held that Temple had calculated his last book to help celebrate the King,[13] the dedication to William seems entirely in keeping with Temple's practice—in all but the timing and choice of books, that is. It presents Temple's literary executor in the best possible light: innocently dutiful to the great man's memory, and sharing his nonpartisan patriotism and his connections with the great of the world.[14]

A similar attention to context and detail may clear up some other oddities in the prefaces. In the preface to the *Memoirs, Part III* (1709), for instance, Swift spends half his time defending Temple from criticism levelled at his earlier works, especially the *Memoirs of What Past in Christendom* (1691).[15] It is a becoming show of loyalty: Ehrenpreis calls it "an instructive demonstration of his fidelity to his patron."[16] Unfortunately, it also tends to dignify and emphasize the criticism made against Temple. Worse, the criticism all touches on an especially sensitive spot, Temple's imputed vanity. Swift's defense seems remarkably ignorant and inept, considering Temple's history, his earlier publications, and Swift's intimate knowledge of them. He begins by noting the title of Temple's earlier volume of memoirs, the *Memoirs of What Past in Christendom*. Instead, he volunteers, the title should have been a less grandiose *Memoirs of the Treaty of Nimeguen*, because the book centers on "a Relation of that famous Treaty." The reason, it appears, was a rascally publisher "who sent them into the World without the Author's Privity" —although, as Woodbridge shows, Temple almost certainly approved and concerted publication himself.[17] Unfortunately, anyone familiar with the 1699 *Letters* would have realized that *Memoirs of What Past in Christendom* was a title wholly typical of Temple, who favored the word "Christendom" so much that it sometimes seems as if his every move, as a diplomat, is fraught with consequences for it.[18] What is worse, Swift had incorporated the same grandiose phrase into the title for the 1699 *Letters*. By rights, they should have received a title like *Letters Relating to Negotiations in Flanders and Holland, 1665-70*, or *Letters Relating to the Munster Alliance, the Triple Alliance, and the Treaty of Aix*. Instead Swift had called them (probably on Temple's instructions) *Letters Written by Sir W. Temple Bar.* And Other *Ministers of State, Both at Home and Abroad. Containing, An Account of the most* Important Transactions *that pass'd in* Christendom *from 1665 to 1672.*[19] Retitling the *Memoirs* might have passed off smoothly enough, even so, but Swift also sounds odd in suggesting that the *Memoirs* title should have centered on "that famous Treaty" of

Nimeguen. Famous for what? Though ineffectual, the Triple Alliance of 1668 at least remained a popular treaty, but as Ehrenpreis notes, the Treaty of Nimeguen was ludicrous in its genesis and piffling in its results, "a joke, which only postponed the judgment to come."[20] By proposing a title which reflects "that famous Treaty" instead of the affairs of Christendom, Swift not only proposes a more accurate name but, in all apparent earnestness, reduces the sublime to the ridiculous.

The preface to *Memoirs, Part III* continues with a loyal defense of Temple on another point, his habit of speaking too much of himself in his narrative. Temple dwells on himself, it appears, because he is always the chief actor in the events unfolding around him. After a plausible review of Temple's position at Nimeguen, as chief mediator, Swift turns to the narrative itself. "The same may be offer'd in Defence of the following papers," he observes,

> because during the greatest part of the Period they treat of, *the Author was in chief Confidence with the King his Master.* To which it may be added, That in the few Preliminary Lines at the Head of the first Page, the Author professes he writ those Papers *for the Satisfaction of his Friends hereafter, upon the Grounds of his Retirement, and his Resolution never to meddle again with publick Affairs.*[21]

Even in Swift's day Charles II was famous for deviousness and secrecy. Any claim of close confidence between him and Temple seems inherently dubious, and Temple's narrative further belies it. Temple resolved "never to meddle again with publick Affairs" not because he enjoyed the King's confidence but because he lacked it—and began to think it impossible. "I found, the Arts of a Court were Contrary to the Franckness and Openness of my Nature," Temple explains in his conclusion. His reasons include "the Uncertainty of Princes" and "the Unsteddyness of Counsels," not to mention his own inability "to follow the present Humour of the Prince, whatever it is. . . ."[22] From 1679 to 1681, the time described in the narrative, Temple seems to have served Charles's purposes as handily (and as unwittingly) as he did a decade earlier with the Triple Alliance.[23] As Temple opens his narrative, it is true, Charles urges him to join the government and showers him with marks of special confidence.[24] Thereafter, and for "the greatest part of the Period" at stake, the confidences seem all on Temple's side, as he openly rebukes the King for dealing behind his back.[25] As an artistic construct, the memoirs dramatize a process of disabuse and disillusionment, but Temple's literary executor appears blind to their nature, almost as if he had never read, copied, or helped prepare them for the press.

Nor is this the only oddity in the preface. In his sturdily loyal fashion, Swift continues by defending Temple's habit of affecting French expressions in the earlier volume of memoirs. Although Swift had witnessed, at first hand, his master's struggles with French usage, he implies that Temple's gallicisms stemmed from his deep fluency and familiarity with the language, arising in turn from his long immersion in it on the Continent, so that "it was hardly possible for him to write upon publick Affairs without some Tincture of it in his Style. . . ."[26] Even stranger is Swift's exaggerated flattery of three Whig lords, especially the Lord Treasurer Godolphin, who is

> represented by this impartial Author [Temple], as a Person at that time deservedly entrusted with so great a Part in the Prime Ministry; an Office he now Executes again with such universal Applause, so much to the Queen's Honour and his own, and to the Advantage of his Country, as well as of the whole Confederacy.[27]

As Middleton Murry points out, Temple's narrative not only fails to confirm Swift's assertion but if anything suggests the opposite, that Godolphin was an ungrateful and self-serving hypocrite.[28] Only in the cynical sense, that knaves prosper most in Courts, could he deserve "so great a Part in the Prime Ministry." At the time he probably composed the portrait, in the spring of 1709,[29] Swift was preparing to return to Ireland after failing in his twin objectives, to wring concessions from Godolphin's ministry for the Church of Ireland, and to win advancement for himself, preferably in England. Louis Landa calls the winter of 1708–9 a time of deepening disillusionment for Swift.[30] By April he had nothing more to hope from the Godolphin ministry, much as he had nothing to hope from King William when dedicating to him ten years before.[31] Godolphin continued to push for removing the Sacramental Test in Ireland—a threat to the Church and anathema to Swift—and Swift's antipathy to him probably grew even stronger than it had been a year earlier, when Swift first discovered Godolphin's price for granting the Church any financial concessions.[32] Considering Swift's convictions, and those of the strongly Anglican Queen, who had reportedly grown disenchanted with Godolphin herself,[33] his preface seems to reflect a certain private irony in claiming Godolphin's ministry to be "so much to the Queen's Honour and his own." By comparing preface with narrative, anyone familiar with Swift's mission in England would have sensed something amiss in the flattery.

Possibly Swift meant the preface to signal a final warning to the Whig leadership, or even an encouraging hint to his potential allies in the opposite camp.[34] Though not yet famous in England, Swift was earning a reputation among the people who mattered, as a pamphleteer and the putative author of *A Tale of a Tub*. It may be no coincidence that, when he next returned to England in September 1710, he found himself actively courted by both parties, though coldly received by Godolphin himself.[35] Whatever the case, the truth will emerge only after a thorough study and collation of all the evidence—Swift's work with the *Memoirs,* the *Memoirs* themselves, Swift's mission between 1707 and 1709, and his position in the spring of 1709. What Swift meant the average reader to see is plainer, because the average reader would neither know of Swift's lobbying for the Church nor bother to compare the text with its preface. Instead of ironies or veiled warnings, such a reader would find little beyond the conventional flattery of a conventional place-seeker. When Swift moves from praising potential patrons to defending a past patron, nothing would seem more in character. His earnest loyalties, it appears, are easily secured. Here is another context for evaluating the praise of Temple which follows in the preface.

Besides the prefaces he wrote for Temple's posthumous books, Swift contributed occasional notes as well. They too deserve attention. In *Miscellanea, The Third Part* (London: for Ben. Tooke, 1701), for example, Temple left a long hiatus at the crucial juncture of his argument in the essay *Some Thoughts Upon Reviewing the Essay of Antient and Modern Learning.* The young scholar William Wotton had attacked Temple most successfully for pretending that the ancients were more sophisticated and knowledgeable scientifically than the moderns. The hiatus occurs just as Temple is about to launch into a triumphant self-justification, the very heart of his argument. (As Wotton later remarked, "Just where the Pinch of the Question lay, there the Copy fails. . . .") Swift knew all about Temple's intentions in the essay. He had copied the earlier Ancient-Modern essay, studied the replies to it, in 1696 or 1697 made a fair copy of the "Hints: written at the Desire of Dr. F. and of His Friend," which Temple soon afterwards began expanding into the second essay, and knew Temple's intentions for them. At first he wanted another man to incorporate the "Hints" into an answer to Wotton, and later (when the project fell through) he decided to let the "Hints" 'take its fortune abroad' on its own, perhaps privately at first and later by expanding into an essay for publication. (We shall return to these "Hints" later in this chapter.) In his note, though, Swift sounds suspiciously innocent, almost humorously so. No, he says, the author's intentions are not known —and in his ignorance he gives a fair summary of them. (Even in his preface Swift had announced, in all solemnity, that "I cannot well Inform the Reader upon what Occasion it [the essay] was writ.") In the essay itself, after a line of dots indicating a break in Temple's narrative, Swift announces in the impersonal dignity of italics that

> *Here it is supposed, the Knowledge of the Antients and Moderns in the Sciences last mentioned* [chemistry, anatomy, the natural history of minerals, plants, and animals, "the Invention of Instruments," astronomy and optics, music, medicine, "Natural Philosophy," philology, and theology], *was to have been compared; But, whether the Author designed to have gone through such a work Himself, or intended these Papers only for Hints to some body else that desired them, is not known.*

In this deadpan fashion Swift gets over an awkward spot in the essay without actually detailing the less-than-inspiring history of Temple's "Hints," but in the process he raises the pertinent questions about the essay's origins and effectively guarantees that no one will miss the essay's basic argumentative feebleness. Temple's position is complete except for his evidence and reasoning. Wotton found both hiatus and note something of a joke, although his ironical squint at Swift is unfounded (". . . and I take it for granted, Dr. Swift had express Orders to print these Fragments of an Answer"). He remarks on the oddity of "This way of printing Bits of Books that in their Nature are intended for Continued Discourses," and notes that he has seen few other examples except "one more which may be supposed to imitate this, *The Tale of a Tub*. . . ." In fact, at one crucial juncture in the *Tale* (in the Digression on Madness), Swift triumphantly solves an especially "knotty Point" ("the most abstracted that ever I engaged in") with a hiatus of stars, and the italic note, *"Hic multa desiderantur."*[36]

Swift's Ode to Temple *and Other Moor Park Verse*

An even richer vein of Temple references occurs in Swift's earliest poetry, his Pindaric odes and other heroic verse composed before 1695. There Swift hymns Temple's praises in high and sometimes ludicrous strains. Like Swift's prefaces, the early poetry deserves closer attention. Most often the odes have been treated as the productions of a callow, insecure, and essentially humorless youth, apparently written to little purpose beyond practice and to little effect beyond semiconscious self-revelation.[37] After charting the themes and imagery in the *Ode to the Hon*[ble] *Sir William Temple*, for instance, Ehrenpreis finds that the poem "will be found to mirror the whole relationship between patron and pupil at the time when it was written," that it shows Swift in "the role of a son," and that it "proves that Swift in turn not only shared but correctly understood the ideals of the foster-parent from whom he differed so profoundly in character."[38] Other critics see Swift struggling to accommodate himself to a genre either uncongenial to his character or unsuited to his purposes, whether satiric negation or indirect affirmation.[39] Here the emphasis is more literary than biographical, but it entails similar difficulties. If it avoids treating the poetry as straightforward biographical evidence, it still depends on unproved assumptions about Swift's character and purposes in the 1690s.

As yet these remain unclear. The available evidence is scanty, has yet to receive careful evaluation, and even then may yield insufficient results. Aside from the poetry, the available documents consist almost exclusively of Swift's few surviving letters.[40] Probably the most often quoted—at face value and usually out of context—is his early letter of 3 May 1692 to his cousin Thomas Swift, to whom he seemingly unburdens himself on a number of topics, chiefly his poetry-writing, while lavishing some highly questionable flattery on Thomas's and Temple's literary output. This is the letter in which Swift claims that he had "usd the Court above two years ago" in 1689 or 1690, when there is nothing to suggest that he had;[41] speaks of sending a poem to "my Bookseller and make him print it with my name and all," when there is no evidence that Swift had a regular publisher this early;[42] and pretends to find a remarkable "likeness of humors" in his temperamental opposite, Temple.[43] The style is oddly breathless and chaotic, reminiscent of his early persona-poem *The Humble Petition of Frances Harris* (1700), which it nearly equals in the number of run-on sentences. He confides his "desperate weakness" in loving his own bad verse ("I know farther, that I am wholly in the wrong" to do so), claims "the same pretence the Baboon had to praise her Children," and next informs Thomas, in all apparent innocence, that "I am just the same way" in loving Thomas's verse— and in loving Temple's writings, "Which I suppose is all but a piece of selflove, and the likeness of humors makes one fond of them as if they were ones own. . . ."[44] Like the man-of-the-world letter to his young Lisbon cousin Deane Swift, the letter to Thomas requires caution from readers approaching any of its contents which reflect value judgments or depend on Swift's tone. The character presented may not be Jonathan's. From what we have seen of Thomas in 1694–95, especially his enthusiasm, his lack of judgment, and his curiously flexible sense of truth, Jonathan's letter may well contain more sly reflections of his cousin than artless confessions of his own.

If Swift's feelings and character remain subject to doubt, his audience in the odes is easier to determine. Although the question of readership has attracted little or no attention since Maurice Johnson implicitly raised it in 1950,[45] it is unavoidable in the work of any man who, like Swift, seldom set out consciously to address the ages. For people not schooled to the contrary, writing remains a form of communication, a practical matter undertaken under certain circumstances, directed towards a certain readership, and designed for certain goals. Writing in a gardening magazine, for instance, a man can expect his readers to catch arcane references to layering, tetraploid hybrids, and pH, but he may have to explain even the most basic references to astronomy, couture, or international economics. His work will seem odd or unaccountable when taken out of context. Other writings aimed at limited readerships may run the same risks.

Judging from his later pamphlets and satires, Swift enjoyed a superb sense of writing as a purposeful activity, and with it a superb sense of audience. It is dangerous to assume the reverse when he was writing his odes at the age of twenty-three or twenty-six. Whatever extended readership he may have had in mind—and for two of the poems an ultimate destination is fairly clear[46]—he seemingly wrote his odes primarily for a Moor Park audience. In his long letter to his cousin Thomas, Swift speaks at length of composing a verse translation of the *Aeneid,* Book vi, for Temple and Lady Giffard. He has just shown them an installment, and observes that "She and Sr W. T. like it as I would have them."[47] Since Swift recounts actions just past—and since the passage hinges only slightly on matters of value judgment, which his tone and purposes could call into question—the account seems fairly reliable. Earlier in the same letter, Swift reports his success with the *Ode to the Athenian Society,* which has just been printed by the Athenians themselves, and suggests that here too he was writing for Temple. (In 1692, Temple had not yet broken with the chief Athenian, John Dunton, over the *Introduction to the History of England,* and Swift had not yet written his *Tale of a Tub,* with its assorted reflections on Dunton in particular and Grub Street in general.) Though he dashed off the poem in less than ten days, Swift avers,

> yet it is so well thought of that the unknown Gentlemen printed it before one of their Books, and the Bookseller writes me word that another Gentleman has in a book calld the History of the Athen Society, quoted my Poem very Honorably (as the fellow calld it) so that perhaps I was in a good humor all the week, *or at least S^r W^m T speaking to me so much in their Praise made me zealous for their cause,* for I really take that to be a part of the Honesty of Poets that they can not write well except they think the subject deserves it.[48]

In his covering letter to the Athenian Society, printed before the *Ode,* Swift confirms the impression. He dates his letter from "Moorpark," well known as Temple's country retreat, and goes out of his way to mention the "Person of very great Learning and Honour" to whom he showed the poem for approval and from whom (among others) he received the suggestion to submit it for publication.[49] In an even more personal way, the poem seems intended for a Moor Park audience. Since Temple apparently contributed to the *Athenian Mercury* himself, a good two months before Swift dated his covering letter,[50] the *Ode* seems to flatter the great man along with the regular Athenians, when it invokes "Ye great Unknown" in the majesty of black letter.[51] If the early poems primarily addressed themselves to the limited circle at Moor Park, it is probably no accident that Swift never included them in any of his authorized collections of works—any more than he included most of his other pieces meant for a highly limited readership, like many of the Market Hill poems, his trifles, and pieces in Anglo-Latinus.[52]

The poems themselves confirm the impression that Swift wrote with Temple and Lady Giffard in mind. Working in a different context, Ehrenpreis has already established that Cowley influenced Swift's Pindaric verse, and that Waller and Dryden probably influenced Swift's heroic couplets of the period.[53] By the same token, he argues that it was Temple who steered Swift towards such heroic models.[54] The case is persuasive. Although Temple ventured little in print about modern English poets,[55] Cowley's and Waller's heroic verse came closest to his tastes. Temple half distrusted ridicule and satire in literature, felt that among human endeavors "Heroick Virtue and Poetry" alone deserve "the honour of being called Divine,"[56] and once observed that

> I would have been glad to have seen Mr. Cowley, before he died, celebrate Captain Douglas his Death, who stood and burnt in one of our Ships at Chatham when his Soldiers left him, because it should never be said, a Douglas quitted his Post without Order; whether it be wise in Men to do such Actions or no, I am sure it is so in States, to honour them; and if they can, to turn the Vein of Wits, to raise up the Esteem of some Qualities, above their real Value, rather than bring every Thing to Burlesque. . . .[57]

Heroic virtue, it appears, is the poet's proper theme, and exaggeration his stock in trade. A page later Temple sadly notes that, among wits, "Mr. Waller is turned to Burlesque among them, while he is alive, which never hapned to old Poets, till many Ages after their Death," and observes that, if Waller must be counted

> enough out of Fashion, yet I am apt to think some of the old cut-work Bands, were of as fine Thread, and as well wrought, as any of our new Points; and at least, that all the Wit, he and his Company spent, in heightening Love and Friendship, was better employ'd, than what is laid out so prodigally, by the modern Wits, in the Mockery of all sorts of Religion and Government.

By the same token, Temple believed that the truest poetry reflects a heightened state of mind, not only an intensity of feeling but also a certain God-given "Elevation of Genius" which spurs poetic invention. Both music and poetry spring from "a certain Noble and Vital Heat of Temper, but especially of the Brain," he explains in the essay *Of Poetry:* "This was that Coelestial fire, which gave such a pleasing Motion and Agitation to the minds of those Men, that have been so much admired in the World, that raises such infinite images of things so agreeable and delightful to Mankind. . . ."[58] Temple's formula especially suits Cowley's most celebrated genre, the Pindaric ode, which encourages wild poetic inventiveness, insists on strong personal feeling, and permits the digressiveness which fosters them.

In the Pindaric *Ode to the Hon*ble *Sir William Temple,* Swift certainly appears to follow Temple's advice. Not only does he seem to lay out all his wit "in heightening Love and Friendship," in the most fervent but chaotic way, but he also seems to "raise up the esteem" of Temple's qualities "above their real value"—just as Temple had recently done for other great heroes in the essay *Of Heroick Virtue.* No one could sound more admiring than Swift when he exclaims that "Those mighty Epithets, Learn'd, Good, and Great,/ Which we ne'er join'd before, but in Romances meet,/ We find in you at last united grown."[59] Here is a proper confluence of poetry and heroic virtue, the two human productions worthy of being called divine. In the process, of course, Swift addresses Temple directly.[60] It is more than a poetic device. When he mentions meeting the three mighty epithets in *romances,* Swift makes an apposite and private allusion to one of Temple's favorite genres. As a youth, Temple had written romances of his own,[61] and apparently loved the genre. While he professed scorn for most modern literature, he made an exception for romance in general and Sir Philip Sidney in particular, seemingly for producing that archetypal romance, *The Countess of Pembroke's Arcadia.* Temple calls romance a "kind of Poetry in Prose," provides it with lost or fragmentary classical antecedents, and asserts that "the true Spirit or Vein of Ancient Poetry in this kind, seems to shine most in Sir Philip Sidney, whom I esteem both the greatest Poet and Noblest Genius of any that have left Writings behind them, and published in ours or any other modern Language. . . ."[62] To see his own virtues linked with so shining a genre—which, in Sidney's hands, Temple felt, was capable "not only of forming the greatest Ideas, but of leaving the noblest Examples"[63]—could only have given Temple a special pleasure, unavailable to readers outside Moor Park.

Swift's Moor Park audience may also explain the many echoes of Temple in the *Ode to the Hon*ble *Sir William Temple* and in the other early poems. Some time ago Maurice Johnson and Herbert Davis suggested that, in some of the pessimistic and valetudinarian passages in it and the *Ode to the Athenian Society,* Swift may write in Temple's voice more than his own.[64] Since then, Ehrenpreis has traced a number of general thematic parallels.[65] In at least one instance, though, the ode to Temple reflects conscious borrowing rather than general influence. In a paragraph towards the end of his essay *Upon Ancient and Modern Learning,* Temple deplores bookish pedantry and the general scorn of learning which it inspires in others. In lines 42–58 of his ode, Swift paraphrases Temple and, in the process, borrows Temple's metaphors.[66] Almost certainly, Swift had the passage fresh in mind, either from transcribing it shortly before or from having the published book open as he composed his verse.[67] Temple charges that pedants have earned general scorn "by broaching [their knowledge] in all places, at all times, upon all occasions, and by living so much among themselves, or in their Closets and Cells, as to make them unfit for all other business, and ridiculous in all other Conversations." As Swift works himself up to the same crowning charge against pedants—their unfitness in polite company—the ode similarly emphasizes their social shortcomings:

> They purchase Knowledge at the Expence
> Of common Breeding, common Sense,
> And at once grow Scholars and Fools;
> Affect ill-manner'd Pedantry,
> Rudeness, Ill-nature, Incivility. . . .

Temple next launches into an elaborate conceit comparing pedantry to a "Contagion" which "grows very generall" and either infects the neighbors or inspires fear, loathing, and scorn in them. In a less drastic sense, Swift borrows the image of contagious sickness to complete his own bill of indictment:

> And sick with Dregs of Knowledge grown,
> Which greedily they swallow down,
> Still cast it up and nauseate Company.

When Swift exempts Temple from charges of being pedantic or of scorning knowledge, several lines later, he reverts to the image, this time in Temple's graver sense of contagion: "Thrice happy you have 'scap't this gen'ral Pest. . . ." In the interim, Swift curses either the pedant who started the process or the man who first scorned learning (which one is not clear), and concludes with two more images from the Temple passage. Whoever he is, the wretch should be curst who first "Taught us, like Spaniards, to be proud and poor,/ And fling our Scraps before our Door." Temple had likewise concluded by linking pride and poverty—in pedants, who have brought loathing and scorn upon themselves. Temple contrasts them with the inherent wealth of true friends of learning, who "began to be ashamed" at the pedants' excesses and fearful of the ridicule which they attract.[68] Next he launches into an illustrative anecdote, attributed to a Spaniard in Brussels, about moral and physical degeneration in the Spaniards, apparently the inspiration for Swift's own reference to Spaniards.

However awkward the poem may sound to a general reader, it should have done Swift no harm at Moor Park. Not only does he parrot Temple's thoughts and words with considerable fidelity, but he also implicitly follows Temple's preferred manner of verse-writing ("to raise up the Esteem of some Qualities above their real Value"). More gratifyingly, he employs it on a subject close to Temple's heart, Temple's own greatness and goodness. Even when he slips from panegyric to condemnation, as in the passage on pedantry, his views echo Temple's. To his cousin Thomas, Swift had claimed to love Temple's writings out of a principle of self-love, "and the likeness of humors makes one fond of them as if they were his own." Swift's ode to Temple seems to reflect a canny application of the same principle, assuming that Temple was fond enough of his own work to appreciate its reflection in his secretary's verse. Accordingly the master of Moor Park and his sister should have been indulgent to any quavers in Swift's poetic voice.

Assuredly there are enough such quavers, both in the *Ode to the Hon*[ble] *Sir William Temple* and in Swift's other early verse. Temple might have appreciated seeing his three "mighty Epithets" meet in romance, but another reader would find the passage ambivalent. To most people, romances ranked fairly low in the literary hierarchy, as a kind of literary make-believe written for women. Swift himself held them in contempt both before and after his stay at Moor Park—if not then as well. In his earlier Pindaric *Ode to the King*, for instance, Swift imagines William III prevailing in battle almost single-handedly and (with a somewhat ambivalent effect) terms the imagined heroism "what I us'd to laugh at in *Romance*."[69] In the ode to Temple, Swift's effect is equally ambivalent. The emphasis falls much less on the magnitude than the implausibility of Temple's astonishing greatness, goodness, and learning, "Which we ne'er join'd before, but in Romances meet. . . ." Despite the air of fervor, Swift does not assert that Temple actually possessed greatness, goodness, and learning—only that he had the *epithets,* or the reputation for them. These epithets, says Swift, "We find in you at last united grown," but he does not identify the gardener who planted and cultivated them there.

Swift cannot even manage a direct paraphrase from Temple without injecting bathos or absurdity. When he restates Temple's opinions on pedantry, for instance, he exaggerates the element of snobbery and concludes his first bill of indictment (as well as the stanza) with a thumping anticlimax. Pedants are guilty of folly, incivility, rudeness, ill nature, and a metaphorical sickness. The stanza ends with the final, unforgivable offense, that having swallowed down the dregs of knowledge, they "Still cast it up and *nauseate Company.*"[70] At Moor Park the line would probably have passed unchallenged because Temple and his sister attached great value to polite conversation and polite company. In her *Character* of Temple, Lady Giffard boasts that "no body was welcomer in all company" than her brother, and that he "Turn'd his conversation to what was more easy & pleasant, especially at table where he use to say ill humor never ought to come. . . ."[71] In point of fact, Swift's phrase "nauseate Company" sounds like something spoken by a genteel and disapproving dowager like Lady Giffard herself.

Elsewhere, when Temple makes clear the relationship between contemptible pedantry and the growing contempt for learning, Swift confuses the two hopelessly. At first his indignation with pedants seems to carry over into the next stanza, with "Curst be the Wretch, nay doubly curst," who "learnt himself that Heresy first . . . That Knowledge forfeits all Humanity; / Taught us, like Spaniards, to be proud and poor. . . ." But who is the wretch? In the original, Temple vented his ultimate scorn not on pedants but on people who ridicule learning. Knowing Swift's original as he did, Temple should have had no difficulty supplying his own meaning, but another reader would expect more anger against the pedants and would find Swift's attack shifting confusingly. Instead of pedants, Swift now seems to condemn people like Temple who hate pedantry—people who believe that "Knowledge forfeits all Humanity" (since Swift has just defined pedantry by its "Rudeness, Ill-nature, Incivility," half a dozen lines before) and who remain "proud and poor" as a result. Where Temple made a distinction between scorning pedantry (as he himself did) and scorning true learning (as commoner people do), Swift never succeeds in separating the two. Accordingly his ode shows contempt for pedantry in one stanza, in terms drawn from Temple, and in the next turns the tables on itself.

The curious treatment of pedantry is hardly an isolated phenomenon. Temple himself receives similar handling in the poem. In the opening stanza, for instance, Swift presents a postlapsarian view of the empire of Virtue, which through Man's rebellion has fallen and broken "into small States and Principalities" which "ne'er since" have been "seated in one single Breast." It is Temple who must play the part of

Christ, the second Adam, in restoring the empire of Virtue. Much later, in stanza x, Swift repeats the analogy with less subtlety. In Temple's garden retirement "we expect from you/ More than your Predecessor, Adam, knew," Swift exclaims: "You strove to cultivate a barren Court in vain,/ Your Garden's better worth your noble Pain,/ Hence Mankind fell, and here must rise again."[72] Even in the opening stanza the flattery is fulsome enough and the implications slightly blasphemous, though Temple and Lady Giffard might not have found much amiss with it.

A certain Miltonic element compounds the problem. With its darkly heroic diction, its paucity of rhyme and end-stops, and its exaggerated periodicity—the verb of the first sentence does not rear its head until line 4—the opening passage is more than a little Miltonic:

> Virtue, the greatest of all Monarchies,
>   Till its first Emperor rebellious Man
>   Depos'd from off his Seat
> It fell, and broke with its own Weight
> Into small States and Principalities,
>   By many a petty Lord possess'd,
>   But ne'er since seated in one single Breast.

The effect is subversive, though to all appearances well-meaning. If Swift's theme suits *Paradise Regained,* his handling of it recalls *Paradise Lost* instead. In Miltonic terms, the emphasis upon imperial imagery, upon rebellion, and upon falling ("its first Emperor rebellious Man/ Depos'd" and "it fell") better suits Satan than Adam. The person who will reconquer the empire of Virtue must necessarily be a great Redeemer (Temple in Christ's robes), but the imperative quality sounds more like a tinhorn Satan or Beelzebub holding forth in Pandaemonium:

> 'Tis you who must this Land subdue,
> The mighty Conquest's left for you,
> The Conquest and Discovery too:
> Search out this *Utopian* Ground,
> Virtue's *Terra Incognita,*
> Where none ever led the Way. . . .

In the first rush of enthusiasm, the narrator stumbles into an anticlimax here, first urging conquest and then on second thought "Discovery too," without which conquest is naturally impossible. Oddly enough, Satan faced the same problem in Milton's epic: where to find the rumored new creation, Earth, the search for which leads him on his long voyage of discovery. Like Temple, Satan receives his followers' applause for volunteering his services as a scout as well as a would-be conqueror or redeemer. The praise they give him is the praise Swift gives Temple as the second Adam: "Towards him they bend/ With awful reverence prone; and as a God/ Extol him equal to the highest in Heav'n" (*Paradise Lost*, II, 477–79).

To a reader familiar with Milton, such self-destructing praise may raise questions about Swift's sincerity and intent in the poem. Few if any questions should have troubled Temple, though. Unlike Swift, he apparently did not know Milton's work. Milton is not mentioned in the essay *Of Poetry* or in Temple's other essays. In matters personal, poetic, political, and religious, Milton and he inhabited different worlds. In fact, as David P. French has suggested, Swift's various comparisons of Temple to the second Adam should have made Temple an acceptable compliment. Temple himself had paved the way for equating Adam and himself. In the essay *Upon the Gardens of Epicurus*, well before the section in which Temple congratulates himself upon his own retirement to a garden, Temple had noted God's favor towards the gardening life, by placing Adam there. "If we believe the Scripture," Temple reflects, "we must allow that God Almighty esteemed the Life of a man in a Garden, the happiest he could give him, or else he would not have placed Adam in that of Eden; that it was the state of Innocence and Pleasure. . . ." There too, it develops, Temple has managed "to escape" from the world of public affairs and, innocent of worldly concerns, has found full recompense in "the sweetness and satisfaction of this Retreat."[73] By the terms of his own argument, Temple has inherited the estate once enjoyed by Adam.

Perhaps because he works from Temple's point of view, French fails to notice that the Adam in Swift's poem is not just Adam but Christ as well—the second Adam, inhabiting a garden in which or through which Paradise will be restored to men ("Your Garden's better worth your noble Pain,/ Hence Mankind fell, and here must rise again"). From a less idiosyncratic view than Temple's, it may seem somewhat presuming for a postlapsarian mortal like Temple to claim the same garden pleasures which Adam enjoyed before the fall. Earlier, in stanza I, where Swift speaks of the empire of Virtue in terms which suggest Adam's fall, he at least manages the business less obtrusively (for Temple) by using imperial imagery drawn not just from the unfamiliar Milton but also from Temple's own essay *Upon Ancient and Modern Learning*. Temple had applied it to his beloved Ancients. After noting the rapid disintegration of empires like Tamerlane's and Alexander's, Temple moves on to the "several Empires of Science," which have suffered a like fate. Thales, Pythagoras, Democritus, Hippocrates, Plato,

Aristotle, and Epicurus, he notes, "were the first mighty Conquerors of Ignorance in our World, and made greater progresses in the several Empires of Science, than any of their Successors have been since able to reach." Like Swift's petty barons of Virtue, these successors content themselves with smaller dominions: They "have hardly ever pretended more, than to learn what the others taught, to remember what they invented, and not able to compass that it self, they have set up for Authors, upon some parcels of those great Stocks. . . ."[74] Virtue is as great an empire as learning, and to imagine Temple reconquering it all is to range him among the greatest of the Ancients. The borrowed imagery should have gratified Temple or at least distracted his attention from the subversive elements in Swift's flattery.

Intentionally or otherwise, other references to Temple's writings serve much the same function. In the same stanza, Swift had urged Temple to "Search out this *Utopian* Ground,/ Virtue's *Terra Incognita.*" The reference should have been gratifying enough, if only because Temple believed in the value of searching out *terrae incognitae.* In the first Ancient-Modern essay, Temple spent some time berating the Moderns for not using their supposed invention, the compass, to seek out more unknown lands, as the Greeks and the Romans doubtless would have done.[75] Even here, unfortunately, the narrator's enthusiasm carries him away. In the end his imagery emphasizes the improbability and unreality of Temple's glorious undertaking. Temple must seek out the *"Utopian* Ground" of Virtue,

> Where none ever led the Way,
> Nor ever since but in Descriptions found,
> Like the Philosopher's Stone,
> With Rules to search it, yet obtain'd by none.

Not only must Temple reconquer an empire left shattered since Adam's time, but merely to rediscover its whereabouts he must also achieve the impossible—"obtain'd by none." Besides *terrae incognitae* Swift deals in Utopias and the Philosopher's Stone, both objects of general scepticism. Judging from his later essay, *Some Thoughts Upon Reviewing the Essay of Antient and Modern Learning,* Temple vehemently scorned the Philosopher's Stone and those who sought it. It is "a wild Vision or Imagination of some shatter'd Heads," he suggests, "or else, a Practice of Knaves upon Fools, as well as sometimes of Fools upon themselves." Indeed, the next stanza in Swift's *Ode* duly likens scholastic philosophy to "The Roguery of Alchymy,/ And we the bubbled Fools/ Spend all our present Stock in hopes of golden Rules."[76] In the opening stanza, though, Temple is exhorted to seek where no one else has gone, find something found only in "Descriptions," "Like the Philosopher's Stone,/ With Rules to search it, yet obtain'd by none." Trying to emphasize the magnitude of Temple's task, the blundering poet instead brings out its unlikelihood and its associations with folly.

The many anomalies in the *Ode to the Hon*ble *Sir William Temple*, and in Swift's other early verse, have not escaped comment. In the most careful treatment to date, Robert Uphaus remarks on Swift's penchant for inadvertently collapsing the ideals which he supposedly means to celebrate. Uphaus charts the strikingly "close relationship between the pervasive disunity of the odes and Swift's use of satire in *A Tale of a Tub.*" He diagnoses this "consistent pattern of failure" as an impasse between Swift's panegyrical intentions and his irreducibly satirical nature, "the disjunction between the poet's intent and his own awareness."[77] Considered from the assumptions now current, the diagnosis seems unimpeachable: that is, if Swift aimed only at an expression of his personal feelings, if he lacked the skill to turn his satiric gift to genuine panegyric, and if he definitely worshiped Temple at the time.

More realistic assumptions produce a different diagnosis. No matter how awkward the results, Swift's manner, substance, and sentiments flatter his employer's vanity, but what satisfaction if any did the poem hold for Swift himself? In his forties Swift amused himself by suggesting tactics to a madman who claimed to command a 200,000-man army ready to serve Queen Anne.[78] In his sixties, on his first meeting with a conventional-minded young woman, he amused himself by drawing her apart from her husband, ushering her into his library, and confiding his great secret:

> "Well," says he, "I have brought you here to shew you all the Money I got when I was in the Ministry, but do not steal any of it." "I will not indeed, Sir," says I; so he opened a Cabinet, and shewed me a whole Parcel of empty Drawers; "Bless me," says he, "the Money is flown. . . ."[79]

In both cases Swift's mischievousness smacks more of the prankster than the grave divine, and in both cases his primary motive was his own amusement—a frequent motive in his later occasional verse as well. If he enjoyed such hoaxes in his forties and sixties, what then of his twenties at Moor Park?

Swift's heroic odes sometimes commit gaffes so unaccountable that, behind their earnest and lumbering exterior, the poet seems to be laughing up his sleeve. In stanza v of the ode to Temple, for example, Swift seems to hymn Temple's praises as a peace-maker by reflecting on the vanity of war (attended with its "usual bloody Scar"). War is

> . . . that mad Game, the World so loves to play,
> And for it does so dearly pay;
> For though with Loss or Victory awhile
> Fortune the Gamesters does beguile,
> Yet at the last the Box sweeps all away.[80]

Uphaus rightly notes that Swift's imagery only downgrades Temple's diplomatic achievements, especially in the gambling metaphor. The impermanence of victory or defeat either negates any permanence in diplomacy based on them, or leaves the world too subject to chance for diplomacy to make much difference.[81] On the next throw of Fortune's dice box, any victories, defeats, or settlements may be swept away. In a Moor Park context, the gambling metaphor is even more unfortunate than Uphaus notes. In Temple, Swift praises a man who, by his own sister's admission, "naturaly loved play & very deep"—and praises him by a scornful reference to beguiled gamesters.[82] To make matters worse, Temple's two major peace treaties, that of Aix (based on the Triple Alliance) and the farcical accord at Nimeguen, suffered precisely the fate which Swift describes. Fortune beguiled the gamesters—much as Charles II beguiled Temple, in a literal sense—and "at last the Box sweeps all away," with prompt defections, realignments, and further warfare.

If the reference to gamesters did not blunt Temple's pleasure in the passage, Swift's treatment of warfare should have completed the job. In a general sense, Swift's source for the stanza is Temple's last peroration in the essay *Of Heroick Virtue,* with its assertion that in matters of heroic virtue the arts of peace take precedence over those of war. To sharpen an antithesis, Temple had conceded that "the designs and effects of Conquests, are but the slaughter and ruin of Mankind, the ravaging of Countries, and defacing the world," while those of statecraft produce only blessings.[83] Swift picks up the disapproving reference to slaughter (in war's "usual bloody Scar") but soon shifts his tone to open contempt. Temple had showed disapproval enough, but only momentary disapproval. Conquests and conquerors still hold "the second Rank in the pretensions to Heroick Virtue." In the bulk of his essay, Temple exhibits a naive veneration for his great empire-builders with their wars of conquest. The five pages immediately preceding his peroration provide an enthusiastic recipe for victory in battle, including a discourse on the strategic superiority of foot over horse. (By the time Temple wrote his second Ancient-Modern essay, later in the 1690s, he had so far forgotten himself as to deny the title of "history" to Fra Paolo Sarpi's celebrated *History of the Council of Trent,* because history requires "a noble and great Subject," that is, "great Actions and Revolutions," and Sarpi's book is "only an Account of a long and artificial Negotiation, between the Court and Prelates of Rome, and those of other Christian Princes."[84]) If war is merely some "mad Game" when compared to diplomacy, as Swift would have it, then its heroism becomes a mockery. Diplomat though he was, Temple could not wholly have relished Swift's praise, but with Swift basing it so closely on Temple's own ideas, Temple could not have taken offense either.

Even in the passage about pedantry, the ode is strikingly infelicitous for a Moor Park production, although Swift specifically excludes Temple a few lines later. It is awkward enough when Swift's condemnation shifts unexpectedly from pedantry to the people who, nauseated like Temple by it, seem to hold that "Knowledge forfeits all Humanity." To make matters worse, when Swift borrows Temple's image of Spaniards, he makes the description fit Temple more closely: ". . . Taught us, like Spaniards, to be proud and poor,/ And fling our Scraps before our Door." Not only does the description of flinging out scraps of knowledge sit awkwardly with a partial paraphrase of *Upon Ancient and Modern Learning*—which scornfully belittles or casts aside the Moderns' few acknowledged advances in the sciences, and parades a vague and superficial learning about the ancient "Brachmans" of India and the antiquity of Phalaris—but the reference to proud Spaniards also sits awkwardly in a poem addressed to a man with Spanish tastes and a firm sense of his own dignity.[85] Most oddly yet, the passage paraphrased by Swift introduces an observation at which Swift could only have wondered. In the essay *Upon Ancient and Modern Learning*, Temple's strictures against pedantry and the scorn of learning preface his final attack on the Moderns—for indulging in satire and ridicule. When he mentions the Spanish, Temple does so in relating the opinion of a Spaniard who believed that *Don Quixote* (one of Swift's favorite books) had caused moral and physical decay among the Spaniards by making them laugh at honor and romance. Temple cannot quite endorse the Spaniard's opinion, but he accepts the principle at stake:

> Whatever effect, the Ridicule of Knight-Errantry might have had upon that Monarchy, I believe that of Pedantry has had a very ill one upon the Commonwealth of Learning; and I wish, the Vein of Ridiculing all that is serious and good, all Honour and Virtue, as well as Learning and Piety, may have no worse effects on any other State: 'Tis the Itch of our Age and Clymate. . . .[86]

Somehow it seems more than fortuitous that a future satirist should have chosen to paraphrase a passage linked so closely with Temple's strictures against satire and then, in all apparent innocence, make a hash of the work. Not that Temple had any cause for anger: Swift skirts any overt ridicule and shows no demonstrable disloyalty (something about which Temple was touchy, according to Lady Giffard[87]). Indeed, Swift caps his muddled paraphrase by attributing to Temple practically everything which Temple claimed too precious for ridicule—"all that is serious and good, all Honour and Virtue, as well as Learning and Piety." Except perhaps for the piety, Swift sums them up as "Those mighty Epithets, Learn'd, Good, and Great" (never joined except in Romance), through which "Thrice happy you have 'scap't this gen'ral Pest."

In the ode to Temple, then, there is as much reason to suspect Swift's ingenuousness as to believe that Temple accepted it. Possibly the young secretary was laughing up his sleeve at the great man's foibles and pretensions—a dangerous game when he writes for Temple himself, but an especially tempting one for a lover of hoaxes and mischief. Possibly too Swift had another practical motive beyond recommending himself to Temple. With his enthusiasm for romance, Temple may have been a relatively unsophisticated reader, but even he must have found Swift's poetry old fashioned and somewhat flat in effect, despite its many gratifying features. In his own writings Temple always managed to skate gracefully over the occasional muddle and contradiction in his own thinking, but all too often his ardent disciple, clumping along behind, seems to crash through the ice. Temple stood on thin ice in his notions about heroic virtue (often naive and militaristic) and in his scorn for modern learning (with his scorn for those who scorn learning).

His strictures against ridicule reflect an equally basic self-contradiction. When writing of *Don Quixote* and the decay of Spain, he cannot wholly accept his Spanish friend's theory, and takes pains to emphasize the attribution.[88] Cervantes may mock the sort of romantically heightened love and honor which Temple felt most necessary, but along the way Temple still makes a bow to Cervantes' "inimitable Wit and Humor." In fact, only ten pages earlier, Temple had ranked Cervantes as one of the two "great Wits among the moderns" in Spain.[89] Although he could not approve of satire, Temple never seems to have freed himself from enjoying it occasionally, at least in its more obvious forms. Lady Giffard insists that, as a younger man, Temple showed "more spirit & life in his humor then ever I saw in any body," with "soe agreable turns of witt and fancy."[90] Her extreme partiality and general humorlessness may weaken her testimony, but without doubt Temple possessed enough wit and fancy to enjoy at times what he could not approve. Even when summing up his condemnation of modern ridicule, he cannot resist borrowing some himself, in this case from Lord Rochester's cruel but apt impromptu on Charles II. The itch of modern ridicule has invaded public affairs as well as private, he mourns, "and I have known in my Life, more than one or two Ministers of State, *that would rather have said a Witty thing, than done a Wise one;* and made the Company Laugh, rather than the Kingdom Rejoice."[91] Temple's half-suppressed appreciation for ridicule is even clearer in his later essay, *Some Thoughts Upon Reviewing the Essay of Antient and Modern Learning,* written in the period after 1694. There, on occasion, he indulges in sarcasm of his own. Summing up the wondrous advances which modern scientists "are like to make" in the coming age, he lists "An Universal Language, which may serve all Mens Turn, when they have forgot their own," "The Art of Flying, till a Man happens to fall down and break his Neck," and, echoing a scoffing report in the *Athenian Mercury* some years before, "The Transfusion of young Blood into old Men's Veins, which will make them as gamesom as the Lambs, from which, 'tis to be derived. . . ."[92] Earlier in the essay he takes evident satisfaction in reporting and quoting the satiric abuse heaped on his French opponents, the Moderns in the Académie. Inspired by his own essay *Upon Ancient and Modern Learning,* it seems, the Ancients' partisans there "began to pelt them with Satyrs and Epigrams in writing, and with bitter Railleries in their Discourses and Conversations; and led them such a Life, that they soon grew weary of their new-fangled Opinions. . . ."[93]

Undoubtedly Swift recognized his master's ambivalence towards satire. Writing for a man whose natural tastes sat so uneasily with his literary prescriptions, Swift may well have meant not just to gratify his master's vanity, but also dose him with his own medicine—and by making him slightly queasy with it, inspire him to reconsider his position. Certainly the ode follows Temple's prescription for exaggerated panegyric, and deviates from it only to introduce Temple's pet peeves. Swift makes a glorious hash of the job and, whether intentionally or not, demonstrates the unproductiveness of Temple's position. The ode's conclusion not only safeguards his tone of innocent inadvertence, but may also point a moral. Temple will accept "this worthless Verse," Swift hopes, as "The Tribute of an humble Muse." Though worthless, the verse satisfies Temple's chief requirement for poetic composition, as laid down in the essay *Of Poetry*—that it stem from what Temple called "a certain Noble and Vital Heat of Temper" which, as "the free Gift of Heaven or of Nature," is "a fire kindled out of some hidden spark of the very first Conception." Swift claims to possess this same poetic fire. In strikingly similar language he explains that "Nature the hidden Spark did at my Birth infuse,/ And kindled first with Indolence and

Ease." Because the spark has been "too oft debauch'd by Praise," Swift continues, it has now become "an incurable Disease,"[94] an eventuality unaccounted for in Temple's theory. Swift has tried "In vain to quench this foolish Fire" with wisdom and philosophy, presumably Temple's too. Even so, it continues to flourish, and (as Swift changes the metaphor yet again) to flourish with "an *equivocal* Birth":

> In vain all wholsome Herbs I sow,
> > Where nought but Weeds will grow.
> What e'er I plant (like Corn on barren Earth)
> > By an equivocal Birth
> Seeds and runs up to Poetry.

The word "Poetry," in the final line, carries a double burden. Not only has Swift defined and practiced poetry in Temple's way, but now the word's connotations are decidedly negative. Swift may plant "wholsome Herbs," but what sprouts and grows is "Poetry," a kind of weed. Its birth is "equivocal." For the word "Poetry," he could as justly have substituted "ambivalence," "inadvertent ridicule," or even "worthless verse," the fruits of poetry springing from Temple's prescriptions. Although Swift tactfully attributes the problem to his own personal failings—he plants in soil "Where nought but Weeds will grow"—he reinforces the moral (as well as his good intentions) by echoing Temple's imagery early in the essay *Of Health and Long Life.* There Temple reflects on his own writing, uniformly inspired by his own good intentions, and confesses that he has "never written any thing for the Publick without the Intention of some Publick Good." It is not for him to judge how he has succeeded, but others give him reports which "may deceive either me or themselves" (compare Swift's being "debauched by Praise"). "Good Intentions," Temple reflects, "are at least the Seed of good Actions; and every Man ought to sow them, and leave it to the Soil and the Seasons, whether they come up or no, and whether He, or any other gathers the Fruit."[95] Along with good intentions, it appears, a man may sow poetry, but the end of Swift's ode does not spell out which man he meant to gather its fruit.

Whatever the final verdict on the *Ode to the Hon*ble *Sir William Temple* (and much has yet to be evaluated) Swift's other early poetry will probably share it in some degree. In their tone, imagery, awkwardnesses, and limited readership, they seem much of a piece, part of the "consistent pattern of failure" which Uphaus finds in the first three odes. What remains is to subject each poem to a close and thorough examination, both textual and contextual, while suspending any untested assumption that the earnest but digressive narrator must necessarily represent the genuine Swift, speaking (for once in his life) in his private voice. If the ode to Temple serves as a guide, close inspection may reveal not an adolescent's moony incompetence—or at most an unconscious rehearsal of the satiric narrative in *A Tale of a Tub*—but the conscious exercise of the same sort of strategy, aimed at a different readership for different purposes.

The work is long overdue. It is suspicious enough in itself, for instance, that Swift should address an ode to the Athenian Society, John Dunton's imaginary secret conclave of virtuosi who supposedly write the *Athenian Mercury*, that grab bag of miscellaneous curiosities and advice to the lovelorn. In his covering letter to the Athenian Society (duly printed along with the ode) Swift left a standing invitation to scholars. When he first heard about the Athenians' project, he writes, he "believed the design to be only some new *Folly* just suitable to the Age. . . ." After digressing about his movements during the past few weeks and his arrival at Moor Park, Swift reports that he has at last seen the Athenians' productions, all four volumes' worth, "which answering my Expectation. The perusal has produced, what you find inclosed." Although he had heard at Oxford an unspecified "Account and Opinion" of the Athenians, Swift says in effect that he expected folly and found his expectations answered.[96] Better yet, Swift gravely suggests that the Athenians print the enclosed *Ode to the Athenian Society* before the next bound volume of the *Athenian Mercury,* in the manner of the commendatory verses traditionally prefaced to great works of literature or scholarship—like those in Casaubon's Strabo (1620), Milton's *Paradise Lost* (1678), Gale's Herodotus (1679), or Ben Jonson's *Workes* (1640), to cite editions then or later owned by Swift.[97] The same wide-eyed flattery and digressiveness which lulled Temple and the Athenians into approving the work should instantly alert anyone familiar with *A Tale of a Tub*.

Temple in the Journal to Stella *and Swift's Annotations of Burnet*

If Swift's references to Temple in his early poetry, his prefaces, and his early letters seem to reflect his purposes and readership more clearly than his private opinions, what then of the references in his more private writings? In his intimate *Journal to Stella,* for instance, Swift also mentions Temple. Years later, in Burnet's *History of His Own Time,* Swift annotated Burnet's character of Temple. About the time of Temple's death, Swift also composed two appreciations of the great man, one in a lost journal and the other in a lost Bible. How far do such references reveal Swift's feelings?

The letters to Stella seem especially promising, if only because

Swift never wrote more freely and because Stella too had lived in the
Temple household. The references to Temple, though, are scanty and
ambivalent at best, neither strongly negative nor strongly positive.
Swift gives the impression even here of being slightly on his guard. In
fact he should have been. Stella had every reason to venerate Temple,
in whose house she had grown up with unusual privileges, and from
whom she had inherited enough to support her in later life.[98] On 3 April
1711, for instance, Swift recounts somewhat playfully "a very proper
speech" he gave to Henry St. John, the secretary of state. St. John,
thought Swift, had slighted him two days before. When he charges him
with coldness and condescension, he associates his being "treated like
a school-boy" with Temple. The "one thing I warned him of," Swift
recounts, was

> Never to appear cold to me, for I would not be treated like a school-boy;
> that I had felt too much of that in my life already (meaning from sir
> William Temple); that I expected every great minister, who honoured me
> with his acquaintance, if he heard or saw any thing to my disadvantage,
> would let me know it in plain words, and not put me in pain to guess by
> the change or coldness of his countenance or behaviour; for it was what
> I would hardly bear from a crowned head. . . .[99]

As he continues, Swift gradually exaggerates his anger into something
close to humor ("what I would hardly bear from a crowned head"). St.
John promptly apologizes, owns himself in the wrong, and "to make up
matters" asks Swift to a special dinner, which Swift huffily refuses
(actually, he tells Stella, because he remembers a prior engagement).
The next day, though, Swift worries about how Stella will take the
entry. He finds "mistakes of the pen," suspects Stella's puzzlement,
apparently over his speech to St. John, but in fact corrects himself about
the reference to Temple. Now the emphasis shifts from Temple's
condescension ("treated like a school-boy") to the safer and more neutral
subject of Temple's bad moods, which even Lady Giffard acknowledged.[100] In the process, Swift further removes the sting by laughing at
his own reaction to the moods:

> [April] 4. I sometimes look a line or two back, and see plaguy mistakes of
> the pen; how do you get over them? You are puzzled sometimes. Why, I
> think what I said to Mr. secretary was right. Don't you remember how I
> used to be in pain when Sir William Temple would look cold and out of
> humour for three or four days, and I used to suspect a hundred reasons?
> I have pluckt up my spirit since then, faith; he spoiled a fine gentleman.[101]

A touch of the same tact appears a few months earlier, when Swift
recounts an informal and playful evening with Prior and St. John.

Struck by the contrast to Temple, Swift observes without transition that "I am thinking what a veneration we used to have for sir William Temple, because he might have been secretary of state at fifty; and here is a young fellow, hardly thirty, in that employment."[102] In context, Swift's remark draws attention to the abyss between the young man's informality and Sir William's implied self-importance, but Swift is tactful enough to subscribe to the "veneration" which Stella feels. A year later, though, he states the contrast more cruelly. After confirming a rumor which Stella has heard, apparently about St. John chaffing Swift, Swift explains that

> The secretary is as easy with me as Mr. Addison was. I have often thought what a splutter Sir William Temple makes about being secretary of state; I think Mr. St. John the greatest young man I ever knew; wit, capacity, beauty, quickness of apprehension, good learning, and an excellent taste. . . .[103]

Gone is the polite pretense of "veneration," in favor of the humorous or mildly contemptuous tone of "splutter." Swift's superlatives ("the greatest young man I know . . .") seem as much directed against Stella's veneration of Temple as towards Swift's fondness for St. John. In the end, if the *Journal*'s remarks hint at a clear-eyed attitude towards Temple, they resemble Swift's more public pronouncements even more, by seeming so well tailored to his reader.

The same phenomenon occurs in Swift's marginalia for Burnet's *History,* except that Swift wrote for the benefit of a friend far less intimate than Stella. Swift entered his comments not in his own copy of the book, but in one belonging to the impressionable young clergyman and antiquary, John Lyon. Swift wrote in pencil so that (as he told Lyon) "you may rub it out, when you please," or so Lyon later reported.[104] Since Swift was already famous at the time, the admiring young man naturally treasured the volumes. Swift enjoyed rapping out the most immoderate reactions—entries like "Dog," "Treacherous Villain," "Rogue," or "False and detracting"[105]—but when he came to Burnet's attack on Temple he exercised surprising moderation. When Burnet remarked that "Temple was a vain man, much blown up in his own conceit, which he shewed too indecently on all occasions," Swift apparently held his peace. In the text edited by Herbert Davis, there is no entry opposite the sentence.[106] A few lines later, Burnet charges that Temple "thought religion was fit only for the mob," and here Swift rouses himself—not to defend Temple but to condemn the neologism "mob," short for *mobile vulgus.* "A word of dignity for an historian," Swift fumes.[107] Only when Burnet reaches the bounds of the imaginary does Swift rouse himself for his former employer.[108] Burnet calls Temple "a corrupter of all that came near him" (including his secretaries, presumably) who "delivered himself up wholly to study ease and pleasure." Here Swift comments that "Sir William Temple was a man of virtue, to which Burnet was a stranger." Considering Swift's expletives in the surrounding pages, the comment seems surprisingly restrained, aimed more at condemning Burnet than defending Temple. If Swift had been writing privately in his own copy, three or four decades earlier than he did (the late 1730s), his comments would surely indicate something about his feelings for Temple. Under the circumstances, though, they may simply indicate that the subject no longer interested him, or that he did not care to illuminate Lyon on it.

The Journal d'Estat *and Bible Flyleaf Eulogies of Temple*

Swift's lost but oft-quoted inscriptions of 1699 constitute far more important evidence, though almost impossible to evaluate with any hope of certainty. As Swift's court-appointed guardian during senility, Lyon preserved a number of Swift manuscripts which have since disappeared.[109] Among them may have been a paper somewhat grandiosely entitled *Journal d'Estat de M^r T—— devant sa Mort*. As Lyon reported, it appeared that in June 1698 Temple "began to decline in his Health, but Swift's Love and attention to him was such that he kept a Register of ye variations, wch appeared in his Constitution, from 1 July 1698 to 27th of Jan: following," which was the date of Temple's death. Lyon quotes only Swift's final entry, that "He dyed at one o clock in the morning & with him all that was great & good among Men."[110] Since the journal itself has disappeared,[111] it is impossible to inspect the other entries to determine its overall tone, purpose, and intended readership. Lyon thought that the journal reflected Swift's "Love and attention" for Temple, but Lyon's credulity and ear for language are open to challenge on other counts.[112] Even his inference about Temple's failing health in June may be open to question. When taken ill, Temple customarily withdrew from even his own family's sight, but on 17 July—less than three weeks after Swift allegedly grew worried enough to begin the journal—Temple was gaily summoning a young stranger, the Hon. Charles Boyle, to visit him at Moor Park. He says not a word of any ill health.[113] A touch of gout seems to have followed in August (or so Lady Giffard wrote her nephew-in-law) but by 7 September Temple felt well enough to go off visiting himself. Lady Giffard reported home that "Papa I thank God [is] very well, and so insufferably pert with winning 12 guineas at Crimp last night."[114]

Under the circumstances, interpreting Swift's final entry in the

Journal d'Estat becomes more difficult yet. If Swift kept the journal for his own eyes only, the entry may still indicate that Swift's heart somehow kept alive a flame of hero-worship, which Temple's death could fan into full grief, despite the contrary implications of Swift's odes, prefaces, letters, and other references during and after the 1690s. Even here, though, much could depend on the provisions which Temple had made for his secretary's career following his own death. When Temple died, Swift was thirty-one and had been pushing his prospects unsuccessfully for at least seven years. If Temple had finally made arrangements satisfactory to him, no matter how unsuccessful they eventually proved, Swift's words most probably reflect grief. If Temple had continued to defer arrangements—and (as it actually happened) then died leaving Swift unprovided for—a natural bitterness might put Swift's entry in a different light. As it is, the words "all that was great & good among Men" sound uncomfortably close to Swift's self-destructing praise in the ode to Temple, about "Those mighty Epithets, Learn'd, Good, and Great," found in Temple and in romances. His later Moor Park poem, *To Mr. Congreve* (1693), flatters Temple in terms even closer to the journal entry's. On and off through the poem, Swift contrasts the Muse of his obscure country retreat—pure, virtuous, and noble—with the tasteless and corrupt city milieu in which struggles the Muse of poor successful Congreve. His own Muse, Swift boasts, is "Happy beyond a private muse's fate, / In pleasing *all that's good among the great.* . . . "[115] Greatness and goodness sum up the image which Temple wished for himself, but as qualities to inspire private grief, from a longtime personal associate in 1699, they seem somewhat formal and eulogistic.

It is not certain, however, that Swift kept his *Journal d'Estat* solely for himself. In the Moor Park household it was Lady Giffard, not Swift, who found Temple's health a subject of engrossing interest. Five of her six surviving letters of 1697–98 take pains to report on the latest developments in Temple's condition, and the sixth illustrates it indirectly.[116] Writing at the beginning of Swift's tenure at Moor Park, in 1690, she reported the onset of Temple's gout more than ten years before and mentioned his impatience under the pain which "he has had lately great & frequent returns off." For the years after 1689, she later reported that Temple "had bin long in great extremity afflicted with ye gout, wch with age & decay of strength & spirits at last [MS. breaks off]." Undoubtedly she meant to write "at last wore out his life," as the passage came to read when printed with her *Life* of Temple.[117] But for Lady Giffard and other outside sources, Swift's surviving writings would suggest that Temple enjoyed fairly unexceptionable health. Except when writing for Temple or Lady Giffard, he never even mentions Temple's condition one way or the other.[118] Even in his three letters of 1698–99, including a long one dated two weeks before Temple's death, Swift never raises the subject, although he once reports the health of Lady Giffard's parrot.[119] Perhaps the subject obsessed him even so, but under the circumstances the *Journal d'Estat* looks like a project undertaken to please Temple's solicitous sister. Its portentous French title gives the subject the kind of importance she expected, and may well date from the crucial weeks following Temple's death. (Swift would never have used the phrase *"devant sa Mort"* while Temple still lived.) So too with the tone of the journal's final entry: more than anyone else, it was Lady Giffard who felt in her bones that with Temple died "all that was great & good among Men."

Lady Giffard would have had time enough to read Swift's entry, if in fact he meant it for her eyes. The secretary stayed on at Moor Park for four or five weeks after Temple died.[120] During the same period she concerned herself with a more formal but similarly exaggerated eulogy of her brother, a memorial sermon delivered in the local church by a clergyman named Savage. She sent it off to London for advice about publication. On 16 February her nephew-in-law William Berkeley, fourth Baron Berkeley of Stratton, returned word that he himself "liked it extreamly" but that he acquiesced in the negative judgment of her two other friends, John Danvers (Lady Temple's first cousin) and Anthony Henley (the wealthy wit, M.P., and patron of aspiring writers).[121] Miss Julia Longe, who read the entire sermon in manuscript, assumes that it was too fulsome even for Temple's admirers.[122] She quotes a paragraph containing a line strikingly similar to Swift's. "Rivers of tears and hecatombs of sighs would I with this my voluntary elegie offer to thee," writes Savage, *"thou all that was excellent in Man,* did it suit with the privacy of thy life, and thy modest desires, to have such pompous obsequies."[123] Miss Longe also quotes Swift's journal entry in almost the same words—"He died at 1 o'clock in the morning, and with him *all that was good and excellent in man"*—instead of Lyon's "all that was great and good among Men," which is still strikingly close to Savage's phrase.[124] Whether or not she quotes from an independent source, the likeness of phrasing suggests the possibility of some sort of cross-pollination. Perhaps both Swift and Savage had a common source in Lady Giffard's own expressions about Temple or in the standard clichés of formal eulogy. Perhaps Savage had seen Swift's journal entry, or a transcript of it, through Lady Giffard; perhaps Swift echoes the sermon. Whatever the case, Swift later expressed a certain humorous contempt for Savage, his eulogy, and the efforts to publish it. A day after his own *Conduct of the Allies* appeared in 1711 (anonymously, as was usual with Swift), he re-

counted for Stella the first signs of its popular reception. Several people
advised him to read it because, as they said, "it was something very
extraordinary." Although he will be suspected for the author, and although "several paultry answers" are bound to appear, Swift gravely
reflects that "It must take its fate, as Savage said of his sermon that he
preached at Farnham on Sir William Temple's death." He then reports
that a friend saw Savage in Italy "and says he is a coxcomb, and half
mad: he goes in red, and with yellow waistcoats. . . ."[125]

Swift's second eulogistic inscription of 1699 would have suited Lady
Giffard even better than the first, thanks to its emphasis on Temple's
transcendent virtues, in the tradition of Boyer's character sketch and of
Temple's essay *Of Heroick Virtue*. As George Mayhew reconstructs it,
Swift entered the eulogy on the flyleaf of the quarto Bible which he
acquired in either 1697 or 1698, next to his notation of Temple's death:

> Jan^{ry}. 27. 1698/9 Dyed S^r. W^m. Temple Bar^t. at one O Clock in the Morning
> aged 71 years—
> He was a Person of the greatest Wisdom, Justice, Liberality, Politeness,
> Eloquence, of his age or Nation; the truest Lover of his Country, and one
> that deserved more from it by his eminent publick services, than any Man
> before or since: Besides his great deserving from the Commonwealth of
> Learning; having been universally esteemed the most accomplisht writer
> of his time.[126]

If Swift seems to describe a near demigod, he responds in precisely the
way in which common men are supposed to respond in the presence of
heroic virtue. Whatever its precise components, Temple had implied,
heroic virtue is a public quality, to be viewed from afar. It gives

> such a lustre to those who have possest it, as made them appear to common
> eyes, something more than Mortals, and to have been born of some mix-
> ture, between Divine and Humane Race; To have been honoured and
> obey'd in their Lives, and after their Deaths bewailed and adored.

A true hero is a patriot and lover of mankind, and by his services in
private or public life he earns his nation's thanks and remembrance.
Temple finds all heroic actions summed up in three lines translated
from Vergil: "Here such, as for their Country, wounds receiv'd/ Or
who by Arts invented, Life improv'd,/ Or by deserving made themselves remembred." In sum, he says, "the Character of Heroick Virtue
seems to be in short, The deserving well of Mankind."[127] Appropriately
enough, Swift's emphasis is likewise on Temple's great deservings from
the public. As the truest lover of his country, Temple "deserves more
from it" than any man before or since, and his reputation as a writer

vouches for "his great deserving from the Commonwealth of Learning."
If Swift's flyleaf preserves a cry from the heart—a formally eulogistic
one, admittedly—it is a cry which conforms closely to Temple's specifi-
cations for heroic virtue, and which, if overheard, should have met with
certain approval from Temple's most ardent student and admirer, Lady
Giffard.

Like Swift's briefer inscription in the *Journal d'Estat,* the Bible
tribute ultimately depends on a context now uncertain. Did Swift write
for his own eyes only, or as his terms suggest, for Lady Giffard's as well?
What provisions had Temple made for Swift's future, and how strong
were they? What function did Swift's Bible itself serve at Moor Park?
In many households, after all, Bibles are free of access to everyone, and
the Swift who lived at Moor Park after 1696 was an ordained clergyman,
sworn to "be diligent in prayers, and in reading of the holy Scrip-
tures."[128] When Thomas Swift replaced Jonathan at Moor Park, from
1694 to 1696, he apparently fulfilled at least a few ecclesiastical functions.
In February 1694/95 Thomas wrote the bookseller Bentley at Temple's
behest, and Bentley endorsed the letter "Mr. Swift's (Sir William Temple's chaplain) letter about the History of England." In later years as
well, Thomas styled himself "formerly Chaplain to Sir William Temple."[129] To exalt his own dignity at Moor Park, Thomas probably exaggerated his priestly duties, but at least when gout sent Sir William to
his bed, someone had to lead family prayers.[130] When Jonathan returned
to Moor Park in the summer of 1696, he probably took on the same
minor responsibilities.[131] It would help to know whether the Bible
which he later acquired served him only privately, or for household
duties as well, and thus whether or not Swift could expect others to view
it. (It would also help to know if Swift was troubled by snooping or
tale-bearing servants at Moor Park. Among his amusing resolutions
"When I come to be old," dated the year of Temple's death, appears the
entry, "Not to be influenced by, or give ear to knavish tatling Servants,
or others."[132])

Certainly nothing very personal appears on the flyleaf. However
ardent his feelings at the time, Swift describes a public hero rather than
a private personality, and the description itself appears in a formal,
almost impersonal, location. As Mayhew reconstructs it, the tribute to
Temple was sandwiched between two Latin memoranda recording natural wonders. The first, dated 3 May 1698, records in solemn detail an
unseasonable snowfall, which "non solum nocte, verum etiam ad cras-
tini diei partem meridianam, confe[r]ta humi jacuit. . . ."[133] Mayhew
observes that Swift chose to enter "such cosmological omens and portents as traditionally accompany the death of a great man"—although

traditionally they appear only for the mightiest princes and prophets, not former ambassadors. In May 1698, to be sure, Temple was still alive, Swift had not yet begun compiling his *Journal d'Estat,* and the precise significance of the portentous snowfall may not have been clear. It is only the second Latin memorandum, written after Temple's death, which definitely turns the flyleaf into a page on the fall of princes.

For the first memorandum, at least, Swift's inspiration most likely came from Temple himself. The atmosphere at Moor Park was sympathetic to such scientific observations. Temple's admired Athenians often dealt with natural wonders and portents, which they tried to explain naturalistically, and from time to time the *Athenian Mercury* encouraged its readers to record and contribute more such accounts.[134] Temple seemed to share the Athenian point of view. In his essay *Of Popular Discontents,* he could speculate that comets and meteors may affect human minds as well as bodies (and so may lead to civil commotions in a state), and in the essay *Upon Ancient and Modern Learning,* he could praise "the more ancient Sages of Greece" for their remarkable understanding of nature, which allowed them to foretell the most unusual phenomena:

> not only Eclipses in the Heavens, but Earthquakes at Land, and Storms at Sea, great Drowths and great Plagues, much Plenty, or much Scarcity of certain sorts of Fruits or Grain, not to mention the Magical Powers, attributed to several of them, to allay Storms, to raise Gales, to appease Commotions of People, to make Plagues cease; which qualities, whether upon any ground of Truth or no, yet if well believed, must have raised them, to that strange height they were at, of common esteem and honour. . . .

Elsewhere in the essay he implied his belief in the talismans and other "Magick" of the ancient Indians, Chaldaeans, and Egyptians, who likewise (said Temple) must have possessed "some excelling Knowledge of Nature."[135] Still uncertain of his facts, he later sent the *Athenian Mercury* a query about the validity of ancient talismans and magic. After considering such arts at length, the Athenians finally dismissed them as "a wicked, superstitious, ridiculous Juggle."[136] When Temple next raised the subject, he adapted his discussion to the Athenians' criticism. In *Some Thoughts Upon Reviewing the Essay of Antient and Modern Learning*— which he began in fragmentary form about 1695, and then decided to continue and expand in 1697—Temple drops the subject of talismans altogether, concedes a number of gross cheats and superstitions among ancient priests and magicians, but holds fast to his central point, that the ancient *illuminati* possessed an excelling knowledge of nature, now lost, which allowed them to make predictions, work cures, and control natural phenomena in ways which seem almost magical. Empedocles, for example, actually knew how to stop the plague and foretell "many strange Events." Temple credits the Delphic oracle with "discovering Secrets in Natural or Mathematical Matters," but dismisses its mouthpiece, the Pythia, as a pious fraud who did the bidding of the Delphic priests—"a Colledge or Society of wise and learned Men, in all sorts of Sciences. . . ." Temple credits reports of the portentous lightning and thunder which defended Delphi, but is apt to think that the priests either had "some admirable Knowledg of that kind, which was called Magical; or that they knew the Use and Force of Gun-powder, so many Ages since, and reserved it, as they did the Effects of all their Sciences, for the Service of their God. . . ."[137]

Temple's continuing interest in "Magick," scientific secrets, oracles, and natural wonders seems to have involved Swift as well. Early in 1698—a few months after Temple decided to expand his essay, and two or three months before Swift entered his meteorological memorandum about the May snowfall—Swift had read Isaac Vossius' treatise *De Sibyllinis aliisque quae Christi natalem praecessere Oraculis,* an unorthodox study concerned with the validity of pagan oracles which, before the coming of Christ, had supposedly forecast the advent of a Great King.[138] The reading list in which Swift mentions the book shows signs of Temple's influence,[139] and Temple apparently made Swift a present of the volume. The Rothschild Collection preserves Swift's copy, at least twice rebound and complete with a tipped-in endpaper which bears Swift's note, *"Jon: Swift. Donum Illus*[mi] *D.D. G. Temple Febr. 2. 1697."*[140] With the adjustment for New Style, the inscription therefore dates from the period indicated on Swift's reading list, where the Vossius appears as the third and final book listed under the heading "From Jan: 7th 1697/8."[141] While it is less than certain that Swift recorded the portentous snowfall for Temple's benefit, or on Temple's suggestion, the evidence points in that direction. In doing so, it lessens the possibility that Swift inscribed his Bible flyleaf with material meant for his own eyes only.

When Swift entered his next inscription on the flyleaf, the eulogy of Temple, any outside inspiration would have come from Lady Giffard instead. Swift's eulogy resembles his tribute to Temple in the *Journal d'Estat.* In both he praises the public Temple, or at least the heroic public image which Temple had worked so hard to achieve through his writings. The point deserves emphasis because, as Temple's greatest admirer, Lady Giffard shared this view of Temple. Both she and her last surviving brother, Sir John Temple, were anxious that the public should derive its notion of their brother's character not from his private life but from his published writings. As early as 1690 she wrote that "Sr Wm Temples character will be best knowne by his writeings, & to that picture of him I leave those that care either to know or imitate him," much as Temple had commended his readers to the illustrious examples of heroes, as depicted in the essay *Of Heroick Virtue.*[142] Some time "not long before" Sir John himself died in 1704, she showed him her *Life* of Temple and approvingly quoted his reaction. At the end of her manuscript, she said, Sir John had written that their brother's "parts & abilitys will be best knowne by his writeings. . . ."[143] Indeed, it was probably Lady Giffard who was responsible for Boyer's refusal to dwell on Temple's private life and character, and instead assert that "Any intelligent Reader will, from the Account of his [public] *Life* and *Writings,* readily form to himself the *Idea* of an *accomplish'd Gentleman,* a *sound Politician,* a *Patriot,* and a *great Scholar. . . .*"[144] Boyer goes out of his way to flatter Lady Giffard in the next paragraph, after giving a physical description of Temple jointly based (it seems) on the one which Lady Giffard had written in 1690 and on the Lely portrait of Temple to which she had also referred.[145] Boyer's preface acknowledges help in "several Particulars which I have learn'd from Sir William Temple's *intimate Friends,*" a term especially appropriate for Lady Giffard, who was even prouder of being his closest friend than of being his sister.[146]

The same preface mentions Temple in terms even closer to Swift's flyleaf than Boyer's later characterization. In his eulogy Swift had called Temple "the truest Lover of his Country, and one that deserved more from it by his eminent publick services, than any Man before or since: Besides his great deserving from the Commonwealth of Learning. . . ." Boyer's preface presents the same two ideas in the same order, with some of the same phrasing. Temple is "one who has so well deserv'd of *Mankind* in general, and of his *Country* in particular; one who has left so great a Name in the *Commonwealth of Learning. . . .*"[147] Since Boyer had no access to books in Swift's library, any direct influence could only have come through a transcript of Swift's eulogy in Lady Giffard's possession. If so, she had indeed read the flyleaf in the Bible, and with approval. On the other hand, the resemblance may be only a coincidence stemming from a mutual source. One possibility is Temple, whose accents and ideas always found an appreciative audience in Lady Giffard. In his essays Temple often spoke of "the Commonwealth of Learning" and those who deserve well or ill from it. In *Of Poetry,* for instance, Temple had earnestly noted that "a clear Account of Enthusiasm and Fascination from their natural Causes, would very much deserve from Mankind in general, as well as from the Commonwealth of

Learning," and in *Of Heroick Virtue* he celebrated the prosody of one Regnor Ladbrog, a snake-bitten Viking chieftain whose dying verses have been preserved by the antiquary Olaus Wormius, "who has very much deserved from the Commonwealth of Learning."[148] Lady Giffard herself is another, even likelier source for the verbal similarities in Swift and Boyer. If Boyer consulted her about Temple, as is probable, he would have heard much the same sort of praise that Swift had, some years before. Even her friend Anthony Henley, who discouraged her from publishing Savage's funeral sermon, knew how to phrase his objections in terms consonant with her ideas about Temple. Henley professes to love Savage "for his good will," suspects that no one could have done better, but tactfully admits to having the same thoughts of the sermon "that I am like to have of everything that aims att giving a character that I think nobody should dare to pretend to attempt."[149] Only Temple's public life or writings, presumably, can convey so exalted a character.

When such relative strangers as Boyer, Savage, and Henley knew how to suit their words to Lady Giffard, what then of Swift, who had lived so long under the same roof? If ever he needed to stay in her good graces, it was early in 1699, when he made his final entry in the *Journal d'Estat* and his eulogistic inscription in the Bible. As soon as the great man died, on 27 January, Swift's career entered a crucial phase. Both in a positive and a negative sense, it depended on the good will of Temple's sister and, to a lesser extent, on that of Sir John Temple. Lady Giffard was Temple's chief mourner, and as such commanded the sympathy and assistance of Temple's friends, including the King himself. She and Sir John were also Temple's executors, charged with fulfilling the terms of Temple's will.[150] One of Swift's chief legacies, after so many years in Temple's service, was the reputation for having worked for so great a man, but a few well-placed complaints from Temple's lifelong companion could ruin any prospect of advancement on that score. Swift's less abstract legacies also depended on her and Sir John. By the terms of Temple's codicil, Swift was to receive a £100 bequest payable from Sir John's share of the estate, but the executors had it in their power to delay or otherwise complicate payment. Sir John earmarked Swift's £100 to be paid "out of my store," but by assigning a mortgage to Lady Giffard, he transferred the debt to her. She was to pay Swift interest on it.[151] More valuable than the cash legacy was Swift's literary executorship. By publishing Temple's posthumous works, Swift stood to gain by linking his name publicly with Temple's and by selling the copyrights.[152] Lady Giffard and Sir John were under no legal obligation to honor the arrangement. Neither the will nor the codicil specified anything about it. Legally, Temple's unpublished papers belonged either to "all my goods, stock, and furniture whatsoever at Moore Parke" (books specifically included), which with Moor Park itself went to Lady Giffard during her life, or to the "whole remainder of any and all such personal estate" not already disposed of, which Temple ordered divided among Lady Giffard, Sir John, and the two Temple granddaughters.[153] To carry away the appropriate manuscripts, Swift needed the executors' permission. Up to a point, he apparently received it.[154] Had they refused him the appropriate manuscripts, including the Downton transcript and its successor, Swift could never have published what he did.

Compared with Swift's immediate prospects, however, the legacies would have mattered only slightly. Here Lady Giffard figured more centrally than ever, unless Temple had made foolproof arrangements for Swift before dying. Almost certainly he had not. Nothing from Swift's letters in the 1690s, including the one written two weeks before Temple's death, suggests that the great man had made clear provisions for his secretary.[155] If Temple were procrastinating, he had little opportunity to make good at the end. Death probably came "with rather unexpected suddenness," as Miss Longe reports.[156] For what it is worth, Swift's sister Jane later wrote that Temple had promised to find Swift a living in England, "but death came in between, and has left him unprovided both of friend and living."[157] Certainly he found himself unprovided for at Court, where he went after leaving Moor Park to petition the King through Temple's friend the Earl of Romney, supposedly "upon the Claym of a Promise his Majesty had mad[e] to Sir W T that he would give Mr Swift a Prebend of Canterbury or Westminster."[158]

If Swift possessed any common sense in the days following Temple's death, he would have realized how valuable Lady Giffard had suddenly become. As the sad news spread, she began receiving offers of sympathy and assistance from her brother's powerful friends. The Earl of Sunderland, through whom Swift had hoped for advancement a year earlier, promptly wrote from Northamptonshire that, "to the uttermost of what I am Capable of, you may depend upon my service as Long as I have a being for his [Temple's] sake and for your owne."[159] On the same day, 2 February, Henley wrote from London to express his own sympathy and that of the King, who "talked to mee about a quarter of an hour yesterday morning about y^r La^p and y^r losse and exprest the greatest concern for both that ever I saw him doe. . . ."[160] Lady Giffard needed a favor of some sort from the King, and on the 16th her attentive young nephew-in-law, Lord Berkeley of Stratton, returned a hopeful answer. Although he had been delayed in reporting "how your message was received" by the King, he is now "very glad to tell you now, y^t I think it was very well taken and ye King said you might be assured y^t no body could take greater part in what concern'd you then he did."[161] A day earlier, Lord Romney himself had reported progress. He would be "glad to give you other testimonies" of his love for Temple, "then onely my saying it:

> I think I never failed in any thing that I thought would contribute to your service or your satisfaction, and I am sure that I never will if it lies in my power, I have done somthing towards it already, and will let you know the perticulars in a short time. . . .[162]

With Romney, Henley, and Berkeley of Stratton representing her interests at Court, the King anxious to oblige her, and Sunderland offering his utmost from Northamptonshire, Lady Giffard was well equipped to speed the claims of her late brother's secretary—or at least would have seemed so at the time. Even without reading the letters, Swift would have known the situation. He may well have delivered letters containing Lady Giffard's "message," or carried news of Temple's death to her London correspondents. The Moor Park estate papers reveal that he had gone to London on Temple family business—important enough to justify buying mourning clothes there—some time between January 28, the day after Temple's death, and February 2, the day of the early letter from Henley, whom Swift probably knew at this time.[163] Whatever the case, it is worth noting that when Swift returned to London four weeks later to press his own advancement, he turned to Lord Romney, who "professed much friendship for him." Failing at Court, he next turned to the Earl of Berkeley, on whom Lord Berkeley of Stratton seems to have had particular claims.[164] Both earls had been acquainted with Temple, Romney in particular. Lady Giffard may have done nothing to smooth Swift's way with them, although Swift probably required an introduction to Berkeley.[165] What matters is not the result of Swift's search for preferment, but Lady Giffard's impressive connections when Swift needed them most. In the end, it may prove impossible to fix Swift's intentions in the *Journal d'Estat* and the Bible eulogy—and with his intentions, the sincerity of his praise—but it is no longer possible to assume that the inscriptions show Swift writing in a vacuum, spilling out his deepest feelings. If anything, the reverse is the safer bet. In tone, approach, and subject matter, his praise of Temple suits his circumstances far too closely, as in most of his other references to Temple.

Swift had more to write on the flyleaf of his Bible, but its significance is again uncertain. Before the eulogy of Temple he had made the Latin entry about the unusual May snowfall in 1698, and a month or two after the eulogy, he entered another natural wonder: "Mensa Martio A.D. 1698/9 saevit, pestis inter equos, Non solum per Insulas Britannicas, sed fere [omnino] Europam grassata."[166] The entry completes the necessary portents which surround the death of princes, but it also changes the flyleaf's tone. There is something unsettling in an epidemic among *horses,* no matter how universal its scope or unsmiling Swift's Latin. As in the ode to Temple—where Temple restores the empire of Virtue much as men find the Philosopher's Stone, or where the mightiest attributes meet only in Temple and romance—the final entry adds a faint flavor of absurdity. It is all very well for Nature to mourn the death of princes with earthquakes, comets, plagues, or even freakish snowfalls, but when she takes it out on horses, even a great number of them, her tribute seems somehow dispensable. Whatever the case, there is less circumstantial evidence to help pin down Swift's intentions. By April he must have been at Court, pressing his petition through the dilatory Lord Romney, but in March he may still have been at Moor Park, trying to secure Lady Giffard's support, despairing of it, or simply finishing his household duties. Until more evidence turns up, the final entry's purposes remain hazy.

The same holds true for Swift's final alterations on the Bible flyleaf. He crossed out his eulogy of Temple. Quoting the man who transcribed the flyleaf inscriptions in 1811, Mayhew reports that "Swift had after-wards 'effaced the entire of it (except for the date)' of Temple's death with the same circular cancellations he later used for parts of the *Journal to Stella.*"[167] Although a cancelled eulogy does not carry great conviction, Sir Walter Scott printed its text without qualification.[168] There the matter stood until Mayhew sought out Scott's sources and announced his findings in 1971. Explaining the cancellation largely depends on the nature and purposes of the eulogy itself. If Swift's praise in fact represents a hero-worshipper's admiration, then the cancellation may represent later disillusionment, revulsion with Temple, embarrassment over such boyish sentiments, or an instinct to hide outpourings of cherished private emotions. If the praise represents a practical way of coping with an uncertain future, or an outlet for Swift's sense of irony, then the cancellation may represent a wish to expunge evidence of the maneuvre, some second thoughts about introducing Temple's death into its equine and faintly mocking context, or even a flash of anger when, despite his best efforts, suitable preferment failed to materialize that spring, or when (a decade later) he broke with Lady Giffard over her efforts to discredit his edition of Temple's *Memoirs, Part III.*

Inscriptions in Temple's Gift Books

Although seldom remarked, Swift owned other books with similar cancellations. They help to narrow the field of possible explanations, but do not resolve the problem entirely. On the flyleaf tipped into Swift's copy of *De Sibyllinis*, Swift had entered a formal inscription of ownership, but he later obliterated the words *"Donum Illus*^{mi} *D.D. G. Temple"* with circular scrawlings not unlike the ones described on the Bible flyleaf.[169] About six years before, Temple had given him Archbishop Laud's *Relation* of the conference with the Jesuit Fisher (published in 1639), in which he entered a similar inscription. Again he later crossed out Temple's name in it.[170] The same thing happened with a copy of Temple's *Miscellanea* (a double volume containing the first and second parts, Wing T651 and Wing T655, London, 1697, 1696), now at the Public Library, Armagh. On the preliminary blanks, Swift had inscribed it *"Illustrissimo Authore/ Donante/ Dec*^{bre}*1697,"* and *"Jon: Swift./ Donum Illustrissimi/ D.D. W. Temple/ Dec*^{bre}*1697."* Except for the dates and Swift's name, both inscriptions have been crossed out with circular scrawlings.[171]

In a fourth gift book, recently discovered in Ireland, the inscription remains unaltered, but the evidence suggests that Swift had lost or given the book away before Temple's death. The book is Thomas White's *Institutionum Ethicarum, sive Staterae Morum, Aptis Rationum momentis libratae, Tomus Primus (—Secundus, —Tertius)*, 3 vols. in 1, 12mo (London: n.p., 1660). Swift's signature is on the title page, and on the free endpaper appears the inscription (in his formal copy-hand) *"Jon. Swift./ Donavit Excellent*^{mus}*/ D. D. Will Temple/ April 16*^{tho}*/ 1692/* [flourish]." The inscription date is the same as in Swift's copy of Laud's *Relation*. The author, who writes under the pseudonym Thomas Anglus, was an eccentric Roman Catholic priest who had earlier collaborated with Sir Kenelm Digby in speculations of natural philosophy which were of interest to Temple. Until 1973 the book lay unrecognized in an Irish country house. Unlike the Vossius, the Laud, and the Armagh *Miscellanea*, it appears in neither the 1715 nor the 1745 Swift library lists. There are no marginalia in Swift's hand, and the book is in generally mint condition, another sign of sparing use. When Swift left his cure at Kilroot in 1696, he left behind many or most of his books, about which he wrote to his friend John Winder two years later, with instructions about disposing of them. Some, it appears, have been lent to other people. After Winder collects them all (and keeps a few specified titles for himself), he is to send them on to Dublin.[172] The White volume may belong to the "few and inconsiderable" books still missing from the list which Winder sent Swift, or may have been lost thereafter in transit to Dublin. At any rate it is the only such gift book known in which Swift has not blotted out the inscription mentioning Temple.

Whatever the story behind the cancellations, they do not represent an effort to hide emotions too private for the world to see. The epithet *"Illustrissimus"* may be a superlative, but if florid or flattering, it is still part of a conventional formula. Judging from the Bible flyleaf, the four other cancellations probably date from a period following Temple's death. More certainly, those in the books inscribed 1697 or 1698 date from a period following Swift's only known rift with Temple, in 1694. Their exact implications may be impossible to fix, but they surely represent some sort of negative reaction in Swift—perhaps against Temple personally, but also perhaps against the recollection of Swift's experience at Moor Park, against his longtime flattery of Temple, against the doting Lady Giffard, or even against himself. If anything, they offer a rare if tantalizing glimpse behind Swift's continuing show of respect and admiration for the great man, which he maintained fairly steadily through his frustrations in 1699 and his irritation a decade later. As such they stand out from the bulk of Swift's allusions to Temple, which aim themselves at a Moor Park readership, at the public, or at others whom Swift wrote with set purposes in mind. Any account of Swift and Temple in the 1690s must take the cancellations into consideration.

Temple in the Commonwealth of Learning: The "Hints" and Other Follies

Another question worth pursuing concerns Temple's intellectual attainments, at least in the days when Swift knew him at Moor Park. Even apart from his personal vanities and foibles, how much was there for a bright young secretary to look up to? Not long after Temple set himself up as an arbiter of learning in his essay *Upon Ancient and Modern Learning*, after all, Swift found Temple using Dunton's dubious *Athenian Mercury* as a kind of research service (or at least as a sounding board for his hypotheses) and altering his later arguments to square with the Athenians' opinion. Then too, in his published works, Temple demonstrated a sometimes amazing propensity for self-contradiction. At least in Swift's time, its most distinctive hallmark was Temple's penchant for despising ideas or attitudes which he himself maintained elsewhere.

In its treatment of the origins of the ancient Picts and Scots, Temple's *Introduction to the History of England* (1694) provides a case in point. Having confidently conjectured that the Picts were actually ancient Britons driven the length of the island by Romans, Temple can smile at the considerable "Pains and Invention" which have been "employed by many Authors, to make them a Foreign Race of People, who, from they know not what Country, and at they know not what Time, invaded and possessed Caledonia. . . ." The case is wholly different, to be sure, with that second ancient Northern people, the Scots of northern Ireland and Scotland. After ridiculing Buchanan and other historians for hazarding no conjectures about the Scots' origin before Ireland, Temple launches into a long mythico-etymological discursus tending to show that the Scots must have been a foreign race, Scythians who somehow made their way into the British Isles from somewhere in Asia, doubtless by way of Norway. Aside from the striking etymological evidence ('Scyths' being so close to 'Scots') and the close anthropological parallels (both peoples were semi-nomadic and wore mantles), Temple chiefly relies upon "the Runick Learning and Stories," which reveal that "the Asiatick Scythians, under the Names of Getes or Goths, and the Conduct of Odin their Captain, (their Lawgiver at first, and afterwards one of their Gods)" set up a mighty kingdom around the Baltic, from the geography of which region "'tis necessary, Norway must have been the last they possessed in their Western Progress. . . ." Having settled matters to his own satisfaction—"This is the best Account I have been ever able to give my self," he notes—Temple pours contempt upon earlier historians, who (it seems) have been guilty of the flimsiest kind of conjectures, based on mere tradition or fable. Questions of Picts, Scots, and the earliest periods in North British history have

> implyed so many unskilful Pens, in so much idle Trash, and worthless Stuff, as they have left upon it; but all involved in such groundless Traditions and vanity of Fables, so obscured by the length of Time, and darkness of unlearned Ages, or covered over with such gross Forgeries, made at Pleasure by their first Inventers. . . .

Of course it goes without saying that "the Runick Learning and Stories," with their insights about Odin, that captain and lawgiver of the Goths, have nothing to do with the fables which Temple finds so contemptible a source for history.[173] Although more striking than most in its verve, Temple's Picto-Scottish discursus is typical enough in its proceedings, and if anyone was in a position to recognize the oddities of Temple's thinking, it was the secretary who had read, copied, and reread Temple's working manuscripts. Between Temple's continuing (if much diminished) reputation as an original thinker, and Swift's unmerited reputation as an inferior student at Trinity College, Dublin, it is also easy to forget that the master's formal training hardly equalled his employee's, especially in the classics, the heart of most academic curricula. After two years largely spent in "Entertainments" (including tennis and doubtless the gambling which Lady Giffard said that he enjoyed as a young man) Temple dropped out of Cambridge without taking a degree.[174] What book-learning he boasted he owed to his grammar-school days and to independent reading in later years. By contrast Swift had spent nearly seven years in Trinity College, Dublin, before troubled conditions in Ireland drove him to England, and the M.A. which he nearly attained in Dublin he soon afterwards received from Oxford—all this besides the heavy schedule of independent reading he maintained at Moor Park.[175]

It is interesting, then, to note Temple's intellect at work in a pair of passages which Swift transcribed at Moor Park. The first concerns Regnor Ladbrog [Ragnar Lothbrok], the dying Viking chieftain whose verse Temple quotes in the essay *Of Heroick Virtue* as printed in *Miscellanea, The Second Part*, which Swift had helped Temple ready for the press in 1689–90. Although Temple tended to despise philology (a Modern invention) he sometimes fancied himself an etymologist, and a few pages after praising the Viking's verse, he invokes Regnor to demonstrate the antiquity of the word *baro*, Late Latin for 'baron.' *Baro* is an ancient Northern word, Temple argues, because he finds it "used above eight hundred years ago, in the Verses mentioned of King Lodbrog, when one of his Exploits was, to have conquered eight Barons." Unfortunately, the word which Temple finds Regnor using comes not from the original Old Norse but rather a seventeenth-century Latin translation of it. As Clara Marburg has noted, Temple's source for Regnor's verse was Olaus Wormius' 1636 treatise, *[Runir]: Seu Danica Literatura Antiquissima, Vulgo Gothica luci reddita . . .* (Hafniae, Typis Melchioris Martzan), which provides a sampling of Old Norse verse in an appendix. Sure enough, among some of the verse associated with the mythic Ragnar Lothbrok appears the translated line "vicimus octo Barones" (p. 199). At least for the moment, Temple has forgotten that his ancient Viking hero spoke Old Norse rather than barbaric Latin. Probably the appendix's format had confused Temple. Olaus Wormius had printed the original Old Norse in the runic alphabet, not the Roman, and between the lines had provided a word-for-word Latin gloss. By turning to one of Wormius' tables earlier in the book, Temple could easily have discovered that the five-rune word translated by "Barones" actually reads "iarla"—'jarls' or 'earls,' to give the English cognate forms. But did Temple know of the tables' existence? Did he even know that Olaus'

Latin follows the runic words word for word? How much, if at all, had he bothered to consult Olaus' apparatus and elaborate treatise before dabbling in the Latin 'verse' at the end?

Temple's appreciation of Regnor's poetry raises more questions than it answers. This time Temple seems vaguely aware that the poetry which he quotes has been, in some sense, "translated into Latin by Olaus," as he says, but his praise of the verse is squarely based on the accidental effects of the gloss. If nothing else, a word-for-word translation can seldom capture much of the meter, alliteration, or rhythm in an original, and the syntax is bound to seem disjointed or odd. So it happens that Regnor's dying verses, in the Latin gloss, sound suitably halting and barbaric to an ear used to regular syntax (whether Latin or English, poetic or prosaic) and regular versification in some form or other: "Pugnavimus ensibus/ Hoc ridere me facit semper/ Quod Balderi Patris Scamna/ Parata scio in aula,/ Bibemus cerevisiam/ Ex concavis crateribus craniorum. . . ." Nowadays we might recognize something vaguely Whitmanesque in such verse, but to Temple the most recognizable parallel would have been with contemporary Pindarics, with their heightened emotions and irregular lines. In his judgment, at any rate, here is "a vein truly Poetical, and in its kind Pindarick, taking it with the allowance of the different Climats, Fashions, Opinions, and Languages of such distant Countries." Despite the final vague proviso, about different "Languages" in Regnor's day, Temple has based his appreciation squarely upon the unintentional effects of a kind of translation which he seemingly fails to recognize, from a language of which (thanks to the runic alphabet) he may never have seen a word—"the Runick Language," as he earlier calls it in his confusion.[176] Someone with Swift's training should have noticed such anomalies—and with them Temple's pleasure in even unintentional pindarics—but Temple himself apparently sensed no difficulty. After all, the French that he wrote was practically interchangeable with his English, when translated word for word: why shouldn't there be an equal parity between Latin and whatever language Regnor happened to speak? If the intelligible lines say something about eight "Barones," no doubt the unintelligible ones do much the same, thus proving that Regnor knew the word.

To judge from a second passage, which Swift transcribed around 1697, Temple approached classical scholarship with much the same care as he had etymology, Viking prosody, and early North British history. The passage occurs in the "Hints" which Temple eventually expanded into *Some Thoughts Upon Reviewing the Essay of Antient and Modern Learning,* easily his weakest essay, and the only major piece that he seems to have composed during his last five years, when Swift himself was working on *A Tale of a Tub*. As the passage eventually appeared in print, Temple made a strong distinction between Renaissance and modern critics—that is, between the critics whose work restored ancient learning and the critics who now try to tear it down again. Philology is a subject he hardly knows what to make of, Temple writes, but "If it be only Criticism upon antient Authors and Languages; he must be a Conjurer that can make those Moderns with their Comments, and Glossaries, and Annotations, more learned, than the Authors themselves in their own Languages. . . ." On the other hand, he says, we owe much to the critics who worked in the period "after the Restoration of Learning in these western Parts," those employed "for the first hundred Years." They established texts of the ancient authors, corrected transcribers' mistakes, explained obscurities, and in short tried "to recover those old Jewels out of the Dust and Rubbish, wherein they had been so long lost or soiled. . . ." Instead of such meritorious service, Modern critics only rake into trifles, repeat what their Renaissance forebears have already written, and enviously denigrate the ancients, to make them seem "as mean and wretched as themselves." By Temple's time, he concludes, "there has been so much written of this kind of Stuff, that the World is surfeited" with it.[177] What Swift copied in 1697 tells a different story, before second thoughts or wiser heads intervened. In the early manuscript version, probably first composed about 1695, not long after Wotton's *Reflections* appeared, Temple makes no distinction between the Renaissance critics who helped restore learning and the petty detractors who now undermine it. They are all Moderns. If philology means criticism upon ancient authors and languages, he writes,

> He must be a Conjurer to make those Moderns with their Comments, and Glossaryes, and Annotations, more learned than the Authors themselves in their own Languages as well as the Subjects they treat. *The Truth is, there was so much writt of this Kind of Stuff in the first hundred and fifty Years after the Recovery of the Greek and Latin Tongues, that the World has for some Time been quite surfeited,* and I should have thought, without Mr Wotton's Authority, that one might make Tautology a Science, as well as Philology.[178]

In the corrected, much expanded published version, Temple praised "the Criticks for the first hundred Years" after the restoration of learning, but here he shows nothing but contempt for them. That their labors —glossaries, commentary, annotations, and all—played a part in the restoration of ancient texts and ancient languages, Temple seems blissfully unaware. The "Recovery of the Greek and Latin Tongues," he implies, was something unconnected. Coming from a country gentleman who had never progressed beyond a grammar-school level of competence in dealing with the classics, such comments might be understandable, if regrettable. In a man of Temple's intellectual pretensions, they are astonishing. It would be less distressing, today, to discover that one of our most celebrated gardening writers had no inkling of the connection between botanical research and the development of the hybrid strains which he recommends for our gardens, and so damns all past and present botanists for triviality and irrelevance.

Thanks to the unusual freedom he permitted himself, Temple's "Hints" are revealing in other ways as well. Temple had composed them as a rejoinder to Wotton, who had questioned his scholarship, but originally Temple had not meant them to appear under his own name. Instead they were to be incorporated in the work of another man engaged in answering Wotton—a "M^r H" at Oxford, the friend of "Dr Fullham" (possibly Dr. George Fulham of Magdalen).[179] As a result, writing of himself in the third person, Temple attacked Wotton and praised himself much more frankly and directly than he would otherwise have dared. This led to difficulties, as it turned out. According to the anonymous note which accompanies the "Hints," both Fullham and Mr. H. informed Temple that "the Style of these ['Hints'] could not agree in any kind, or all look of a piece with that of the other," and accordingly proposed that they appear as an appendix instead—thus isolating the "Hints" from Mr. H's text and increasing the likelihood that readers would identify them as Temple's. Naturally Temple "absolutely refused" the proposal and in an apparent fit of pique "desired the Doctor to prevayl with his Friend to suppress the whole Thing; which was accordingly done." (Considerable pressure may have been needed: even before Temple began writing the "Hints," Fullham had "brought Him a good Part of the inte[n]ded Treatise [by Mr. H], & told Him tht it had cost His Friend so much Pains, that He found He was loath to lose it. . . ." Later Fullham even brought Mr. H. to meet Temple.[180])

Of the six sections which Temple originally composed as his "Hints," five fragments survive, with parts scored through or otherwise marked for revision—revisions which eventually appeared in Temple's more finished product, *Some Thoughts Upon Reviewing the Essay of Antient and Modern Learning*. Here and there in the "Hints," whenever the opportunity arises, Temple allows himself sarcastic asides about Wotton—Wotton the asinine alchemist (though Wotton was actually more sceptical than Temple about alchemy), Wotton the tautologist, Wotton the philologist or pretentious lover of talk. It is in the fragments of section 6 that Wotton and Temple receive Temple's full attention. At the beginning of section 6 Temple asserts that "The whole Cause between the Pretensions of Antient and Modern Learning will be best decided by the Comparison of the Persons and the Things that have been produced under the Institutions and Discipline of the one or the other." After a few introductory comments about the kind of "Persons" to be discussed, he begins his inquiry into the "Things" ("Hints," pp. 13–14). In the next surviving fragment (pp. 15–16), Temple seemingly returns to a comparison of the "Persons"—in this case, Temple for the Ancients *versus* Wotton for the Moderns, much as in the single combat through which Swift's *Battle of the Books* was to reach its climax, or rather its anticlimax. Temple's comparison never appeared in his revised essay, published in *Miscellanea, The Third Part*. There, instead of featuring himself, he expanded his preliminary comments and gave a list of such ancient heroes as Epaminondas, Julius Caesar, Philip of Macedon, Trajan, and the two Scipios.[181] Originally, it seems, Temple meant his comparison of Wotton and himself to supplement or replace something similar in Mr. H's treatise: at the end of the manuscript note accompanying the "Hints" appears a short, barely legible memorandum, "Memad^m. that wht He sd of Himself was to putt as wht Mr H sayd abt Scipio."

In themselves, Temple's remarks on Wotton and himself show anger and wounded vanity. They effectively serve to challenge Wotton's credentials as a commentator—as a critic of Temple on questions of ancient and modern learning—and in the process they justify Temple's credentials in the field. In 1694–95, when Temple approached the publishers Dunton and Bentley through Thomas Swift, Temple had proposed a composite history of England drawn from himself and other "authors of name and estimation," "approved and esteemed authors" only—personages like More, Bacon, and Herbert of Cherbury, famous for their public careers as well as their public writings. In Temple's "Hints" the same criteria apply. As a commentator on ancient and modern learning, Temple stands beyond Wotton's criticism because Temple is a great man, a gentleman who has mingled with the great and become famous for his distinguished public career as well as for his published writings. It is worth considering, writes Temple, at what sort of person Wotton has directed his cavils:

> One brought up and long conversant with Persons of the greatest Quality at home and abroad; In Courts, in Parliaments, in privy Councils, in Foreign Embassyes, in the Mediations of generall Peace in Christendom, And the great Assemblyes met upon those Occasions; And yet perhaps more knowne by his Writings than by the great Employments He has had or refused. . . .

That Wotton happens to be wrong in the specific cavil he makes comes as an afterthought, barely worth mentioning. "And this is the Person Mr Wotton pursues so insolently with a pitifull Grammaticall Criticism," Temple continues, "and a mistaken one too."

The tone changes to sarcasm as Temple turns to Wotton. "One would wonder who this great man should be," Temple remarks, "that uses both Antients and Moderns with such an Arrogance...." Wotton's problem is less that he is a "superficiall Sciolist," whose learning is presumably unequal to the task, than that he is Temple's opposite in what really matters in a commentator on ancient and modern learning. Wotton is a man of no worldly note or experience. He proves to be a teacher of children and a would-be private chaplain—a man

> that knows no more of Men or Manners than He has learnt in His Study; A superficiall Sciolist, that by Force of Memory and Scraps of Learning, has been indeed, Raysed, as He calls it; But, to what? why, to teach Mr Finch's Children; He tells us indeed in the Title-Page, of a greater Character, which is that of Chaplain to the Earl of Nottingham, but confesses in the End of His Epistle that He assumed this Stile to sett Himself upon a Level with S^r W T, from whom He takes the Freedom so often to dissent. . . .[182]

Obscure, inexperienced in the great world, ambitious enough to lie, Wotton is not even a gentleman.

If nothing else, Temple's angry sarcasms sound surprising in a man who disapproved of sarcasm in others. When Swift published the expanded "Hints" in essay form in 1701—lacking the frontal attack on Wotton's credentials, but retaining some sarcastic asides elsewhere in the text—he followed the essay with two sets of other fragments or notes ("Heads"), for essays which Temple had thought of writing. In "Heads, Designed for an Essay on Conversation," Temple speaks out boldly against coarse personal raillery and other invidious comparisons:

> Offensive and undistinguish'd Raillery comes from ill Nature, and desire of Harm to others, tho' without Good to ones self.
> Or Vanity and a Desire of valuing our selves, by showing others Faults and Follies, and the Comparison with our selves, as free from them.[183]

Perhaps Temple made a distinction between personal raillery ill natured enough to put into the mouth of others (like Mr. H.) and the more delicate variety which one may permit oneself *in propria persona.* In the finished essay, at any rate, Temple makes a more lightsome hit at Wotton's supposed fondness for applauding himself, a very despicable trait. It is not enough that the Moderns attack all the ancients, says Temple,

> but one of them, I find, will not be satisfied to condemn the rest of the World, without applauding himself; and therefore falling into a Rapture upon the Contemplation of his own Wonderful Performance, he tells us;

Hitherto in the main I please my self, that there cannot be much said against what I have asserted, &c.[184]

As clearly as anything save the Downton transcript and Thomas Swift's two letters for Temple, the "Hints" throw unexpected light upon Swift's master, his attitudes and sense of priorities, the workings of the mind behind the published prose. What Swift asked himself as he copied the "Hints" we cannot know for certain, but we cannot ignore the evidence of Temple's unvarnished views on classical criticism, on Wotton and Wotton's disabilities as a critic, and on the great Sir William Temple himself. Likewise we cannot ignore the secretarial handwriting in which they survive. What Temple wrote for Mr. H. to use, Swift witnessed in the most painstaking way possible. This is the same Temple, we must remind ourselves, in whom are met "Those mighty Epithets, Learn'd, Good, and Great," the same Temple whom Swift was to praise (about two years after transcribing the "Hints") for his "great deserving from the Commonwealth of Learning." If nothing else had survived to make us suspect the candor and motivation behind such praise, Swift's transcription of the "Hints" should be sufficient. Even the most solemn hero-worshipping booby should have sensed something uncomfortable, something with possible applications to himself, in Temple's diatribe on Wotton, the mere teacher and would-be chaplain who 'knows no more of men and manners than he has learnt in his study'. "One would wonder who this great man should be," Temple had begun, and then at first answered: "Why, 'tis a young Scholar that confesses He owes all the Comforts of His Life to His Patrons Bounty...." After Swift returned from his Ulster living in 1696, his life and career depended more than ever upon his own patron's bounty. How did he feel in 1697 (at age twenty-nine, a year younger than Wotton) as he copied Temple's scornful words? And on a lighter note, how did he feel as he copied the passage which ends the fragment as it now survives? Having received his sister's adulation, his secretary's adoring odes, Dunton's occasional flattery (before they quarrelled), his friends' assurance that his works successfully serve the public good[185] —having received, in short, what looks like a steady stream of flattery at Moor Park—Temple exclaims scornfully over the flattery which Wotton lavishes on his own patron, Lord Nottingham, in the Epistle Dedicatory to the *Reflections*. Wotton calls himself Nottingham's chaplain in order "to sett Himself upon a Level with S^r W T," Temple had complained:

> Now, to bring this fairly about, He shews indeed a very extraordinary Contrivance; He affirms in His Epistle that all the severall Characters that

make a true "Hero are united in the Earl of Nottingham, in as eminent a Degree, as they are found asunder in the true Characters of the antient Worthyes, and are yet rendered more illustrious by another Quality, which indeed they wanted, which was their Concern. . . ."[186]

In other words, Wotton tries to put himself on Temple's level first by calling himself an earl's chaplain, and then by making the earl the greatest hero who ever lived, thus raising the chaplain's stock in the process. Here the fragment breaks off. What Temple meant to say next does not appear, but his scorn is visible enough ("indeed a very extraordinary Contrivance"). So is his preoccupation with Wotton's flattery.

At first it may seem curious that Temple should harp about a mere dedication. Dedications, after all, were traditionally full of high flattery, which no one but a patron would take seriously. Nottingham is obviously no paragon of greatness, and having the ancient worthies' virtues applied so baldly and improbably makes them sound a touch absurd in themselves. But in his own way, with his own dependents, Temple was a patron who seems to have taken both himself and the heroic virtues very seriously indeed. Apparently he had been willing to hear his secretary compare him to the Second Adam in the *Ode to the Hon*^ble *Sir William Temple,* and (apropos the heroic qualities gathered together in Nottingham) to hear the secretary say that the attributed qualities of learning, goodness, and greatness, "Which we ne'er join'd before, but in Romances meet,/ We find in you at last united grown." In Swift's 'penitential' letter of 1694, Swift had addressed Temple as if he were royalty, and far from being offended, Temple promptly obliged with the testimonial which Swift requested. It was Temple, not Wotton, who worshipped the ancients; heroes and heroic virtue had engrossed Temple's thinking as they never did Wotton's. In fact Wotton did not use either term when describing Nottingham: it is Temple who supplies the word "Hero" when quoting Wotton's flattery. In sum, the tribute which Wotton paid Nottingham was precisely the tribute which, at some level, Temple would have felt his own due—to be praised as a compendium of the greatest virtues exhibited by the greatest ancient heroes. When Temple expanded his "Hints" into an essay, it may be no coincidence that, when comparing the "Persons" by whom Ancients and Moderns may be judged, he compensated for suppressing his praise of himself by adding some lines praising Epaminondas, Julius Caesar, the two Scipios, and the rest, thus parcelling out his own virtues, as it were, among some ancient worthies. To find his own virtues commandeered for the patron of his worst critic (a Modern at that!) and to see them thus made absurd may have irked Temple more than he cared to admit. And as he copied

out Temple's scornful reactions, his secretary would have been a remarkable man not to have sensed a certain irony in the situation.

Temple's Second Secretary, and Other Matters

Temple's "Hints" raise questions in another area as well. The manuscript notes which accompany Swift's draft and which explain the
work's genesis up to 1697 are not in Swift's hand but in someone else's
—someone whose autograph does not appear in the voluminous Moor
Park household account papers preserved in the Osborn Collection, or
in the Farnham parish registers.[187] Whoever it was, the scribe was
obviously working under Temple's direction, setting forth the official
account of how Temple came to write the "Hints" and why he has just
decided (1697) to let them "take their Fortune abroad."[188] Two memoranda at the end tell the reader where Temple meant his comments on
himself to appear, and explain "that these Remarks refer to his [Wot-
ton's] first Edition." Not long afterwards Temple began expanding his
"Hints" into essay form, and Sir Harold Williams acquired some manuscript fragments from this time—two quarto leaves, in Temple's hand,
containing revisions for two of the passages scored through or otherwise marked for further work in Swift's fair copy of the "Hints." The
same hand which wrote the notes to the "Hints" has added various
corrections here—a revised sentence, a few minor insertions, a note
about a paragraph's placement, and (less certainly) the few X's and
scorings-through which appear (Appendix D). Clearly Temple used the
person to read him the passages aloud and enter the appropriate revisions—an important part of composition, in which a clever secretary
could hope to show his worth with queries and suggestions. Both here
and in the "Hints" notes, in other words, Temple employed someone
other than Swift in the work which Swift usually did, while he retained
Swift for the humbler and more tedious task of transcribing the fair
copy of the "Hints" (and presumably the fair copy of the later essay as
well). What the circumstances were, there is as yet no telling. Perhaps
Swift happened to be absent from Moor Park during the appropriate
times in 1697 or 1698, thus compelling Temple to turn to the other man.
(If so, Swift must have been absent fairly often. The same unknown
hand appears on a loose draft of a letter which Temple was readying for
publication about this time—a letter which Swift afterwards copied into
the Downton transcript.[189]) Whatever the explanation, the unidentified
secretarial hand indicates that Swift was not the only helper working
for Temple between 1696 and 1698. We have seen that Temple used

Boyer or some other Frenchman to correct his French letters while Swift was dutifully making his word-for-word translation of the superseded text. In 1697 Swift may have been "the secretary" at Moor Park, as Lady Giffard referred to him then, but it looks as if he enjoyed no monopoly on the secretarial functions there—at least, no monopoly above the level of a copyist.

By bypassing any direct mention of Temple, a few other documents may also give some hints about Swift's Moor Park experience, and with them his private responses to Temple. Among them is the amusing *jeu d'esprit* which he wrote in 1699, under the title "When I come to be old."[190] In form it comprises a list of rules to follow in old age: "Not to be peevish or morose, or suspicious," "Not to tell the same Story over & over to the same People," "Not to talk much, nor of my self," "Not to boast of my former beauty, or strength, or favor with the Ladyes, &c.," "Not to be positive and opiniatre," and so on. In practice the list adds up to a caricature of an old geezer—querulous, vain, and egotistical —and in the process betrays an occasional peevishness of its own ("Not to be fond of Children, ⌐ or let them come near me hardly⌐ "). It gathers a kind of momentum and culminates with an admonition of terse and snappish anticlimax, "Not to sett up for observing all these Rules, for fear I should observe none." In 1699, Swift had just left a situation which afforded matchless opportunities for watching the foibles of old age, and Ehrenpreis sensibly points out that Temple probably inspired a number of the reflections.[191] It is not so clear, though, that Swift wrote in utter seriousness or naively expected to follow a set of rules made pointless by the admonition "Not to sett up for observing all these Rules."[192] Instead, the piece looks like a private amusement, meant to while away the time alone or with a friend or two, in Lord Berkeley's establishment or wherever else Swift composed it.[193] Its biographical significance figures less in any condemnation of faults attributable to Temple, than in the mental associations which put thoughts of Temple in a light and mildly satirical context. Hero worship could not have inspired such a piece, but neither could a settled resentment.

Indeed, if Temple's vanity, condescension, or occasional querulousness had grated insufferably on his secretary, Swift would hardly have continued the association through most of a decade. Somewhere he undoubtedly achieved an accommodation of sorts, or at least discovered compensations for any frustration or irritation. To an ironist, after all, Temple's chronic self-esteem must have exerted a certain appeal. Even the great man's disapproval of satire, generally at odds with his involuntary taste for it, has an endearing quality. The late H. L. Mencken, who in a more boisterous way was an ironist himself, fondly described his

fellow Americans as "the most timorous, sniveling, poltroonish, igno-
minious mob of serfs and goose-steppers ever gathered under one flag
in Christendom since the end of the Middle Ages," distinguished the
nation for its "unending procession of governmental extortions and
chicaneries, of commercial brigandages and throat-slittings, of theological buffooneries, or aesthetic ribaldries, of legal swindles and harlotries,
of miscellaneous rogueries, villainies, imbecilities, grotesqueries, and
extravagances." Far from wishing to flee it, though, Mencken professed
to "awake every morning with all the eager, unflagging expectation of
a Sunday-school superintendent touring the Paris peep shows."[194] With
Swift at Moor Park, it is impossible to dismiss the suspicion of a kindred
appreciation, on a more easygoing, less moralistic, and more occasional
scale. Whatever his areas of philosophical agreement with the great
man, Swift's most characteristic function in life was to smile at solemn
human pretense, which all too often it was Temple's unhappy fate—
despite his best intentions—to embody.

While Temple lived (and with him, Swift's chances for preferment
through him) those good intentions must have counted for something
with Swift, if only to deflect some anger or exasperation. Despite his
vanity on the score, Temple usually seems to have acted honorably and
honestly in an age not much given to public virtue.[195] He lacked the
capacity for deviousness. Although Lady Giffard protested too much
about her brother's good nature, good humor, and easy familiarity with
even the "meanest servants,"[196] he undoubtedly had his moments of
charm or warmth with underlings. The books which he gave Swift may
not always have suited Swift's tastes, but they bespeak an attempt at
kindliness or graciousness. Years later, as we have seen, when Swift
lived on intimate terms with the two chief men in Queen Anne's Tory
ministry, he occasionally mentioned Temple in implied contrast with
the easy, unaffected St. John. Once, though, he mentioned him in an
implied parallel with the older, more cautious, and occasionally rheu-
matic Robert Harley, of whom he also was fond. As Lord Treasurer,
Harley controlled the flow of millions each year, and Swift takes evident
pleasure in describing him playing a penny-ante card game at home:

> Ld Treasr has hd an ugly fit of the Rheumatism, but is now near quite well,
> I was playing at one and thirty with him and his Family tother night. he
> gave us all 12 pence apiece to begin with: it put me in mind of Sr W T.[197]

As Ehrenpreis remarks, the incident reflects a certain "cosiness" in
Swift's life at Moor Park,[198] but the tone reflects a touch of humor as
well as warmth. He names Harley by his official function, Lord Treasurer, to describe his dispensing pennies, and he associates the resulting

scene, warm yet faintly ridiculous, with that well-to-do landowner and reformed gambler, Sir William Temple.

While many circumstances suggest that Swift managed some sort of accommodation with Temple, others hint at continuing areas of friction. Swift shows little lightness or warmth, for instance, in crossing out the inscriptions in his books. Almost certainly, much of the friction arose from Temple's failure to push for Swift's advancement. As early as 1690, Swift won Temple's vague recommendation to a Dublin-bound official, that Swift might merit an appointment as his clerk or attendant, or eventually a fellowship at Trinity College, Dublin. Apparently nothing came of it, and though he travelled to Ireland anyway he soon returned to England.[199] In 1694, probably in anger, he broke with Temple over the great man's failure to secure him an English living, and tried to make a career in the Church of Ireland. The adventure ended unsatisfactorily in Ulster, and Swift returned to Moor Park with "better prospect of interest," as he claimed to Jane Waring at the time.[200] Three or four months after Temple's death, he was as far to seek as ever. Meanwhile he had exhausted the limits of his own or his family's influence, which had found him his place with Temple in 1689 and which (five years later) had seemingly secured his dismal living at Kilroot.[201] His other alternatives, as Ehrenpreis charts them, were to publish arguments on theological controversies, in the hopes of making a name for himself within the Church, or to find himself a more powerful and active patron.[202] The first involved the sort of professional theological disputation which went so strongly against his bent.[203] Without guaranteeing advancement from strangers, it would also have hurt him with Temple, who scorned theological controversy as a waste of time and talent, a hindrance to the progress of learning, and potentially a menace to the peace itself.[204] The second alternative meant leaving Temple (and what Ehrenpreis terms the "dying order of Temple's circle"[205]) to secure a new patron out of nowhere—in practical terms, to take his chances on Grub Street in hopes that a dedication hit home. In the first four volumes and supplements of the *Athenian Mercury,* which he said that he studied in 1691/2, he had seen how his Grub Street brethren (one in fact an Oxford man and an unbeneficed Anglican clergyman) managed to subsist between patrons.[206] With its preface and digressions narrated by a half-mad hack starving in a garret, *A Tale of a Tub* suggests that Swift had more than once considered the opportunities which beckoned.

In brief, Swift did not have to love Temple to stay with him so long, and it is far from certain that he deserved the charges since levelled at him, of showing ineptness, naïveté, over-reliance on Temple, poor judgment in his choice of employer, and a general lack of self-confidence.[207] Swift's autobiographical fragment—with its reference to that "old illiterate Rake," Lord Romney, who was "without any sense of Truth or Honor"—betrays anger more than two decades after the Earl failed to win Swift an English living, in the weeks following Temple's death. Very likely Swift was even angrier at the time. Ehrenpreis states that "he poured over Romney's character the acid which ought to have fallen on Temple's" (thereby sacrificing "his small faith in Romney to save his deep admiration for Temple"), and suggests that the transfer of blame may signal Swift's realization that his own miscalculations had cost him his preferment.[208] It may also signal Swift's unwillingness to undermine the earlier part of his narrative, which, as we have seen, had made the most of his standing with Temple and King William. In 1727–29, the approximate time of composition, Temple's name still stood for something in England, and the publication of Lady Giffard's flattering *Life* of Temple, in 1728, should have jogged any uncertain memories.[209] Although he abandoned his own narrative before carrying it past the year 1700, Swift had treated the fragment as if he once thought to publish it —making a careful fair copy down the right-hand side of his pages, with the left-hand column free for additions and corrections.[210] The slap at Romney may betray a genuine note of anger, but the transfer of blame does not necessarily imply any deep love or admiration of Temple. If anything, it pays tribute to a certain bare competence in Swift as a writer. If it must also reflect on anyone besides Romney (whom Swift had enough reason to dislike), the best candidate is the man whose name and praises Swift had blotted from the flyleaves of his books.

Whatever Swift's reactions in the four or five months following Temple's death, the core of his Moor Park experience belongs to the decade preceding it. Here we have found surprisingly little to set it above or apart from the experience of Thomas Downton, William Blathwayt, and Thomas Swift, the other men known to have served Temple as secretary at one time or another. What evidence survives suggests that they worked faithfully and hard for Temple, that they enjoyed no unusual degree of initiative, and that they left Temple's service not much better off professionally than when they began. Downton had served Temple during his first Dutch embassy, accompanied him back to England in 1670, and continued serving him privately for at least a couple of years until he dropped out of sight for good. His colleague Blathwayt wisely remained with the foreign service and did much better. Eventually he became secretary-at-war and a commissioner of trade, but like Swift's his later career seemingly owed little to Temple in any concrete sense. In neither Temple's papers nor Blathwayt's (many in the Osborn Collection at Yale) have I found any evidence of continuing contacts, though they might always have kept up a passing acquaintance by other means.[211] For Thomas Swift, it is true, Temple provided a modest country living, but here he may have consulted his own interests as much as Thomas's, to bring a potential helper into the neighborhood at a time when his regular secretary was threatening to decamp. When Thomas completed his period of service he received nothing further. Except for one published sermon (*Noah's Dove*, 1710) and his claims to authorship in *A Tale of a Tub*, he disappears from sight almost as completely as Downton did.

With Downton, Blathwayt, and the two Swifts in mind, it is instructive to read Temple's observations on the art of managing secretaries and other "servants," in an early unpublished letter from the Temple family records (Palmerston line) from Broadlands. The year was 1666 but Temple's words carry a prescient ring. From Brussels he writes to William Godolphin, a fellow diplomat and disciple of Lord Arlington's, to thank him for the despatch of a secretary named Collerd whom Godolphin has just recruited for him in England ("I know you have chosen for me as you would for yourself . . ."). When Mr. Collerd arrives, says Temple, he "must run the Venture of being spoil'd at first with good Usage," because "that is both agreable to my Nature and to my Reason too with all the Servants I take. . . ." Psychology and sound management techniques dictate this policy. It is "ones first Business to know them well," Temple explains, "and Good Humour & being pleased opens every body unawares whereas Sullenness or Fear shuts them up, a hard Condition and hard Weather having the same Effect upon Ground and Men." Godolphin need not worry about Mr. Collerd's taking advantage of Temple, who has fathomed the great secret of managing servants:

> But yet I am not Honey to have the Flies eat me up and I know very well that both in great and little whoever will be well served must compass it by the continual Employment of those two general and natural Governors of Mankind, Hope and Fear, and he that is capable of giving most of them is so of being the best served. Yet I who in the common kind can give the least of them have made some good Servants and I think spoiled few.

In the broad sense here are many of the elements perceptible in the situation at Moor Park twenty-five and thirty years later: the dangling of hopes for preferment, the occasional moments of warmth, the occasional worrisome chills, the sense of bounds and hierarchy, of service owed and to whom, and most of all the faintly ludicrous character of Temple's self-satisfaction ("made some good Servants and I think spoiled few," as if Temple at thirty-seven were a greybeard with decades of experience). When Temple uses the word "servants," of course, he means professional retainers as well as mere domestics, the more exclusive sense of the word today. Still it is interesting that he makes no distinction in practice in the manner of managing the two classes. His central metaphor is one of governance ("those two general and natural Governors of Mankind, Hope and Fear"), which could as easily have appeared in his later essay praising enlightened absolutism in China ("the two great hinges of all Governments, Reward and Punishment"[212]).

Temple presents his servant policy as something deep, hidden, and psychologically original, like statecraft, but somehow it is not hard to imagine Mr. Collerd taking the measure of Temple fairly easily. Temple demonstrates a fresh-faced naiveté not to be found in the later master of Moor Park, still subject to enthusiasms but more practiced in expressing them. In January 1666 Temple had been a diplomat for less than a year, on a mission fated to end in failure by April. He had known the Spanish viceroy in Brussels, the Marquis of Castel-Rodrigo, for a bare two months. "I believe no publick Minister has been used with greater Confidence or Testimony of good Opinion in all Kinds than I am by his Excellency here," Temple exclaims, "and I dare promise all the Advantages to his Majestys Service which that can yield." By his Moor Park days Temple would have managed the thought better, and did. In his *Letters* and *Memoirs* volumes, all copied by Swift, his air is more modest and his detail more convincing as he retails scene after scene illustrating the remarkable trust and confidence he received from Charles II, Jan de Witt, William of Orange, and other noteworthy statesmen. The treatment seems more obsessive but not nearly so boyish. By the same token we may reasonably wonder how increasing experience and eccentricity affected Temple's self-esteem as a molder and manager of secretaries. To what degree did Swift encounter the same servant-training techniques which Temple had outlined in 1666? In what form might he have encountered them? To what extent would they help explain his two withdrawals from Moor Park to seek his fortune in Ireland, in 1690 (ostensibly for reasons of health) and again, more angrily, in 1694?

Speculation is always tempting, but with Swift and Temple it is wiser not to push matters too far. More reliable insights come from documents which neither cite Temple years before nor Swift years later, but instead show Swift carrying out his regular duties at Moor Park in the 1690s. With its evidence that the great statesman tinkered obsessively with his French phrasing (before sending it out for further rewriting), and its evidence that his secretary worked on so short a tether, the Downton transcript not only provides a glimpse of the Moor Park life which Swift found convenient not to dwell on, but also helps to place his existing testimony in a more realistic context. So does the transcript which Swift made of Temple's "Hints," that unfortunate exercise in illogic, vilification, and wounded vanity. The "Hints" and the Downton transcript are probably the most important such documents in the Rothschild Collection, but by no means exhaust it—just as the Rothschild Collection by no means exhausts the resources in England, or England those of Scotland, America, or Ireland. More such work should add to the picture. For Swift in the 1690s, research materials of all sorts (both printed and manuscript) are admittedly so scattered and fragmentary that the truth may never emerge with full certainty, or in full detail. Still, if Swift ranks as a major writer, and if his *Tale of a Tub* counts for much in his canon, the effort needs to be made. One important obstacle probably lies in the influence of theories now current: that in his middle and late twenties, Swift worshipped Temple with the faith of an adolescent, that his earliest known writings show a poetic incompetence equalled only by their good intentions, and that, by extension, further research should reveal only more of the same. By investigating Swift's work as a translator, and by evaluating much of the evidence on which these theories rest, this study means to illustrate the difficulties and contradictions which they entail. If anything, the evidence conveys a markedly different impression of Swift at Moor Park —a strong sense of his pragmatism (at times with a hint of mischievousness, at others with a hint of clear-eyed ambivalence towards Temple) and most of all, beneath his habitual praise of the great man, the sense of a complex character, still largely unknown, coping with a complex experience. A sense of privacy also comes across. In all his written comments on Temple, Swift gives remarkably little of himself away, except his ability to suit his words to his readers, his purposes, and the circumstances under which he writes. If Swift served as anyone's true disciple in the 1690s, I suspect, it was as his own. Of necessity these impressions must remain somewhat vague and tentative, subject to the evaluation and discovery of further evidence. Meanwhile there is still much to investigate in Swift's work with Temple manuscripts, in Swift's prefaces for the posthumous Temple publications, in his early correspondence, his odes and other early poetry, his part in the DuCros pamphlet controversy in 1692/3, and his use of Temple materials in *A Tale of a Tub*.

CHAPTER FOUR

Moor Park and the Traditions of Swift Biography

Traditional and Proscribed Interpretations of Swift at Moor Park, Samuel Richardson's Anecdote on the Subject, the Moor Park Household Staff

For all questions concerning Swift in the 1690s, a fresh approach has long been overdue. For more than two centuries now, biographies of Swift have bred other biographies of Swift by a process of reaction, synthesis, repetition, and general accretion.[1] Certain traditional ways of viewing Swift at Moor Park have emerged, with traditional taboos to match. Whether accepted or rejected, they can function as blinders which make an either/or proposition out of an unusually problematic period in an unusually complex man's life. It may be unjust to hold Murry or Ehrenpreis accountable for biographical clichés which, in their substance, go all the way back to Thomas Sheridan's *Life of the Rev. Dr. Jonathan Swift* (London: for C. Bathurst, W. Strahan, et al., 1784) and the younger Deane Swift's *Essay upon the Life, Writings, and Character of Dr. Jonathan Swift* (London: for Bathurst, 1755). Together Sheridan and Deane Swift established what has become the traditional approach to Swift at Moor Park, but in both cases it was an approach grounded in bias and special pleading. To defend Swift's reputation from scandal and denigration, or what they perceived as such, they exaggerated heavily in the opposite direction.

For the Moor Park period, Deane Swift was chiefly concerned with countering impressions left by Lord Orrery's *Remarks on the Life and Writings of Dr. Jonathan Swift* (1751) which, as Deane Swift saw it, had made outrageous insinuations about Swift and the Swift family. Orrery had repeated a rumor that Swift might have been Temple's bastard, and though Orrery thought the rumor groundless he had speculated that Swift himself might have acquiesced in it to dignify himself in his friends' eyes. Such comments Deane Swift finds unforgivable, both on Swift's account and the Swift family's. Elsewhere Orrery had referred to the Swifts in terms which Deane Swift found objectionably conde-scending.[2] In the first two chapters of the *Essay*, accordingly, Deane Swift paints a picture designed to counter Orrery's. The Swifts, it seems, were a worthy family with whom the Temples were glad to associate. Temple first received Swift not because he had fathered him, but because he remembered that Swift was a distant kinsman of his beloved wife's and the nephew of his dear father's bosom friend, God-win Swift. Similarly, Deane Swift explains, the pecuniary assistance which Swift received from time to time through the 1690s came not from Temple but from Swift kinsmen.

Barring some exaggeration, Deane Swift's explanations carry a respectable authority thus far. He had access to many of Swift's papers (including Swift's autobiographical fragment) as well as other family papers which he is able to reproduce for the reader. In the process, though, he nearly paints himself into a corner. If Temple had no close blood ties with Swift and furnished him no substantial aid during the Moor Park years, how does a worshipful biographer account for the two men's long association? How does one explain Swift's flattering refer-ences to Temple? Deane Swift accordingly postulates a bond of close personal friendship between the two, cemented by a great admiration for each other's transcendent abilities. The admiration of so great a man as Temple helps establish Swift's greatness, and vice versa. It is "a moral impossibility," Deane Swift asserts,

> that so great and wise a statesman thoroughly versed in all the windings and turnings of human nature, as Sir William undoubtedly was from his great experience both at home and abroad, should not immediately per-ceive, what a treasure was offered to his friendship by this amazing and exalted young genius. . . .

Swift profits in his turn. "The politicks of our young aspiring genius," notes his biographer-cousin, "were enlarged day after day by the wis-dom and conversation of this old experienced counsellor. . . ." Most of all, it is Temple's favor and friendship, "infinitely superior to any pecuniary presents," which lay an obligation upon Swift: "The greatest obligation that Swift had to Sir William Temple, and which in fact was the source of all the rest, was the honour of his being thought not unworthy to be the domestick friend and companion of so wise, so learned, and so accomplished a statesman."[3] From here it is not too far to a theory of active discipleship.

Taking over many of Deane Swift's materials (despite his professed contempt for Deane Swift's efforts[4]), Swift's godson Thomas Sheridan extended, modified, and romanticized Deane Swift's treatment of Swift at Moor Park. Sheridan sets out to champion his godfather against all comers—in his own words, to "rescue his good name from the aspersions thrown on it by foulmouthed calumny." Like Deane Swift, Sheridan is anxious to counter the effects of Orrery's widely-read biography, which (says Sheridan) has revived the torrents of Whiggish abuse heaped upon Swift in his own time. Similarly Sheridan wishes to counter the generally dyspeptic treatment given Swift in Samuel Johnson's *Lives of the Poets*. Personal animus may also have entered here. Johnson and Sheridan had been on bad terms for years ("Why, Sir, Sherry is dull, naturally dull; but it must have taken him a great deal of pains to become what we now see him. Such an excess of stupidity, Sir, is not in Nature"). It is hardly surprising, then, to discover in Sheridan what one modern observer terms an "idolatrous attitude" towards Swift which "reaches a degree that embarrasses the reader." Not only was Swift the first writer of the age, says Sheridan in the dedication, but Swift also afforded in himself "a pattern of such perfect virtue, as was rarely to be found in the annals of the ancient Republic of Rome, when virtue was the mode . . . :

> In the following history Swift has been represented as a man of the most disinterested principles, regardless of self, and constantly employed in doing good to others. In acts of charity and liberality, in proportion to his means, perhaps without an equal, in his days. A warm champion in the cause of liberty, and support of the English Constitution. A firm Patriot, in withstanding all attempts against his country, either by oppression, or corruption; and indefatigable in pointing out, and encouraging the means to render her state more flourishing. Of incorruptible integrity, inviolable truth, and steadiness in friendship. Utterly free from vice, and living in the constant discharge of all Moral and Christian duties.[5]

It is for the service of such panegyric, even more exalted than Deane Swift's, that Sheridan designs his account of Swift at Moor Park. Thanks to advantages denied Deane Swift, Sheridan produces a much more appealing account, psychologically speaking. Former actor and stage manager that he was, Sheridan knew how to inject drama where it was needed. If Swift was a perfect paragon, how did he become one in the first place? Deane Swift had been saddled with the need to dignify the whole race of Swifts and never really tackled the question. Sheridan does so with panache. His Swift is the poor boy who makes good, the rough gem in need of polishing, the Cinderella who, guided by the hand of Providence, finds her genuine Fairy Godmother. Deane Swift had credited Temple with enlarging Swift's political awareness, but Sheridan gives Temple credit for bringing out everything else as well. The Swift who leaves Dublin in 1689 has little enough to recommend him —undistinguished family, no money, no powerful backers, no learning of the sort "necessary to put a young man forward in the world." Reclusive and splenetic in temper, he has not yet acquired the skills necessary for making friends. Indeed, says Sheridan,

> at that juncture perhaps there were few living less qualified than he to do any thing for his own support.
>> The world was all before him where to choose
>> His place of rest, and Providence his guide.
> And he seems indeed to have been then under the immediate guidance of Providence; for, hopeless as the end of such a journey might at that time have appeared, it proved in fact the means of all his future greatness.

Naturally this "unseen hand of Providence," as Sheridan later calls it, guides Swift "to the means of all his future greatness, in placing him under the hospitable roof of Sir William Temple." At first, Sheridan concedes, Temple might not have recognized the genius of his raw young secretary, but he supposes that Swift must have showed Temple a draft of *A Tale of a Tub* early in the 1690s: "A work, bearing such a stamp of original genius, must, in a man of Sir William Temple's delicate taste, and nice discernment, have at once raised the author into a high place in his esteem, and made him look upon him afterwards with very different eyes." Temple accordingly entrusts Swift with great business, helps him overcome his lack of education through independent reading, and generally fits him for his great role in history. "His situation at Sir William Temple's," Sheridan hypothesizes,

> was indeed in every respect the happiest that could have been chosen, to prepare this great genius for the complicated part he was to act in the world. Swift was to figure as a Writer, as a Politician, as a Patriot. And where could a young man have found such a director and assistant in fitting him for the performance of these several parts, as Sir William Temple; who was himself one of the finest writers, one of the ablest statesmen, and the truest lover of his country, that had been produced in that, or perhaps in any other age?[6]

Here is the direct forebear of Swift the admiring disciple, as he figures in Murry and Ehrenpreis.

While it is easy to fault Sheridan as a scholar—to point out (as Phillip Sun has done) his lack of genuine research, his strategic omissions and inventions, his transparent bias, his haste in composition, and his venal motives[7]—it is foolish to discount the psychological appeal of his portrait. It is a canny performance. No matter how his biographers trick him out, Swift's remains a formidable name to conjure with. It is hard enough to make him appealing, much less to make him both appealing and impossibly virtuous at once. Paragons are notoriously difficult to warm to. Sheridan surmounts all difficulties by reducing Swift to a stereotype, by showing him weak and ignorant, despite his native talents, and then making him the beneficiary of a providential good luck which transforms him into a great man. The poor, ignorant, reclusive, and eminently vulnerable Swift who leaves Trinity College in 1688 is a figure whom any reader can feel comfortably superior to—an inspired stroke when presenting a personage whose hallmark as a satirist is the vague sense of discomfort, of being somehow mocked, which he leaves in his readers. Considering the weaknesses which Sheridan portrays in Swift, we can hardly grudge the young fellow the fortune which soon lifts him above the common fate. Deep in their hearts, after all, most readers recognize in themselves some rare talent which needs only the spark of special circumstance to flame forth into greatness. Swift was merely lucky, the recipient of the perfect guidance at the perfect time. In Sheridan his story serves to point a moral which, in comparably happy circumstances, each reader could apply to himself:

> When we reflect that Swift was first brought up in the school of Adversity, (who though she be a severe mistress, yet does she generally make the best scholars) and that he was thence removed to another Lyceum, where presided a sage, in whom were blended Socratic wisdom, Stoical virtue, and Epicurean elegance; we must allow his lot to have been most happily cast for forming a great and distinguished character in life. Nor did he fail to answer the high expectation that might be raised of a young man endowed by nature with uncommon talents, which were improved to the utmost by a singular felicity of situation, into which fortune had thrown him.[8]

Richardson's Moor Park Anecdote and Its Legacy in Swift Biography

In one way or another, Sheridan's account of Swift has left its mark on every subsequent biography, although changing tastes in the nineteenth century left Swift's reputation very different from what Sheridan had tried to establish. Far from a paragon, the author of Gulliver's *Travels* became in the public mind a bitter and nasty-minded misanthrope, haunted by fears of the madness which eventually triumphed over him. In the new stereotype of Swift, the Moor Park years figured even more centrally than they had in Sheridan's. For very different purposes, Sheridan had exaggerated Swift's ignorance and antisocial qualities before meeting Temple, and in the process had labelled young Swift "naturally splenetic" in temper. In 1804 appeared a report which allowed Sheridan's assessment to be adapted for different ends. In that year Mrs. Barbauld brought out Samuel Richardson's *Correspondence*, taken (as the title page announces) "from the Original Manuscripts, Bequeathed by Him to His Family." Early in 1752 Richardson and his friend Lady Bradshaigh had been corresponding about Orrery's *Remarks*, just recently published. What does Richardson think of the Orrery book and of Swift? In his letter of 22 April Richardson forwards a mixed gleaning of tidbits about Orrery and Swift, not always reliable, including a secondhand report about the situation at Moor Park:

> Mr. [Jack] Temple, nephew to Sir William Temple, and brother to Lord Palmerston, who lately died at Bath, declared, to a friend of mine, that Sir William hired Swift, at his first entrance into the world, to read to him, and sometimes to be his amanuensis, at the rate of 20 l. a year and his board, which was then high preferment to him; but that Sir William never favoured him with his conversation, because of his ill qualities, nor allowed him to sit down at table with him. Swift, your Ladyship will easily see by his writings, had bitterness, satire, moroseness, that must make him insufferable both to equals and inferiors, and unsafe for his superiors to countenance.

Temple was wise enough to see through Swift, Richardson concludes, and as a notably polite man would presumably not have mixed with a minor employee who probably was "always unpolite, and never could be a man of breeding."[9]

Thomas Babington Macaulay and William Makepeace Thackeray took up the incident and dramatized it in an *Edinburgh Review* essay (1838) and a popular lecture (1851), respectively. Neither was a work of serious scholarship, nor pretended to be. Both reappeared in books which reached an enormous popular readership. Together Macaulay and Thackeray painted a picture of Swift likely to appeal to Victorian tastes —an uncouth, misanthropic young Swift, relegated to the servants' table and chafing bitterly under an ignoble regimen.

In Macaulay's essay on Temple, Swift enters only briefly but with a dramatic flair reminiscent of Sheridan. Following Sheridan, Macaulay supposes Swift antisocial and ill-educated at first. Eventually he hypothesizes that, in political awareness, "the obligations which the mind of Swift owed to that of Temple were not inconsiderable." Pri-

marily, though, Macaulay draws upon the Richardson anecdote and
paints a picture of genius slighted and neglected. Macaulay had been
saying that Lady Giffard continued preeminent at Moor Park after
Lady Temple's death in 1694:

> But there were other inmates of Moor Park to whom a far higher
> interest belongs. An eccentric, uncouth, disagreeable young Irishman, who
> had narrowly escaped plucking at Dublin, attended Sir William as an
> amanuensis, for board and twenty pounds a year, dined at the second table,
> wrote bad verses in praise of his employer, and made love to a very pretty,
> dark-eyed young girl, who waited on Lady Giffard. Little did Temple
> imagine that the coarse exterior of his dependent concealed a genius
> equally suited to politics and to letters, a genius destined to shake great
> kingdoms, to stir the laughter and the rage of millions, and to leave to
> posterity memorials which can perish only with the English language.
> Little did he think that the flirtation in his servants' hall, which he perhaps
> scarcely deigned to make the subject of a jest, was the beginning of a long
> unprosperous love, which was to be as widely famed as the passion of
> Petrarch or of Abelard. Sir William's secretary was Jonathan Swift. Lady
> Giffard's waiting maid was poor Stella.

On Swift's side there was only suppressed bitterness, Macaulay claims.
Swift "retained no pleasing recollection of Moor Park," he says: "And
we may easily suppose a situation like his to have been intolerably
painful to a mind haughty, irascible, and conscious of preeminent ability."[10]

In his Swift lecture published in *English Humourists of the Eighteenth
Century*, Thackeray echoes Macaulay's treatment and adds a further
note of melodrama. Basically, he says, Swift's "youth was bitter, as that
of a great genius bound down by ignoble ties, and powerless in a mean
dependence. . . ." Once again appears Richardson's anecdote from Jack
Temple about the £20 salary and dining apart from Temple:

> It was at Sheen and at Moor Park, with a salary of twenty pounds and a
> dinner at the upper servants' table, that this great and lonely Swift passed
> a ten years' apprenticeship—wore a cassock that was only not a livery—
> bent down a knee as proud as Lucifer's to supplicate my lady's good graces,
> or run on his honour's errands.

Thackeray wonders whether it ever struck Temple that "the swarthy,
uncouth Irish secretary" was actually Temple's superior. No, he answers, Temple could never then have lived with Swift. Meanwhile
Swift "sickened, rebelled, left the service,—ate humble pie and came
back again; and so for ten years went on, gathering learning, swallowing
scorn, and submitting with a stealthy rage to his fortune." Indeed,

Thackeray hints a bit later, Swift's gnawing resentments may even presage the insanity which Thackeray finds everywhere in Swift's later works, struggling to burst forth. He has quoted a few lines from Swift's poem of 1693, *Occasioned by Sir W—— T——'s Late Illness and Recovery*, and now notes that even there, for all the "courtly condolence," Swift "breaks out of the funereal procession with a mad shriek, as it were, and rushes away crying his own grief, cursing his own fate, foreboding madness, and forsaken by fortune, and even hope."[11] This, it develops, is the story of Swift's life: frustration, impotence, suffering, accompanied by a terrible hatred of self and of all around him. Thackeray concludes Swift a sceptic in matters of religion, for instance. Swift entered the church anyway, he notes, and "having put that cassock on, it poisoned him: he was strangled in his bands. He goes through life, tearing, like a man possessed with a devil." In the *Drapier's Letters*, says Thackeray, "the assault is wonderful for its activity and terrible rage . . . one admires not the cause so much as the strength, the anger, the fury of the champion." And Book IV of Gulliver's *Travels* is of course "Yahoo language; a monster gibbering shrieks, and gnashing imprecations against mankind . . . filthy in word, filthy in thought, furious, raging, obscene."[12] Just as Sheridan's account of Swift at Moor Park prepares the reader for panegyric, so Thackeray's account lays the groundwork for the thesis of Swift the half-crazed genius, lacerated and lacerating.

Readers who somehow had missed Macaulay's essay on Temple (reissued in *Essays Critical and Historical*, 1843) or Thackeray's lecture on Swift (in the *English Humourists*, 1853) would have absorbed similar views of Swift from sources deriving from them. In chapter 19 of his *History of England*, published not long after Thackeray's *English Humourists* came out, Macaulay repeated and elaborated upon his own earlier sketch of Swift at Moor Park. Once again appears the anecdote about Swift's wages and dining arrangements, the flirtation with the "pretty waitingmaid" in the servants' hall, the generally slighting attitude which Temple adopted towards his secretary ("Sometimes, indeed, when better company was not to be had," Swift was "honoured by being invited to play at cards with his patron . . ."). With a footnote referring the reader to Swift's 'penitential' letter to Temple of 1694, Macaulay now asserts that Swift habitually addressed Temple in the language "of a lacquey, or rather of a beggar." Although he stops short of Thackeray's melodrama of half-mad stealthy rage, Macaulay moves a step closer to it. On the outside, he says, Temple's secretary must have seemed a tame fellow: "But this tameness was merely the tameness with which a tiger, caught, caged, and starved, submits to the keeper who brings him food. The humble menial was at heart the haughtiest, the most aspiring, the most vindictive, the most despotic of men."[13] Macaulay's *History of England* enjoyed phenomenal sales, of course. Between him and Thackeray it is hardly surprising that, during the late nineteenth and early twentieth centuries, most popular accounts of Swift at least partly followed their lead. Temple's modern biographer, Woodbridge, indignantly offers a short list of offenders: John Churton Collins (articles of 1882–83; reissued 1893), Sophie S. Smith (1910), Gerald P. Moriarty (1893), Sir Shane Leslie (1929), and Carl Van Doren (1930), not to mention the more responsible Sir Henry Craik (1882; rev. ed. 1894).[14]

Tastes and values have changed since Thackeray's day, but not enough to remove the threat posed by his and Macaulay's indictment. A self-consciously tolerant and humanistic age is less likely to tolerate the nay-saying satirist, who tears down without building up, than it is to tolerate such worthies as the gossip columnist or the soft-core pornographer, who for all their infirmities at least remain basically life-affirming. To win popular acceptance the satirist still needs to be furnished with a heart as big as all outdoors, a glowing humanitarian conscience, personal harmlessness, and (if possible) a reassuringly tub-thumping predictability in his work. Macaulay's Swift fails on all counts. Thackeray's fails even more dismally, if possible. Unfortunately the two Victorians and their followers reached a far wider readership than Sheridan ever had. As a result, Thackeray's name in particular has become something of a dirty word to Swift specialists. Much of modern Swift scholarship has been taken up with attempts to counter the view of Swift which he helped popularize. A certain defensiveness, even closed-mindedness, has also resulted. Thanks to nineteenth-century views of Swift, Arthur H. Scouten remarked in his 1979 Clark Lecture, Swift scholars even now sometimes resort to a "role of protective silence" when confronted with uncomfortable findings about Swift. "In the academic world as late as forty years ago," he explained, "a promising young graduate student who elected to specialize in Swift was looked down upon or treated in a condescending manner." As a result, Swift scholars "banded together to resist hostile criticism, and fiercely beat down any publications which insinuated" inconvenient or unflattering interpretations of Swift's life—that Swift might have acted in a brutal way towards some of his friends, for instance, or that he did not always tell the truth in his personal correspondence. Considering Swift's growing popularity in recent years, Scouten says that such protective action "is no longer obligatory" and suggests that "problems no longer need be hushed up." Old attitudes die hard, however. Scouten's comment is as much a plea as a statement of fact.[15]

Meantime the strategic use which Sheridan and Thackeray made of Swift's Moor Park period has left it something of a football between contending views of Swift, the proprietary and the hostile. Like Sheridan, both Murry and Ehrenpreis have thrown in their lot with the proprietary team—and then some. Sheridan had made Temple responsible for all Swift's attainments, but despite his exaggeration not even he had pretended that Swift naively idolized Temple or (as Ehrenpreis claims) set him up as a father-figure and Christian hero. Instead this new wrinkle seems traceable to Thackeray, by way of simple contradiction. Assuming a comparable humorlessness in Swift, Thackeray had pretended just the opposite—that serving Temple filled Swift with secret rage and resentment. Then too, for all his hostility and melodrama, Thackeray had granted Swift genuine stature. Swift repels Thackeray but remains "a great genius" even in youth, a "giant" who must "live apart" from ordinary men, a figure who is all too likely ("with a great respect for all persons present") to be superior in capacity to Thackeray's auditors.[16] In direct contradiction, Ehrenpreis provides an unusually ordinary Swift—a not atypical product of the times who, in his twenties, remains basically an adolescent and (to judge by his worship of Temple) is seemingly something of a booby as well. Sheridan had exaggerated Swift's lack of attainments before his Moor Park period, but not even Sheridan went to such lengths. Lack of attainments is one thing, lack of genius quite another. Basic outlines of personality and intelligence, we now recognize, generally emerge in early childhood or even in infancy, as some psychologists claim. Whether they celebrated Swift or deplored him, contemporaries usually agreed that he had a markedly original genius—that he possessed a high degree of intelligence, and that it burst forth in original, surprising, and often disconcerting ways.

Lord Orrery is a case in point. The least admiring of the half-dozen biographical writers who had known Swift personally, Orrery emphasizes Swift's various weaknesses and faults, deplores many of Swift's writings (from Anglo-Latinus word games to Gulliver's *Travels*), and generally presents an unheroic, sometimes patronizing portrait of the Dean. Orrery still pays tribute—sometimes unwitting—to the force of Swift's mind and the complexity of Swift's personality. Swift "was in the decline of life when I knew him," writes Orrery, but a few lines later he recollects that Swift's "capacity and strength of mind were undoubtedly equal to any task whatever." Although Orrery offers many confident generalizations about Swift's character, he sometimes betrays a certain awestruck incomprehension. At one point he concedes apparent contradictions as he pursues Swift "through the mazy turnings of his

character." Rather lamely he explains that, "of all mankind, Swift perhaps had the greatest contrasts in his temper." In Swift's poetry as in
the prose writings, he says somewhat later, the reader will find Swift
"an uncommon, surprizing, heteroclite genius." Many of the poems
Orrery finds trifling or uneven—the result, he claims, of a restless imagination soured by thwarted ambition.

Orrery's explanations may be facile, even patronizing, but in his
search for something to cinch his point he offers a simile which is more
revealing than he intends. Swift, it seems, is like a chained eagle, unable
to seek his natural prey: he "diverts his confinement, and appeases his
hunger, by destroying the gnats, butterflies, and other wretched insects,
that unluckily happen to buzz, or flutter within his reach."[17] In real life,
Swift may or may not have been a chained eagle snapping at gnats: what
matters is that a favored acquaintance like Orrery should have thought
him so. It is the wretched insects more than Swift for whom Orrery
betrays a feeling of empathy and understanding. Ten or eleven years
after Orrery had last visited the Dean, it looks as if the memory of Swift
was enough to stir up feelings of vulnerability.[18] His various analyses
of Swift may inspire little confidence, but by communicating incomprehension Orrery gives us one measure of the personality, otherwise
unknown, which had confronted him. Unfortunately, Orrery's unwitting testimony has been swallowed up by more hostile critics and so
rendered distasteful. Thackeray adapted much from Orrery, including
the notion of thwarted ambition, and turned it into the melodrama of
the raging and self-lacerating lone titan. Where Orrery imagines a
chained eagle tearing at gnats, Thackeray paints a Promethean giant
torn by a vulture which turns out to be one and the same with himself
("what a lonely rage and long agony—what a vulture that tore the heart
of that giant!"). Macaulay in turn imagines Swift as a "tiger, caught,
caged, and starved," but still raging and vindictive at heart. Would we
have liked to live with Swift? Thackeray asks the question and un-
hesitatingly answers in the negative. With the reaction against nineteenth-century stereotypes of Swift have come attempts to substitute an
equally unhesitating affirmative, to domesticate Swift into something
comfortable and easily understood. Evidence like Orrery's is not always
welcome.

To all appearances, the association with Macaulay and Thackeray
has also affected the welcome afforded Richardson's anecdote about
Swift's starting salary and table privileges at Moor Park. In substance
it is an anecdote impossible either to build upon or to reject out of hand.
For most of the past century and a quarter, though, it has either been
enthusiastically built upon or contemptuously rejected out of hand.

The atmosphere seems to have been calmer when the anecdote was first published, in 1804. Only ten years later—but still a generation before Macaulay first romanticized it—Sir Walter Scott took a reasonably sensible and evenhanded approach. In his memoir of Swift's life he relegated the anecdote to a footnote. After all, Richardson had heard about Swift only at second hand—not directly from Jack Temple but from a mutual friend. As Scott prints it, the thrust of the anecdote is that Temple held himself aloof from his secretary. Scott can only endorse the notion with heavy qualifications. "The outlines of this unfavourable statement are probably true," he notes, but only "if restricted to the earlier part of Swift's residence at Moor-park"—that is, before Temple became better acquainted with Swift. On the other hand, Scott cautions, there had been considerable ill-feeling between Swift and Temple's heirs: Jack Temple's hostility may well have colored the account. Similarly Scott hazards no specific opinion about the details which Jack Temple reports, either the £20 with board which Swift supposedly received as his starting salary or Temple's refusal to sit down at table with Swift.[19]

The next scholarly assessment of Richardson's anecdote came in 1876, when John Forster published his careful but incomplete *Life of Swift*. Macaulay and Thackeray had meantime embedded the anecdote into their melodramatic accounts of Moor Park. In Forster the results are all too apparent. Normally a judicious scholar, Forster shows little of Scott's cautious weighing of pros and cons. Instead he goes on the attack—and spends nearly twice as much time inveighing against Macaulay's version as the original in Richardson. Significantly, Forster brings little that is new to the argument and chiefly elaborates facts earlier available to Scott: that Richardson's account is secondhand, that one of his other miscellaneous gleanings about Swift is unreliable, that Swift had quarrelled with or snubbed various Temples (Lady Giffard, Lord Palmerston, Jack Temple himself) whose reliability is thus open to question. "There is no authority but this," Forster indignantly remarks, "for either the sum said to have been paid or the treatment alleged to have been received; and such authority should at once have condemned both averments."[20]

In 1876 there was reason for Forster to sound like a defense lawyer confronting a damaging witness. He was swimming against a strong tide of public opinion set in motion by Thackeray and Macaulay. When the tide slowly began to turn in the twentieth century, Richardson's inconvenient anecdote met even readier hostility—enough to justify A. H. Scouten's remark about the "protective silence" sometimes exercised by modern commentators. In his glowing biography of Temple (1941), Woodbridge cannot even bring himself to reproduce the anecdote accurately, much less rebut it as Forster had. An early believer in Swift's hero-worship and vast intellectual debt to Temple, Woodbridge waxes indignant about "the discreditable and really calumnious legend" (derived from Macaulay and Thackeray) that Swift chafed in bitter servitude at Moor Park. The actual evidence for such a view is either trifling or nonexistent, he maintains. In his list of such evidence he barely mentions "a story derived from second-hand hearsay, that he [Swift] had to eat at the second table."[21] No footnote is given referring the reader to Richardson. No further discussion is vouchsafed. In fact Woodbridge seems less concerned with the actual anecdote than with the "story derived" from it.

Granted, Woodbridge's account at least hints that some such anecdote existed before rejecting it out of hand. This is further than Ehrenpreis is willing to go. What attention he gives comes in his preface. In the following book, he says, he has been "less concerned to add than to eliminate fables," and the reader will search in vain for Ehrenpreis's views "on a long train of legendary Swiftiana." Thus, among other matters, "Temple does not seat Swift and Stella at the servants' table."[22] Richardson had said nothing about Stella's table privileges and in fact never actually assigned Swift himself to the servants' table—only reported that Temple never "allowed him to sit down at table with him." The 'fable' with which Ehrenpreis will not concern himself belongs instead to Macaulay, Thackeray, and their followers. So far as Ehrenpreis's reader can tell, Richardson's more factual account never even existed. Given Ehrenpreis's thesis, this may be just as well. To reject the anecdote as Richardson reported would involve recognizing its existence and marshalling evidence against it—that is, taking it seriously for a moment and in the process raising the inevitable questions of salary, house privileges, and other pragmatic arrangements which exist between employers and their household employees. Was Swift paid quarterly or semiannually? Did he get a suit of free clothing each year, as did many secretaries and retainers in other households? Did he ever try to negotiate a raise, and for how much? Such questions have no business obtruding into the drama of a fatherless young hero-worshipper, sitting at the feet of a bereaved and sonless father-figure who fears "to play Daedalus a second time, and to Swift's Icarus."[23]

Richardson's Anecdote Reconsidered: The Moor Park Household

Between eager credulity on the one hand and defensive hostility on the other, there have been few sober attempts to sort out Richardson's anecdote since Sir Walter Scott's time. Certainly it needs sorting out.

A gossipy and generally unsympathetic observer, Richardson was surely not the most rigorous researcher, but on the other hand there is no reason to think he invented or set out to falsify what he had learned. Similarly there is little reason to doubt his claim that a friend heard the report from Jack Temple. Richardson knew enough of Jack Temple's movements to be able to tell Lady Bradshaigh, in April 1752, that the man had "lately died at Bath."

By the same token, Jack Temple's credentials have their strengths as well as their admitted weaknesses. As Forster pointed out, he was a decidedly hostile witness—the nephew of Lady Giffard with whom Swift quarrelled in 1709, and the brother of Lord Palmerston, with whom Swift quarrelled sixteen years later. In 1710 Swift told Stella he had snubbed Jack Temple in the street. Where Swift was concerned, we may safely assume that Jack Temple would exaggerate and put the worst possible interpretation on matters. It is far less certain that he would make up stories out of whole cloth.

With his resources, he probably would not have found that necessary. Although Forster conveniently overlooks the fact, no other man alive in 1751 was better equipped to report upon, though not to interpret, the terms of Swift's service at Moor Park. There Jack Temple had access to records which none of Swift's early biographers had seen. He was himself a good deal more than Temple's brother's son. The favorite nephew and later the executor of Lady Giffard, the lady of the house in Swift's time at Moor Park, he was also the husband of Temple's granddaughter and co-heiress, Elizabeth Temple. By arrangement with his aunt (who preferred to divide her time between her houses in London and East Sheen) the young couple lived at Moor Park from about 1704 onwards. Jack Temple took an interest in the family papers there. Several which Swift had copied or worked with carry dockets in his autograph. His interest in Sir William's household extended to Swift himself. It is Jack Temple's endorsement which gives the name "penitential" to the "May it please Your Honour" letter which Swift sent to Temple from Dublin, late in 1694.[24] To some degree his interest was shared by his brother Henry, the first Viscount Palmerston, who had inherited Sir William's funeral and final Moor Park estate papers from their father Sir John, the chief executor of the estate. Jack had allowed Henry to make a copy of the "penitential" letter at Moor Park and presumably had access in turn to the estate papers in his brother's keeping, which included the final wage and legacy receipts for the Moor Park staff.[25]

Whatever Jack Temple found among the various Moor Park papers, all the same, he would have been imperfectly equipped to interpret. He

had not lived at Moor Park during his uncle's time, and I have found
no record of any visits. For firsthand accounts of Temple's personal
relationship with Swift he would have been largely dependent upon
Lady Giffard or upon his wife Elizabeth—the first a blindly emotional
witness whom Swift had angered, the second only a girl in her grandfather's time, when she occasionally visited Moor Park. What their memory preserved, poor judgment or lack of experience might well have
distorted.

Considering Jack Temple's varying sources and hostile motivation,
and allowing for some possible distortion in the transmission of his
report, a good deal can be discounted in what Richardson reports. That
Temple disliked Swift sounds like Lady Giffard in a mood of wishful
thinking, as does the corollary that Swift was too morose and uncouth
for a man of Temple's great discernment to countenance. That Temple
never favored Swift with his conversation or *never* sat down at table with
him is an obvious impossibility. As an overseer, if nothing else, Temple
had worked far too long and far too closely with Swift to let us imagine
that the two men never conversed out of the study. From Swift's letter
to his cousin Thomas in 1692, we have also seen that Swift composed and
submitted verse for Temple to read—a good sign that Temple neither
discouraged nor avoided his secretary. Indeed it appears that Swift
wrote most of his surviving Moor Park poetry with a Moor Park readership in mind. Swift's later allusion to Stella about playing cards with
Temple suggests that, at least occasionally, Swift might have dined with
him as well. And Temple would hardly have willed the care of his
unpublished writings to a man whom he actively disliked or distrusted.

Thus far the objections to Richardson have a solid grounding. In
what remains there is nothing intrinsically impossible, or even unlikely.
Stripped of its hostile interpretive element, Jack Temple's report
merely suggests that Swift's starting salary had been £20 plus board, that
(however much the rule might have been waived from day to day)
Swift's place at meal times was not properly with the family, and that
in other respects as well Temple acted as if he considered himself
Swift's superior. Given Temple's limitations there is nothing surprising
or discreditable in all this, and nothing to suggest strained relations. In
fact it would have been somewhat surprising if a vain old gentleman
with family of his own—wife and sister at home, with brother, granddaughters, nieces and nephews within a day's journey—had ordered
matters any differently.

Jack Temple seems to suggest that £20 a year with board were
shameful wages for a beginning secretary, but in fact they seem to have
been fair enough for the times. Although he largely subscribes to the

worshipful-disciple theory of Swift, Murry finds £20 an unexceptionable figure. He notes that Swift's contemporary, Edmund Gibson, received the same salary when appointed resident librarian at Lambeth
Palace in 1696.[26] At Hamilton Palace in Lanarkshire, a generously-paid
household in a prosperous part of the poorer sister kingdom, most of the
professional employees received not quite £17 a year, including the tutor
and the chaplain (usually a young man fresh from one of the universi-
ties).[27]

Certainly the figure assigned Swift seems in keeping with the
known wage scale at Moor Park. There seem to have been twenty-two
full-time employees there including the shepherd but excluding Stella's
younger brother Neddy Johnson and a young woman named Mary
Davis (probably a daughter or sister of a maid named Martha Davis),
both of whom figure in the mourning expenses at Temple's death but
not in the wage receipts. The surviving Moor Park estate papers for
1698–99, now in the Osborn Collection, include wage and legacy receipts
for the sixteen lower servants and partial receipts for two of the six
higher employees. The Broadlands Archive preserves a copy of Temple's deed of settlement, dated 1–2 July 1697 and hitherto untraced, which
supplements these figures. Thanks to the tabulations of J. Jean Hecht,
we can compare the Moor Park figures with the range of salaries which
Hecht records for many categories of domestic servants during the first
third of the eighteenth century, before a rising trend in servant wage
scales made itself felt.[28] (Unfortunately, following modern social distinctions, Hecht gives no figures for secretaries or chaplains and treats
them nowhere in his book.)

For the lower servants, Temple paid standard wages or a little
better. In 1698, salaries at Moor Park ranged from £4 a year for one
Hester Foster, perhaps a laundry or scullery maid, to a high of £10 for
Thomas Jones and £12 to £14 for the gardener James Plumridge (paid
jointly with his wife Mary, the dairy maid, who earned at least £6 of
their £20 total). Judging from Temple's expenditures in outfitting him,
Jones was the butler. His £10 was a standard wage for butlers (compare
Hecht's £10, £10, £6, £15). Most of the female servants, presumably maids
of various types, worked for £5 a year, a standard figure (£4–£6 in
Hecht). Temple's coachman received £8 (versus Hecht's £6–£12), the
postilion £6 (versus £5–£6), and the two footmen £5 (versus £4–£6).
Because Hecht's tables include some wages paid in the city, where the
scale tended to run higher than in the country, the Moor Park figures
may gain a little by comparison. In addition, Temple was somewhat
more generous than average with perquisites, though people of his rank
traditionally offered better terms than lesser folk did. Except for the

livery servants (at Moor Park the coachman, groom, postilion, porter, and two footmen) employers were not strictly required to provide new clothes for their households, but like many gentlemen Temple seems to have done at least a little in this way.[29]

If Temple's maids, butler, and livery servants received average or slightly above-average terms, the situation with the higher employees is more problematic. In Swift's case and several others, the 1698–99 wage receipts have been lost. Even so, circumstantial evidence suggests that salaries were noticeably less generous higher up the ladder at Moor Park, although Temple's largesse with new clothing (and presumably cast clothing from the family) continued in effect. In his settlement of 1697 Temple gave his trustees elaborate instructions for the continued upkeep of Moor Park, the "possession or jewel I most love and esteem" as he had called it in his will. For interim periods when no heir was in possession, Temple provided for a skeleton staff of five to maintain the place in the same good condition in which he should leave it at his death. Besides an allowance for board wages, necessary when the house was tenantless, the steward Ralph Mose is to receive £12 a year, the housekeeper Bridget Johnson (Stella's mother) is to receive £10, the gardener Plumridge £10, his wife the dairy maid £6, and "one Shepheard" £6. (Interestingly enough the board wages, at 3s. 6d. a week, were the same for everyone from steward to shepherd, as if there were no traditional distinction to be made between the upper and lower staff.) Although Temple sets the shepherd down for a little more than his regular salary (£5), the others' caretaker salaries are probably a little lower than what they would receive with the house occupied. The Plumridges received £20 between them in 1698, but as caretakers are set down for £16. Adding the same 25 per cent to his caretaker salary would give the steward Mose only £15 a year in Temple's time, or £18 a year if we double the differential to be as generous as possible. This was a miserable salary for a steward, even on a relatively small estate with few tenants. The smallest steward's wage which Hecht lists for the fifty years following Temple's death is almost twice as high, at £30, and the mean is closer to £50. At first glance Bridget Johnson fares better. Hecht's figures suggest a mean of £10 to £15, but her own long service and that of her late husband, a former steward, should have entitled her to more than her £10 as a caretaker housekeeper or her possible £12 during Temple's life. (A partial receipt for her 1698 wages survives, and depending on the number of quarters for which she was paid, her salary falls in the range between £7 6s. od. and £16, with the likeliest figure £10 or £12.[30])

At £10 a year as a caretaker and £12 to £14 normally, James Plumridge's salary is even more surprising. Gardeners did not quite rank with stewards or housekeepers in the social hierarchy but still occupied a more important position than they do today. Even apart from their specialist training, Hecht notes that they had to be presentable and articulate enough to usher visitors around—no doubt a common occurrence at Moor Park thanks to Temple's essay *Upon the Gardens of Epicurus* and the reputation it gained him as a great horticulturist. Building and planting "have not been the least" of Temple's follies, he boasted there, "and have cost me more than I have the confidence to own. . . ."[31] For the size of the house, the Moor Park gardens were disproportionately large, and as at Sheen Temple seems to have spent freely on them. In his deed of settlement he even gives his trustees instructions about "all the plants and trees in potts & tubs in the garden." For all his concern and prodigal ways, however, Temple spent little enough on his gardener. From Hecht's tables we might expect an average gardener to receive something like £16 or £18, but for a major situation under a celebrated horticulturist like Temple, we would expect to see something at the upper end of the scale, £25 or £30, rather than the paltry £12 to £14 which Plumridge actually received.

What then of Swift? If Temple's steward received about £15 a year, his gardener £12 to £14, and his housekeeper £10 to £12, £20 certainly seems reasonable enough for his secretary, especially during his early days at Moor Park. Indeed Richardson indicates that the £20 figure represents Swift's wages when Temple first hired him, "at his first entrance into the world." Why the qualification? If Jack Temple had invented the figure out of malice and thin air, he should have had no compunction in applying it to Swift's entire tenure with Temple, not just to the beginning. Instead it looks as if Jack Temple had really investigated the question, found that Swift's salary had risen, and in his eagerness to disparage Swift then confined himself to the lowest figure available, suitably but unobtrusively qualified. If Swift began work at £20 a year, it is possible that he left Temple's service making appreciably more. At Hamilton Palace the secretary had proved himself over many years—eventually, forty—and perhaps even more than Swift had developed special talents (in this case legal) which had made him indispensable to his employers. As the best-paid employee in the household, the Hamilton secretary earned nearly £45 a year, though apparently without full board.[32]

Of course it is also possible that by the late 1690s Swift was still making only about £20 a year. We have seen that Temple was more tightfisted with his higher-ranking employees than with the maids and livery servants. By 1698 Swift had served him on and off for a long time, but not nearly so long as Bridget Johnson, who was scarcely overpaid. Similarly Swift occupied a position of authority in the household. So did Ralph Mose, many of whose duties Swift shared. Mose's salary was minimal. Many of Swift's secretarial duties involved work close to Temple's heart, his literary projects, but Plumridge the gardener could say much the same in his way. Plumridge was not overpaid either. If none of these factors weighed much with Temple in itself, it is still possible that the combination of them could loosen Temple's purse strings. Until Swift's actual salary receipts turn up, we can hardly be sure. In the meantime, £20 seems an eminently reasonable wage for the beginning of Swift's tenure, and not impossible for the end of it.

Comparison with the Hamilton household also sheds some light on the question of Swift's table privileges. With its emphasis on class lines, nineteenth- and twentieth-century social usage implies something shameful about sitting at the second table, in the servants' hall. Late seventeenth-century usage seems to have been a little less fussy. At Hamilton Palace in 1703, the second table served not only the servants proper but also the chaplain, the Duchess's gentlewomen, and the pages —the first hired for his professional qualifications, the others most usually on the basis of blood or family connections.[33] Nor is it unrealistic to compare Hamilton Palace with Moor Park, despite the disparity in rank between Temple, a mere baronet, and the Duchess of Hamilton, whose pedigree few in Scotland could match. The Scottish nobility have always lived closer to the people than their counterparts in England, and in the Duchess Anne her employees found a fair-minded and approachable mistress. Living modestly but decently in the country, on only a moderate budget, she directed a staff of perhaps thirty-five in 1703 —not too many more than the twenty-two employed at Moor Park in 1698.[34]

On his own side, Temple liked to present Moor Park as a simple rural retreat, the abode of philosophy and greatness of mind. It is significant, though, that among the neighboring gentry he and his sister worked to cultivate a connection with Petworth, where the Duke and Duchess of Somerset maintained a magnificent establishment.[35] When Temple received the young Swiss traveller Béat-Louis de Muralt, probably in the summer of 1694, he arranged to have him invited to Petworth. Muralt was suitably impressed by the sumptuous "Retraite" of Temple's friends, where "il se trouve plus de cent Domestiques" in "un Palais plus beau que celui du Roi." As a man of sophisticated taste and judgment, Muralt could still see the superiority of the house he had just left. He found himself thinking nostalgically of Temple's simpler and more pleasingly countrified little establishment.[36]

In Muralt's case, country simplicity was in the eye of the beholder. He recalls "le petit Jardin" at Moor Park, but in a surviving drawing of Moor Park in the 1690s the gardens look something like a scaled-down version (not much more than eight or ten acres) of the Prince of Orange's gardens at Het Loo, the Dutch Versailles, begun the same year that Temple moved to Moor Park. This is not to say that Moor Park provides an exact replica. Among other things, its gardens extend less far into the distance and boast a raised terrace walkway on only one side of the main garden square (substituting walls on the other two), with less statuary overall and the canal (differently aligned) laid out closer to the house. Still there is resemblance enough to show that much of Temple's inspiration came not from some cosy rustic model but from the current Franco-Dutch style in palace landscape architecture. Appropriately enough, in the foreground the drawing shows a splendid coach and six preceded by two mounted servants bearing batons.[37] Temple's rusticity was not the rusticity of a Squire Western but instead the product of a tasteful and distinguished cosmopolitan who self-consciously turned his back—but only so far—on the world of courtly ostentation. In some respects the Duchess Anne's establishment in Lanarkshire seems the more informal of the two. At Moor Park we should not expect to find Temple's young secretary dining with the family as a matter of course, especially in the period before Swift entered the Church. So far as we can tell Temple neither disliked nor despised his secretary, any more than the secretary showed himself morose or ill-bred. Still it was with a certain amount of justice that Jack Temple remarked (or Richardson for him) that Temple "was one of the politest men of his time." If affability and an easy grace sit well with a gentleman, so does the sense of who he is and what is owing him. Temple's household arrangements probably tallied with those described in Mark Girouard's recent study, *Life in the English Country House,* though no doubt scaled down to fit the less palatial dimensions of Moor Park. Instead of taking their meals with household servants and retainers in the hall, in the old baronial fashion, gentlemen increasingly sought privacy for themselves in their living arrangements, a trend reaching its peak not long after Temple's death. At least in the grander establishments there were fewer positions of the sort formerly reserved for dependent gentlemen and gentlewomen, and increasingly their occupants exhibited a somewhat less distinguished social origin—like Swift himself (son of a legal functionary, grandson of a clergyman, nephew of three lawyers and a clergyman), hailing less from the gentry proper than from the respectable professional classes.[38]

All this, of course, does not pinpoint the precise dining arrangements at Moor Park. We know a good deal more about Hamilton Palace, where most of the employees (professional and otherwise) ate downstairs in the 'Lattermeat Hall.' Did Moor Park have a similar catchall arrangement, or did the higher employees normally take their meals elsewhere, at a second sitting in the dining room or at a separate table there or elsewhere? At larger country houses, after all, there was often a separate 'steward's table.'[39] If Jack Temple could have placed Swift among the ordinary servants at meal times he probably would have done so, instead of merely saying that his uncle would not sit down with Swift at table.

Staff Hierarchy at Moor Park

Typically for the times, the higher-ranking employees at Moor Park seem to have formed a fairly distinct category, separate from the family on the one hand and on the other from the servants and more menial employees. In surviving accounts from early 1699—chiefly to do with the costs of mourning clothes—they are almost always entered first as if by precedence (sometimes set off as a group from the ordinary servants) and invariably receive the honorific "M^r" or "M^{rs}." Among the men the group consisted of Swift, the steward Ralph Mose, and Leonard Robinson (possibly Temple's valet or personal attendant); among the women, the housekeeper Bridget Johnson, her daughter Esther (Swift's Stella, who was then Lady Giffard's principal waiting woman and as such the ranking female employee), and Rebecca Dingley (a poor relation of Temple's, likewise in attendance on Lady Giffard).[40] Most had received separate legacies under Temple's will besides the standard half-year's wages given to all employees. The wage and legacy receipts for the sixteen lower-ranking employees (drawn up by Swift) seem to have survived nearly intact, but for Swift and most of the other higher-ranking employees there is nothing to show the final settlement. Probably this is because Sir John Temple, as Temple's executor, completed the business himself some weeks after Swift had taken care of the lesser folk. The one such final receipt to survive was prepared by Sir John for Robinson's special legacy of £20. It is dated 9 Mar. 1698/99.[41] By contrast, the receipts which Swift prepared bear dates between 3 and 17 February. Temple's will and deed of settlement had referred to all his employees by the catchall term "servants," but a memo in Sir John's hand suggests a practical distinction between "the servants" on the one hand and the higher-ranking employees on the other. After listing the separate legacies due to Mose, Robinson, and Bridget Johnson—beyond their half-year's wages, that is—he enters an estimate, "To all the servants halfe a yeare wages about 40–00–0."[42] Unless Sir John had no notion at all of the wages paid at Moor Park, he would seem to be referring only to the sixteen lower-ranking employees for whom Swift was drawing up receipts. Their yearly wages came to £102, requiring legacies of £51, not too far beyond Sir John's estimate.

Distinguished from the "servants" on the one side, Swift and the other higher-ranking employees were still in no danger of being confounded with family. Among the many bills in the 1698–99 account papers, items chargeable to them almost never appear in company with those chargeable to Lady Giffard, Temple, or Sir John. In such matters as yard goods, sundries, and tailoring, for instance, different tradesmen usually handled the needs of the staff and of the family—local tradesmen in the first instance, London tradesmen in the second.[43] Although Stella and Rebecca Dingley would almost certainly have accompanied Lady Giffard when she travelled to London for Temple's funeral, her own mourning expenses appear on the account sheet drawn up by the family's London agent, Charles Hanbury, while Stella's and Dingley's appear on various local bills covering the Moor Park staff. Swift had earlier travelled up to London on family business, and in the funeral procession sat in Lady Giffard's coach. Of necessity he had purchased some mourning clothes in London, but instead of appearing on Hanbury's list (which includes mourning costs for some of Temple's London retainers) his various London charges were reimbursed back at Moor Park, where he received an additional waistcoat and breeches made by the tailor who handled everyone else on the staff. Ralph Mose and another man hired by the day had also made trips to London immediately after Temple's death and like Swift were reimbursed upon their return. Despite his appearance in a family coach at the funeral—an appropriate place for a clergyman—Swift's expenses were chargeable not to the estate as a whole, as the family's were, but to the household at Moor Park. First and last, he was a Moor Park employee.

The scale of mourning costs tells a similar story. As chief mourners the Temple family would have required much more elaborate attire, but even allowing for such differences there is something of a gap between Lady Giffard's charges of £38 15s. od. or Temple's daughter-in-law's £150 on the one hand, and the highest charges incurred among the female staff at Moor Park—a little under £6 for Stella, a little over £5 for her mother and for Rebecca Dingley. Swift's exact charges here are impossible to compute because we have no itemization for his London trip, but they probably did not run much higher than the steward's £6 10s. 4d.[44] By comparison Sir John Temple's costs were £110. Even Hanbury and his wife, though hardly family, received £20 between them for mourning. In the sums paid out, it is much more reasonable to compare Swift's group with the ordinary "servants" at Moor Park. Where Stella, her mother, and Dingley incurred charges of five shillings each for tailoring (plus an extra five shillings for Stella's "mantowoman," or dressmaker), the female servants were charged at the rate of four shillings each. On the same tailoring bill Mose is put down at thirteen shillings, Swift at eight shillings (waistcoat and breeches only), and the groom and shepherd at twelve shillings each. The drapier's bill shows only a little more disparity: yard goods for Mose come to £5 17s. 14d., for Swift (who needed less material) £3 14s. 7 1/2d., for the shepherd £4 0s. 1d. Only the honorific "M^r" does justice to the difference in status.[45] With her veneration for her brother, it is unlikely that Lady Giffard would have permitted Sir John to innovate too far in his treatment of the staff. Probably they had long been used to such relatively evenhanded distributions of perquisites. By 1698 Swift was easily the most trusted employee at Moor Park and, like some other personal secretaries of the time, exercised greater authority in the household than the steward did.[46] For all the trust and authority, though, it does not appear that he was overwhelmed with inducements to forget his place.

In the arrangements at Moor Park there is nothing particularly unusual or discreditable. As at Hamilton Palace, the surviving documents give little hint of the more finely calibrated class consciousness which we like to imagine in genteel English households. Respectable family background seems to have exacted few special privileges here. As a university graduate, a clergyman of respectable origins, and the kinsman of an old family business associate, Swift would nowadays receive very different treatment from that accorded the more yeomanly Ralph Mose. As Temple's distant cousin, Rebecca Dingley should have inhabited a higher sphere than Bridget Johnson, whose humble origins Swift was later to comment upon.[47] Yet they did not. Ehrenpreis, who briefly inspected the Moor Park accounts in the Osborn Collection, finds a special significance in the honorific "Mrs" which Stella receives in the drapier's bill ("Mrs: Hetty")—"suggesting," he says, "a very young gentlewoman."[48] Undoubtedly Stella was much petted at Moor Park, but as we have seen, the honorific "Mrs" and "Mr" were standard for all the higher-ranking retainers, of gentle blood and otherwise. The titles reflect household function rather than gentle family background or the treatment now thought proper for gentlefolk. In fact the drapier, as an outsider, seems to have been a little too free with the honorifics in his bill. Temple's underpaid gardener and two other lower-ranking employees, whose receipts Swift drew up a little later, appear there with

"Mr" and "Mrs."[49] Similarly, some rough jottings by Sir John Temple suggest that the family did not take the honorifics too seriously. They duly appear on documents drawn up by tradesmen, by Swift, and by his Moor Park co-workers, but Sir John himself largely dispenses with them. With respect to his cloth Swift remains "Mr Swift," but Mrs. Johnson becomes plain "Bridget," Mr. Mose simply "Ralfe," and Mr. Robinson "Leonard."[50]

★ ★ ★

Major questions lie behind the various trivialities of drapier's bills, salaries, forms of address, and table privileges at Moor Park. Did Temple ever realize that he had a man of Swift's abilities working for him? Did he treat the man accordingly? On both heads the Jack Temple anecdote implies that the answer was no, and here everything else we have learned about his uncle bears him out. Whatever talents Temple possessed in his prime, perception and logic had ceased to be strengths by the 1690s. Although he elsewhere argues that Temple treated Swift as one of the family, Ehrenpreis himself remarks upon Temple's "inability to judge character."[51] In his dealings with Dunton in 1694–95 and his later response to Wotton's critique, Temple demonstrated a petty vindictiveness which says even less for his intelligence. Graceful and appealing though they are, his writings of the period show superficial scholarship, fuzzy thinking, and a larger-than-life opinion of himself. Judging from Swift's various duties at Moor Park, Temple found him a generally competent, literate, and trustworthy secretary—but little more. Swift was allowed to carry an important message or two for Temple. He was allowed to work with his master's papers. Temple even had him translate his French and Latin letters. Here we have seen the nature of Swift's labors, and on Temple's side they argue scant recognition of the talents which he could command in his secretary. An unexceptional parson with a modest command of French could have managed as much, and would have required the same short leash and careful supervision. With distressing regularity the evidence keeps suggesting that Temple was too much taken up with his own greatness as a statesman, a philosopher, a gardener, a scholar, an author and literary critic, a patriot, a benefactor of humanity, and a gentleman, to recognize anything extraordinary in Swift.

Perhaps Swift came to prefer it that way. As yet we do not know. Whatever the case, the result is something of an anomaly. By rights, Swift's position at Moor Park ought to have been a good deal less ordinary and conventional than it seems to have been. What were his reactions? For a man of exceptional talents and satiric tastes, what was it like working on and off for a decade, unrecognized, in the house of a comparative mediocrity whom the world (and the mediocrity himself) counted a great man? How could a Swift serve someone like Temple so long, so fruitlessly, and yet to most appearances, so complaisantly?

For different reasons, as we have seen, both Sheridan and Deane Swift chose to find nothing especially odd in Swift's position at Moor Park. Instead, to do them justice, it was Macaulay and Thackeray who first intuited the problem and stressed its importance. For the most part we may safely disregard the solutions that they proposed, much as we discount their melodrama and their casual scholarship. Imagination and intuition are usually poor substitutes for the labors of research, but to recognize the basic oddity of Swift's position at Moor Park may require something of the kind—not just intuition, perhaps, but intuition in a man of similar talents and habits of mind.

Here Macaulay and Thackeray boasted unusually strong credentials. In intelligence and literary abilities, including a sensitivity to sham and a gift for journalism, no other commentators have brought a more Swiftian capacity to bear on Swift's early career. A talent for burlesque first brought Thackeray to public notice, and although his attitudes remained ambivalent he had satire in his blood—certainly enough (three years before his Swift lecture) to give us *Vanity Fair* and Becky Sharp, whom he allows nearly as many ironic insights as himself but then consigns to a suitably Victorian comeuppance. In some respects Macaulay stood even closer to Swift, despite his Whiggish principles. It has become commonplace to exclaim over the sheer range of Swift's reading as reflected in *A Tale of a Tub*, but for omnivorous reading habits Macaulay equalled or exceeded him. Among Macaulay's basic traits, his biographer John Clive notes a well-developed ability "to spot imposture and affectation" and an "irrepressible sense of the ludicrous," both of which come to the fore in the essay on Temple. Clive also notes a "fondness for self-dramatization and fantasy," especially in Macaulay's letters to his adored younger sisters, Hannah and Margaret.[52] Here Macaulay recognized a parallel between himself and Swift, and in an odd turn of self-dramatization even gave himself the nickname "Poor Presto"—Swift's nickname for himself in the *Journal to Stella*, as transcribed by Deane Swift. Early in his career, at least, Macaulay seems to have found parallels in other areas as well. At the height of his first fame in the House of Commons, during the Reform Bill debates of 1832, he sent Hannah some nonsense verse adapted from an exuberant couplet which Swift had sent Stella during the first weeks of his own rise to power in 1710. Swift pretended to cite "an old saying, and a true one, Be you lords, or be you earls, you must write to naughty girls." Macaulay brings the saying up to date—"Be you Foxes, be you Pitts/ You must write to silly chits"—and for good measure then gives a reprise, "Be you Tories, be you Whigs,/ You must write to sad young gigs."[53] At least in 1832, Macaulay felt sufficiently attuned to Swift to imagine himself in Swift's place. A similar process seems to have been at work six years later, when he first described Swift at Moor Park.

At the same time it would be foolish to identify Swift too closely with Macaulay or Thackeray, as if either could infallibly answer for what Swift might have thought or felt. In their different ways both were more conventional personalities than Swift, and as Eminent Victorians they inhabited a society which had put considerable distance between itself and Temple's. Having recognized the problem of Swift at Moor Park, they offered solutions which probably say more about themselves than about Swift. Certainly in the evidence we have examined it is difficult to recognize a neglected young genius swelling with secret rage or resentment. On only two occasions can we point to signs of anger, and both coincide with crises in Swift's career. In 1694 Swift had angrily broken with Temple and gone to Ireland to seek a place in the Church. In the 'penitential' letter which he then had to write to Temple, we may accordingly recognize signs of sarcasm or suppressed anger. Similarly, in the months following Swift's disappointment at Court in 1699, we may again recognize signs of anger or frustration which perhaps account for Swift's obliterating the various inscriptions in his books—the eulogy of Temple in the Bible and the ownership inscriptions in books received from Temple. For the rest of Swift's time with Temple—as far as we can gauge them—his attitudes seem to have been a good deal more equable and complex. The hints of mischievousness which are noticeable here and there certainly suggest no gnashing of teeth, no helpless rage. Having sensed the anomalies of Swift's position at Moor Park, Macaulay and Thackeray could only imagine a relatively conventional response to it—and a humorless one at that.

In the reaction against Thackeray's and Macaulay's views of Swift, more recent commentators have rejected the Victorians' one worthwhile insight while retaining the shaky assumptions which had led them astray. Macaulay and Thackeray sensed a fundamental imbalance between the master and secretary at Moor Park, but Woodbridge, Murry, and Ehrenpreis have variously sidestepped the issue by exaggerating Temple's stature, underrating Swift's, or hypothesizing paternal affection on Temple's side balancing filial veneration on Swift's. The new stereotype of Swift is certainly more appealing than the old but leaves Swift just as humorless and conventional as before. The earnest young hero-worshipper ultimately follows in the same tradition as the embittered young genius. Given the situation prepared for him, the one is as easily imagined and as predictable as the other—as much a projection of his creator (or of ourselves) as a reflection of Sir William Temple's actual secretary. For a more realistic assessment it is necessary to travel beyond the self-perpetuating traditions of Swift biography, both hostile and proprietary, and settle for something a good deal less comforting than simple certainties. After all we are not Swifts ourselves to put ourselves in his place. Instead the wisest course is to keep an open mind, investigate the evidence as closely as possible, and fragmentary though it is, see if some sort of pattern does not emerge, some faint outline of a personality different from our own. If we cannot readily account for it, project ourselves into it, or comfortably condescend to it, we may well have glimpsed the same personality which so impressed and mystified the Dean of Saint Patrick's contemporaries in later years.

CHAPTER FIVE

The Temple Element in the Satires:
A Tale of a Tub *and* The Battle of the Books *in a Moor Park Context*

To anyone studying Swift at Moor Park, the problems of *A Tale of a Tub* loom especially large. How does the *Tale* reflect Swift's attitude towards Temple, that champion of the ancients against the Moderns? By the same token, how does it reflect Swift's circumstances during the most active period of the book's composition? When the *Tale* eventually reached print in 1704, two or three years after the Ancient-Modern controversy had finally petered out, it addressed the general reading public. Is it safe to assume, as most critics seem to do, that Swift wrote with the same conditions in mind six or seven years earlier at Moor Park? Again, what are we to make of the curious tensions and anomalies present in the *Tale* and its companion piece, the *Battle of the Books?* The myth of Swift's admiring discipleship has made all these questions awkward, even impolitic to dwell much upon. Practically everyone who reads the *Tale* or the *Battle* will notice the inconvenient way in which Swift's satire of the Moderns can spill over onto the defenders of the ancients, but for all the attention traditionally given to the intellectual background of the Ancient-Modern controversy, there have been relatively few attempts to acknowledge the problem of these ambivalent passages and trace their connections with Temple. Even here, in most cases, the need for conforming to traditional views of Swift has led not to a careful inductive analysis but instead to brief conjectural forays in armchair psychology or to theorizings about the *furor satyricus* which supposedly possesses a satirist's mind during the heat of composition. In the end such treatments may beg the question.

Certainly signs of Temple's influence are everywhere in the *Tale of a Tub*. In his essay *Of Poetry* Temple had called for "a clear Account of Enthusiasm and Fascination from their natural Causes," which "would very much deserve from Mankind in general, as well as from the Commonwealth of Learning."[1] Portions of the *Tale* surely answer the prescription, especially the Digression on Madness. On the unambiguous side of Swift's satire, critics have long tied Temple to the *Tale*'s dispraise of Moderns and implicit praise of Ancients. Quoting Swift's later statement about the convenience of having "some eminent person in our eye, from whence we copy our description" of human virtues and vices, Ehrenpreis observes that "For the virtues implicitly recommended by *A Tale of a Tub*, the eminent person is of course most often Sir William Temple," and for the vices, Temple's chief antagonists William Wotton and Dr. Richard Bentley, along with some lesser foes. Ehrenpreis and Gerald J. Pierre have found an impressive number of echoes, parallels, and thematic analogues, and Ehrenpreis once observes (about Swift's attack on Wotton in the Digression on Critics) that "Swift may be said to have borrowed his [Temple's] emotion" as well.[2] Like some other contemporaries of Swift, Wotton himself identified enough echoes of Temple's phrasing to imagine that the great man had written the *Tale*. In more general terms, the modern critic John Traugott has observed that Swift appropriated "not only Sir William's manner but the ideas and attitudes in which the retired courtier specialized in his declining years." In the *Tale*'s relation to the "gentlemanly notions" of Temple, Traugott suggests that we may trace "the evolution of Swift's peculiar irony of foolery which pervades the work."[3] The idea deserves investigation.

Meanwhile the Temple element in the *Tale* raises an even more elementary issue, largely ignored in recent years. Did Swift write portions of the *Tale* for Temple to read, as he apparently did with the ode to Temple and some of his other Moor Park verse? The internal and external evidence has long pointed to Swift's final stay at Moor Park, especially the year 1697, as a notably active period of composition.[4] Even so, Ehrenpreis never faces the question directly, and neither do Traugott or the *Tale*'s modern editors, A. C. Guthkelch and D. Nichol Smith.[5] But if Temple generally disapproved of satire (as Ehrenpreis points out) he never lost a sneaking appreciation for it, especially when it attacked the objects of his own scorn. If anything, his tolerance seems to have grown with the years. In the period 1696–98, as we have seen, he was actively working on his occasionally sarcastic essay against Wotton, *Some Thoughts upon Reviewing the Essay of Antient and Modern Learning.* Ten years after Swift died, the younger Deane Swift raised the possibility that Temple had not only seen the *Tale*'s Digressions but had also helped to correct them. "It was at Moore-Park," he asserts, "that Swift corrected the *Tale of a Tub,* and writ his famous *Digressions,* every section of which, one after another, he submitted to the judgment and correction of his learned friend." In itself the idea of Temple actually correcting the Digressions sounds farfetched, and because Deane Swift provides neither source nor corroboration for his assertion, it is usually classed among apocrypha.[6] In the *Tale*'s "Bookseller to the Reader" section, composed about 1704, the bookseller mentions a lost copy. The author supposedly "lent it to a Person, since dead"—possibly an allusion to Temple, and if so an indication that Temple had seen the *Tale.* On the other hand, the reference may be pure invention, part of the deliberate mystifications with which Swift surrounded the book's publication.[7]

The Digression on Madness and Temple's Formula for Tranquillity of Mind

So far, at least, there has been little enough on one side or the other to allow safe assumptions about Temple's access to the *Tale* in the late 1690s and its likely effects upon composition. The conditions and purposes which inspired Swift's work in the period 1696–98 are not necessarily the same as those which applied when Swift at last published the piece in 1704, a good five years after Temple's death. New evidence must now be weighed in the balance. While arguing other conclusions from different premises, David P. French's article on "Swift, Temple, and 'A Digression on Madness' " unwittingly provides further reason to suspect that, as Swift first conceived them in the late 1690s, the *Tale*'s Digressions may have begun as a kind of prose *Ode to Temple*—a tribute originally framed for Temple's eyes, containing some of Temple's phrasing and arguments, yet pursued at times with enough pretended ineptitude and enthusiasm to collapse them.

Especially in the essay *Upon the Gardens of Epicurus,* Temple had argued for a mild if muddled Epicureanism. At the outset he labels human reason the "greatest Default of Human Nature" which "subjects it to more Troubles, Miseries, or at least Disquiets of Life, than any of its Fellow-Creatures." Ultimately he seeks peace of mind in the innocent pleasures of gardening, equally far from the passionate scramblings of public life and the numbing asceticisms of the extremist philosophers who would have a man use reason to suppress its own effects, a principle which "pretends to make us wise no other way, than by rendring us insensible."[8] Arguing that the Digression on Madness reflects much in

Temple's thinking, French traces Temple's influence through the Digression and identifies some parallels with Temple's works. He draws up short at the Digression's dramatic high point. Here, in perhaps the best known passage he ever wrote, Swift gravely raises the question of happiness, gives the preference to surface over substance, exalts the senses over reason, and concludes that

> He that can with Epicurus content his Ideas with the *Films* and *Images* that fly off upon his Senses from the *Superficies* of Things; Such a Man truly wise, creams off Nature, leaving the Sower and the Dregs, for Philosophy and Reason to lap up. This is the sublime and refined Point of Felicity, called, *the Possession of being well deceived;* The Serene Peaceful State of being a Fool among Knaves.

French readily concedes that the passage "seems to contradict everything in my essay: it calls Epicureanism shallow, it limits its disciple to the flashy surfaces of life only, and it calls him a fool." To avoid the difficulty he concludes that Swift "means here literally to praise the man who can restrict himself to the films and images of things," and that Swift's manner of speaking (at worst "sardonically, not cynically") indicates an inner emotional conflict ("though he may intellectually accept Temple's views, he must reject them emotionally").[9] With Ehrenpreis he assumes that Swift was Temple's admiring disciple, which would account for Swift's active championing of Temple in the *Tale*'s first companion piece, *The Battle of the Books,* and explain Swift's many echoes of Temple in the *Tale* itself. Accordingly, French reasons, Swift's talk of Epicurus and "The Serene Peaceful State of being a Fool among Knaves" cannot possibly refer to Temple's Epicurean scepticism. "In addition to the fact that the clearest candidate for such a 'Fool' was Temple himself," he explains, "the very phrase 'Fool among Knaves' possibly echoes the latter's *Of Popular Discontents,* which speaks of the power of demagogic 'knaves upon fools' in a faction-ridden state." (French forgets that faction-ridden states are the kind from which Epicurus and others most strongly urge retirement, as the prerequisite for achieving a properly philosophical wisdom and tranquillity. "But where Factions were once entred and rooted in a State," says Temple in the gardening essay, "they thought it madness for good men to meddle with Publick Affairs. . . ."[10])

As for the phrase "a Fool among Knaves," French might also have recalled Temple's response to the search for the Philosopher's Stone: "a Practise of Knaves upon Fools, as well as sometimes, of Fools upon themselves," words which Swift himself had copied out for Temple about 1697, in the early draft fragments of *Some Thoughts Upon Reviewing the Essay of Antient and Modern Learning.* In these draft "Hints," Temple had associated the phrase with William Wotton, the Modern he most resented. Elsewhere in the "Hints," as we have seen, Temple sputtered angrily about this "superficiall Sciolist," who "knows no more of Men or Manners than He has learnt in His Study. . . ." On the subject of alchemy and the Philosopher's Stone—pursuits he roundly despised—Temple asserts that Wotton confuses alchemy with chemistry and is a crack-brained alchemist himself. Alchemy is "that Part of Chymistry which is conversant about the Transmutation of Metals, and applyed to the Search of the Philosopher's Stone," he charges, "which our Reflecter [Wotton] seems chiefly to mean by Chymistry. . . ." Indeed, Temple sneers, wise men could never determine

> whether Alchimy was any Thing more than a wild Vision or Imagination of some shattered Heads, or else, a Practise of Knaves upon Fools, as well as sometimes, of Fools upon themselves: For, however Borrichius, or any others, may attribute the vast Expences of the Pyramids and Treasures of Solomon, to the Philosophers Stone, I am apt to believe, none ever yet had it except it were Midas, and His Possession seems a little discredited by his Asses Ears; And I wish the Pursuit of many others may not fall under the same Prejudice: Much indeed may be expected from Mr Wotton, who I find is very deep gone in this Science, as He calls it. . . .

Swift's phrase about fools among knaves does not merely echo Temple. It echoes Temple at his most openly contemptuous, berating the man he most despised.[11]

Given French's assumptions, an echo of Temple's contempt in a passage implicitly contemptuous of Temple's own position must indeed seem unaccountable without recourse to armchair psychologizing. It is hardly without parallel, though. We have seen a similar pattern asserting itself again and again in Swift's self-destructing *Ode to the Honble Sir William Temple*, with its intermittent echoes of Temple. In his stanzas about the scorn of pedantry, for instance, Swift had based his argument on a muddled passage in Temple, and while following Temple's lead managed to throw its weaknesses into relief. In a more careful but pointed way, the same process holds true with Swift's formula for happiness in the Digression. His immediate inspiration, I believe, came from an early section in Temple's gardening essay, *Upon the Gardens of Epicurus.* Before proceeding to his chief business—the innocent joys of gardening at Sheen, in retirement from public affairs—Temple attempts a philosophical justification for the quiet life, from the teachings and examples of the ancients. In one passage, Temple tries to define Epicureanism and Stoicism, and relate them to his formula for happiness.[12] He muddles the job badly, although his meandering periods help dull or divert a casual reader's attention from the problem. In retrospect, a charitable critic may guess that Temple fails to make a crucial distinction between the better Stoics and Epicureans, whom he generally agrees with, and the extreme Stoics, whose teachings he rejects out of hand.[13] Instead he inadvertently equates them, and in rejecting them together he effectively argues against part of his own position. In the process, Temple projects a much stronger impression of fuzzymindedness and self-indulgence than he could have intended. His passage also reflects most of the same basic elements present in Swift's satiric definition of happiness.

Passing from theories of natural philosophy, which vary wildly, Temple begins the section by asserting that the ancients largely agreed in their moral philosophy. Here he finds little difference between "the most reasonable of the Stoicks" and "the best of the Epicureans." Both parties, he asserts, agreed in the "Ultimate End of man, which was his Happiness." Both agreed in valuing the pleasure of virtue attained by using reason to moderate the desires, fears, and other passions originally raised by reason itself. Here Temple sounds positive, even admiring. Among other things, he says, they agreed "To place true Riches in wanting little, rather than in possessing much; and true pleasure in Temperance, rather than in satisfying the Senses," and they agreed "not to disturb our minds with sad Reflections upon what is past, nor with anxious Cares or raving Hopes about what is to come"—virtues by which Temple sets great store, later in the essay.[14] It is this use of reason to "cure its own Wounds," he continues, which "pretends to make us wise no other way, than by rendring us insensible." Suddenly the tone has turned scornful. What Temple has just defined as common ground between the better Stoics and Epicureans suddenly becomes the property of the extreme Stoics as well: "This at least was the Profession of many rigid Stoicks, who would have had a wise Man, not only without any sort of Passion, but without any Sense of pain, as well as pleasure, and to injoy Himself in the midst of Diseases and Torments, as well as of Health and Ease. . . ."[15] To Temple, this is "against common Nature and common Sense." What he condemns in the extreme Stoics is what he has apparently praised in the better Stoics and Epicureans—the principle of rational control. By rejecting the one group he rejects the other, and with it the praiseworthy rational virtues which he has just held up for approval. Against such unnatural nonsense he approvingly contrasts "the Epicureans," as if they differed from the "best" Epicureans who subscribed to the principle of rational control. "The Epicureans," he announces, "were more intelligible in their Notion, and fortunate in their Expression, when they placed a man's Happiness in the Tranquility of Mind, and Indolence of Body; for while we are composed of both, I doubt both must have a share in the good or ill we feel." In the end it is this antirational ideal of "true Quiet and Content of mind" which Temple accepts as "the best account that can be given of the Happiness of man, since no man can pretend to be happy without it." Along the way, Temple observes that other philosophers call his Epicurean tranquillity of mind by other names (including the "Apathy, or Dispassion" which Temple has just condemned in the extreme Stoic and Stoic-Epicurean position), and he notes that it may proceed from almost any cause—including, to a usurer, the retention of one's estate. "As Men of several Languages, say the same things in very different words," observes Temple,

> so in several Ages, Countries, Constitutions of Laws and Religion, the same thing seems to be meant by very different expressions; what is called by the Stoicks Apathy, or Dispassion; by the Scepticks Indisturbance; by the Molinists Quietism; by common men, Peace of Conscience; seems all to mean but great Tranquility of Mind, though it be made to proceed from so diverse Causes, as Human Wisdom, Innocence of Life, or Resignation to the Will of God. An old Usurer had the same Notion, when He said, No man could have Peace of Conscience, that run out of his Estate; not comprehending what else was meant by that Phrase, besides true Quiet and Content of mind; which however expressed, is, I suppose, meant by all, to be the best account that can be given of the Happiness of man. . . .

Whatever Temple meant to say, and I suspect that he meant to make a strong distinction between real and imputed causes of tranquillity,[16] he projects the idea that his Epicurean tranquillity is an end which justifies the means, that the ideals of competing philosophical and religious systems amount to mere mental tranquillity in disguise, and that even mistaken, inexperienced, or self-deceived people may achieve it. The Christian who seeks inner peace through "Resignation to the Will of God" is seeking nothing more than an Epicurean ideal. "Peace of Conscience" becomes no more than a phrase for mental tranquillity, stripped of moral and religious implications about the duty of suppressing base and selfish desires. Such "Peace of Conscience" is the goal of mere "common men," and it is the prize of the man who keeps from running out of his estate—at least in the eyes of the usurer who cites him. "Human Wisdom" seems to rate no higher than "Innocence of Life"—a somewhat ambivalent phrase which denotes harmlessness of life but also suggests inexperience or ignorance. Among mortals only Adam and Eve ever lived in innocence, and it ended when they gained knowledge. The Christian's reward for "Resignation to the Will of God" and the Stoic's "Apathy, or Dispassion" rate no higher, in the end, than the fruits of careful estate-management. Temple's line of argument leaves happiness defined purely as a state of mind, achieved whatever way it may. In rejecting the use of reason to "cure its own wounds"—to control passions and to achieve a pleasure based on virtue—Temple unwittingly rejects the need for moral or rational standards in happiness, whether internally or externally applied. By implication, then, a man may achieve true happiness by indulging himself, deluding himself, or stultifying himself. So long as he feels at peace with himself, he has achieved the highest good.

Here, in most of its essentials, is Swift's approach in the Digression on Madness. In his definition of happiness the ideas run especially close. Like Temple, Swift professes to find the greatest good in happiness, and like Temple he associates it with the Epicurean school ("He that can *with Epicurus* content his Ideas . . ."). Just as Temple associates painful or disagreeable qualities with using reason to restrain the passions ("rendring us insensible," expecting a man "to injoy Himself in the midst of Diseases and Torments"), so Swift would leave "the Sower and the Dregs, for Philosophy and Reason to lap up"—just a few lines after he illustrates the disappointments of rational inquiry in inspecting a flayed woman and a dissected beau. On the positive side, both locate happiness entirely in the mind, and both define it in terms of its peacefulness: "Tranquility of Mind" or "true Quiet and Content of Mind" for Temple, and for Swift a "Serene Peaceful State" of being deceived. In Temple's argument, happiness can be attained by almost anyone, including the innocent in life and the man who preserves his estate from usurers. Since Temple unwittingly rejects the need for reason and morality, true happiness arrives with whatever happens to make the mind tranquil. Swift accepts the principle, draws its logical inference, carries the argument a step further, and reconciles the apparent self-contradictions in Temple. Because reason shows a man faults in himself and others, pure happiness *only* comes through self-deception and folly. Through them he achieves "the sublime and refined Point of Felicity, called, *the Possession of being well deceived;* The Serene Peaceful State of being a Fool among Knaves." What is more, such serenity is the path of true wisdom. For Temple, the principle of rational self-control not only violates "common Nature and common Sense," but also "might have told us in fewer words, or with less circumstance, that a man to be wise, should not be a man. . . ." By implication, then, wisdom must lie in the opposite direction, which Temple recommends. In Swift, it is the fool who goes blithely with Epicurus who is "truly wise" and skims off the cream of Nature. In a word, Temple's argument claims wisdom in happiness achieved through Epicurean tranquillity—the peace of a mind answerable only to itself—and opposes such tranquillity to the dismal life of rational and moral control. Swift maintains the same basic philosophy, only in clear and heightened terms which advance the argument one step further and which carry it into the realm of satire. In doing so he repeats each basic element in Temple's argument.

At first glance, it may seem harsh in Swift to base his satire on so faulty a passage in Temple. Unfortunately, the great man's muddle about Epicurean tranquillity was all too typical. He was always ready to condemn the "Sufficiency" of man, especially the Modern, who seeks truth no further than within himself. Pride and ignorance supply "what he wants in Knowledge," and he makes his own individual reason "the certain measure of truth," though his opinions may "change every Week or every Day."[17] At the same time, Temple often claimed that happiness (and even true wisdom) came from the same source—the mind operating within itself, seemingly without much external guidance or restraint. Although "a Man may grow Learned by other Mens Thoughts," Temple remarks elsewhere, "yet He will grow Wise or Happy only by his own. . . ."[18] Other men's thoughts may even prove a hindrance, as Temple remarks in the essay *Upon Ancient and Modern Learning* (in which he later reproves men for "Sufficiency"). Recovering the ancients' knowledge may make men losers rather than gainers, he says: they "may lessen the Force and Growth of their own Genius, by constraining and forming it upon that of others; may have less Knowledge of their own, for contenting themselves with that of those before them."[19]

Temple comes even closer to Swift's satire in an unfinished essay which Swift eventually published as "Heads, Designed for an Essay upon the Different Conditions of Life and Fortune." In several places Temple waxes eloquent about the necessity of wisdom and self-knowledge, but along the way he can contrast fools who attain happiness with wise men who fall short. At first all seems in order. "The Good of Wisdom, [is] as it most conduces to Happiness," he notes at one point, and then, "A Man's Wisdom, his best Friend; Folly, his worst Enemy." Ten pages later he can again say that "The End of all Wisdom, [is] Happiness," and that "Pride and Sufficiency, in Opinion of ones self, and Scorn, in that of others; [are] the great Bane of Knowledge and Life." Between the two sets of observations, Temple discusses the vanity of riches and other "Conditions of Fortune" for which men strive. Without the right "Temper" of mind and body, he notes, such gifts will only bring misery, not happiness. "A Man's Happiness, all in his own

Opinion of himself and other Things," Temple continues: "A Fool happier in thinking well of himself, than a wise Man, in others thinking well of him."[20] Temple only means a mild digression to illustrate his point about the uselessness of riches without the right "Temper," but his love of antithesis and aphorism betrays him into contradicting himself. Wisdom may be a man's best friend and guide to happiness, but for the moment it appears that the fool does better after all "in thinking well of himself," because a man's happiness lies "all in his own Opinion of himself." Temple brings in no allusion to Epicurus nor discussion of reason and tranquillity, but he stumbles into much the same position that he did in the gardening essay. So long as a man can think well of himself—even in folly—he has reached true happiness. More clearly than in the gardening essay, here is the final element in Swift's definition: the outright fool and his *"Possession of being well deceived."*

To judge from the parallels, then, Swift caps his Digression (elsewhere so often indebted to Temple's influence) with a travesty of Temple's ideas about happiness, or at least a travesty of the ideas which struggle across in the *Heads* for an essay on life and fortune and in the essay *Upon the Gardens of Epicurus.* He concludes with a sneer ("a Fool among Knaves") of precisely the sort which Temple used against people he scorned, Wotton and the dupes of demagogues and alchemists. In Swift's version Temple himself becomes the fool among knaves—not only as the follower of Epicurus ("He that can with Epicurus . . ."), but also as the partly unconscious propounder of Swift's theory of happiness. Worse, he is accused out of his own mouth—all too appropriately accused, as it turns out. If Swift speaks of the man, "truly wise," who achieves happiness by living as a fool among knaves, so had Temple in speaking of himself.

Temple could never have imagined himself a 'fool among knaves' in good earnest, but as Denis Donoghue has briefly noted, Temple managed to call himself one in the gardening essay all the same. In a digression set among his gardening hints, late in the essay, Temple turns to his own retirement from public life. Indeed, he has never sought any of the "great Employments that have fallen to my share" in public life, he confesses, but instead often tried to escape from them "into the ease and freedom of a private Scene. . . ." Where indeed may true tranquillity be found? Quoting and translating Horace's famous lines on the *secretum iter* of retirement, Temple modestly congratulates himself for the solution he has found in his own life:

> But above all, the Learned read and ask
> By what means you may gently pass your Age,

> *What lessens Care, what makes thee thine own Friend,*
> *What truly calms the Mind, Honour or Wealth,*
> *Or else a private path of stealing Life.*

These are Questions that a man ought at least to ask himself, whether he asks others or no, and to chuse his course of Life rather by his own Humour and Temper, than by common Accidents, or Advice of Friends, *at least if the Spanish Proverb be true, That a Fool knows more in his own House, than a Wise Man in another's.*

The measure of chusing well, is, Whether a Man likes what he has chosen, which I thank God has befallen me; *and though among the follies of my Life, Building and Planting have not been the least,* and have cost me more than I have the confidence to own; *yet they have been fully recompenced by the sweetness and satisfaction of this Retreat. . . .*[21]

It is to himself in retirement that Temple applies the Spanish proverb, "That a Fool knows more in his own House, than a Wise Man in another's," and though expressed with fetching ruefulness, Temple's expensive "follies" of retirement have more than repaid him in happiness.

Here indeed is the wise and happy fool, but where are the knaves? Early in the same essay Temple had cited the wise philosophers who "thought it madness" to serve a state in which faction was rife. When the essay appeared in 1690, after some fifty years of English factionalism and disorder, Temple's readers should have had little difficulty in recognizing the kind of public life from which Temple had retired, less than a decade earlier. In his essay *Of Popular Discontents,* Temple was soon to discuss such situations. When storms of faction arise, and "All regard of Merit is lost in Persons imploy'd," Temple explains, "the Wise and the Good are either disgraced, or laid aside, or retire of themselves, and leave the Scene free to such as are most eager or most active to get upon the Stage. . . ." And who are these applicants? "The Needy, the Ambitious, the Half-witted, the Proud, the Covetous, are ever restless to get into publick Employments," notes Temple, "and many others, that are uneasy or ill entertained at home."[22] Retired from such a scene of knavery, Temple is indeed a man, truly wise, who finds happiness in country "follies," just as his earlier digressions on philosophy and the *summum bonum* of tranquillity demonstrate how a "Fool" may know more in his own house than a wise man in another's.

Of course Temple does not mean us to think him a fool in any literal sense of the word. Speaking of his own retirement, Temple could hardly call himself anything more flattering, or seem to take himself any more seriously than he does here, without risking the imputation of vanity. An offhand manner, a touch of self-disparagement, and an air of inadvertence are essential to the kind of praise for which Temple angles. Having philosophized earlier in the essay about the elusive mental tranquillity in which all philosophers (he claims) find the *summum bonum* —a tranquillity practically unobtainable for a creature so naturally restless and irrational as man—Temple modestly confesses his own tranquil happiness in retirement, the "follies" of which have been so amply "recompenced by the sweetness and satisfaction of this Retreat" that he has spent five full years there without once going up to London, where he has a house ready to receive him at all times. And having likewise celebrated the virtue and wisdom of the great Epicurus and other philosophers who retired to their gardens, as well as the virtue and wisdom of Epicurus' great followers—Maecenas, Lucretius, Vergil, Horace, great Caesar himself—he now inadvertently places himself in the same wise and glorious tradition. He sounds apologetic about his wish to elude the "many great Employments" once thrust upon him, and with rueful good humor he compares himself in retirement to the fool in the Spanish proverb. In the context of the essay, it is not folly but an excess of virtuous wisdom to which Temple confesses. Indeed there is no other motive, conscious or unconscious, which can account so well for the digressive structure of the gardening essay—its early philosophical ruminations about reason, human nature, and philosophy (Temple is a philosopher himself!); its generous praise for Epicurus and other ancient philosophers who preferred gardens to public life, and of great writers and statesmen who followed Epicurus' teachings; its disquisition on the earliest gardens and their great makers (God, Semiramis and the Assyrian kings, Solomon, Lucullus); its long humble section of Temple's own gardening hints; and, preceding a few final pointers on fruit-growing (offered in the public interest), its brief and innocent digression on Temple himself. Unless the reader has forgotten the early parts of the essay as completely as Temple seems to, the 'fool' at Moor Park should seem nothing less than the heir of the wise and virtuous ancients, the rediscoverer and possessor of the *summum bonum*, the man who has transcended common human nature.[23] Under the circumstances, it seems the keenest injustice for Swift to call such a self-confessed fool among knaves "a Fool among Knaves," in the fool's own contemptuous phrase, and speak of his serene happiness in *"the Possession of being well deceived."*

To a lover of irony or mischief, there might be strong attractions in such shenanigans. At first it appears improbable, if not impossible, that Swift would actually have dared to show Temple the Digression, as he probably had done with the *Ode to Temple* not many years before. Whatever his love of irony and mischief, Swift knew his own interest.

It is hard to imagine that he would ever have risked insulting his employer. But would Temple have caught Swift's allusions and realized that Swift's definition of happiness mocks his own? The answer must be a qualified no, even after giving Temple all possible credit for reading carefully. Briefly put, Swift's discussion of happiness contains no clear verbal echoes of Temple's discussions on the subject, no borrowings of the sort which readily jog the memory. Admittedly, Swift equates the "Man truly wise" with a fool—in substance recalling Temple on the "follies" of his wise retirement, in phrasing half echoing his antithesis between fool and wise man ("A Fool happier in his own opinion of himself, than a wise Man, in others thinking well of him"). Still, Swift completes his equation with the phrase "a Fool among Knaves," which more closely echoes Temple in a different context, sneering at the dupes of people he despised. Ready enough to despise others, even to despise his own ideas in others, Temple was hardly the man to include himself consciously in his scorn. He would never have made the connection between Swift's fool and himself. Elsewhere in Swift's passage, Temple's arguments are present, but not the phrases he used to express them. Swift's Epicurean phrasing belongs instead to another context, a philosophy which Temple specifically rejected only a page before he began his own Epicurean definition of happiness.

More important, Swift mocks a philosophical position which Temple could not consciously have condoned. In the *Heads* for an essay on life and fortune, Temple had repeatedly claimed that wisdom helped a man towards happiness and that folly only hurt him. In the gardening essay, he chiefly illustrates the wisdom and happiness of a life passed in retirement from public affairs, especially in gardening. As Temple describes it, such a life includes most of the quiet virtues and rational pleasures prescribed by the better Stoics and Epicureans whose position he had inadvertently rejected. He makes himself a case in point: happy in his own retirement, he modestly offers himself as a wise man, knowing that his readers will discount his pretense of folly. No man can resent or even recognize mockery when it levels itself at a proposition which he never thought he had made in the first place, or when it laughs at a failing which he could never acknowledge in himself. Indeed, Swift goes out of his way to make the point in the *Tale*. No man makes bold to apply satire against himself, Swift notes in the Preface. A satirist may suit his attack to his audience, but the satire is "but a *Ball* bandied to and fro, and every Man carries a *Racket* about Him to strike it from himself among the rest of the Company."[24] (Though clever and unusual in itself, the metaphor seems unfortunate, perhaps intentionally so. Until Temple's mid-forties—about a dozen years before Swift joined his household—tennis had been Temple's "favorite form of exercise," in Woodbridge's phrase, and he only seems to have given it up when gout forced him to.[25]) In the Digression on Madness, Swift's observation on satire would probably have held true. Temple should have had difficulty associating Swift's Epicurean definition of happiness with his own, although he might have felt instinctively at ease with it at first, before the ironies multiply too far and yield Swift's final words of contempt.[26] The passage also occurs towards the end of the Digression, which is perhaps the densest, most brilliant flight of irony which Swift ever composed. Even on the second or third perusal, a reader will find himself continually off balance, a step or two behind Swift's satiric intentions. Under the circumstances, then, it is hard to imagine Temple recognizing his own confused formulation or undergoing any reaction stronger than a vague sense of discomfort as Swift's ironies grow sharper at the end.

In point of fact, Temple might even have felt obliged to agree with the passage. It satirizes a self-indulgent view of happiness, an internal pleasure based on simple self-satisfaction, no matter what the external realities may suggest. Even so, Swift never openly states the idea he chiefly mocks, that the source of happiness is purely internal and that the happy fool depends (in Temple's phrase) "all in his own Opinion of himself." Instead Swift satirizes something very different, something which Temple himself specifically rejected. Ostensibly Swift mocks Epicurus' theory of sense impression, in which pleasures arise not from the mind's own powers but from impressions received from the outside —the thin surfaces of objects which register on the sense organs. The happy man, Swift claims, is the follower of Epicurus' natural philosophy. "He that can with Epicurus content his Ideas with the *Films* and *Images* that fly off upon his Senses from the *Superficies* of Things" is truly wise. He "creams off Nature," achieves happiness ("This is the sublime and refined Point of Felicity . . ."), and is "well deceived," whether by the films and images or by the knaves who surround him ("a Fool among Knaves"). Swift's use of "films," surfaces, images, and the action of 'creaming off' (physically removing a surface) stems directly from Epicurus' atomist theory of perception. A standard summary of the pertinent details in Epicurus' Letter to Herodotus (46–52; in Diogenes Laertius, x) and in Lucretius (*De Rerum Natura*, iv) suggests the extent of Swift's indebtedness. Epicurus taught that

> sense perception, the mechanics of which are explained in the physics, is reliable, in the sense that the mental image formed by means of sensation always corresponds to the physical object which caused the sensation. *This*

physical object is always an eidōlon *(idol)—an extremely fine "film" of atoms given off from the surface of compounds in the physical world.*

In normal sense-perception, a stream of similar *eidōla* proceeding from the surface of an object without intermission activate the soul-atoms of the perceiver in the sense-organs, and the soul-atoms by their motions somehow picture the characteristics of the external object.[27]

Temple may have championed Epicurean moral philosophy, as he understood it, but he specifically rejected Epicurean natural philosophy. Shortly before discussing the nature of happiness in his gardening essay, he had digressed to attack all systematic natural philosophy, concerning "the Faculties of the Mind, and the Judgment of the Senses," as well as the nature of matter and the universe. Like "the pursuit of a Stag by a little Spaniel," he notes, it "may serve to amuse and to weary us, but will never be hunted down." Accordingly he doubts that any such philosophic system is susceptible of proof. Some, "like Juglers Tricks," may appear more plausible than others because of their authors' superior "Wit and Eloquence," but Temple sceptically suspects that, even "if we were capable of knowing Truth and Nature, these fine Schemes would prove like Rover Shots, some nearer and some further off, but all at great distance from the mark. . . ."

Temple specifically includes Epicurus in the partial list of philosophers who advanced such "Schemes of Nature." He alludes to Epicurus' atomist theories in his list of dubious speculations—specifically in the propositions that the world, if not eternal, has been produced "by the fortuitous Concourse of Atoms," and that the human soul is "Corporeal" rather than eternal.[28] In his essay *Of Health and Long Life,* Temple shows even more contempt for "Philosophers" and their theories of happiness based on external sense impressions. There is "no Mistake so gross, or Opinion so impertinent," he says, "as to think, Pleasures arise from what is without us"—that is, "from the Impression given us of Objects." Accordingly Temple's view corresponds closely with Swift's ostensible attack on the followers of Epicurus who content their ideas with the films and images which fly off from objects.

Unfortunately, Temple seems to be building unconsciously on an Epicurean foundation all the while. He indignantly rejects the paramount importance of physical sense impressions, but he unwittingly confirms it by exalting the importance of the organs which receive them —and all to fit a theory of human pleasure which ultimately arises from within a man rather than from the world outside him:

Let Philosophers reason and differ about the Chief Good or Happiness of Man: Let them find it where they can, and place it where they please: But there is no Mistake so gross, or Opinion so impertinent (how common soever) as to think, Pleasures arise from what is without us, rather than from what is within; from the Impression given us of Objects, rather than from the Disposition of the Organs that receive them: The various Effects of the same Objects upon different Persons, or upon the same Persons at different times, make the contrary most evident. . . . From all which, 'tis easy, without being a great Naturalist, to conclude, that our Perceptions are formed, and our Imaginations raised upon them, in a very great measure, by the Dispositions of the Organs, thro' which the several Objects make their Impressions. . . .[29]

Temple concludes that "Pleasures depend upon the Temper of the Body," and after apologizing for digressing into natural philosophy, he proceeds to the essay's more mundane concerns of health and long life. As in the essay *Upon the Gardens of Epicurus,* with its own philosophical digression about happiness, Temple has half betrayed a belief that happiness consists in mere self-sufficiency, that pleasures arise from "what is within" a man rather than "what is without," at least in permitting the proper reception of sense impressions. This time he omits reason entirely from the formula, although he makes room for it elsewhere in the essay.[30] To maintain a neat antithesis and to emphasize his point about happiness and health, he considers only the organs of sense and the impressions which they receive.

To all outward appearances, then, Swift's satire of Epicurean natural philosophy follows Temple's own lead. Its ironic implications for moral philosophy have little in common with the ideals which Temple consciously understood and supported in Epicurus' moral philosophy. Because Temple knew Epicurean atomism and rejected it with mild contempt—as one of the "Schemes of Nature" likened to "Juglers Tricks" in their persuasiveness and to "Rover Shots" in their chances of validity—Temple could not have reasonably objected to an attack on a theory of happiness directly derived from it. Because he specifically rejected sense impressions as the chief cause of pleasures (a "gross" and "impertinent" mistake, he said) he could not have objected to an attack on this theory in turn.

All the same, if he ever read the Digression, he could not have felt too comfortable at times—much like the reader first encountering Temple's sudden if unwitting *volte-face* in the gardening essay.[31] Epicurus may be wrong about films and images, but Swift pours too much scorn on his followers. Worse yet, the contemptuous phrase "a Fool among Knaves" seems to come out of Temple's own mouth. Temple rejected Epicurus' natural philosophy, or thought he did, but he still admired Epicurus personally and counted himself a follower in the moral sphere.

In the paragraph directly following his garbled definition of tranquillity, in the gardening essay, Temple says that he has

> often wondred, how such sharp and violent Invectives came to be made so generally against Epicurus, by the Ages that followed Him, whose Admirable Wit, Felicity of Expression, Excellence of Nature, Sweetness of Conversation, Temperance of Life, and Constancy of Death, made Him so beloved by His Friends, admired by his Scholars, and honoured by the Athenians.

Temple thinks these "sharp and violent Invectives" are the result of malign envy in the Stoics, the "Mistakes of some gross Pretenders to His Sect (who took pleasure only to be sensual)," and "the Piety of the Primitive Christians, who esteemed his Principles of Natural Philosophy, more opposite to those of our Religion" than those of the competing philosophic schools.[32] At least on the surface, the Epicurean disciple whom Swift mocks is just such a 'gross pretender to the sect', for anchoring his happiness on sense impression ("who took pleasure only to be sensual," in Temple's phrase). As Temple saw the situation, he himself had never been guilty of arguing for such sensuality (though in effect he had) and Epicurus' *moral* philosophy could present no objections (though he himself objected to the Epicurean moral philosophy which he blunderingly defined). Swift's satiric definition of happiness, in effect, takes advantage of Temple's self-contradictions on both counts, and seems to encourage Temple's scorn against the beliefs which he had betrayed in himself. Where Temple effectively argued for folly and self-sufficiency, on the moral side, Swift ironically praises the same qualities, in tacit agreement with Temple's more conscious call for wisdom and reasonable temperance. Where Temple condemned the Epicureans' theories of sense impression and sensual pleasure, in natural philosophy, so too does Swift—only to attack Temple's half-conscious belief in the same pleasures of sense impression, once received. In effect, Swift's passage holds up a kind of satiric mirror for Temple, and makes sure that he would discover in it every face but his own. In another sense, it is also a trap, though not the kind which its prey could have recognized as such. For at least forty years critics have sensed some sort of trap in the passage, but have failed to reach a consensus in interpreting it. In a recent essay Neil Schaeffer cites the conflicting views of F. R. Leavis (in 1934) and Robert C. Elliott (in 1951), before propounding a different theory of his own.[33] Examining the passage in its Moor Park context not only helps to reconcile these difficulties but also accounts for the allusions, ideas, phrasing, and twists of logic in what both Schaeffer and Elliott call the emotional and intellectual center of the *Tale*. At least in its construction, the passage is indeed a trap, but much less neatly for the world in general than for the unusually self-contradictory but all-too-human philosophizer at Moor Park.

Other Echoes of Temple in the Digression on Madness

Swift's definition of happiness would seem remarkable enough if it stood alone in the Digression, but from Temple's point of view it is far from being the only odd passage there. A few pages earlier Epicurus figures again, in much the same way. Swift attacks "the great Introducers of new Schemes in Philosophy"—people who "advance new Systems with such an eager Zeal, in things agreed on all hands impossible to be known." Swift specifically includes Epicurus and his follower Lucretius. So far, at least, he does no more than repeat and exaggerate Temple's strictures on systematizers in natural philosophy, who theorize about matters impossible to know. In the process, however, he treats poor Epicurus with a distinct lack of respect. Temple believed that Epicurus would be "but too well defended by the Excellence of so many of His Sect in all Ages," but Swift, apparently carried away by Temple's ideas on systematizers, argues that Epicurus himself would seem a madman if alive today:

> Of this kind [systematic philosophers] were Epicurus, Diogenes, Apollonius, Lucretius, Paracelsus, Des Cartes, and others; who, if they were now in the World, tied fast, and separate from their Followers, would in this our undistinguishing Age, incur manifest Danger of *Phlebotomy*, and *Whips*, and *Chains*, and *dark Chambers*, and *Straw*. [34]

These are hard words for a philosopher whose virtues Temple felt so keenly—even harder when they follow a reference to the philosophers' "present undoubted Successors in the *Academy* of *Modern Bedlam* (whose Merits and Principles I shall farther examine in due Place)." Had Swift reversed the order of his statements—citing first the madmen Epicurus and Lucretius, and *then* their Modern successors—Temple might have supposed himself included in Bedlam because he counted himself a follower of Epicurus. Under the circumstances, though, the only result should have been a growing feeling of discomfort. When Swift mentions the Bedlamites, he has not yet associated them with Epicurus and Lucretius. The Academy belongs to the Moderns—it is the "*Academy* of *Modern Bedlam*"—and its inmates accept what Temple rejects, the worth of systematic natural philosophy. Temple, of course, counted himself firmly on the Ancient side, and would never have imagined himself among the Moderns. He nourished a healthy contempt for them, and indeed for most developments in the modern world. If it is disagreeable to find Epicurus threatened with dark chambers and straw, along with the other systematizers, it still follows Temple's distinction between Epicurus' natural and moral philosophies.

For that matter, how indeed would the modern world have treated a good man like Epicurus? In his essays on ancient and modern learning, Temple had bitterly complained about the insolent treatment which the ancients now receive.[35] Indeed, he blamed Paracelsus and Descartes (whom Swift lumps with Epicurus) for setting up systems in competition with the ancients'.[36] Swift's speaker makes the point that only "this our undistinguishing Age" would have treated such great men so shabbily. Here again is something for Temple to agree with. In doing so, however, he would only have placed himself in a dilemma. The speaker approves of the systematizers, whom Temple has rejected, and he likewise approves of their Modern successors in Bedlam. To agree with the speaker about "this our undistinguishing Age"—as Temple undoubtedly would have, under any other circumstances—would make Temple a half-conscious sympathizer with systematic philosophy and with the Academy of Modern Bedlam. After reasserting the asininity of systematic philosophers—what man, asks Swift, "did ever conceive it in his Power, to reduce the Notions of all Mankind, exactly to the same Length, and Breadth, and Height of his own?"[37]—Swift continues with another fling at Epicurus and any reader who felt as Temple did about him. Swift seems to satirize Epicurus' physics (at least he makes fun of its jargon) but the laughter masks mockery of Epicurus' personal vanity:

> Epicurus modestly hoped, that one Time or other, a certain Fortuitous Concourse of all Mens Opinions, after perpetual Justlings, the Sharp with the Smooth, the Light and the Heavy, the Round and the Square, would be certain *Clinamina*, unite in the Notion of *Atoms* and *Void*, as these did in the Originals of all Things.[38]

To a reader who looked askance at atoms and void, as Temple did, the passage would be amusing. If he also thought Epicurus a modest and virtuous man, his laughter might have felt a little uncomfortable as well.[39]

Summing up the rhetorical methods which Swift used in the Digression, David French makes an observation which may possibly apply here. With considerable justice, he argues that all Swift's methods "have the same goal of shocking the reader into attention through re-examination of his own assumptions."[40] French assumes that Swift genuinely admired Temple and that the anomalies in the Digression stem from opposing forces in Swift's personality. By "the reader" he means the reader outside Moor Park, but his words may also apply to an intended Moor Park reader—and an author who was less the admiring disciple than he seemed.

A second look at the Digression reveals much else which reads as if once intended for Temple, though less perhaps to shock him than to leave him feeling vaguely uncomfortable. One of Swift's unsettling rhetorical methods, says French, is his energy in "showing traditional ideas in a new light." He cites the surprising analogies and images used to "force us to review the pompous solemnities of history." Swift's treatment of the great Sun King, Louis XIV, seems a case in point. Swift calls him "a mighty King," of whom he has read "in a very antient Author," and then proceeds to describe him as a small antic bully, a manic child who "amused himself" (as only a little boy can) "to take and lose Towns; beat Armies, and be beaten; drive Princes out of their Dominions; fright Children from their Bread and Butter; burn, lay waste, plunder, dragoon, massacre Subject and Stranger, Friend and Foe, Male and Female."[41] In an unexpected way, the description reflects a good deal of truth. Seen purely in terms of their concrete effects, Louis's expansionist policies lose much of their lustre and coherence. This is not the usual vantage point, and even today the Sun King remains a figure of some *éclat*. To an ordinary English reader around the turn of the eighteenth century, he would have figured more highly yet. Louis was powerful, menacing, brilliant, unpredictable, and frequently at war with England. Besides money and soldiers, he controlled the English Pretender, and with him a claim to the kingdom itself. To present his thirty years of military aggression as the play of a hyperactive child could only have surprised and amused an English reader. It debunks the myth, removes the threat, and presents the overgrown child underneath—all with a measure of truth. If Swift's description of Louis XIV would appeal to an average English reader, it should have appealed even more to Temple, at least in theory. Unlike the average Englishman, Temple had spent the greater part of his active career trying to plumb the depths of Louis's mind and to counter his foreign policy. In both aims Temple largely failed. More than most of his contemporaries, Temple had reason to fear and detest the French king, and while he would write of him with quiet sarcasm at times,[42] he loomed especially large in Temple's mind. As a frustrated peacemaker, Temple should also have welcomed an attack on Louis's militarism. On both counts Swift seems to cater to Temple—but only in a way which would have left him curiously unrefreshed. In his analysis of French foreign policy, Temple had stated that a France under Louis's rule posed graver threats, in the way of conquest, "than have been seen in Christendom since that of Charlemaign." Louis himself is "a Prince of great aspiring thoughts, unwearied application to whatever is in pursuit, severe in the institution and preservation of Order and Discipline."[43] Despite his job as peacemaker, Temple also admired the ethos of war. The essay *Of Heroick Virtue* repeatedly celebrates the hero-king who makes history while leading his people to civilization and conquest. Temple may have disapproved of Louis, but by associating him with Charlemagne he almost seems to concede him a hero, unintentionally. By implication, of course, the French king's dark eminence also gives stature to those who, like Temple, set their wits against him.

But if that king "of great aspiring thoughts," no matter how malign, is actually a kind of antic child, where does it leave the hard-working opponents and analysts who think him a genius? " 'Tis recorded," Swift continues in his description, "that the Philosophers of each Country were in grave Dispute, upon Causes Natural, Moral, and Political, to find out where they should assign an original Solution of this *Phaenomenon.*" Louis is an antic bully, but the solemn folk who analyze him cannot seem to recognize the obvious. Temple could not have felt too comfortable with the observation, if he read it, but he would never have consciously applied it to himself. Although he often generalized about politics and the nature of man, he maintained an outspoken scepticism about systems of natural and political philosophy, the "Causes Natural" and "Political" which the grave "Philosophers" dispute. For that matter, the narrator seems to join such philosophers himself, by presenting his own theory, and in the process draws the laughter on his own head. The cause of the king's antics, it appears, is a "*Vapour* or *Spirit,* which animated the Hero's Brain." This the speaker traces (with much solemn jargon) in its circulation from brain to anus, where gathering into a tumor it "left the rest of the World for that Time in Peace." Besides distrusting such theories, Temple thought the condition called "Vapours" an amusing modern delusion—at least he thought he did.[44] He could readily have joined in the laugh, even though it scarcely restores much dignity to the French king or those who solemnly analyze him. It also prepares for Swift's conclusion about Louis. Again the imagery comes from the theory of vapors: "Of such mighty Consequence it is, where those Exhalations fix; and of so little, from whence they proceed. The same Spirits which in the superior Progress would conquer a Kingdom, descending upon the *Anus,* conclude in a *Fistula.*" All this is good fun, of course, and for Temple it would also have carried the ring of truth. In effect, Swift raises one of Temple's favorite points about history. As Ehrenpreis has observed, Temple often theorized that great events stemmed from small or secret causes. At various times, he had noted the "poor small Springs" from which "the Torrents of Factions first arise," remarked "upon how small accidents the greatest Councels and Revolutions turn," and observed that a "perfect Accident" (trivial in itself) had accounted for a general's taking the field, which "will serve for a Moral to shew how small Shadows and Accidents sometimes give a Rise to great Actions among Mankind. . . ."[45]

In effect, Swift has turned Temple's argument against him. While appearing perfectly loyal to Temple's theory of history, he has associated it with a theory of vapors which Temple found foolish, and employed it to trivialize a man on whose darkly heroic stature Temple's professional self-esteem had rested. Swift's ludicrous details assure amusement, just as the echo of Temple would assure some assent, but in laughing or agreeing Temple would be unconsciously laughing or agreeing against himself. For an ordinary reader, the paragraph about Louis may inspire some second thoughts about "the pompous solemnities of history," as French puts it. For Temple as a reader, the satire may not inspire conscious reconsideration, but as the best satire will do, it touches uncomfortably on matters much more basic to the ego than any philosophy of history. The ultimate target seems to be the reader himself, his own pompous solemnities and self-contradictions. As in the passages on Epicurus and Epicurean happiness, Temple's attitudes appear to dictate Swift's particular choice of subject and imagery, the unpredictable turnings in his argument, and his shifts of satiric focus. The passage is tailor-made for a reader who, like Temple, opposed Louis XIV yet thought him brilliant and potentially heroic, who could sound scornful about Louis yet based his own self-esteem on him, who praised the virtues of peace yet thought a hero's conquests glorious, who condemned systematic philosophy yet liked to generalize philosophically, who considered "Vapours" foolish yet half believed in them, and who rejected political science while theorizing that great events flow from petty causes.

Of course, Temple was more a man of his time than he liked to think, and most of his contemporaries probably shared a number of the same views, inconsistencies and all. For a public readership, the passage works well enough, if less probingly or disturbingly. Even so, few Englishmen besides Temple held *all* the attitudes on which the passage capitalizes, much less attached the same degree of importance to each of them in turn. By the same token, few English readers felt obliged to favor the world with their views, inconsistent or otherwise, by publishing whole volumes of genteel generalizing essays—most often speculative in their approach, wide-ranging in their show of learning, digressive in their structure, and public-spirited in their proclaimed intentions. As Temple modestly noted in the essay *Of Health and Long Life*, "I have never written any thing for the Publick without the Intention of some Publick Good."[46]

The passage about Louis and the two about Epicurus suggest an unusual strategy in the Digression on Madness, but firm and unequivocal conclusions (if attainable at all) must await further research. Unless new evidence materializes, for instance, it seems impossible to determine conclusively whether or not Temple actually saw portions of the *Tale* at Moor Park, much less to ascertain the *Tale*'s text as it stood in 1698, six years before Swift published the book with some additions and, perhaps, revisions. Then too, it is always possible that the three telltale passages represent mere coincidence—that Swift was merely a master of unconscious writing, and that he borrowed Temple's ideas, details, and even phrasing without any thought of serving them back to him.

Innocence and unconscious writing are the usual explanations for the anomalies which critics occasionally recognize in the *Tale*. Explaining such explanations usually requires a measure of psychological theorizing at least as tenuous as Ehrenpreis's talk of father-figures and discipleship. For David French, as we have seen, the subversive tendencies in the 'Fool among Knaves' passage demonstrate a conflict in Swift's personality, between conscious acceptance of Temple's views and unconscious emotional discomfort with them. Kathleen Williams notes "the curious tensions of parts of *A Tale of a Tub*," and like French effectively attributes them to a momentary loss of full artistic control caused by Swift's inner conflicts. These occasions in the *Tale*, she says, show Swift's "inner tensions," when "conscious allegiance is at odds with personal tendencies." Recognizing Temple's presence in the *Tale* even more fully than French does, John Traugott postulates a kind of demonic possession—with Swift setting out to fight Temple's battles in acceptably genteel fashion, only to fall prey to a kind of *furor satyricus* when the various feigned voices in which he speaks begin to take control over him. "As he adopts the extravagances of his enemies," Traugott theorizes, "his invention takes fire and he becomes his enemy, working out his own sceptical ideas in the enemy's guise." So it happens that parody, "the satiric device encouraged in Swift by the snobberies of the Temple circle, led him to a sympathy (perhaps largely unconscious, though not entirely so) with the enemy he mocked. . . ." Most of all, the *Tale* becomes a study in anxiety and abnormal psychology. Self-hatred turns to hatred, and from thence to an irony of "tragic overtone."

Harking back to Thackeray, Traugott asserts that Swift's is a "diabolist personality" and that in the *Tale* Swift conjures up his cast of voices with "demonic joy." At Moor Park, Traugott supposes, Swift both smarted under Temple's cold looks and identified with him. Because of an unsettled and presumably insecure childhood, Swift must have been "a kind of psychological 'bastard,' " a repressive type who would refuse to acknowledge any master or cause but still would "naturally" identify with his patron Temple, accept Temple's wrong-headed notions without thinking, "adopt his top-lofty attitude, and displace his hatred upon the vulgar." In the emotional crucible of the *Tale*, the vulgar reclaim their own as Swift reveals the thought processes by which he "found his own genius after a false start as Temple's minion in the school of gentlemanly irony."[47]

Given the broadly synthesizing qualities which we prize in literary criticism, it would be unfair to subject Traugott's assertions to the kind of scholarly scrutiny reserved for full-dress biography. The critic's accepted function, after all, is to get at the truth without the encumbrance of too much documentation or demonstration. As a critic Traugott makes a strong case because he makes an appealing case. His Swift borrows something from the romantic appeal of Thackeray's Swift, the tormented genius, and caters to the popular assumption that great literature must come from strong emotion (the poet's eye in its fine frenzy rolling). Traugott's argument likewise appeals to the complementary belief, popular among armchair Freudians, that creativity itself is an expression of inner conflict and psychic dysfunction. In Swift's case, the result is to preserve some of Swift's stature, in stereotyped form, while reducing the threat that he poses to his readers. Who can blame Swift for the *Tale*'s discomforts when he is not fully conscious of what he is doing and when, by his own lights, the *Tale* must be counted a failure? If Swift leaves us with a burden of anxiety in the *Tale*, at least it is a burden "that is his own." If we "can almost imagine" that Swift's 'Fool among Knaves' is Temple himself, what else can we expect of a scarred psyche seeking semiconsciously to liberate itself from the influence of an unconsciously-resented rôle-model? True, Traugott concedes, there is a "characteristic entrapment of the reader in Swift's irony," but it is only a natural by-product of Swift's "obsession" to follow the ideas that he satirizes to extreme and nihilistic conclusions. In such a scenario, artistic function and control must take a back seat to guesswork about the author's assumed psychic conflicts.[48]

Appealing though they may be, Traugott's theories have little power to account for the oddities we have so far seen in the Digression on Madness. In Swift's satiric definition of happiness, in his treatment of Louis XIV and of Epicurus, he capitalizes far too cleverly upon Temple's various prejudices, weaknesses, and inconsistencies to permit us to imagine that he remained largely unconscious of what he was doing. Possibly we could try to dismiss the passages as anomalous phenomena, isolated coincidences which prove nothing when set against the rest of Swift's prose.

If so, there seems to be a good deal of such coincidence and unconscious writing going on elsewhere in the Digression as well. Considered in a Moor Park context, the bulk of it reads suspiciously. Even on the intellectual plane, Swift's crack-brained narrator demonstrates a certain kinship with Temple, though not the sort which Temple would have recognized or relished. The narrator's praise of surface over substance, for instance, begins with an echo from Bacon, but as the passage unfolds it sounds more like Temple's attack on Modern critics in *Some Thoughts Upon Reviewing the Essay of Antient and Modern Learning*. Both Temple and Swift's narrator deplore people who value themselves for exposing others' faults—in the manuscript version Temple cited the detestable Wotton, who had exposed his own arguments—and both resort to metaphors of cutting and opening. For both, the reality of the faults weighs less than other considerations, and ultimately both seem to confuse the discovery of faults with their creation, as if identifying flaws meant widening or creating them. Where Swift's mad narrator objects to men who "reckon among their high Points of Wisdom, the Art of exposing weak Sides, and publishing Infirmities," Temple damns trivial-minded critics who "can at best pretend, but to value themselves, by discovering the Defaults of other Men." Their object, says Temple, is "to find some Occasion of censuring and defaming such Writers as are, or have been most esteemed in the World: Raking into slight Wounds where they find any, or scratching till they make some, where there were none before." Swift's narrator carries the metaphor a good deal further, into anatomy. Disapprovingly he describes the arrival of Reason "with Tools for cutting, and opening, and mangling, and piercing" the exteriors of bodies, "offering to demonstrate, that they are not of the same consistency quite thro'." Using the standard of social utility habitually invoked by Temple, the narrator concludes with a thought implicit in Temple's argument, that a man should seek beauties instead of raking into wounds—or, in the narrator's words,

> That whatever Philosopher or Projector can find out an Art to sodder and patch up the Flaws and Imperfections of Nature, will deserve much better of Mankind, and teach us a more useful Science, than that so much in present Esteem, of widening and exposing them (like him who held *Anatomy* to be the ultimate end of *Physick*).

As for social utility (invoked in Swift's phrase about those "who will deserve much better of Mankind"), Temple had said that his much-admired heroic virtue was "in short, The deserving well of Mankind," and had denigrated Harvey's anatomical discoveries because even if true they "have made no change" in the practice of medicine, "and so have been of little use to the world."[49]

Heroic virtue, as such, does not appear in the Digression on Madness, but the narrator demonstrates much the same enthusiasm for madness that Temple did for heroic virtue—and for good reason, because in each case the result is that incomparable blessing, human greatness. In such essays as *Upon the Gardens of Epicurus* Temple praised the greatness of ancients who philosophized virtuously in retirement, while the essay *Of Heroick Virtue* hymns the greatness of ancient or exotic empire-builders and (with obvious fascination) charts the rise of Mohammed, whose cunning religious inventions brought him an equally dazzling empire.

To account for the England of his own day, Temple took a different tack, and instead of an exalted theory of heroic virtue (an innate quality helped towards great deeds by birth, good fortune, and education) he resorted to a more mechanistic approach based on the interactions of diet, weather, and temperament. Because of the hearty English diet and the uncertainty and sudden changes in the English weather—"And how much these affect the Heads and Hearts, especially of the finest Tempers," he notes, "is hard to be believed by Men, whose Thoughts are not turned to such Speculations"—the English temperament runs the full gamut and produces a bewildering variety of enthusiasts and hypocrites, not just in religion but also in politics, chemistry, philosophy, and practically everything else. Temple can praise the solid virtues of the English, but at times he sounds as if he is describing a nation of madmen as well. Thanks to the effects of diet and climate, he notes at one point, "We are not only more unlike one another, than any Nation I know, but we are more unlike our selves too, at several times. . . ." In the end, Temple observes,

> it may happen that there is no where more true Zeal in the many different Forms of Devotion, and yet no where more Knavery under the Shews and Pretences. There are no where so many Disputers upon Religion, so many Reasoners upon Government, so many Refiners in Politicks, so many Curious Inquisitives, so many Pretenders to Business and State-Imployments, greater Porers upon Books, nor Plodders after Wealth. And yet no where more Abandoned Libertines, more Refined Luxurists, Extravagant Debauches, Conceited Gallants, more Dabblers in Poetry as well as Politics, in Philosophy and Chymistry. I have had several Servants far gone in

Divinity, others in Poetry; have known in the Families of some Friends, a Keeper deep in the Rosycrucia Principles, and a Laundress firm in those of Epicurus.[50]

Here is a world reminiscent of Swift's *Tale,* especially in the Digression on Madness. Swift's narrator takes a similarly mechanistic view of behavior. Onto it he fuses an enthusiasm for heroism equally characteristic of Temple. On the one hand, the narrator reflects Temple's fascination with greatness in empire-builders, philosophers, and even successful religious innovators like Mohammed, and on the other, he echoes Temple's belief in diet, climate, and their effects on human temperament and actions. In his scorn for English fanatics like Jack (the first hero cited in the Digression), Temple would never have recognized the double likeness when Swift's narrator announces his great theme:

> For, if we take a Survey of the greatest Actions that have been performed in the World, under the Influence of Single Men; which are, *The Establishment of New Empires by Conquest: The Advance and Progress of New Schemes in Philosophy; and the contriving, as well as the propagating of New Religions:* We shall find the Authors of them all, to have been Persons, whose natural Reason hath admitted great Revolutions from their Dyet, their Education, the Prevalency of some certain Temper, together with the particular Influence of Air and Climate.[51]

When propped on such underpinnings, human greatness forfeits something of its glory, but at least Swift reconciles Temple's thinking with itself. Temple thought true greatness an impossibility and heroic virtue a rarity in a degenerate age like his own, and hence had applied more cynical criteria to it. The greatness that he celebrated he celebrated only in other ages or in other parts of the world. "Some Ages produce many great Men and few great Occasions," he once explained in his essay *Of Popular Discontents:*

> other times on the Contrary, raise great Occasions, and few or no great Men: And that sometimes happens to a Country, which was said by the Fool of Brederode; who going about the Fields, with the motions of one sowing Corn, was asked what he sowed; He said I sow Fools, t'other replied, why do you not sow Wisemen? Why, said the Fool, *C'est que la Terre ne les porte pas.*

At other times, Temple continues, "the Races of Men may be so decayed" by disease, luxuriousness, "the Viciousness or Negligence of Education," or poor examples from those in authority, that even the best prince will find no suitable men to rule under him. In short, the greatness a man can achieve depends on his timing—on the age into which he is born and the occasions which it provides him. Later in the same essay Temple indicates that his own worthless age will take him for a fool when he proposes reforms "of great Consequence, and publick Utility to the Constitution of our Kingdom." His proposals are the sort associated with an "Utopian Scheme" and would make him appear "either Visionary or impertinent, if I should imagine, they could either be resolved in our Age and Country, or be made farther use of, than for the present Humour of our Times to Censure and to Ridicule them."[52] It is interesting, then, to find Swift's narrator maintaining the same idea. Had he lived "in this our undistinguishing Age," Epicurus himself might be chained fast. Indeed, if madness causes greatness, and if excessive vapors cause madness, then

> the main Point of Skill and Address, is to furnish Employment for this Redundancy of *Vapour*, and prudently to adjust the Seasons of it; by which means it may certainly become of Cardinal and Catholick Emolument in a Commonwealth. Thus one Man chusing a proper Juncture, leaps into a Gulph, from thence proceeds a Hero, and is called the Saver of his Country; Another atchieves the same Enterprise, but unluckily timing it, has left the Brand of *Madness*, fixt as a Reproach upon his Memory. . . .[53]

There is even a touch of Temple in the narrator's final proposal, based on the strongly utilitarian economic argument about population and prosperity. By adopting the "Reformation" that he proposes for Bedlam—freeing the inmates for work in the appropriate spheres outside—the world will not only recover a "vast Number of *Beaux, Fidlers, Poets,* and *Politicians,*" but England will enjoy a "clear Gain redounding to the Commonwealth, by so large an Acquisition of Persons to employ, whose Talents and Acquirements, if I may be so bold to affirm it, are now buried, or at least misapplied. . . ." A similarly utilitarian economic argument figures in Temple's *Of Popular Discontents,* among his many proposals for reforming England. Temple has nothing to propose about madmen, but urges the nation to put its convicted robbers to better use. Because current laws require the execution of robbers, "they deprive us of so many Subjects, whose Lives are every Year cut off in great Numbers, and which might otherwise be of use to the Kingdom; whose Strength consists in the Number, and Riches, and the Labour of the Inhabitants. . . ." Instead, Temple proposes, it would be more profitable (and more agreeable "with the Mildness and Clemency of our Government") to set robbers at forced labor for the rest of their lives or some other reasonable period (and thus "change the usual Punishment by short and easy Deaths, into some others of painful and uneasy Lives, which they will find much harder to bear").[54] Swift's narrator has nothing to say about robbers or clemency, to be sure, and Temple would hardly have recognized the likeness. Yet here as elsewhere in the Digression Swift seems to be capitalizing upon Temple's arguments and attitudes as if he once meant the section for Temple's eyes—and meant Temple to laugh at arguments and attitudes which, beneath their Modern veneer, are all too typical of Temple.

Of the many odd echoes and parallels with Temple which I have noticed, I have given only a selection here—weighted towards the larger intellectual issues which the Digression plays with, and traced with something less than full thoroughness. What I have so far noticed may also represent only a moiety of what a more painstaking search would uncover. For more definite conclusions we must await the results of such work, but the odd yet consistent pattern discernible in the Digression becomes increasingly difficult to explain in other ways.

Temple Elsewhere in the Tale *and in the* Battle

The rest of the *Tale* deserves attention, too—at least the sections on which Swift apparently worked while living at Moor Park, or sections which bear obvious signs of Temple's influence. In his discussion of Swift's part in the Ancient-Modern controversy, for instance, Philip Pinkus draws attention to the long passage in the Digression in the Modern Kind, in which Swift's speaker modestly compares himself to Homer, his nearest competitor, who likewise "design'd his Work for a compleat Body of all Knowledge Human, Divine, Political, and Mechanick." The speaker lists Homer's omissions in several branches of Modern knowledge, including occultism, English common law, and Christian theology, "A Defect indeed, for which both he and all the Ancients stand most justly censured by my worthy and ingenious Friend Mr. W–tt–n, Batchelor of Divinity, in his incomparable Treatise of *Ancient and Modern Learning.* . . ." After praising Wotton for "his sublime Discoveries upon the Subject of *Flies* and *Spittle,*" among other things, the speaker turns from Homer's omissions to defects for which Homer may be less accountable. "For whereas every Branch of Knowledge has received such wonderful Acquirements since his Age, especially within these last three Years, or thereabouts," the speaker continues,

> it is almost impossible, he could be so very perfect in Modern Discoveries, as his Advocates pretend. We freely acknowledge Him to be the Inventor of the *Compass,* of *Gun-Powder,* and the *Circulation of the Blood:* But, I challenge any of his Admirers to shew me in all his Writings, a compleat Account of the *Spleen.* . . .

Pinkus sensibly observes that "the satire moves in two directions" in the passage, not only "against the Moderns who find in the ancients almost nothing at all," but also "against the antiquarians who find in Homer and the ancients all knowledge and all beauty."[55] He concludes that Swift "is taking the hallowed materials of the controversy to laugh both sides out of Court," and that, to Swift, "even following the ancients is modern."

Overt laughter at the antiquarians may be fleeting—over two pages and more, only a line or two comes across strongly[56]—but it brings out a vein of satire implicit all through the section. As Homer's advocates are foolish to credit him with the compass and gunpowder, so they are foolish to seek there in the first place, just as the regular Moderns are foolish to accept their opponents' claims about the compass and gunpowder, and foolish to consult Homer for elucidations on Christian theology and English common law. As Pinkus points out, the discovery of the compass, gunpowder, and the circulation of the blood were "generally conceded to be the supreme achievements of Modern inventiveness."

Pinkus neglects to mention an even more important point, however. Much like Homer's "Advocates," Temple himself refused to concede the Moderns any of the three great discoveries. Of the circulation of the blood (and the Copernican theory of astronomy), Temple complained that the Moderns usually took credit, "But whether either of these be modern discoveries, or derived from old Fountains, is disputed: Nay, it is so too, whether they are true or no. . . ."[57] He felt the same way about gunpowder and the compass: "Nor can we say, that they are the Inventions of this Age, wherein Learning and Knowledge are pretended to be so wonderfully encreased and advanced." If the Chinese did not actually use gunpowder "many Ages before it came into Europe," he observes, then the ancient priests at Delphi may well have invented it.[58] Temple had never actually claimed the discoveries for Homer, or any other ancient, but the glove fits him even so. Among the ancients' popular advocates in England, he was probably the most unwilling to concede the Moderns credit for anything worthwhile.

Had Temple read Swift's mocking passage he should have felt vaguely uncomfortable, but Swift springs it in a way which should have kept him laughing at the same time. It is a Modern who speaks, after all, and Temple would never have knowingly ranged himself among them, 'Modern' though his reasoning often seems. Then too, Swift's subject was dear to Temple's heart. "Homer," he once announced, "was without Dispute, the most Universal *Genius* that has been known in the World," and "must be allowed, the most fertile [poetic] Invention, the richest Vein, the most general Knowledge, and the most lively Expression." Temple approvingly notes that "there cannot be a greater Testimony given, than what has been by some observed, that . . . the Greatest Masters have found in his Works the best and truest Principles of all their Sciences or Arts. . . ."[59] Here is Homer's "compleat Body of all Knowledge Human, Divine, Political, and Mechanick," as Swift attributes the idea to Xenophon. The distance is not too great between "the most Universal *Genius*" or "the most general Knowledge" on the one hand, and on the other the ability to invent gunpowder or compasses. Attacks on the ancients filled Temple with "a just Indignation" and "gave me the same kind of Horror I should have had, in seeing some young barbarous Goths or Vandals, breaking or defacing the admirable Statues of those antient Heroes. . . ." When Charles Perrault, a Frenchman who had found faults in Homer, recanted before the Académie, Temple incorporated the recantation and gloated over it in his second Ancient-Modern essay.[60]

Not only does Swift's passage appeal to Temple's sentiments by defending Homer and satirizing Goths like Perrault, it also satirizes the despicable Wotton, who had challenged Temple's claims for the ancients and incurred his anger in the answering "Hints." There Temple accused Wotton of being a "superficiall Sciolist" and egregious Modern, who "knows no more of Men or Manners than He has learnt in His Study," who dabbles in alchemy and the search for the Philosopher's Stone, and who insolently dares set himself on a level with that great and worldly gentleman, Sir William Temple.[61] In Swift's passage, Wotton figures as "my worthy and ingenious Friend," receives the speaker's praise for the *Reflections'* "sublime Discoveries upon the Subject of *Flies* and *Spittle,*"[62] and "my publick Acknowledgments, for the great *Helps* and *Liftings* I had out of his incomparable Piece, while I was penning this Treatise." Half as admirer and half as plagiarist, the speaker identifies himself with Wotton. Much more than the average reader, Temple should have relished Swift's satire against such Wottonian Moderns, and his momentum should have carried him safely over the line about compasses and gunpowder. It is a Wottonian speaking, after all—a reminder comes only three or four lines before—and unlike Temple, who did not descend to evidence, Wotton had investigated (before rejecting) the evidence that an ancient might have discovered the circulation of the blood.[63]

Safely on the other side of the line about blood and compasses, Temple should have felt any discomfort pass. Among other defects, the speaker charges, Homer fails to give a "compleat Account of the *Spleen.*" Temple would have recognized another 'help' from Wotton, who had devoted a page to the spleen's workings. Between the line's implicit absurdity and its welcome thrust at Wotton, Temple should have enjoyed it, and in the process missed another barb. Like Wotton, Temple had himself written on the subject, two brief (one- or two-page) accounts not of the organ itself but of that psychosomatic yet somehow dangerous English malady, "the Spleen." Here Temple takes "the Spleen" in dead earnest and gives out broad hints (confirmed by his sister) that he had been a sufferer himself.[64] As a commentator upon the Spleen, Homer alone is deficient. In the end, Swift's principles of construction and choice of imagery reflect the same pattern at work in the Digression on Madness. Swift provides good fun for a reader with no knowledge of Temple and no strong feelings about Ancients and Moderns. Even so, in both the laughter and the discomfort involved, the passage would work even more strongly on a reader who shared Temple's sometimes contradictory attitudes and found them echoed there.

If the *Tale* is worth searching for signs that Swift designed sections for Temple to read, so is its companion piece, *The Battle of the Books*. In the *Battle* Swift thumps Wotton and Bentley with at least as much vigor as he had in the *Tale*. Perhaps more gratifyingly,[65] he advances Temple to center stage, especially in the climactic single combat between Wotton and Temple. There Swift presents him not as Swift knew him—fulminating angrily in the "Hints"—but in great dignity, wholly unconscious of the combat in which he figures.[66] After so many lesser single combats, Temple's inactivity may seem a touch anticlimactic, but it precisely suits the guise in which Temple wished the world to see him.[67] Partly because so much else in the book seems carefully calculated to suit Temple, Swift's modern editors entertain the suspicion that Temple may have read the *Battle*.[68] It is especially interesting, then, to find a critic noting "a basic confusion" in the book's conception. Swift's first aim, suggests Philip Pinkus, "was to defend Sir William Temple against his opponents and put them in their place," but Swift also "felt obliged to ridicule the controversy and keep Temple's ideas at a distance."[69] Among other instances, Pinkus cites the narrative's opening paragraph, in which Swift generalizes about the origins of quarrels and traces how resentments arise in "the Republick of *Dogs*," who inhabit a street where only one bitch is in heat and who exhibit "Plenty of Heartburning, and Envy, and Snarling" when some dog "of more Courage, Conduct, or Fortune than the rest, seizes and enjoys the Prize." Swift then applies his findings to the "Commonwealth of Learning," to "discover the first Ground of Disagreement" between the Ancients and Moderns.[70] As Pinkus observes, the analogy does little to dignify their controversy, and creates an absurd and faintly mocking context for the grand battle which follows, no matter who its ostensible heroes and villains.

Closer inspection indicates that the passage fits the pattern already seen in sections of the *Tale*. On the surface, at least, Swift echoes Temple's writings and appears to follow his thinking implicitly. Temple sometimes fancied pithy or aphoristic generalizations, and at different times had noted that conquests "have generally proceeded from North to South," that like men even sociable animals "quarrel in hunger and in lust," and (more ambitiously) that "Plenty begets Wantonness and Pride, Wantonness is apt to Invent, and Pride scorns to Imitate; Liberty begets Stomach or Heart, and Stomach will not be Constrained."[71] Adopting Temple's manner, and sometimes echoing Temple's phrasing as well, Swift begins the *Battle* with a similar jumble of nuggets. Among other matters, he mentions "Invasions usually travelling from *North* to *South*, that is to say, from Poverty upon Plenty," and remarks that "The most antient and natural Grounds of Quarrels, are *Lust* and *Avarice*; which, tho' we may allow to be Brethren or collateral Branches of *Pride*, are certainly the Issues of *Want.*" He had opened the passage with the maxims that "*War is the Child of Pride,* and *Pride the Daughter of Riches,*" but then suggested that, on the other hand, "*Pride* is nearly related to Beggary and *Want*, either by Father or Mother, and sometimes by both. . . ." (Temple had used the simple verb "begets" with his personified abstractions, but Swift, it seems, needs to trace the family tree with greater exactitude.)

His discussion of dogs also recalls Temple. In an attempt to discredit political theory, especially theories which account for government by a social contract, Temple had spoken out against philosophies like Hooker's and Hobbes's, which assume a social contract arising from man's innate sociability or from his innate aggressiveness. Temple both compares and dismisses the philosophies by applying them to groups of animals—sociable herbivores like sheep on the one hand, aggressive carnivores like ravens or wolves on the other. Not only do the sociable animals often quarrel in hunger or in lust, he notes, but the aggressive ones often join together in packs. Since men can resemble both kinds of animals, Temple cannot see which model they would fit:

> Nor do I know, if men are like sheep, why they need any Government: or if they are like Wolves, how they can suffer it. Nor have I read where the Orders of any State have been agreed on by mutual Contract among great numbers of men, meeting together in that natural state of War, where every man takes himself to have equal right to every thing.[72]

Not only does Swift seem to take a hint from Temple's analogy to animals in packs—dogs fit neatly between the aggressive wolves and the sociable sheep—but he uses his analogy to smile at Hobbesian theories of man in a natural state of war. Complaints and civil dissensions arise within "the Republick of *Dogs*," he observes, when "some *leading Dog*" appropriates a large bone. When a bitch in heat appears, "Jealousies and Suspicions do so abound, that the whole Commonwealth of that Street, is reduced to a manifest *State of War*, of every Citizen against every *Citizen....*" Here are Temple's animals quarreling in lust and hunger, along with an amusing send-up of the Hobbesian view of man in his natural state of war.

All this should have been gratifying enough, had Temple read it, but the passage also has its uncomfortable side. Swift may follow Temple's lead, but his aphoristic observations do not sit as gratefully as they might. Temple indeed held that invasions proceed from north to south, but to the invaders he usually attributed a more heroic vigor and courage—not a superior greed and beggary, as Swift does.[73] If Temple enjoyed aphoristic assertions about Plenty, Wantonness, and Pride, he could not have felt too comfortable seeing similar aphorisims attributed to Mary Clarke's vulgar penny almanac, although, in the closest parallel, he had waxed aphoristic not about war but the rise of the English drama of humors.[74] Swift means to equate the Moderns with the invading northerners, the offspring of Pride and Want, but before he can make the equation he digresses about dogs. Here it is hard to tell which dogs represent the proud and beggarly northern invaders. They all live on the same street and share the same lust and hunger, except that some enjoy greater success than others. Swift may pleasingly echo the imagery from Temple's observation on Hobbes, but his ideas come from a different and more awkward source. Swift in fact is theorizing about the genesis of civil quarrels and unrest in a state. In the essay *Of Popular Discontents*, Temple had addressed the same issue. His arguments had combined the same basic elements as Swift's, but he had used them to very different effect. Like Swift, Temple makes an extended comparison between animals and men (who share almost all the same faculties, including reason and the passions), derives civil unrest from man's envy and passionate restlessness (an abuse of his reason), and emphasizes the workings of a natural inequality among men and the equally natural tendency to complain under the rule of others.[75] In each instance Swift follows suit, in a general way. But where Swift attributes the same selfish behavior to all the dogs, including their happy leader, Temple makes a strong implicit distinction between government and the rabble. Not only can "this restless Humor, so general and natural to Mankind" grow in all soils, he notes, but it "seems to thrive most, and grow fastest, in the best." From man's natural restlessness "issue those Streams of Faction" which "overflow the wisest Constitutions of Governments and Laws," which "bring such Men to Scaffolds, that deserved Statues," and which tragically sacrifice "the Wisest, the best of Men," including the heroes Solon, Pythagoras, the two Gracchi, Scipio, Hannibal, and Temple's friend De Witt.[76] In Temple's thinking, to be sure, great men somehow transcend the sorry human condition about which he so often philosophizes. Heroic virtue springs "from some great and native Excellency of Temper or Genius transcending the common race of Mankind, in Wisdom, Goodness, and Fortitude."[77] While smiling at Swift's "Republick of *Dogs*," with its happy *"leading Dog"* and its pleasing mockery of Hobbes, the great man would in fact have been smiling at the hero under whose leadership dissensions spring up. Instead of a Scipio or a Solon, the leader is merely another dog, whose greater "Courage, Conduct, or Fortune" leads him to seize the bone, mount the bitch, and bring down on himself "Plenty of Heartburning, and Envy, and Snarling." The tragedy of heroic virtue becomes the comedy of greed and lechery, successfully pursued.

As in the passages from the *Tale*, Swift again seems to tailor his words for Temple—that is, he writes for a reader holding Temple's attitudes, contradictions and all, and he incorporates snippets echoing Temple's published statements. In the process, while maintaining Temple's stated position and satirizing the objects of Temple's scorn or disapproval, Swift somehow manages to include part of Temple in the laugh he raises, without giving the least sign of conscious disloyalty. The ironies are often private: at least they are not easily accessible to anyone less familiar than Swift with Temple's character and writings, vanities and inconsistencies included. A casual reader of Temple would only find some admiring echoes and the occasional outright praise. Much the same pattern appears in Swift's earlier *Ode to Temple*, but the ode manages to collapse Temple's ideals while attempting serious panegyric and invective. For an outside reader, the poem seems at best an embarrassment, well-meaning but awkward. In the *Tale* and the *Battle* passages, Swift attempts satire instead, and it is through his success, not his apparent failure, that Temple comes under the gun. In the poem Swift seems to mock him by praising him ineptly, not in itself the most demanding task for a satirist but still a challenge when writing for Temple himself. In the *Tale* and *Battle* passages, he seems to mock Temple while succeeding all too well in mocking what Temple opposed —usually something in which Temple also half believed or unconsciously shared. The opponent of speculative Modern scholarship, after all, often indulged in it while defending the ancients. The critic of "Sufficiency" in learning could recommend its uses in wisdom and happiness, though under a different name, and the man who philosophized about the vanity of human reason (yet distrusted systematic philosophy anyway) drew his strength from a considerable confidence in his own. Neither modesty nor consistency was Temple's long suit, and Swift's covert satire seems to capitalize on his failings. For a scholar willing to immerse himself repeatedly in Temple, and then read Swift with Temple's works open beside him, the *Battle* and the Moor Park sections of the *Tale* may well reveal a recurrent, perhaps even continuous vein of secondary satire, an additional source of ironies which parallel and interact with those available to the general reader. In the process, he will approximate Swift's point of view while writing at Moor Park, and may recapture part of the pleasure which Swift took in his task.

Certainly there are enough passages which raise suspicions. In the *Tale*'s Digression on Critics, for instance, Swift expands on a conceit which he had first employed in the *Ode to Temple*. In the ode Swift had hymned Temple's heroism for fighting the monstrous Serpent which drives virtue from royal courts and palaces, but though Temple "oft renew'd the Fight," he never quite succeeded. In the end Temple grants England peace by retiring from the fray: "Till at last tir'd with loss of Time and Ease,/ Resolv'd to give himself, as well as Country Peace."[78] In the *Tale*, Swift borrows and extends the same idea—that crusading heroes constitute a worse nuisance than the monsters they combat. In an extended analogy between bad critics and what he calls "Heroick Virtue," Swift's narrator defines heroic virtue much as Temple had in the essay *Of Heroick Virtue*, in terms of the divinity which men attribute to the successful hero. The narrator suggests that critics in the line of Bentley and Wotton resemble "those Antient Heroes, famous for their Combating so many Giants, and Dragons, and Robbers," heroes whom some people think "were in their own Persons a greater Nuisance to Mankind, than any of those Monsters they subdued." He concludes that such critics should emulate the hero Hercules, who earned men's thanks and worship by doing away with himself.[79] Recommending ratsbane to a Wotton or a Bentley should have gratified Temple tremendously, but to relish the attack on such critics, the reader must also be ready to smile at the semidivine heroism so near Temple's heart. In fact the Digression on Critics seems almost as full of suspicious passages as the Digression on Madness, while they seem to occur more sporadically, if still with some regularity, in the *Tale*'s Preface, its remaining Digressions, and the *Battle*.[80]

Sometimes a resemblance or parallel turns up in the most unexpected places, for instance in the *Battle*'s fable of the Bee and the Spider. To a general reader it seems straightforward enough, and Temple and his contemporaries would have noted a resemblance between that coarse and railing Modern, the Spider, and Temple's two chief antagonists, especially the blunt Richard Bentley. In his own lifetime, after all, Temple had never deigned a reply to Wotton or Bentley, much less showed any anger publicly. Nothing could seem less like Temple than the rage of the Spider, who "when beholding the Chasms, and Ruins, and Dilapidations of his Fortress," was "very near at his Wit's end, . . . stormed and swore like a Mad-man, and swelled till he was ready to burst." But Temple's secretary knew better. We cannot reconstruct the form which Temple's anger took when he first read Wotton's *Reflections,* but in the manuscript "Hints" which Swift transcribed about 1697, Temple's anger is plain enough to see. Temple associates Wotton with the alchemists, implies that Wotton will grow ass's ears like Midas's, and accuses him of *hybris* in general and in particular. (If philology is "as the Word signifyes, A Love of Talk," Temple says, and if Wotton "can make it pass for a Science, He will indeed at the same Time make Himself pass for a very learned man," and because Wotton supposedly called himself "Wottoni" when in Italy, Temple advises him "that it should be Wottoni in His next Edition.") Most of all, as we have seen, Wotton showed insolence in setting himself up against Sir William Temple, a man long conversant with the great world and well known both from his writings and the great offices he either held or refused ("And this is the Person Mr Wotton pursues so insolently . . ."). Who, then, is Wotton? "One would wonder who this great man should be," Temple sputters,

> that uses both Antients and Moderns with such an Arrogance; Why, 'tis a young Scholar that confesses He owes all the Comforts of His Life to His Patrons Bounty, that knows no more of Men or Manners than He has learnt in His Study; A superficiall Sciolist, that by Force of Memory and Scraps of Learning, has been indeed, Raysed, as He calls it; But, to what? why, to teach Mr Finch's Children; He tells us indeed in the Title-Page, of a greater Character, which is that of Chaplain to the Earl of Nottingham, but confesses in the End of His Epistle that He assumed this Stile to sett Himself upon a Level with S^r W T, from whom He takes the Freedom so often to dissent. . . .[81]

It is significant, then, to find the Spider boasting a comparable social superiority over the Bee. When the Bee dares to reply to the Spider's idle threat to *"come and teach you better Manners,"* the Spider waxes angry: *"Rogue, Rogue,* replied the Spider, *yet, methinks, you should have more Respect to a Person, whom all the World allows to be so much your Betters.* " Like Temple with Wotton, the Spider finds it degrading to be considered in the same breath with the Bee, but makes the comparison anyway. The Bee, it seems, has no home of his own or intrinsic means of support. *"Not to disparage my self,"* says the Spider, *"by the Comparison with such a Rascal; What art thou but a Vagabond without House or Home, without Stock or Inheritance; Born to no Possession of your own, but a Pair of Wings, and a Drone-Pipe. . . .* " In his revised attack on Wottonian critics, published posthumously in *Some Thoughts Upon Reviewing the Essay of Antient and Modern Learning,* Temple also employed a metaphor which suggests the Bee's lack of "Stock or Inheritance." Temple has always considered critics to be "like Brokers," low tradesmen "who having no Stock of their own, set up and trade with that of other Men; buying here, and selling there, and commonly abusing both sides, to make out a little paultry Gain"—not too far from the Bee's roving life (as the Spider describes it) as *"a Freebooter over Fields and Gardens,"* who *"for the sake of Stealing, will rob a Nettle as readily as a Violet."*[82]

Temple's retort to Wotton, both in the privately circulated "Hints" and the published essay which succeeded it, also suggests another parallel with the Spider:

> . . . the Spider having swelled himself into the Size and Posture of a Disputant, began his Argument in the true Spirit of Controversy, with a Resolution to be heartily scurrilous and angry, to urge *on* his own Reasons, without the least Regard to the Answers or Objections of his Opposite; and fully predetermined in his Mind against all Conviction.

Temple and his contemporaries would have seen Wotton or Bentley here,[83] but Temple fits the description even better. His opponents had poked holes in his arguments about the ancients' scientific preeminence, but Temple had nothing new to urge in reply. The "Hints" chiefly reveal his anger and scurrility towards Wotton, and the published essay *Some Thoughts* (ostensibly a refutation of Wotton's *Reflections*) feebly repeats Temple's original arguments, this time with a sharper attack on Modern pride and ignorance. (Temple's greatest modern champion, Homer Woodbridge, finds the essay so repetitious, wrongheaded, and "argumentatively feeble" that he declines to summarize it.[84]) If nothing else, the essay furnishes a demonstration of his resolution "to urge *on* his own Reasons, without the least Regard to the Answers or Objections of his Opposite; and fully predetermined in his Mind against all Conviction." Swift's handling of the Spider ought to have gratified Temple, but all too often Swift encourages contempt for the traits which Temple unwittingly shared with the Moderns he despised.

Although described as distinctively "Modern," for instance, the Spider's boasted accomplishments in mathematics and military architecture reflect Temple's claims for the ancients as much as Wotton's for the Moderns. As Guthkelch and Nichol Smith suggest, Wotton had argued the Moderns' superiority in military architecture, and Temple had held up ancient architecture as a proof of the ancients' superiority in mathematics.[85] Actually it was Temple who first raised the issue of preeminence in the *military* applications of mathematics, the Spider's special fiefdom. Wotton had only picked up the gauntlet which Temple threw down. "The stupendious Effects of this Science [the ancients' architecture], sufficiently evince, at what Heighths the Mathematicks were among the Ancients," Temple had said:

> but if this be not enough, whoever would be satisfied, need go no further than the Siege of Syracuse, and that mighty Defence made against the Roman Power, more by the wonderful Science and Arts of Archimedes, and almost Magical Force of his Engines, than by all the Strength of the City, or Number and Bravery of the Inhabitants.[86]

With additional examples of the ancients' architecture (military as well as civil) and of their military machinery, drawn from fact and fable, Temple repeats the old claim in his second Ancient-Modern essay: he cannot conceive how such astounding things could have been done "without some other Mathematical Skill and Engins, than have been since known in the World."[87]

It is also worth noting that, as much as for Bentley (at the Saint James's library) and more than for Wotton (at Lord Nottingham's house), the Spider resembles Temple in his choice of a retired life in a house safely away from the world ("In this Mansion he had for some Time dwelt in Peace and Plenty, without Danger to his *Person* by *Swallows* from above, or to his *Palace* by *Brooms* from below . . ."), and that, like the Temple who steered clear of involvement in the Glorious Revolution, the Spider believes in avoiding dangerous conflicts *("an old Custom in our Family, never to stir abroad against an Enemy")*. In the Moor Park context which produced Temple's "Hints" and second Ancient-Modern essay, the Bee's final summation of Modern pride and pretension in the Spider takes on special resonance, especially since Temple would have despised the Spider and identified himself with that diligent, studious, and tasteful nobleman, the Bee:

> *So that in short* [says the Bee], *the Question comes all to this; Whether is the nobler Being of the two, That which by a lazy Contemplation of four Inches round; by an over-weening Pride, which feeding and engendering on it self, turns all into Excrement and Venom; producing nothing at last, but Fly-bane and a Cobweb: Or That,*

which, by an universal Range, with long Search, much Study, true Judgment, and Distinction of Things, brings home Honey and Wax.[88]

Without forfeiting anything of its satire on Wotton and Bentley, Swift's fable of the Spider and the Bee appears to work equally well as a trap for Temple.

If Swift was laughing at Temple here and there in his Moor Park satires, he had nothing to gain by asking the general public to join in. In the *Tale* itself, an average reader of 1704 would have identified Temple (if at all) only as Wotton's opponent, the "Friend" of Prince Posterity's Governor, Time.[89] (By the fifth edition of 1710, readers should also have recognized Temple in the 'Apology,' as "a certain great Man then alive, and universally reverenced for every good Quality that could possibly enter into the Composition of the most accomplish'd Person" —identified a few lines later as "Sir W. T."[90]) By 1704 the Temple-Wotton, Bentley-Boyle controversy about ancients and Moderns had generally petered out, and with it the likelihood that readers might recognize echoes of Temple's specific arguments, imagery, or phrasing, from his Ancient-Modern essays. By 1704, in fact, the most recent printing of the first two sets of *Miscellanea* essays was already seven years old, and the third set three years old. Had the *Tale* and the *Battle* appeared before Temple died early in 1699 or in the year or two immediately following, publication would have helped the book thrive with the controversy, but more men than Wotton might have found odd or suspicious traces of Temple in it. If Swift actually initiated publication, as most people assume, its long delay served him well.

In the *Tale*'s preface, dated August 1697, Swift seems to guard his privacy from exposure, whether by Temple or the general reader who succeeded him years later. To explain the seeming dulness of Modern wit, Swift's narrator announces that *"Wit* has its Walks and Purlieus, out of which it may not stray the breadth of a Hair, upon peril of being lost." Hence he concludes that

> Whatever Reader desires to have a thorow Comprehension of an Author's Thoughts, cannot take a better Method, than by putting himself into the Circumstances and Postures of Life, that the Writer was in, upon every important Passage as it flow'd from his Pen; For this will introduce a Parity and strict Correspondence of Idea's between the Reader and the Author.

So far so good: Temple and most other readers would probably agree in theory. Though a little exaggerated, the principle promises help in evaluating a writer's intentions, though not necessarily his success in fulfilling them. In fact it follows from some of Temple's own beliefs, including his conviction that human greatness and learning have their walks and purlieus, and cannot flourish outside them.[91] Most important, it also serves as bait for a satiric trap. Further development reduces the idea to absurdity, and the reader must either relinquish the principle itself or laugh at himself for holding it. The speaker indicates that "the shrewdest Pieces of this Treatise, were conceived in Bed, in a Garret," that he "thought fit to sharpen my Invention with Hunger," and that he began and completed it "under a long Course of Physick, and a great want of Money." With impeccable logic, he makes the final application:

> I do affirm, it will be absolutely impossible for the candid Peruser to go along with me in a great many bright Passages, unless upon the several Difficulties emergent, he will please to capacitate and prepare himself by these Directions. And this I lay down as my principal *Postulatum.*[92]

Here Swift satirizes the inane subjectivities of Modern wit, which sparkle only in the eyes of each individual author, but the passage also serves to discourage any attempt to consider the *Tale* in terms of Swift's circumstances at the time of writing. By implication, the "candid Peruser" should content his ideas with whatever Swift gives him, without inquiring into the circumstances which may have inspired them. Otherwise the reader must make a fool of himself—must agree to shut himself up in a garret, go hungry, and catch a disease (probably venereal) requiring a "long Course of Physick." Worse, he must join in the laughter which Swift directs against those who accept this "principal *Postulatum.*" Temple was hardly the man to concede himself a fool and laugh at himself.[93] To a lesser if still substantial degree, neither was the average Englishman in 1704, nor most readers who have succeeded him, including the twentieth-century critic or scholar. Whoever the reader, Swift makes sure that he will not venture too far behind the scenes, while teasing him in the same breath with the intelligence that he writes wit "calculated for this present Month of August, 1697"—which for Swift means Moor Park, Temple, and Temple's exasperation over the new and expanded edition of Wotton's *Reflections,* published a couple of months before.[94]

* * *

Still, it is best to proceed with caution. More work remains before suitably firm conclusions can be drawn about either the *Tale* and the *Battle* as a whole, or Swift's inspirations and private feelings. The worklist is substantial: further research on Swift's experience at Moor Park; on Swift's private and public attitudes towards Temple, both then and later; on Temple himself, including his little-known ties with Grub

Street and the *Athenian Mercury,* as well as his abilities (or disabilities) in classical learning and his interests in natural "Magick" and other phenomena beloved of the Moderns; on the creation of Temple's public image and its maintenance in Swift's lifetime; on Temple's writings and other works which touched Temple closely, including Wotton's and Bentley's reflections on him; on Swift's reliance upon all such sources in his Moor Park writings; and on those writings themselves, considered as the product of Swift's attitudes, circumstances, ambitions, and intended readership, both immediate and eventual, limited and extensive.

Meantime Swift's Moor Park satires remain enjoyable enough for the standard reader, quite apart from any private pleasure that they may originally have given Swift. For the modern critic, however, the pattern of telltale passages in the *Tale* and the *Battle* raises important questions. In a paradoxical way it provides new support for the hypothesis on which Ehrenpreis has based so much of his work—that Swift drew his literary inspiration not from his reaction to abstract ideas but from his reactions to people he knew.[95] Over the past generation, much academic criticism of the *Tale* has instead centered on assigning Swift a label in philosophy or intellectual history. Until more can be learned about the *Tale*'s origins and inspirations, it may be wise to table further attempts to prove that the *Tale* reveals Swift as an Epicurean sceptic, a Christian humanist, a secret Man of Feeling, a neo-Stoic, an Anglican rationalist, a pyrrhonist, an existentialist, an orthodox Augustinian Christian, a nihilist, or whatever other designation comes to mind. Does Swift's ironic definition of Epicurean happiness represent a bitter comment on the nature of happiness, does it instead satirize the libertine rejection of rational control, or does it mock Temple's muddled and self-indulgent philosophizings? When Swift deflates Louis XIV, does he reveal his own belief in the theory that small accidents determine history, or does he only borrow Temple's in order to tweak Temple's vanity and inconsistency on the subject? If Swift follows Temple and Boyle in satirizing pedantry as the kind of 'written ill-breeding' exemplified in Wotton, does it indeed mark a change in his belief (as one critic implies) when years later he expresses contempt for such notions?[96] In the telltale passages from the *Tale* and the *Battle,* Swift appears to borrow Temple's beliefs for use in glancing at Temple's conflicting beliefs, often to reveal his vanities and follies along the way. What then was Swift's own personal philosophy, if any, and if his motives were as mischievous as the evidence so often suggests, how much does it actually figure in the *Tale?*

Even purely literary analysis may gain from better information about the *Tale*'s inspiration and origins. Many critics have traced

Swift's strength to his choice and manipulation of imagery, his inconsistent use of voice or persona, the mutability or continuing redefinition of the terms of his arguments, or the shifting satiric focus which results. What blueprint did he follow? When he mixes dogs, Hobbes, and portentous aphorism early in the *Battle*, what dictates his choice—the consciousness of certain principles of satiric imagery, or an awareness of a particular reader's needs? What is going on, in the *Tale*, when the Wottonian Modern who catalogues Homer's faults begins to sound like an advocate of the ancients, or when the crack-brained enthusiast who praises systematic philosophers and the Academy of Modern Bedlam suddenly mutters (more like a wise man) about "this our undiscriminating Age"? What holds the key—certain types of Empsonian ambiguity, for instance, or the vagaries of Sir William Temple? Admittedly, an author's working blueprint may sometimes lead to writings which operate according to principles which he never fully conceptualized or even knowingly intended. In theory, a critic need not concern himself with an author or his conscious principles of construction, but in practice such matters impinge on literary analysis. If Swift wrote for human consumption, his work must be analyzed accordingly. For a William Temple, the *Battle* and the *Tale* would operate in a somewhat different way than for the average Englishman in 1704, and for a modern American academic they may function somewhat differently in turn. Ultimately any definition of Swift's satiric art must depend on the reader involved, and here Swift's intentions should be taken into account. If this study serves any purpose, it is to encourage a more careful evaluation and comparison of existing evidence, biographical together with textual, and a more thorough attention to the immediate practical contexts which so often inform, inspire, and give meaning to Swift's words. Otherwise we risk erecting our critical apparatus on shaky foundations.

Certainly the *Tale* and the *Battle* deserve any attention which offers to provide a clearer understanding of Swift's satiric art. By general admission, both works show Swift operating at the top of his form. What holds true with them should also apply in some way to his later work. Whatever Swift's original inspiration in the *Tale*, he eventually had it published, and if it so often appears tailor-made for Temple, it still works well enough (if less neatly and probingly) for the general reader of the day. In his thinking, in his inconsistencies, and in his basic self-regard, Temple was as much a man of his time as what he liked to imagine himself, an original who transcended it. To some degree—the most considerable one, I now believe—writing for Temple in the 1690s should have prepared Swift for his later career of writing for wider contemporary audiences.

As the departure point for his recent book of criticism, C. J. Rawson speaks of a certain "undermining effect" in Swift's satire, a "curious precariousness to the reader's grasp of what is going on," along with "the imposition of an exceptional immediacy of involvement with the reader." Rawson considers it a kind of "aggressiveness towards the reader," and describes its effect "approximately in terms of the edgy intimacy of a personal quarrel that does not quite come out into the open. . . ."[97] In an earlier article, "Swift's Satire of the Second Person," Henry W. Sams observes much the same sort of phenomenon, and traces it through Gulliver's *Travels* as well as the *Tale.* There is a "peculiar satiric vibrancy" which occurs, Sams theorizes, when Swift reenters his argument directly as the reader's enemy, after creating a "tacit alliance" with him through a "putative author," whose satiric exordium invites the reader to join him in the laughter. The reader's experience, as Sams explains it, roughly approximates the experience which I think Swift had in mind for Temple in the passages from the *Tale* and the *Battle:*

> Assurance of another's error fosters a state of mind which is stable, confident, secure. Ridicule of persons not so good as ourselves is reassuring. Much of Swift's satire has this effect. His caustic scorn encourages complacency that we are not as one of these. But there are passages of another sort. These passages have a contrary effect. They bring the mind to precarious equilibrium. They prompt a state of being which is unstable, insecure, and afraid.

In addition, he observes, Swift manages the job without giving himself away: "In whatever degree the reader finds himself accused in these passages, he is self-accused."[98]

Admittedly, both Rawson and Sams speak in terms of a twentieth-century reader, apparently of an intellectual stamp.[99] Another reader might feel less actively edgy, fearful, or threatened, or he might laugh and feel uncomfortable not alternately but simultaneously. Even so, both Rawson and Sams point to a certain distinguishing quality in Swift, an odd resonance which sets him apart from other satirists of his time. It ultimately stems, I think, from Swift's literary apprenticeship at Moor Park, his seemingly innocent but progressively more skillful exercises in appealing to Temple's prejudices, fighting Temple's battles, and provoking Temple's scorn or laughter, both consciously against his opponents and, in the same instant, unwittingly against himself. A more thorough understanding of Swift in the 1690s should lead to a more accurate understanding of his most distinctive satiric gift, both then and later.

By the same token, more research on Swift's Moor Park satires may add to the biographical picture, though perhaps not by much. It is always dangerous to try to pin down a presence as protean as Swift's. Still, in the *Tale* and the *Battle*, the telltale passages reflect a certain sense of mischief and a distinct lack of respect for Temple. Possibly Swift meant them constructively—to dose Temple with his own medicine and encourage a spontaneous reevaluation of assumptions. This is far from certain, though. Did Swift write in suppressed bitterness, affectionate contempt, sheer mischievousness, or something more complex and intermediate? At least for the time being there is no saying, and further discoveries in the Moor Park satires may not greatly clarify the situation. In a more positive sense, the *Tale* and the *Battle* passages reveal a remarkable intimacy with Temple and Temple's works—his arguments, images, phrasings, likes, dislikes, perceptions, and blind spots. After working with two volumes of Temple's essays, three of his letters, two of the memoirs, and one of history—copying, reading aloud, entering Temple's corrections, perhaps recopying—Swift could hardly have failed to know his Temple backwards and forwards, more thoroughly than any reader since. At least in 1697 (as we have seen) he seems to have been rereading Temple as well—the *Introduction to the History of England*, the *Memoirs of What Past in Christendom*, and perhaps also the two-volume *Miscellanea* essays which Temple gave him that December. When a man must read slowly and carefully, as he does when copying or reading aloud, the little flaws and inconsistencies in his author tend to emerge from the rhetoric. With repeated readings they may even begin to tickle or grate on the sensibilities. Temple's genteel graces hide a surprising number of such failings, especially in the essays. By occupation as well as intelligence, Swift was not the man to miss them. To all appearances, the *Battle* and the *Tale* contain part of his response. Whether further research extends or modifies my findings so far, the Moor Park satires merit a fresh approach. Under the orthodox assumptions now current, it was a genuine admiration for Temple which inspired Swift in both works, the sort of admiration which would produce much the same sentiments whether or not Temple were looking on. But if Swift deeply admired Temple, as Ehrenpreis maintains, how does so knowledgeable a disciple manage to muddle the job so badly—to turn one borrowing against another, to bring out Temple's inconsistencies and absurdities, and ultimately to include Temple in the laughter directed at the objects of Temple's scorn? Even one such passage should raise suspicions. When Swift collapses Temple's ideals in the early odes, with all apparent innocence, critics have usually accounted for his work by assuming simple incompetence, the loss of artistic control which comes of tackling a personally unsuitable task. *A Tale of a Tub* and *The Battle of the Books,* by contrast, represent a high point in Swift's literary career. Is Swift incompetent here as well? To preserve the hypothesis of Swift's loyal discipleship, it will be necessary to prove him as earnest and bumbling in the *Tale*'s Digression on Madness as he appears in his *Ode to the Hon*ble *Sir William Temple.*

Some Implications for Further Research

In a study of this sort it is wisest not to press conclusions too far, given the nature of the surviving evidence and the amount of work still to be done with it. Even so, there are areas in which it may be helpful to chart potential applications, to point out possibilities for further research beyond Moor Park. We have noted the likelihood that what holds true for Swift's *Tale of a Tub* should in some sense hold true for his later work as well, and that in writing for Temple, very much a man of his time, Swift seemingly prepared himself for addressing a wider readership later on. In Rawson, Sams, and their observations about Swift's unsettling effects we have already encountered one area worth investigating in greater depth.

Of course there are other possible approaches to the literary lessons of Moor Park. Of necessity this study has concentrated upon the things which Swift observed and experienced there. Principally he had viewed the great Sir William Temple at close quarters and Temple's writings perhaps even more closely. Better than anyone else he had been in a position to chart the maze of moles, blotches, and warts behind the smoothly heroic visage which Temple painted for the world to admire. After all, Temple had employed him to pass the brushes and hold the make-up jars. But what inferences did he draw from his experience and observations? Here we are on far less certain ground, though arguably more important to our understanding of Swift. A dull and petty-minded man might have noted the disparity between the real and painted Temple, made a few caustic remarks to himself, and let it go at that. We may guess that Swift, an aspiring artist himself, had the capacity to see further. The fact is that Temple enjoyed a signal success in presenting himself to the world. The reading public took him at face value. His works went through edition after edition, and by the year he died his former secretary could without suspicion of irony write a preface casually invoking, as a matter of fact, the exalted public image which Temple had built up for himself. (Temple is a great and good man, his role in world history pivotal, and his literary reputation peerless: "It is generally believed, that this Author, has advanced our English Tongue, to as great a Perfection as it can well bear. . . ."[100]) Swift's is too private and complex a mind to hypothesize confidently about, but even so it is difficult to imagine him stupid enough to miss the most basic inferences to be drawn, about the nature of the reading public and about the kinds of things which could have such effects on them. Swift's attitude towards Temple, whatever it was, would figure centrally here. If *A Tale of a Tub* and Swift's other Moor Park writings suggest that he first practiced upon Temple the curious games which he later played so successfully with a wider readership, they also suggest that Swift's basic attitude towards the reading public may not have differed too radically from his attitude towards the man who had misled them so successfully. Indeed it is likely that Temple and his readers were somehow associated in Swift's mind. Except for the ode which he sent to Temple's admired Athenian Society and his possible role in Temple's quarrel with Du-Cros, his only extensive first-hand experience with publishing and the public had come through Temple.

Certainly Swift's scattered comments in the *Tale* suggest that he had spent some time thinking (and smiling) about the ways in which successful writers interact with their readers. As with Temple, one promising strategy is self-praise. Repeated often enough, it will convince the world. The author of the *Tale* explains that the Moderns have bought out the fee simple of praise, formerly a pension bestowed by others, and now may freely bestow it upon themselves. He muses upon the formula favored by the Moderns when they set out to praise themselves ("*I speak without Vanity;* which I think plainly shews it to be a Matter of Right and Justice") and tells his reader that the same formula is implied "in every Encounter of this Nature" through the following book, "which I mention, to save the Trouble of repeating it on so many Occasions." A similar strategy of self-praise enjoys "incredible Success" with "Our Great Dryden" in his interminable prefaces: "He has often said to me in Confidence, that the World would never have suspected him to be so great a Poet, if he had not assured them so frequently in his Prefaces, that it was impossible they could either doubt or forget it." Turning to Greatness itself, in the Digression on Madness, Swift asks how philosophers and other great madmen succeed in finding disciples. The reason is easily assigned. A philosopher succeeds when his auditors are tuned to the same pitch and share a "secret necessary Sympathy":

> For, there is a peculiar *String* in the Harmony of Human Understanding, which in several individuals is exactly of the same Tuning. This, if you can dexterously screw up to its right Key, and then strike gently upon it;

Whenever you have the Good Fortune to light among those of the same Pitch, they will by a secret necessary Sympathy, strike exactly at the same time.[101]

If we were to apply Swift's jesting terms to the situation at Moor Park, we might hypothesize that Temple's projected character, with all Temple's vanities and follies behind it, found an answering echo in his gentle readers. Under a hypothesis of this sort, Swift could not have acted more naturally (when the time came) than by subjecting the same reading public to the kind of games which he had seemingly played with Temple.

By the same token we may guess that Swift adapted for his own use, as occasion arose, many of the techniques which he had seen Temple employing so successfully—adapting not as an admiring disciple would, by osmosis and wholesale imitation, but more consciously and selectively, as a professional craftsman might borrow from a gifted but unreflective amateur. In chapter 1 we have seen that Swift seldom imitated Temple's 'style' in the usual sense of the word, except on occasions when it promised special dividends. Swift was never a thoroughgoing self-publicist after Temple's fashion. His motivations as a writer seem to have been a good deal more various and complex than the aging Temple's need for recognition and praise, which shines so steadily through almost everything which he readied for the press during the last ten years of his life. At the same time Swift's business as a writer was, like Temple's, fundamentally that of persuasion, even when his ultimate goal may have been to betray his persuaded reader to the intricacies of his satire. Here I think a critic might be able to trace in Swift certain useful techniques of Temple's: his mode of modest, sincere, but unshakable assertion, which frees him from the need to produce much evidence and carries him safely through subjects only sketchily understood; his ability to express general ideas in concrete terms, which gives an impression of crispness even when the thinking is fuzzy, and helps to reduce the need for evidence even further; his constant implicit flattery of the reader, through the invocation of shared virtues, shared tastes, powers of perception, and common values, especially against widely unpopular aberrations from the norm; and his imperceptibly shifting frames of reference, aided by digressions, which allow him to assert mutually incompatible ideas within a few pages of each other with every appearance of triumphant logic. Systematic analysis should help clarify the nature and extent of Swift's borrowings here and elsewhere, with one likely exception. Even at his vainest and most self-contradictory, Temple writes with undoubted seriousness and sincerity. He is his own first proselyte. In

Swift we may sometimes wonder if this genuineness of feeling will always find its parallel.

Temple's greatest gift as a writer, the string on which he could best strike the note of secret necessary sympathy in the public, was undoubtedly the sense of personality which he succeeded in projecting in book after book. It invites the reader to trust him, admire him, perhaps even identify with him. "No writer whatever has stamped upon his Style a more lively impression of his own character," Hugh Blair observed nearly a century later. "In reading his works, we seem engaged in conversation with him; we become thoroughly acquainted with him, not merely as an author, but as a man; and contract a friendship for him."[102] Of course Blair had no means of knowing Temple's private character, which provides more contrasts than parallels, but Temple's public personality comes through vividly: practical, good-humored, generally open-minded if often sceptical of theorists and specialists, unpretentiously public-spirited, unaffected and down-to-earth despite his genteel graces, and offhand and unselfconscious enough to report the most flattering things of himself without seeming to boast, indeed without seeming to be fully aware. If Swift instead addressed the world through a multiplicity of voices, projecting personality was equally his stock in trade. It is here most of all that we may expect to find Swift drawing upon Temple to strike just the right note required for each occasion. (At the same time, we should not expect to find an evocation meant to remind readers of Temple, but only an adaptation calculated to affect them more directly, without their being aware.) Recasting the public Temple as a small businessman, for instance, leaves us with a personality not too different from the Drapier's—no genteel graces or elegantly cadenced style, but much the same display of pragmatism, distrust of theory and specialists, and winning unselfconsciousness. I believe that careful analysis should reveal an even greater parallel in that representative of the professional classes, the surgeon and ship's captain Lemuel Gulliver, who takes his degree at Temple's alma mater (Emmanuel College, Cambridge) and ends his career in philosophic if disillusioned retirement in his garden at Redriff ("I here take a final Leave of my Courteous Readers, and return to enjoy my own Speculations in my little Garden at Redriff"[103]). Public-spirited yet down-to-earth, Gulliver may lack the public Temple's cadenced style and aristocratic graces, but he possesses more than enough of his other characteristics to inspire the same kind of affectionate confidence in his readers. It is by tracing the Temple element in him, I believe, that we may someday account for the curious and unsettling humor to which Gulliver's adventures subject us in Book IV.

On occasions when he aimed for a mild absurdity from the start, Swift could create speakers who retain Temple's genteel airs, with only a touch of exaggeration to bring out the latent fatuity. By substance, tone, and phrasing, it is sometimes difficult to distinguish the original from the adaptation. In their different ways, for instance, both Swift and Temple valued good conversation and undertook treatises on the subject. One began by announcing that, "As my Life hath been chiefly spent in consulting the Honour and Welfare of my Country, for more than forty Years past; not without answerable Success, if the World, and my Friends, have not flattered me; so, there is no Point wherein I have so much laboured, as that of improving, and polishing all Parts of Conversation. . . ." The other began a treatise with a similar modest confession: "I can truly say, that of all the Paper I have blotted, which has been a great deal in my time; I have never written any thing for the Publick without the Intention of some Publick Good." Whether he has succeeded or not he will not say, "and others, in what they tell me, may deceive either me or themselves. . . ." Which treatise is Temple's, which Swift's? Only the slightly exaggerated element of boasting (his life *"chiefly* spent" in public-spirited occupations, with the "answerable Success" asserted a little more boldly) allows us to identify the first speaker as Swift's, in this case Simon Wagstaff, Esq., in the Introduction to *Polite Conversation.* (We may also recall that Temple never wrote an exordium for his unfinished essay on conversation, and so could not have praised himself there.) Even with Wagstaff, though, Swift makes sure that his readers will not go off on tangents by recognizing his inspiration. Unlike the public Temple, the great worldly philosopher of retirement, Wagstaff is a London gadfly who has made a career of mixing with the most select people "at Court, at publick visiting Days, or great Men's Levées, and other Places of general Meeting," in order to make himself expert in polite conversation. Swift also makes him a much more violent Whig than Temple and assigns him to a younger generation: Wagstaff recalls the year 1695, when he was only thirty-six, and speaks in stereotypical Whiggish terms of "his late Majesty King William the Third, of ever glorious and immortal Memory, who rescued Three Kingdoms from Popery and Slavery. . . ."[104]

Undoubtedly there are other areas worth exploring as well. What sort of readership did Temple set out to address in his various works? He writes with such easy elegance at times that we assume he speaks to the gentry and aristocracy, but his flirtation with Dunton over the General History of England suggests that he cast a much wider net. Did his readership and projected personality vary at all from book to book, and if so can we find something answerable in Swift? Is there any correlation in Swift between the readership which he addresses and the personality or voice through which he speaks?

Here and in all else it is easy to suggest lines of research and to anticipate conclusions. Making broad conjectures can be exhilarating, but what really matters is the more laborious business of documentation and research. From a writer as unaccountable as Swift we may surely expect surprises along the way. For the moment it is enough to emphasize the likely importance of Swift's Moor Park years, even for works which he composed a quarter-century later. While it is pleasing to imagine 'formative' periods into which we can cram all the literary growth of an author's lifetime, reality is not always so obliging. The *Tale* jokes about the narrow confines of Modern wit, which loses its point by the time it can be published, and we recall that Temple was as much a Modern as anyone under Swift's idiosyncratic definition of the term. Had Temple's popularity dissipated as time went on, it is possible that Swift might have taken less seriously the lessons of Moor Park and developed in somewhat different directions.

As it happened, Temple had genuine staying power. Though not quite so frequently as in the 1690s, his best-known works continued to be reprinted in the decade following his death: the *Memoirs of What Past in Christendom* in late 1699 (dated 1700) and again in 1709 (in two different states), *Miscellanea, The First Part* and *Miscellanea, The Second Part* jointly in 1705, *Observations upon the United Provinces* in the same year, and the *Introduction to the History of England* in 1708. None of the posthumous titles left with Swift ran to a second edition, but without a perceived demand for Temple they would never have appeared at all (or Swift received his copy money). During the same time there were occasional attempts to collect copies of the various volumes and bind them together as Temple's "Works."[105] Demand may have temporarily slackened a little in the decade following 1710, during which no new editions appeared, but Temple's name still had enough appeal to push Boyer's *Memoirs of Temple* (1714), itself largely hackwork, into a second edition within a year of publication. The appearance of the collected *Works* of 1720 marks a stablization of demand which continued through the rest of Swift's lifetime and a generation beyond. Reprints appeared in 1731 (two different issues), in 1740, and with fair regularity thereafter. Had Swift ever doubted or begun to forget Temple's fundamental appeal, the continued demand for his works should have periodically reminded him—and reminded him during some of the most active phases of his career, when he had designs of public persuasion himself. Even in our own century we find Temple's biographer Woodbridge endorsing in his enthusiasm the heroic Temple which Temple took such pains to put before the world.[106] No fool himself, Middleton Murry could praise Temple for the "extraordinary" selfless patriotic integrity which Temple's writings so often celebrated in himself. Thanks to the *Letters* and their orchestrated praise of Temple's skill in negotiating the Triple Alliance, the shrewd American John Adams and his shrewder wife Abigail could hold him up to each other as a model of diplomatic virtuosity. Though Temple's personal antithesis in so many ways, Samuel Johnson could tell a sceptical Boswell that Temple had been one of his chief models in prose.[107]

Swift never had the opportunity to observe Johnson or the Adamses, much less Woodbridge and Murry, but he had seen the force of Temple's persuasion as well as its ultimate source. In a sense, Moor Park seems to have served him as a small working laboratory for human nature, a place for observations and experiments with the written word (his own and Temple's) and its power over those who read it. To this extent we may suspect that his experiences there played their part in making Swift an object of such fascination for his contemporaries and a cause of so much confusion, if not discomfort, to critics in our own time. His force and basic originality of mind he was no doubt born with, but more and more it seems likely that it was his tenure at Temple's house which turned them into such unforeseen and effective channels. Whatever more we can learn about his life there—and there is more to be learned—should help us come to grips a little better with the problems which most concern and puzzle us in Swift.

Notes

CHAPTER 1

1. *Letters Written by Sir W. Temple, Bar*ᵗ *and Other Ministers of State, Both at Home and Abroad. Containing, An Account of the most* Important Transactions *that pass'd in* Christendom *from 1665 to 1672. In Two Volumes. Review'd by Sir W. Temple sometime before his Death: And Published by Jonathan Swift Domestick Chaplain to his Excellency the Earl of Berkeley, one of the Lords Justices of Ireland* (London: for J. Tonson et al., "MDCC"). For the date of publication, about 30 November 1699, see Irvin Ehrenpreis, *Swift: The Man, His Works, and the Age* (Cambridge, Mass.: Harvard University Press, 1962–67), II, 34, and Hale Sturges, "The Publishing Career of Jacob Tonson," Dissertation, Yale University, 1936, s.v. Nov. 1699. A third volume followed in 1703. The 1699 *Letters* are hereafter referred to, in the text, simply by volume and page number within parentheses, e.g. (I, 113).

2. Ehrenpreis, *Swift*, I, 18–21, 25–26, 57–71, but see also George Mayhew, "Swift and the Tripos Tradition," *Philological Quarterly*, 45 (1966), 85–101.

3. In his Preface to the *Letters* (I, sig. A2ᵛ). The preface is reprinted in *The Prose Works of Jonathan Swift*, ed. Herbert Davis et al. (1939–68; largely rpt. Oxford: Blackwell, 1959–68), I, 255–59.

4. [Abel Boyer], *Memoirs of the Life and Negotiations of Sir W. Temple, Bar. . . .* (London: for W. Taylor, 1714), p. 421 (Boyer's emphases). Boyer echoes Swift's words in the *Letters* preface, taking responsibility for "whatever faults there may be in the Translation" (I, sig. A2ᵛ). For Boyer's growing Whiggishness and antipathy to Swift, two and three years before, see Henry L. Snyder, "The Contributions of Abel Boyer as Whig Journalist and Writer of the *Protestant Post-Boy*," in *The Dress of Words: Essays on Restoration and 18th Century Literature in Honor of Richmond P. Bond*, ed. Robert B. White, Jr. (Lawrence, Kas.: University of Kansas Libraries, 1978), pp. 142–45.

5. Irwin, "Swift as Translator of the French of Sir William Temple and His Correspondents," *Studies in English Literature* (Rice), 6 (1966), 496.

6. Ehrenpreis, *Swift*, II, 35–36.

7. E.g., ibid., I, 92–93, III, 114–15, 120–21, 141, 174–75, 257–59, 263; Irwin, *Studies in English Literature* 6: 494–96; cf. John Middleton Murry, *Jonathan Swift: A Critical Biography* (1955; rpt. New York: Farrar Straus, n.d.), pp. 28, 34–38, 51.

8. The transcript is numbered 2255 in the Rothschild Collection and described (with some errors) in *The Rothschild Library: A Catalogue of the Collection*

of Eighteenth-Century Printed Books and Manuscripts Formed by Lord Rothschild (1954; rpt. London: Dawson's, 1969), II, 610. Its history after 1745 until Lord Rothschild's acquisition of it can be found in Sir Harold Williams, *Dean Swift's Library* (Cambridge: Cambridge University Press, 1932), p. 26; in Sir Shane Leslie, *The Script of Jonathan Swift* (Philadelphia: University of Pennsylvania Press, 1935), pp. 9–10 (with some errors) and p. 76; and in Edwin Wolf 2nd, *Rosenbach: A Biography* (Cleveland, Ohio: World, 1960), pp. 294, 394–95, 400. The transcript gives all but one of the letters by Temple printed in 1699, but includes none of the letters *to* him. In 1699 these appeared in a separate section at the end of each volume. Swift said that they were prepared in a separate transcript (I, sig. A3^r); this may be part of the transcript of letters to Temple from 1665 to 1681 described among the Palmerston Papers of the Broadlands Archive now on deposit at the Hampshire Record Office (no. 6 in the box of Sir William Temple's letter books, according to the summary list prepared and sent to me by D. F. Lamb shortly before this book went to press). References to the main transcript (letters *from* Temple) in the Rothschild Collection are hereafter given, in the text, simply by the letter *T* and the page number in parentheses, e.g. (T, p. 61). Except as otherwise noted, they uniformly refer to the transcript page on which the letter in question begins. I am grateful to Lord Rothschild and to the Master and Fellows of Trinity College, Cambridge, for permission to inspect and quote from it and other Swift materials in the Rothschild Collection. I acknowledge with thanks the helpful cooperation of the late Mr. Arthur Halcrow, Sub-Librarian of Trinity during my visits there; of his successor, Mr. Trevor Kaye; and of the Librarian, Dr. Philip Gaskell, who was always ready to answer questions or give assistance, both during and after the time of my visits.

9. *The Correspondence of Jonathan Swift*, ed. Sir Harold Williams [and David Woolley] (1963–65; 'rpt. corr.', Oxford: The Clarendon Press, 1965–72), I, 155. The "first Memoirs" was Temple's *Memoirs of What Past in Christendom* (1691). *Miscellanea, The Second Part* came out in 1690, *An Introduction to the History of England* in late 1694. In 1709 Lady Giffard was complaining that the *Memoirs, Part III*, which Swift brought out that year, differed textually from Temple's autograph draft, then in her possession.

10. *Correspondence*, I, 157.

11. Temple, *Letters*, I, sig. A2^v. By the time that Swift began work on the volume, its contents were badly jumbled chronologically. He had to draw up an index of every item then in the volume, as noted in Appendix A. By counting down the list, he arrived at the numbers he assigned to each letter (all but the six in his own autograph, apparently late additions). Between these numbers, the index, and a few marginal directions in Swift's hand, he or another scribe should have been able to produce a fair copy in the proper order.

12. Gertrude Ann Jacobsen, *William Blathwayt: A Late Seventeenth-Century Administrator* (New Haven: Yale University Press, 1932), p. 69.

13. *Prose Works*, I, 266. Some of Temple's loose copies for part of the period covered in the 1703 volume are preserved in the Longe Bequest at the British Library, in Ad. MSS. 9799 and 9800. Excluding materials written by people other than Temple, there are copies of thirty-seven letters and memos here,

mainly from August 1676 through May 1677. None was printed. Three other lots in the Longe Bequest contain ancillary documents (excluding Temple letters) from the periods 1665–68, 1669–70, and 1674–75 (Ad. MSS. 9796, 9797, and 9798). A fourth lot (Ad. MS. 9801) mainly consists of a seventeenth-century bound volume of letter transcripts, of letters by Temple and his fellow English envoys at Nimeguen—120 letters in all, dated from 12 July 1676 through 5 July 1677. Twelve of the letters eventually appeared in the 1703 *Letters to the King*. This transcript volume looks like a contemporary affair, compiled soon after the date of the letters (much as Downton had done with his own transcript in the period 1670–72). It is in the hand of the unidentified scribe (Scribe C) who copied or recopied portions of the Downton transcript about this time, as described in Appendix A. Ad. MS. 9802 represents a companion volume of Nimeguen documents (differently bound), all copied by a different scribe at Nimeguen itself, according to his signed note of 14 May 1677. The Palmerston Papers of the Broadlands Archive now on deposit at the Hampshire Record Office include several other bound volumes of copies of Temple's letters from Nimeguen (nos. 1–3, 5, and 7 in the box of Temple's letter books, according to the summary list), as well as a volume of copies of the despatches received by Temple and the other English negotiators there (no. 4). I have not had the opportunity to inspect these materials, but a note reported in one volume (no. 7) suggests that most of the letters there were eventually printed, presumably in Temple's *Letters to the King* (1703), his authorized sequel to the 1699 *Letters*.

14. Temple to the Marquis of Castel-Rodrigo, 3 April 1670 (II, 173; T, p. 338), and Temple to a Mr. Cary or Carew, 6 Dec. 1669 (II, 129; T, p. 253). The Cary copy is in the hand of William Blathwayt, Temple's other chief secretary at the Hague. The Osborn Collection's two other letters of the period are not among the ones chosen for publication in 1699. All are in Box 98, no. 19. I am grateful to the late James M. Osborn and to the present curator, Stephen R. Parks, for permission to inspect and quote from the Collection's Temple materials.

15. Irwin, *Studies in English Literature* 6: 492.

16. Ehrenpreis, *Swift*, II, 36.

17. Of the thirty French letters from Temple, I have collated fourteen in full against the transcript text, three more in part, and briefly checked the first few lines of the remainder. I exclude the French letters and memos written by people other than Temple. Except for two—the States General to Charles II, 18 February 1668 (I, 207–8; T, p. 159), and De Witt to Lord Arlington, 14 February 1668 (I, 209–11; T, p. 156)—these letters had not been copied into the Downton transcript.

18. He suggests that, in the printed French, Temple was expressing his bitterness at Charles II in the phrase "changer la face de son conseil," with a double-entendre on "son conseil," over Temple's withdrawal from the expanded Privy Council which he had helped to originate (Irwin, *Studies in English Literature* 6: 495). Irwin cannot mean that Temple was bitter at the time of writing, in 1672, which was six or seven years before Temple even joined the Council. If Temple were bitter at Charles in 1672, it was for overthrowing the Dutch alliance and making common cause with France. Since it turns out that

Temple had the phrase cast into its printed form only after Swift had translated it literally, in the 1690s, it may still be possible that Temple intended an additional, bitter allusion in the phrase. What matters, though, is that in his translation Swift was emphatically not trying to hide the allusion and so protect Temple from himself, as Irwin alleges. Swift was merely translating earlier copy word for word.

19. François, duc de La Rochefoucauld, *Oeuvres Complètes*, ed. L. Martin-Chauffier, rev. Jean Marchand (Paris: Gallimard, 1964), maxims 149 (p. 423) and 389 (p. 454). I am grateful to Professor Grace A. Savage, of the Bryn Mawr College French department, for reading the sections of this study which deal with Temple's French, and for offering comments and suggestions. It was she who first alerted me to the archaic element which contributes to Temple's idiosyncratic French usage.

20. A good example of contemporary French usage on this point comes in the French translation of Temple's *Observations upon the United Provinces*. The translator does his best to follow Temple's sometimes tortuous English syntax, but when Temple indulges in elaborate compound-verb constructions, the translator commonly adds a pronoun (personal or relative) or even begins a fresh sentence. Compare the original and translated versions of Temple on the Dutch council of state:

The Council of state executes the Resolutions of the States-General; *consults and proposes* to them the most expedient ways of raising Troops . . . *Superintends* the Milice, the Fortifications, the Contributions out of Enemies Countrey. . . .	Le Conseil d'Etat execute les resolutions des Etats Generaux: *il leur propose & donne advis* touchant les moyens les plus faciles de faire des levées de troupes. . . . *Ce sont les Surintendans de* la Milice, des fortifications, & des contributions, que le Païs ennemy paye.
Observations upon the United Provinces of the Netherlands, 2nd ed. corrected (London: for Sam. Gellibrand, 1673), p. 118 (my emphases).	*Remarques sur l'Etat des Provinces Unies des Pays-Bas* (The Hague: for J. & D. Steuker, 1692), p. 113 (my emphases).

21. Irwin, *Studies in English Literature* 6: 486.

22. Temple, *Miscellanea, The Second Part*, 4th ed. (London: for Richard and Ralph Simpson, 1696), pp. 61–62 (in the essay *Upon Ancient and Modern Learning*). For the date of composition, see Homer E. Woodbridge, *Sir William Temple: The Man and His Works* (New York: Modern Language Association, 1940), p. 242.

23. With the Bishop of Munster in 1665, Temple probably used Latin most of the time. The printed letters to the bishop are in Latin, and writing to his father, Temple remarks that the bishop "speaks the only good Latin that I have yet met with in Germany" (1, 5). To the Spaniards in Flanders, he occasionally writes in Spanish, but more often in French.

24. Homer E. Woodbridge, for instance, points out that Temple probably timed the publication of his *Memoirs of What Past in Christendom* (1691) to help the

sagging popularity of William of Orange, whom the book portrayed in winning terms, and that a similar purpose probably lay behind Temple's *Introduction to the History of England* (late 1694), with its long and generally glowing treatment of an earlier King William (Woodbridge, *Temple*, pp. 246–47, 259–61).

25. This is precisely the view of Temple offered by his admiring modern biographer, Woodbridge. His Temple is something of a white knight with no discernible flaws beyond a propensity to occasional moodiness and the offshoots of a frank and trusting nature (i.e., a tendency to be easily deceived by people, especially highly-placed figures like the Bishop of Munster, Lord Arlington, and Charles II, when they encouraged or made much of him). Though otherwise a solid and responsible study, the biography is untrustworthy on this count, if only for its crusading air. Woodbridge sets out to debunk an earlier orthodoxy —a largely negative interpretation of Temple stemming from Thackeray and Macaulay, who emphasized Temple's flaws while discounting his amiable side (Woodbridge, *Temple*, pp. ix–xi, 238; cf. pp. 120, 205–6, 233). Woodbridge also quotes uncritically from Temple's published accounts of himself—including the letters which Temple had so carefully chosen, edited, revised, and otherwise prepared for public consumption—as if they were documents of unimpeachable historical fact and thus above suspicion. As we shall see, some of them are not.

26. Temple, *Miscellanea, The Second Part*, 4th ed., p. 148 and passim. It was a copy of this edition, published jointly with *Miscellanea, The First Part*, 5th ed., which Temple gave to Swift in 1697, after Swift had left his own copy behind in Ireland (*Correspondence*, 1, 30).

27. Temple, *Miscellanea, The Second Part*, p. 287.

28. Ibid., p. 301.

29. Boyer, *Memoirs of Temple*, p. 418 (Boyer's emphases).

30. Ibid. (Boyer's emphases). As Queen Anne approached death in 1714, the Whigs rallied enthusiastically behind the Hanoverian succession, which would return them to power. Boyer means to appropriate Temple for the Whigs, and to capitalize on his popular anti-French policies and personal connections with George I's spiritual predecessor, William of Orange. Noting the *"unhappy Divisions"* in 1714, Boyer "consider'd, that the fiercest *Popular Contentions* have often been compos'd by the Interposition of a single Person, who by the Dignity of his Appearance, and sober Arguments, asswag'd the Rage of the *unthinking Multitude* [generally Tory in 1714], and brought them back to their Senses." Accordingly, "Sir William Temple appears to me to be the most *proper, unexceptionable,* and *impartial Judge* in the present *Controversy*" (Ibid., pp. v, vi). For an illustration of Temple's healthy self-esteem (in this case sexual), see Woodbridge, *Temple*, p. 190. A less reliable but equally amusing anecdote occurs in a piece of Gulliveriana sometimes attributed to Swift's friend Arbuthnot, and is quoted in T. P. Courtenay, *Memoirs of the Life, Works, and Correspondence of Sir William Temple, Bart.* (London: Longmans, 1836), II, 231 & n. It is possible that Swift reminisced about Temple among his close Scriblerian friends, years after he left Moor Park; cf. Sir Henry Craik, *The Life of Jonathan Swift* (London: Murray, 1882), pp. 24–25. From another Scriblerian source, at any rate, Philip Pinkus has identified an apparent parody of Temple occurring in *The Memoirs*

of Martinus Scriblerus, in which Arbuthnot, Pope, and Swift all had a hand. See Pinkus, "Swift and the Ancients-Moderns Controversy," *University of Toronto Quarterly,* 29 (1959), 51–52.

31. Text established by George Mayhew in "Jonathan Swift's 'On the burning of Whitehall in 1697' Re-examined," *Harvard Library Bulletin,* 19 (1971), 404 n. 7; first printed in Sir Walter Scott, ed., *The Works of Jonathan Swift, D.D.* (Edinburgh: Constable, 1814), I, 43. Compare Swift's rejected draft fragment for the preface to the 1699 Temple *Letters (The Rothschild Library,* no. 2254; printed in *Prose Works,* I, xix). Not only do the *Letters* teach "the true Interest of our Nation both at home and abroad" and "those of the Neighbors we are most concerned in," writes Swift, but they also teach "the Principles, Dispositions, and Abilityes most requisite or necessary to fitt and enable any Gentleman for the Service of His Country." The model patriot, of course, is Temple as he appears in the letters. Because of the dangers of crossing to Ireland, Swift is "more unwilling to venture those Papers than my self; because if the Publication should fayl with me, I am convinced it would be a very generall Loss." For more on Swift's eulogy of Temple and prefaces to Temple's posthumous works, see chapter 3.

32. *A Tale of a Tub,* ed. A. C. Guthkelch and D. Nichol Smith, 2nd ed. (Oxford: The Clarendon Press, 1958), p. 50: "He may ring the Changes as far as it will go, and vary his Phrase till he has talk'd round," Swift notes, "but the Reader quickly finds, it is all *Pork,* with a little variety of Sawce." The editors date the Preface to 1697, little more than a year before the eulogy (p. xlv).

33. Woodbridge, *Temple,* pp. 335–36.

34. As early as 1690, Temple reported that Swift "read to mee" and "writ for mee," as part of his household duties (*Correspondence,* I, I). For an example of the first stage of correction, before Swift's time, see Thomas Downton's copy of the first letter to "the Spanish Ambassador" (T, p. 330; II, 85–91). As Temple's secretary when the letter was written, Downton was uniquely qualified to understand its background (and presumably the hand in which his copy-text was written), but in one especially muddy passage he leaves a long blank for Temple to fill in: "Pourceque V.E. demande pourquoy Mons.ʳ Mareschal ayant dit qu'il n'y auroit point de difficulté a ratifier et conclurre le Concert. Il s'en trouve [Temple: a present.] Je Vous diray. . . ." The printed text shows further revision, including the grammatically necessary step of reuniting the three fragmentary clauses into a sentence (II, 89). For an example of Swift entering Temple's revisions, see Temple's letter to De Witt of 27 May 1668 (T, p. 171; I, 392–97), which in one section of the original transcript (again Downton's hand) reads "sans aigrir l'affaire ny sembler de faire difficultez sur les ratifications de la guarantie au moins jusques a voir les difficultez plus grandes qu'elles ne se semblent . . ." (cf. the printed form, I, 395, beginning "au lieu d'aigrir le different . . ."). Swift's hand is recognizable in altering "l'affaire" to "cette matiere" and "jusques a voir les difficultez" to "de les voir." Someone using a different nib and contrasting ink has stricken the incorrect "se" from "se semblent."

35. The three twice-copied letters are Temple's to the States General "at

first Audience," n.d. [Dec. 1667] (T, pp. 87, 106; 1, 201–2); to the same "At my Audience of Leave," n.d. [Feb. 1668] (T, pp. 88, 158; 1, 203–6); and to De Witt, 3 July 1668 (T, pp. 175 [incomplete], 186; 1, 398–401). Possibly there were others: the transcript shows occasional insertion of material by tipping in leaves or half-leaves, and considerable cutting out of leaves (at least twenty-four, by my count), both before and after someone paginated the transcript (in Temple's time, because Swift's index refers to the same page numbers). Downton originally entered copy in four sections (early English letters, early foreign, later English, later foreign), each separated by blank leaves. On these the later copies were entered. There are still a number of blank leaves remaining in the transcript.

36. Keith Feiling, *British Foreign Policy, 1660–72* (1930; rpt. London: Frank Cass, 1968), pp. 256–63.

37. E.g., his letters to the Grand Duke of Tuscany's secretary (25 February 1715), to Vanessa (12 May 1719), and to the translator of Gulliver's *Travels* (July 1727), in *Correspondence*, II, 156–57, II, 324–26, and III, 225–27, respectively.

38. See Williams, *Swift's Library*, pp. 64–68, and the sale catalogue reprinted there.

39. For the prayer book, see the 1745 library sale catalogue (Ibid., no. 426) and his 1715 library list, in T. P. Le Fanu, "Catalogue of Dean Swift's Library in 1715, with an Inventory of his Personal Property in 1742," *Proceedings of the Royal Irish Academy*, 37 (1927), 273; for the dictionary, sale catalogue no. 220 and Le Fanu, p. 271; for the Shelton translation of *Don Quixote* (London, 1652), Williams, *Swift's Library*, p. 80, and Le Fanu, p. 271; and for the Stevens translation of the same (London, 1700), sale catalogue no. 476.

40. The Osborn Collection at Yale preserves (in her own autograph) a copy of one of Lady Giffard's Spanish translations (Osborn Gift 70.1.5). It is for the letter sent her by Temple, writing under the name of Gabriel Possello on 30 March 1667 (T, p. 184; 1, 84–86). The letter was printed without the translation. According to Lady Giffard's MS. note, Possello was "an old Archer in ye King of Spains Guards who taught her Spanish" at Brussels. As a witty joke, Temple writes her an extravagant Hispanic love letter in Possello's name. Since such brotherly high jinks can easily be misconstrued, it was probably just as well that the letter appeared without the translation.

41. This was for Lady Giffard's translation of some of the verse occurring in Jorge de Montemayor's sixteenth-century romance, *La Diana*, principally the long verse plaint "Cancion de la Ninfa" in Part I, Book II ("Ionto a una verde ribera . . ."). Parts of Lady Giffard's autograph transcript, with the heading "From Diana de Montemayor" in Swift's hand, survive in the Sir Harold Williams bequest, University Library, Cambridge (stored in Box 3 in 1970). As in the Downton transcript of Temple's letters, Swift has entered corrections here and there in the text, suggesting that Lady Giffard had him read the text aloud and enter her corrections. A fair copy by Swift, entitled "The Parting of Sireno and Diana," is now in the Rothschild Collection (*The Rothschild Library*, no. 2251), as is an (earlier?) transcript of the unimproved text, in an unidentified scribal hand (no. 1006). For a representative stanza, both thematically and stylistically, see p. 17 of Swift's fair copy:

But wretched I, who since Thou 'go'st
Know not what will become of Me,
Nor what will become of Thee,
Nor after if Thou ever do'st
Think how oft here Thou didst Me see,
Nor if I was not then deceiv'd,
When first my Pain I did discover
(As I thought) to so true a Lover,
But that which sure may be believ'd,
Is, that my Griefs will ne'er blow over.

Miss Julia Longe reproduces another page, facing p. 218 in her biography, *Martha Lady Giffard: Her Life and Correspondence (1664–1722)* (London: George Allen, 1911). Helping Lady Giffard with such work must have been a rewarding experience for "the secretary," as Lady Giffard referred to him in a letter (Ibid., p. 216). For Swift's depiction of Lady Giffard grieving over Temple's illness, after Temple's recovery from it, see *The Poems of Jonathan Swift*, ed. Sir Harold Williams, 2nd ed. (Oxford: The Clarendon Press, 1958), I, 52–53: "You that would grief describe, come here and trace/ It's watery footsteps in Dorinda's face," &c.

42. According to his admiring sister, in her *Life* of Temple, published in Temple, *Early Essays*, p. 5; cf. Woodbridge, *Temple*, pp. 10–11. On the other hand, Temple received rigorous schooling before reaching Cambridge, according to Lady Giffard.

43. *Correspondence*, I, 2.

44. Ibid., II, 157, my emendation of "Dominautè," a nonsense word which appears to be a typographical error.

45. By 1694 he was teaching Princess Anne's son, the Duke of Gloucester. See *Dictionary of National Biography* and Asa E. Phillips's fragmentary amateur monograph, *Monsieur Boyer: A French Huguenot Who Became an English Man of Letters* (Washington, D.C.: Leet Bros., 1935), pp. 18–19. Phillips works from new but unspecified MS. sources.

46. Woodbridge, *Temple*, pp. 213–14. After Temple's son died in 1689, the widow seems to have lived with her mother in London (Ibid., p. 219; Longe, *Lady Giffard*, pp. 151–52). When the widow herself died in 1710, Swift supposed it to be "much to the outward grief and inward joy of the family"; see his *Journal to Stella*, ed. Sir Harold Williams (1948; rpt. Oxford: The Clarendon Press, 1963), I, 69 & n. She may also have been something of a spendthrift, with expensive tastes in wine and clothing, to judge by an account drawn up by Temple's London agent in 1699 (Osborn Collection, Yale University, fb 182, fol. 64^r). In the weeks following Temple's death that year, there seems to have been trouble over the continuance of a pension claimed by Mrs. Temple since her mother-in-law's death in 1694. Apparently Mrs. Temple was claiming that Lady Giffard had reneged on a promise for the pension benefits, as Anthony Henley secretly reported to Lady Giffard in the unpublished postscript of his letter of 16 February 1698/99 in the Rothschild Collection, MS. no. 1009 (ii).

47. Abel Boyer, *The Royal Dictionary, In Two Parts. First, French and Eng-

lish. Secondly, English and French . . . (London: for R. Clavel et al., 1699), sig.
A2ᵛ-A3ʳ; Temple, *An Introduction to the History of England* (London: Richard and
Ralph Simpson, dated 1695 but publ. autumn 1694), sig. A3ʳ (my italics). Boyer's
dictionary was listed in the Easter 1699 Term Catalogues; Temple had died in
late January. On Boyer's connections with Lady Giffard in 1714, see chapter 3.
For Swift's explanation of the wit and sublimity to be understood in italicized
words or thoughts, see *A Tale of a Tub*, pp. 46–47.

Parts of Boyer's preface to the *Royal Dictionary* read like the archetypal
Modern effusions which Swift satirized in the *Tale* (especially in its own Preface) although the likenesses have apparently not been noticed before. Even
without Boyer's likely links to Moor Park, they are striking enough in themselves to bear mentioning. Boyer speaks confidently of the "proper means to
convey the Wonders of the Reign [of William III] down to the Admiration of
Posterity," which good King William will no doubt afford writers once he turns
to cultivating peacetime activities. At least of dictionaries, Boyer maintains that
"the *Last* are generally the *Best*, as adding all the Wealth of others to their own
Store" (sig. A3ʳ). It is Boyer's opening paragraph, however, which strikes the
most clearly Swiftian note (sig. Al ʳ):

> The Age we live in, is so Learned and Refin'd, and at the same time,
> the Conveniency of Printing has been, of late, such an Encouragement to
> a Multitude of Impertinent Scriblers, that any Author who ventures to
> write on a Subject that has been already blown upon, stands condemned
> *ipso facto*, and must expect to be Exploded, unless by satisfactory Reasons,
> he can justifie the boldness of his Attempt to the judicious *Criticks*, in
> whose power alone it is to reverse the fatal Decree. This consideration
> makes a *Preface* the most necessary part of a Modern Composition; and the
> Reader ought to be so just to the Author, as not to leave his Plea Unperus'd.

48. Boyer, *The Royal Dictionary*, sig. A3ʳ. On the identification of the "Mr.
Savage" who preached at Farnham in early 1699 and was in Italy about 1711, see
chapter 3. In one instance the *D.N.B.* article on John Savage seems to be in error.
It claims that Savage travelled abroad for seven years after leaving Cambridge
(Temple's old college, Emmanuel) in 1698, when he received his M.A. This
would put Savage abroad during the period when the *D.N.B.* itself shows him
publishing furiously in London, and at home when Swift heard reports of him
in Italy. Probably the article should read that Savage travelled abroad after
leaving Oxford, not Cambridge: Savage took his B.D. and D.D. at Oxford in
1707. The *D.N.B.* does not indicate what living, if any, Savage occupied between
1698 and 1701, when Lord Salisbury gave him one in Hertfordshire. His connections with Boyer went back at least to 1695, before he took holy orders. Boyer
wrote some Latin congratulatory verses to Savage as "Candidus" which were
printed in Savage's first book, *Brutes Turn'd Criticks, Or Mankind Moraliz'd by
Beasts*, a translation from the Italian of Carlo Moscheni (London: for Daniel
Dring, 1695), sig. a7ʳ. In the publisher's entry in the Term Catalogues for 1695,
Savage is described as being "of the Middle Temple" in London: see Edward

Arber, *The Term Catalogues, 1668–1709* (London: for Arber, 1903–6), II, 560. Some of Savage's letters were later published in Boyer's and his miscellaneous compendium, *Letters of Wit, Politicks, and Morality*, with Boyer and Savage the chief translators of the foreign letters (London: for J. Hartley et al., 1701). Two of Savage's letters (pp. 264–65, 269–70) show that he was writing from "Mayfield" (probably Mayfield, Sussex, south of Tunbridge Wells) in July 1696. The second letter is to Boyer. In his response (p. 271) Boyer thanks Savage for helping with the dictionary and indicates that, just as Boyer is striving "to improve my self in your Language," so is Savage trying to improve his French. (Besides Savage's "Collections" of words, Boyer acknowledges "the Hints you give me in your Letters, which I will improve into several good Paragraphs, in the Preface to my Dictionary." Could some of the typically Modern statements there, as quoted in the preceding note, have reflected Savage's point of view as well as Boyer's?) Had he been consulted, in short, Savage had the connections and qualifications for giving Temple professional advice about what to do with his French letters.

49. Both transcript and translation make the construction a conditional clause ("Car . . ."; "For . . .") instead of an independent one, and they agree more closely in "aucune chose"/ "one thing" (as against the printed text's "rien") and in "chagrin ou chaleur"/ "Heat or Discontent" (as against "chagrin" alone).

50. See Lady Giffard's letters to her niece, 1697–98, printed in Longe, *Lady Giffard*, pp. 198, 202, 208. In 1693 Swift commemorated an earlier bout in his Walleresque poem, *Occasioned by Sir W—— T——'s Late Illness and Recovery* (*Poems*, I, 51–55).

51. Woodbridge (*Temple*, pp. 147–48) notes that it was "Temple's sole composition [published in] this period which did not have to do with 'public thoughts'," and remarks on the "doubtful taste" of publishing it. But probably Temple either recast the letter for public consumption, or composed it as such in the first place. The title-page of the *Miscellanea* advertises it as "Upon the Excesses of Grief," as if it were an essay, and Woodbridge notes that it "restates the usual arguments persuasively, and in stately and graceful prose" (Ibid.).

52. The transcript reveals that "Mon^r ——" was De Wicquefort (T, p. 342). Like the De Witt letter, it contains many passages in which Swift's translation departs from the transcript text. The other two letters of condolence are to the Earl of Northumberland (II, 204–6) and to the Grand Duke of Tuscany (II, 207–9), on the death of their fathers, but here Temple mixes his usual sympathetic observations with congratulations on the new dignities to which the men succeed. In a later letter to Lord Arlington (II, 221–22), Temple also holds forth condolingly on the death of Madame, Charles II's sister and Louis XIV's sister-in-law, in terms probably intended for the King's eyes as well as his minister's.

53. Woodbridge, *Temple*, pp. 112–37.

54. Compare the printed text, I, 350, beginning "tout le monde voit que la France n'attendra que le moment . . ." with the earlier transcript version (T, p. 168): "tout le monde voit que la ffrance n'attendra que de Nous voir brouillés avec quelq'un de Nos Voisins ou de nous voire de mesme ou de voir entrer entre nous deux Nations la moindre mesintelligence pour venir a bout de tout le reste de ce pais icy en quinze jours du temps."

55. Interestingly enough, the other letter which exhibits several passages in which Swift's translation follows the printed French rather than the transcript's, is Temple's second full-blown letter of condolence, to "Mon^r ——" [De Wicquefort] on the death of his daughter:

. . . so that, to pretend to comfort you by other Considerations than those which your Prudence and above all which your Piety would suggest, would be to attempt an unprofitable Work. . . . (II, 270–71)	Ainsi pretendre vous consoler par d'autres reflexions que celles que votre prudence, & sur tout votre pieté vous suggereront, ce seroit tenter une chose inutile. (II, 271)

The transcript French stands closer to the translation only in the first phrase ("desorte que" rather than "Ainsi," for "so that"). It lacks the final phrases about consolation being "une chose inutile" (somewhat freely, "an unprofitable Work"), and qualifies the fruits of piety and prudence with an idea absent in both the translation and the printed French: ". . . desorte qu'on ne peut pas pretendre de Vous consoler par autres raisons que celles que V^{re} pieté et prudence Vous fourniront *au delà de ce que Je pourrois faire*" (T, p. 342, my emphasis).

56. It was just as well that the phrase never reached print, either in French or English, because the negotiations at Aix were to give Temple good reason for doubting Spain's conduct. The Spanish envoy held up matters for days by pretending to have no proper power to sign the treaty. Infuriated, Temple wrote the Spanish viceroy in Brussels to protest Spain's conduct (I, 362–63).

57. It also provides additional evidence that the author of the final revisions was neither Swift nor Temple, who (as will be seen) are the only likely candidates for the intermediate set of revisions.

58. The intermediate text which Swift translated seems to have survived unchanged in the printed *Letters:* "de representer, que la restitution de Bourgogne dans l'etat ou il est á present, est une offre peu convenable aux promesses du Roy tres Chretien" (I, 396–97).

59. Louis also returned part of his Flemish conquests as well, in a gesture of apparent magnanimity largely dictated by his secret treaty with the Austrian Emperor for the eventual partition of the Spanish dominions. See David Ogg, *England in the Reign of Charles II,* 2nd ed. (1956; rpt. Oxford: Oxford University Press, 1972), pp. 334–35; and Feiling, *British Foreign Policy, 1660–72,* p. 240. For the highly complex background to the Alternative and the Treaty of Aix (though indistinctly treated for the Alternative itself), see Feiling, pp. 239–40, 242–43, 254–58, 260, 263–66, 276–79, 283. The settlement was not a lasting one: in the following January (1669) Temple reports Austrian fears that France will seize the Franche-Comté again (II, 58–59); note that he uses the term "French County" [Franche-Comté] interchangeably with "Burgundy" (I, 328).

60. Ehrenpreis, *Swift,* I, 250, 171; but cf. *Correspondence,* I, 26 n. 1. Swift writes to the Rev. John Winder, his successor in his Irish cure of Kilroot (which Swift resigned in January 1698), and professes his good will towards Winder, whom he had wished as his successor. In suspiciously melodramatic fashion, Swift professes a lofty fatalism about his own fortune ("as late in my Life as it is, I

must een lett it drive on its old Course"), reports that "10 days before my resignation, My Ld Sunderland fell and I with Him"—and then continues with dark hints about "other Courses" which he is now engaged in, "which if they succeed, I shall be proud to own the Methods, or if otherwise, very much ashamed" (Ibid., p. 26). Because of the letter's context—partly a show of lofty benevolence, partly an ambivalent defense against charges of improvidence in resigning Kilroot (Ibid., p. 25), partly an attempt to dazzle a relatively unsophisticated country parson—it is dangerous to read too much into Swift's words or quote them out of context.

61. *Correspondence*, I, 156 & n. 3. With Temple preparing a text showing so little friendship towards Sunderland, it is questionable how much Temple's recommendation would have weighed with him at the time, although Sunderland later wrote in the most obliging terms to Lady Giffard upon Temple's death.

62. Woodbridge, *Temple*, pp. 26, 133–34; Gilbert Burnet, Bishop of Sarum, *History of His Own Time* (London: for Thos. Ward, 1724, 1734), I, 378. For Swift's comments on Burnet, see chapter 3. In the parliamentary elections of 1679, when Temple ran for the Cambridge University seat, he encountered opposition from Peter Gunning, Bishop of Ely, because of the *Observations;* see Temple, *Memoirs, Part III* (London: for Benj. Tooke, 1709), p. 66.

63. Burnet, *History of His Own Time*, I, 378.

64. "Je vous remercie en meme tems de la grace que vous m'avez faite par vôtre dernier lettre, qui me fût rendue il y a quelque tems . . ." (II, 314).

65. See Swift's prefaces to the *Letters*, I, sig. A3ᵛ, and to Temple's *Memoirs, Part III*, pp. x–xiii. The story of the first memoirs' destruction reflects very poorly on Temple's sagacity and judgment of men. Swift dwells on it at length in the later preface but is careful to maintain an air of innocence. Citing Temple's second memoirs, the *Memoirs of What Past in Christendom*, Swift quotes a passage indicating that the first memoirs had been full of praise for Arlington and then paraphrases other passages in which Temple blames Arlington for being one of those who "broke the Triple League; advis'd the Dutch War and French Alliance; and in short, was at the bottom of all those Ruinous Measures which the Court of England was then taking. . . ." Accordingly, Swift hesitantly concludes, "as I have been told from a good Hand, and as it seems very probable," Temple could not have thought Arlington "a Person fit to be celebrated for his Part in forwarding that famous League . . . who had made such Counterpaces to destroy it." In chapter 3 we shall have occasion to return to this and other prefaces which Swift wrote for Temple's posthumous works. In other respects as well they are curious in their show of loyalty to Temple and their damaging if seemingly inadvertent admissions about him.

66. Feiling, *British Foreign Policy, 1660–1672*, p. 153.

67. Mainly these are official despatches to Lord Arlington preserved in the appropriate volumes at the Public Record Office (St. Pap. For., Flanders, vols. 33–38, and St. Pap. For., Holland, vols. 185–86). With the publication of documents to be found in the public archives, admittedly, heavy textual tampering would have incurred greater risks of exposure than with letters to private

correspondents. (Of the seven suspicious letters which Swift and Stella last copied into the Downton transcript, as we shall see, none was an official despatch and four were addressed to Temple's immediate kin.) Two unauthorized volumes of Temple's official despatches were in fact published about the time of the *Letters*, one shortly before, in 1699, and the other in 1701. Both were ostensibly published from the "Originals" in Temple's hand and either taken from Lord Arlington's papers or, as Swift later suggested, taken out of the public records. See his preface to Temple's authorized *Letters to the King* (1703), reprinted in *Prose Works*, 1, 266. Inconsequential collections in themselves, though accurate enough to judge from a few collations I made at the Public Record Office, the volumes are *Letters Written By Sir William Temple, During His being Ambassador at the Hague, To the Earl of Arlington and Sir John Trevor . . .*, ed. D. Jones (London: by and for A. Baldwin, 1699), and *Select Letters, To the Prince of Orange (now King of England,) King Charles the II.^{d} and the Earl of Arlington . . .*, 'Vol. III' (London: for Tho. Bennet, 1701).

68. P.R.O. St. Pap. For., Holland, vol. 185, ff. 84–85 (26 July 1669). More moderate revisions of a similar character can be found in Temple's letter to Arlington dated 13 October 1665, the original at the P.R.O., St. Pap. For., Flanders, vol. 33, ff. 297–98, and the revised text in Temple's *Letters*, 1, 8–12. Temple's alterations do much to temper the original tone of burning enthusiasm for the Bishop of Munster, then impatiently awaiting an overdue subsidy from Charles II which would allow him to invade Holland. Although he had not yet met that great warrior-bishop, Temple adopts the Bishop's cause as his own and reports the pain he feels in "finding so brave a person so desperately engaged upon an encouragement, wch by one accident or other has so unhappily failed. . . ." In his revisions, with the wisdom of hindsight, Temple removes the anguished phrase, rewrites his final paragraph to sound calmer and more dispassionate, and elsewhere inserts a new paragraph not in the original, to add some balance by telling Arlington that he had patiently explained Charles II's financial and political difficulties to the bishop's fretful envoy at Brussels. In the printed version, as a result, Temple sounds less like a wild-eyed enthusiast than a sensible diplomat, weighing the options as best he can and recommending implementation of the subsidy already agreed upon. As with the later letter to Arlington these changes were made before Swift's time, in this instance as early as 1677–79, the likeliest date for the work of the scribe in whose hand the revised text appears in the Downton transcript (T, pp. 3–5, Scribe C; see Appendix A).

69. See Lady Giffard's *Life* of Temple, published in *The Early Essays and Romances of Sir William Temple Bt.*, ed. G. C. Moore Smith (Oxford: The Clarendon Press, 1930), p. 15. For Temple's commercial and maritime negotiations in 1669, see Feiling, *British Foreign Policy, 1660–1672*, pp. 285–89.

70. E.g. Sir George Clark, *The Later Stuarts, 1660–1714*, 2nd ed. (1956; rpt. 1965: Oxford, The Clarendon Press), p. 75: "Very soon after the formation of the Triple Alliance, Temple began to notice an unfriendly tenacity in the way in which Arlington insisted on the ever-recurring commercial disputes with the Dutch. . . ." From reading Temple's unpublished despatches at the P.R.O., I received the impression that he instead took part in these commercial disputes

with a certain amount of enthusiasm. Even the careful historian Herbert H. Rowen, in his massive biography of Jan de Witt, can quote Temple's self-edited letters as if they were undoubted historical documents. Nevertheless, Rowen has access to so many other letters, from more authentic sources, that his argument is affected very little beyond the question of Temple's foresight and sagacity. In his *John de Witt, Grand Pensionary of Holland, 1625–1672* (Princeton: Princeton University Press, 1978) see for example pp. 713–14 and 724, where he paraphrases or quotes from two other suspicious letters in which Temple demonstrates his early suspicions about English intentions over the Triple Alliance. The second letter (Temple to Sir Orlando Bridgeman, 24 April 1669) belongs to a group of seven letters which, as we shall see, Temple seems to have heavily revised or perhaps even composed originally during the late 1690s. The other letter (Temple to his father, 22 July 1668) is suspicious both because of its contents (Temple's prescience asserted at so early a date) and because of its addressee. A good half of the letters which Temple is known to have tampered with are addressed to his brother or father (safe persons in such a case), and these are the letters on which the *Letters* collection chiefly depends for periodic summation and narrative shape. In the light of Lady Giffard's testimony of 1690, I feel little hesitation in assigning the published text of the July 1668 letter to the "dubious" category, although it survives in the Downton transcript (T, pp. 187ff.) in the hand of a scribe working as early as 1677–79 (Scribe C; see Appendix A).

Indeed, far from being one of the first to suspect what was going on at Court, Temple may have been one of the last: in *Temple,* p. 113, Woodbridge plausibly dates the first part of Temple's memoirs to the period 1671–74, when Temple should have known better than to celebrate Arlington so extensively. To judge from a reference in the second part of Temple's memoirs, the *Memoirs of What Past in Christendom,* the first memoirs were still in existence when Temple wrote the second part (eventually published in late 1691, with a prefatory letter by Temple dated 1683).

71. See further, A. C. Elias, "Stella's Writing Master," *Scriblerian,* 9, no. 2 (1977), 134–39.

72. Draft in Box 3, Williams Bequest, Cambridge University Library (Add. MS. 7788). Its date is suggested by the paper which Temple used. It is identical to the paper which Swift used in copying Temple's "Hints" for an attack on William Wotton in 1697 (described in chapter 3). The size is the same (about 5 3/4″ by 7 3/8″ as folded for use), and so is the watermark (a large scrolled shield containing a fleur-de-lys, surmounted by a crown with plain headband, in a design variation not present in Heawood though not too far from nos. 1655, Rochester, 1698; 1657, English, ca. 1682; 1662, London, 1678–80; and 1652, n.p., ca. 1703) and in some of Swift's and Sir John Temple's receipts and expenditure lists in the Moor Park estate papers (Osborn Collection, Yale University, fb 182, fols. 25–27, 29–32, *15, *16, mainly drawn up in Feb. 1698/9).

73. B.M. Ad. MS. 29300 (B). The document also contains some later readings from the Downton transcript text which are entered in what appears to be a third hand, not at all recent, which adds a note identifying the letter as one

which "Dean Swift" copied onto p. 144 of "the Transcript." So it is. In other words, this third hand belonged to someone who had access to both the Downton transcript and the loose draft, some time after Swift became Dean of Saint Patrick's. Possibly this was Lord Chesterfield, who seems to have purchased the Downton transcript at the auction of Swift's library in 1745 (Williams, *Swift's Library*, p. 26). I have not yet had the opportunity to compare the extra autograph to examples of Chesterfield's hand. Whatever the case, the note about "the Transcript" suggests that the two documents were once under the same roof, and perhaps that Swift originally slipped the draft into the transcript volume for safekeeping.

74. For dating portions of the *Tale,* see *A Tale of a Tub,* pp. xlii–xlvii and (for the possibility of work before 1695) pp. xxxiv–xxxvi.

75. *Prose Works,* 1, 266.

76. See Ehrenpreis, *Swift,* II, 340; *Correspondence,* I, 154–55 n. 3; and *Prose Works,* I, 268.

77. *Correspondence,* I, 155–56.

78. She authorized an advertisement accusing him of printing the *Memoirs* from an unfaithful copy. She had retained an uncorrected transcript in Temple's autograph (now in the British Library, Add. MS. 9804), and having literary pretensions herself, no doubt fancied herself suited to serve as Temple's literary executrix. She had considered publishing the *Memoirs* herself, despite Swift's prior claims as Temple's literary executor. (After sending her MS. out to advisers, she decided against it because the text reflected poorly on a friend's late husband.) There is a definite sting in Swift's observation that "since I was not wholly illiterate, I cannot imagine whom else he could leave the Care of his Writings to." For more on the subject, see Woodbridge, *Temple,* pp. 327–28, and below, chapter 3. As for the *Memoirs* text itself, the printed version differs from Lady Giffard's copy in about 55 places (most of them being already underlined in the MS., in pencil). The figure roughly confirms Swift's offhand estimate ("I believe it may in a hundred"–*Correspondence,* I, 156). All the variations seem minor, usually in phrasing alone. In two places (ff. 9^r & 21^v) Temple enters brief notes in the margin; elsewhere he alters phrasing in the text. Like the Downton transcript, the MS. is a working draft, not a finished one. As Williams remarks, Lady Giffard's insinuation that Swift garbled the text "will not bear examination" (Ibid., n. 2).

79. Irwin, *Studies in English Literature* 6: 494–95. We have already noted Swift's literal translation of the passage which he is supposed to have altered in translation to shield Temple from himself.

80. Ehrenpreis, *Swift,* I, 120, 263, 172.

81. Irwin, *Studies in English Literature* 6: 489.

82. On I, 20, for instance, the translation's "For, to speak in your own word, *The World is as round as a* ———, " seems to reflect a text intermediate between the Downton text's "car *Roond is de Werld as een* ———" (without any representation of 'speaking in your own word'), and the printed text, "car (selon votre phrase Allemande) *Roond is de Werld. . . .*" The parenthesis "(according to your Custom)," a page later, may also represent an element present in the intermedi-

ate version. Neither the Downton nor the printed text says anything about Wreden's custom.

83. If "half a dozen" in fact represents "une demi douzaine de," Swift may have suggested the reading in French. At least he knew it well enough to use it himself, in one of his own later letters in French (*Correspondence*, II, 157).

84. Ehrenpreis, *Swift*, II, 36. Taking his cue from Ehrenpreis's description, Clive T. Probyn finds the same qualities in Swift's verse imitation of Scarron (published under the title "The Power of Time"). If Probyn's conclusions are justified, the poem illustrates how far Swift had deviated at Moor Park from his natural manner of translation. See Probyn, " 'The Power of Time': Swift as Translator," *Notes and Queries*, 214 (1969), 337. Even so, his actual evidence suggests that Swift in fact meant to write an *imitation* (inventing new details to fit a modern British context) rather than a straight translation.

85. Temple misquotes slightly, from the *Aeneid*, XI, 425–26: "Multa dies variique labor mutabilis aevi/ Rettulit in melius. . . ." The aptness comes in the phrase "Labor mutabilis Aevi," the 'work of a changeable time', which reflects on Charles II's unpredictable public courses, while the show of optimism in "Detulit in melius" further removes any stigma of anger or bitterness.

86. Temple, *Early Essays*, p. 6 & n. 23. Lady Giffard then deleted the final phrase about suiting "niser people." As for Temple's natural manner, she was probably unaware that in the early essays he imitated Montaigne's.

87. In muting or reversing the tone of Temple's original French, the printed French revisions at least partly provide the elegance and dignity for which Temple strove in his English letters. By the 1690s his desire for a dignified public image may have begun to take precedence over his wish to demonstrate facility in a wide range of styles, suited to the varying characters of his correspondents. The Downton transcript shows that, in English, his standard tone was well established in the late 1660s, and his underlying sense of his own dignity had probably grown rather than dwindled by the time Swift worked for him three decades later. In 1668 Temple was a hopeful young diplomat on his second major assignment abroad, but by the 1690s, with age and gout growing on him, he was living in somewhat ostentatious retirement from public affairs while readying a string of publications meant to demonstrate not only his wisdom in the ways of the world but his virtue in retiring from it. On occasion Temple is capable of tightening his prose enough to provide vigor rather than the usual gentlemanly grace, but the best examples date from Temple's younger days. In them Ehrenpreis finds some similarities to Swift's characteristic style (Ehrenpreis, *Swift*, I, 176, 179–82), but of his three examples of Temple sounding somewhat Swiftian, all were composed fifteen or more years before Swift met Temple. Two of the three passages Swift never had to work with during his years as Temple's secretary (the passage from the essay-letter to the Countess of Essex [Ibid., 181], written in 1674 and published in 1679; the passage from one of the early essays of the 1650s [Ibid., 176], a piece of juvenilia which Temple decided not to publish and which appeared only in 1930).

88. Ibid., p. 179.

89. E.g., Irwin, *Studies in English Literature* 6: 484–85; 486, 489; and 490–93, respectively.

90. See for example the opening paragraphs in the Digression concerning Critics in *A Tale of a Tub* (p. 92) and in his lesser-known but highly characteristic libel, *A Short Character of his Excellency Thomas Earl of Wharton* (*Prose Works*, III, 177).

91. Ehrenpreis, *Swift*, II, 655.

92. Irwin, *Studies in English Literature* 6: 496.

93. For Swift's general epistolary practice, see Oliver W. Ferguson, " 'Nature and Friendship': The Personal Letters of Jonathan Swift," in *The Familiar Letter in the Eighteenth Century*, ed. Howard Anderson et al. (1966; rpt. Lawrence, Kas.: University of Kansas Press, 1968), pp. 14–33. For the Stella letters in particular, see Ehrenpreis, *Swift*, II, 655–57; Frederik N. Smith, "Dramatic Elements in Swift's *Journal to Stella*," *Eighteenth-Century Studies* 1 (1968), 332–52; and A. C. Elias, "Jonathan Swift and Letter-Writing," Dissertation, Yale University, 1973, pp. 46–55.

94. *Correspondence*, III, 417.

95. Ehrenpreis, *Swift*, I, 92.

96. Ibid., I, 168. The letter (*Correspondence*, I, 18–23) is dated 29 Apr. 1696, and elsewhere exhibits a bewildering array of styles and tones, ranging from high romantic cliché to tough colloquialism (in an odd digression about a fistfight between two of Swift's brother professionals, a beggar and a vagabond poet, with reflections suggesting that Swift speaks as a poet himself, that the vagabond poet might ask for Jane's hand, and that she might accept him if he had money enough to give her a separate maintenance).

97. *Correspondence*, I, 14 n. 2, 16; Louis A. Landa, *Swift and the Church of Ireland* (1954; rpt. corr., Oxford: The Clarendon Press, 1965), pp. 3–4. Deane Swift was the father of the better known Deane Swift, Jonathan's later biographer, who first printed the letter. Although Ehrenpreis later mentions the requirement for ordination (*Swift*, I, 150), he interprets Swift's request for the chaplaincy as a mark of Swift's naiveté in foreign affairs and ignorance of "the delays which ordination itself might require" (I, 148). Landa does not mention Swift's request, but it fits with his argument. As early as 1692 Swift showed himself aware of the requirement (Landa, pp. 4–5; *Correspondence*, I, 12). But if Swift only needed to "*certify* that he had a living in readiness," as Landa says, he would not thereby bind himself to accept it, especially if something better came along—as it well might for someone already in orders. A chaplaincy in Lisbon was not much of a plum, and offered few chances of advancement. The well-to-do stepbrother, Swift's cousin Willoughby, was already well disposed to Jonathan: the younger Deane Swift reported that (like Willoughby's father Godwin before him) Willoughby helped support Jonathan financially from 1688 until Swift received his Irish living later in 1694, and John Lyon confirms the view (Deane Swift, *An Essay upon the Life, Writings, and Character, of Dr. Jonathan Swift* [London: for C. Bathurst, 1755], pp. 49–51, 53–55; cf. the Rev. John Lyon, MS. interlineation in Lyon's copy of John Hawkesworth, *The Life of the Revd. Jonathan Swift, D.D.*

[London, printed; rpt. Dublin: 1755], Forster Collection no. 579 [48.D.39], Victoria & Albert Museum, pp. 27–28).

98. The 1694 letter is the only one to survive, although if the elder Deane Swift had kept any others of the sort, his own son would surely have published them. The only other sign of direct correspondence comes nearly two decades later, in Swift's offhand remark to Stella that he has been writing "Cozn Dean in answer to one of his of 4 months old, that I spied by chance routing among my Papers" (28 March 1712, in *Journal to Stella*, II, 526).

99. *Correspondence*, I, 14–15.

100. Swift briefly strikes the same note in the letter to Jane Waring, the Ulster spinster, in a passage which seems calculated to impress. He is alluding to his imminent return to Temple in England. "In short, Madam," he announces, "I am once more offered the advantage to have the same acquaintance with greatness that I formerly enjoyed"—and, he adds, "with better prospect of interest" (Ibid., p. 21). As in most of Swift's references to Temple, the comment sheds more light on Swift's sense of readership and epistolary purpose than it does on his private feelings about Temple and the return to Moor Park, whatever those feelings were.

101. The tone of condescension is somewhat buttressed by Swift's recurrent association of young Deane with reminders of gain and loss, usefulness, and trade generally: "very glad to find you will *spare time from Business*" long enough to write out of friendship, "one of the *idlest* [or least profitable] things in the World"; "to see You *sally out of your Road*, and take Notice of Curiosityes"; "desire You to *set by* some *idle* minutes for a *Commerce*" which "*cannot fail of being useful.*"

102. *Correspondence*, I, 16.

103. Ehrenpreis, *Swift*, I, 126, 141, 263.

CHAPTER 2

1. *Correspondence*, III, 103, 117–18.

2. Elias, "Swift and Letter-Writing," pp. 218–23, 234–47, and passim. There is a complicating factor in Swift's intended readership for the letters themselves —not only Pope personally, but Swift's circle of English friends (pp. 124–36), and at least in later years the public itself (pp. 188–94).

3. Ehrenpreis also suggests that paternal protectiveness may have played a part: since Temple's own son had committed suicide after leaving home, he reasons, Temple might therefore have wished to keep Swift safe at Moor Park without a career (Ehrenpreis, *Swift*, I, 148).

4. Landa, *Swift and the Church of Ireland*, pp. 6–7; *Correspondence*, I, 16–18. This is Swift's famous "penitential" letter to Temple, so termed by Temple's nephew John Temple in an endorsement he later entered on it ("Dr Swifts humble Petition to Sr Wm T. in a Penitential Letter dated Oct. 6. 1694."). See the A.L.s. at Harvard University, fMS Eng. 870 (28a).

5. *Correspondence*, I, 16. For the "great Numbers [of Temple's loose letters] yet lying among his Papers," see Swift's preface to Vol. III of the Temple *Letters*

(1703), reprinted in *Prose Works*, I, 266. For the greeting "May it please Your Majesty," see Temple's letter to Charles II in the 1699 *Letters* (I, 176; T, p. 86) and the several scattered through the 1703 volume, together with those to the Prince of Orange ("May it please Your Highness"). A mere Grand Duke rated only a *"Monsieur,"* or "Sir," (1699 *Letters*, II, 207, 262). For other examples of standard practice, see R. G. Howarth, ed., *Letters and the Second Diary of Samuel Pepys* (London: Dent, 1933), pp. 78, 84, 90 ("May it please your Royall Highness"— Pepys to the Duke of York); p. 184 ("May it please your Honour"—a grovelling letter from Pepys's clerk begging reinstatement, after an unsuccessful earlier letter beginning only "Honourable Sir," p. 181); and p. 57 (the same—a begging letter from a young scapegrace who was indebted to Pepys in various ways and who had fled from other creditors to the Continent). For Swift's joking letter to the Duchess of Queensberry (part of a joint letter to Gay and her), see *Correspondence*, III, 422 & n. Swift's joke is double-edged: not only does the Duchess enjoy royal honors when Swift receives her at the bottom of the stairs, she enjoys a royal condescension as well. When Louis XIV, the great Sun King, received Mary of Modena at the foot of the state stairs, instead of making her climb them first, everyone considered it "an exceptional honor." See Henri and Barbara van der Zee, *William and Mary* (New York: Knopf, 1973), p. 88. For the physical appearance of the "penitential" letter to Temple, see the A.L.s. at the Houghton Library, Harvard University, fMS Eng. 870 (28a). For an example of leaving a large blank space between salutation and text in letters addressed to royalty, see the dedicatory letters "To the Queen" in vols. II and III of Clarendon's *History of the Rebellion and Civil Wars in England* in the first two folio eds. (Oxford: At the Theatre, 1704 and 1707). (This is also the case with the dedicatory letter to Princess Anne in the finely bound MS. copy, apparently the presentation copy, of James Gibbs's *The First Fifteen Psalms of David Translated into English Verse*, 1701, listed as item 340 in Paul Grinke's catalogue 13, London, 1977.) Besides beginning the letter's text at the bottom of the first page, Swift completes it at the top of the third but leaves another long blank space before affixing his signature, with an appearance of exaggerated humility, in the extreme right-hand bottom corner of the page.

    6. See Joseph Foster, *Alumni Oxonienses*, early series (1891; rpt. Liechtenstein: Kraus, 1968), s.v. Swift.

    7. *Correspondence*, I, 12.

    8. For information from the appropriate Subscription Book of the diocese of Winchester, of which Surrey then formed a part, I am grateful to Andrea M. Bassett, Assistant Archivist of the Hampshire Record Office, Winchester. She reports that the records there contain no surviving Bishops Register, Acts Books or other diocesan material for the period in question. Parish registers for Farnham (PSH/FA/1/1), Puttenham (PSH/PUT/1/1[a & b]), and East Clandon (PSH/CL/E/1/1 and the churchwardens' book, PSH/CL/E/7/1) are now in the Guildford Muniment Room of the Surrey Record Office. I am indebted to Mr. J. K. Bridcut of Farnham for making initial inquiries for me there when I could not travel to England myself. Even more I am indebted to Mrs. Shirley F. Corke of the Guildford Muniment Room for providing numerous photocopies and

valuable guidance, not only in the records under her charge but in the often perplexing matter of the autographs represented in them (as well as the practices represented by them). To her care and vigilance I owe many of my findings and the identifications on which they are based, for the accuracy of which, however, I take final responsibility myself.

9. Owen Manning and William Bray, *The History and Antiquities of the County of Surrey* (London: for J. White, by J. Nichols & Son, 1804–14), ii, 22.

10. *Valor Beneficiorum: Or, A Valuation of all Ecclesiastical Preferments in England and Wales* (London: M. Gillyflower et al., 1695), pp. 398 ("A Grant for a Presentation, for the first Turn and next Avoidance"), 400–401 ("A Grant of the next Avoidance of a Parsonage").

11. For John Geree's relationship with Simon Geree (of whose history before 1692 I have so far found no trace), see Alfred Ridley Bax, "The Plundered Ministers of Surrey," *Surrey Archaeological Collections,* 9 (1888), 240 n. 1, which cites Letters of Administration granted on 15 October 1695 to John Geree of Farnham, uncle and next-of-kin and guardian assigned to the three sons of "Simon Geree, late of Puttenham, in Surrey, Clerk." It is John Geree's hand which makes the burial entry for Simon in the Puttenham parish register ("Mr Simon Geree Rector buried Dec: 20 [1694]"). For John Geree's tenure at Farnham (1669–1707/8) and at East Clandon (1674/5–1707/8), see Manning & Bray, *History and Antiquities of Surrey,* iii, 166 and 50. He was in turn the father of the better known John Geree, later Rector of Letcombe Bassett, Berks., with whom Swift spent part of the summer of 1714. The identification of the senior John Geree helps to explain Swift's and Stella's later acquaintance with the son and his two sisters (*Journal to Stella,* ii, 533 & n., 586, 612 & n.) and the Gerees' supposed connection with Moor Park or the vicinity (*Correspondence,* ii, 18 n.).

12. For John Geree's age, see Joseph Foster, *London Marriage Licenses, 1521–1869* (London: Quaritch, 1887), p. 540: in May 1670 Geree was forty-one, which made him an exact contemporary of Temple's. For the death of Simon Geree's predecessor at Puttenham, Henry Bedell (or Beedell), see Manning & Bray, *History and Antiquities of Surrey,* ii, 22.

13. In their note on Thomas Swift, Manning & Bray repeat a tradition that Thomas owed his appointment to Temple's interest with Lord Somers. Almost certainly this points back to William Wotton's *Defense* of his *Reflections upon Ancient and Modern Learning* (printed in the 3rd ed. of the *Reflections,* 1705, and now reprinted in *A Tale of a Tub,* p. 327). Wotton repeats a rumor that Thomas Swift had written the *Tale,* which was dedicated to Lord Somers. Somers's supposed role in sending Thomas to Puttenham seems calculated to lend credence to the claim of authorship, but Wotton disbelieves it and mentions it only for some extra deprecation of the *Tale:* "The World besides will think it odd, that a Man [Thomas Swift] should in a Dedication play upon that Great Man, to whom he is more obliged than to any other Man now living, for it was at Sir William Temple's Request, that my Lord Sommers, then Lord-Keeper of the Great-Seal of England, gave Mr. [Thomas] Swift a very good Benefice in one of the most Delicious Parts of one of the Pleasantest Counties of England." Thanks to Robert Martin Adams in "Jonathan Swift,

Thomas Swift, and the Authorship of *A Tale of a Tub,*" *Modern Philology* 64 (1967), 198–232, Thomas Swift's claims of authorship in the *Tale* are again well known. With its praise of Puttenham's deliciousness, Wotton's account sounds as if it also originated ultimately with Thomas himself (compare Thomas's later praises of Puttenham, printed by Adams, p. 231). But Thomas, as we shall see, was an enthusiast and exaggerator whose literary ambitions and rather flexible sense of ethics leave him a sometimes unreliable witness. While his grant for Puttenham must have passed through Somers's hands, I doubt that Somers was the man with whom Temple had used his interest. (Officially, the benefice was indeed in the Lord Keeper's gift—see the questionnaire which Thomas answered in 1705, reprinted by Adams, pp. 230–31.) Temple had no contacts with Somers that I know of, and indeed Somers was only just beginning to emerge from obscurity by the time Temple had decided to retire from London and from public life. Likelier candidates were his old friends Henry Sidney (soon to be Earl of Romney; at first secretary of state and then after March 1692 lord lieutenant of Ireland) and Sir John Trevor (chief commissioner of the great seal from 1690 until Somers succeeded as lord keeper in March 1692/3, and speaker of the House of Commons), and his cousin and former patron Thomas Osborne, Earl of Danby (president of the council; Duke of Leeds after May 1694).

14. For the patrons of Geree's livings, see Manning & Bray, *History and Antiquities of Surrey*, III, 50 and 166. For his probable kinship with Stephen Geree, Rector of Abinger and onetime preacher at Wonersh and Guildford in Surrey, or with Stephen's brother John, the puritan preacher and controversialist in London, see Bax in *Surrey Archaeological Collections*, 9, 240 & n., and cf. pp. 267–8, 278, 280 & n.; H. E. Malden, "Rectors and Vicars of Surrey Parishes," in ibid., 27 (1914), 93; "Abinger Registers," in ibid., 30 (1917), 106; *Dictionary of National Biography*; and Anthony à Wood, *Athenae Oxonienses*, 3rd ed., ed. Philip Bliss (London: for Rivington et al., 1813–20), III, 244–47 & 428. If the John Geree who received the vicarage of Farnham at age 40 in 1669 is the same as the "John Geree of Abinger in ye Countie of Surrey Gent." reported as having landed from Calais with one Stephen Geree of London, silkman, in April 1657, he must surely have been a son or nephew of the Abinger Stephen Geree. See Bax, "Suspected Persons in Surrey during the Commonwealth," *Surrey Archaeological Collections*, 14 (1899), 185. (The London preacher John Geree, who died poor in 1648/9, left children for whom his brethren in London had to take up a collection, according to Wood: their likeliest destination thereafter would have been the rectory of their beneficed uncle at Abinger.) This link is strengthened by the names current among the Farnham-Puttenham Gerees a generation later, which echo the original John and Stephen: besides his brother and nephew, both John Gerees, Simon Geree had sons named Simon, John, and Stephen. Nor were they the only Gerees in the neighborhood. One of the churchwardens at John Geree's church of East Clandon was a Thomas Geree, grocer, whose son John was buried there on 14 May 1698; the father signs the churchwardens' accounts on 14 April 1696. Given the reproductive capacities of most clerical families, there were probably more Gerees around Guildford, Abinger, and Southwark, where

the widow of the Stephen Geree, silkman, who landed from Calais in 1657 seems to have been living in 1685.

15. William Dingley received a £100 legacy under the codicil to Temple's will (the same amount left to Swift, the only other special legatee named there), and was almost certainly the "Cousen Dingley" who had a place in one of the chariots in Temple's funeral procession in Westminster, on 30 or 31 January 1698/9. The legacy is the more striking because, in his will, Temple leaves nothing at all to any of his friends or distant kin. See Courtenay, *Memoirs of Temple*, II, 486, and Sir John Temple's executor's papers, fb 182, fol. 65^r, Osborn Collection, Yale University.

16. For the university backgrounds of Gerees, Dingleys, and Temples, see Foster, *Alumni Oxonienses*, and John & J. A. Venn, *Alumni Cantabrigienses*, early series (Cambridge: Cambridge University Press, 1922–27). In addition to Temple's cousin Dingley, his nephew Jack Temple (son of the younger Sir John, a Christ Church man) was also to be enrolled at Corpus Christi four years later, in 1695, though he apparently never took a degree. By contrast, Temple and Geree seem to have had nothing to do with Thomas Swift's choice of Oxford college, Balliol, which was the alma mater both of Thomas's late father and of his uncle Charles Davenant (at whose house we find Thomas in December 1694).

17. In the East Clandon parish registers, the entries for the years 1690–1708 (1682–1708 for burials) were made in a separate section of paper sheets, later bound in, apparently to enable them to be carried to Farnham when necessary. Probably Geree arranged this to facilitate the drawing up of affidavits in Farnham, especially those for burials in woollen cloth as mandated by the Act of 1678: see W. E. Tate, *The Parish Chest: A Study of the Records of Parish Administration in England* (Cambridge: Cambridge University Press, 1946), pp. 66–68. Because Geree could have made some entries in Farnham, the appearance of his autograph in the register does not necessarily guarantee his presence in East Clandon or the absence of a curate for whose residence at East Clandon there is other evidence. (The other autographs in the paper register, mainly after 1694, represent an irregular succession of curates and between times seemingly the parish clerk.) The churchwardens' book gives a more reliable guide to presence or absence at East Clandon, because there was an election and other business to be witnessed and certified at the Easter meeting each year. In the 1690s Geree was present to sign every other year, on the average, with curates and churchwardens (or churchwardens alone) the rest of the time.

18. For the annual value of Puttenham in Thomas's time, I have found no certain figures. Mrs. Corke has located an undated assessment made under "a late Act of Parliament, entitled An Act for granting a subsidy to his Majesty for supply of his extraordinary occasions," which lists Henry Bedell for the rectory paying £3 on annual rents of £60 (Guildford Muniment Room, ref. 51/5/67). Bedell was rector between 1636 and 1692, and because the list occurs in a book of notes dating mainly from the 1650s and 1660s, it may refer to one of the Royal Aids granted in 1664/5 and in 1666 for the expenses of the Dutch War. Whatever the benefice's rents, Thomas seemed to draw upon them at face value, without impropriations on the one hand or augmentations on the other as he

reported in 1705 (see Adams, *Modern Philology* 64: 230–31). The 1695 *Valor Benefici-orum* omits Puttenham, and John Ecton's *Liber Valorum & Decimarum* (London: by W. B. for Is. Harrison, 1711), p. 345, lists only the figures as given in the Queen's Books, i.e., the official rents as assessed in 1535, when Puttenham had only a moderate value compared to the surrounding parishes (£11 17s. 11d., compared to a low of £6 7s. 6d. and a high of £29 5s. 5d., which happened to be the vicarage of Farnham).

19. In the autobiographical fragment he wrote a good thirty years later, Jonathan made the curious claim that he had refused Temple's offer of an Irish government job worth £120 a year (perhaps twice as much as the value of Puttenham) so that he could take holy orders on his own in Ireland without "scruple of entring into the Church meerly for support . . ." (*Prose Works*, v, 194). Contemporary evidence suggests otherwise. When he reported his prospects a month after quitting Moor Park in 1694, he was curiously silent about Temple's supposed offer (which in any case seems to echo the choice of career options open to Thomas some months before). Writing his man-of-the-world letter to his young cousin Deane Swift in Portugal, Jonathan insists impressively upon his unconcern and independence, which a spurned job offer would have made even more impressive. Instead he speaks only in general terms which almost certainly refer to Temple's longstanding hints about ecclesiastical preferment in England: Temple "would not oblige Himself any further than upon my good Behaviour, nor would promise any thing *firmly* to Me at all . . ." (*Correspondence*, ii, 16, my emphasis). If Temple had said anything at all about an Irish government job, we may guess it was so pitifully vague and hedged around with qualifications that Jonathan could not think of producing it even for cousin Deane.

20. Unless there was something uncanonical in Thomas's ordination, it took place in Winchester on 4 March, the day before he received his curate's license and signed the Subscription Book there. A bishop ordained candidates only on the Sundays immediately following the four Ember Weeks each year (canon 31), and 4 March was the only such Sunday that year occurring in the period between Thomas's grant of presentation, without which he could not be ordained, and his curate's license, for which he could not qualify unless he were ordained.

Entering the Church of England was of course far preferable to entering the sister Church of Ireland, as Jonathan would soon be reduced to doing. Among other things the English church offered greater opportunities for advancement both in its own and in the Irish church's jurisdiction, as attested by the fairly steady flow of English clerics exported to Irish deaneries and bishoprics.

21. *Correspondence*, i, 13–14.

22. Edward Arber, *The Term Catalogues, 1668–1709* (London: for the author, 1903–6), ii, 522 (announced for Michaelmas Term); *Miscellaneous Letters, Giving an Account of the Works of the Learned, Both at Home and Abroad*, i, no. 4 (7 Nov. 1694), 59–62. Ironically, the previous two issues of *Miscellaneous Letters* (24 and 31 Oct.) had featured a long and glowing account of William Wotton's *Reflections Upon*

Ancient and Modern Learning (London: by J. Leake for Peter Buck, 1694), which had deflated many of Temple's wilder assertions in the essay *Upon Ancient and Modern Learning.*

23. For Temple's surprising admiration of Dunton's Athenian Society and *Athenian Mercury*—an early version of Ann Landers and *Information, Please*— see chapter 3. Political sympathies probably played some part in Temple's admiration: Dunton was an aggressively Williamite Whig, and the *Introduction* itself Woodbridge considers an apologia of sorts for William of Orange, praised through an implied parallel with William the Conqueror (*Temple*, pp. 259–60). For Temple's ideas for a composite history of England, see *An Introduction to the History of England*, sig. A2^v–A3^r.

For Temple's letter to Dunton through Thomas Swift, see the Osborn Collection, Box 67, no. 18. Dunton had already engaged a man to do the history (whether to write it directly, or to assemble it from earlier histories) and also asked Temple to revise or oversee his work. This part Temple declined. Much of Thomas's letter giving Temple's answer to Dunton has been printed in Courtenay, *Memoirs of Temple*, II, 221–23, though with some inaccuracies.

24. *The London Gazette*, no. 3025 (5/8 Nov. 1694), advert. (transcript supplied me through the kindness of Hugh Amory, Houghton Library, Harvard University); *The Athenian Mercury* [alternatively entitled *The Athenian Gazette: Or Casuistical Mercury Resolving all the most Nice and Curious Questions*], 15, no. 21 (Tues. 13 Nov. 1694), advert. Cf. *The Present State of Europe: Or, The Historical and Political Monthly Mercury*, 5, no. 11 (Nov. 1694, licensed 1 Dec.), advert. on obverse of t-p.

25. [Henry Rhodes, John Dunton, John Salusbury, and John Harris], *Proposals For Printing A General History of England From the Flood . . . down to the Reign of Their Present Majesties King William and Queen Mary . . .*, broadside, [London, 21 Nov. 1694], quoted from the seemingly unique copy at Harvard (shelf mark *pEB7.R3464.694p) by permission of the Houghton Library, Harvard University. For the date of publication, see Stephen R. Parks, *John Dunton and the English Book Trade* (New York: Garland, 1976), p. 302 (Dunton bibliography no. 235), and the *Athenian Mercury*, 15, no. 23 (20 Nov. 1694), advert.: "The *Proposals . . .* may be had to morrow morning of John Dunton. . . ." A reprint of the *Proposals* (which I have used in supplying a damaged line in the Harvard copy) appeared at the end of the index to vol. 5 of *The Present State of Europe*, following the December 1694 issue (licensed 3 Jan. 1694/95), sig. 3N3^v–3N4^v. Dunton's fellow undertakers Rhodes and Harris were then the publishers of this journal. Among the three substantive changes is an added line. Before vouching for the industry of "the Learned Gentleman" who will write or assemble the history, the reprint adds that "By this time we doubt not but the Reader is satisfied as to the *Goodness of our Materials*" (original emphasis). This seems to echo Temple's praise of his own idea for a history: a full and just body of history would result from his scheme, says Temple in his preface to the *Introduction*, "for the Architect is only wanting, and not the Materials for such a Building" (*Introduction to the History of England*, sig. A3^r).

26. Tyrrell to Locke, 18 October 1694, printed in J. W. Gough, "James Tyrrell, Whig Historian and Friend of John Locke," *The Historical Journal*, 19,

no. 3 (1976), 602. Writing ten years later, in his *Life and Errors* (1705), Dunton claimed that it was "at the instance of Sir William Temple" that he and his partners put Tyrrell upon writing his *General History of England.* See Dunton, *The Life and Errors of John Dunton, Citizen of London,* ed. John Bowyer Nichols (Westminster: for Nichols et al., 1818), p. 178. Unless Temple had proposed Tyrrell as the editor for a composite history—and proposed him in a later letter than that of 9 November, which does not mention him—this claim appears highly suspect, as we shall see from Temple's angry response to the Dunton-Tyrrell project which took shape.

27. See for instance Temple's account of the origins of the Scots, in *An Introduction to the History of England,* esp. pp. 22–24. Not a great deal, Temple implies, "can be gathered out of the Dust or Rubbish of such barbarous Times and Writings," and accordingly his account proceeds on the basis of native conjecture and some use of unspecified sources. If "their [the Scots'] Authors" are mentioned at all, it is chiefly to note their inability to reach agreement amongst themselves, or as with "Buchanan, or any other Author that I know of," both to deplore their failure to hazard ultimate conjectures on the question, and to deplore their lack of "Authority" for the more modest assertions that they make about the Scots' coming over from Ireland, whatever their ultimate origins (pp. 28–29).

28. Other evidence of a sudden change in plan comes from further disparities within the *Proposals* themselves, and from disparities between the *Proposals* and the first advertisement issued after their publication, apparently prepared beforehand, and only partially altered to fit the new circumstances. In the "Additional Proposals" section of the *Proposals,* Dunton indicates that the first part of Tyrrell's history, containing the period up to William the Conqueror, will be ready "within Six Months from January next ensuing"—i.e., ready about July 1695. The contrasting section which follows in the *Proposals,* apparently retained or imperfectly adapted from the original plan, gives the target date as May ("Within Six Months"), with the rest of the history to follow "with all possible Expedition." The *Proposals* appeared about 21 November, and the first advertisement thereafter ("Proposals more at large are to be had of the Undertakers . . .") comes with the November *Present State of Europe* (5, no. 11), licensed on 1 December. There the undertakers say nothing about the early portion to 1066, but announce that the entire history should be ready "about next Michaelmas Term"—i.e., between September and November 1695. But if the sketchiest parts of English history, up to 1066, will busy Tyrrell until July, it is clearly impossible that the great bulk of the work, from 1066 to the present, could follow within three months or so. Clearly Tyrrell will be working on a much larger scale than the *Present State of Europe* timetable suggests—though not so large as in fact transpired. (It was not until 1704 that Tyrrell's third and last folio volume appeared, and with it Tyrrell had only carried his history as far as Henry III.) In fact, the *Present State of Europe* advertisement has not even registered the change in the kind of history proposed. It says nothing at all about Tyrrell, but instead announces that the history will be "Pursuant to the Model laid down by Sir William Temple," the same phrase used in Dunton's advertise-

ments in the 13 November *Athenian Mercury* and the 8 November *London Gazette*. There is also a disparity in the number of sheets proposed and the price to subscribers—good evidence of a genuine change in plans, rather than mere fraudulent advertising. The *Proposals* themselves indicate that the entire history "will Contain, as near as we can Judge, about *Four Hundred Sheets,*" printed in the same type used in the "Additional Proposals" section, while the *Present State of Europe* advertisement, presumably reflecting the earlier plan, speaks of "about 300 Sheets." In the *Proposals* the price is 40 shillings per book in quires, with 15 shillings prepaid and 25 upon delivery; in the advertisement, 30 shillings per book, with 15 down and 15 upon delivery. For the first time, the *Proposals* also reveal a fourth undertaker, Rhodes, who is not mentioned in the 1 December *Present State of Europe* advertisement or in the three earlier *London Gazette* and *Athenian Mercury* advertisements, all of which list only Dunton, Salusbury, and Harris. Along with Harris, Rhodes was then the publisher of *The Present State of Europe,* and presumably joined the project this way. Probably the new and expanded format of the history required a fourth publisher to help underwrite the heavier printing costs.

In this analysis I am assuming that the lone Harvard copy of the *Proposals* represents the first state, announced as ready for publication on the next day by the 20 November *Athenian Mercury*. It is also conceivable that the Harvard copy represents a second and revised state, and that an earlier version—lacking the "Additional Proposals" section announcing Tyrrell, mentioning only three undertakers, and listing 300 sheets at 30 shillings—is the one referred to in the 20 November *Athenian Mercury* and 1 December *Present State of Europe* advertisements. In other words, it is possible that Dunton's original published *Proposals* in late November were for a history of the sort that Temple wanted, and that, due to some unexpected upset (probably copyright arrangements, as Thomas Swift was to claim), Dunton had to turn hurriedly to Tyrrell and then work up the revised *Proposals* for publication. This would have taken place between early December, when the *Present State of Europe* advertisement appeared, and some time in January, when the same journal reprinted the revised proposals together with its index for the past year's issues. Either way, the result would have been much the same. Dunton had used Temple's name to promote a composite history but then, without warning, had hurriedly had to substitute the very different Tyrrell project.

29. Temple, *Introduction to the History of England,* sig. A2^r–A4^r. Temple's sense of the historian's calling is reflected in the peroration of his preface, in which he calls for "some abler Hand" to continue the noble and patriotic work begun in the *Introduction*. "I have hereby beaten through all the rough and dark Ways of this Journey," he notes; "the rest lies fair and easie through a plain and open Country. . . ." In other words, because the earliest periods of English history are the sketchiest and the most obscure, they present the most onerous task for the historian. Forming conjectures from the few surviving records of Edward the Confessor's time, for instance, would thus be more of a task than dealing with the mountains of documents illustrating Henry VIII's. Temple seems to equate the difficulty of hitting upon sound conclusions (on which he

congratulates himself here) with the burden of investigating all the evidence on which such conclusions, by rights, ought to rest. Unlike Tyrrell and other historians of the day, Temple seems to have engaged in no investigation whatsoever of primary historical sources, further than he found them included in the standard histories which he consulted in writing the *Introduction*. For the probable identity of these, see Woodbridge, *Temple,* pp. 257–58.

30. For Dunton's sale of his share in 1696 or 1697, see Parks, *John Dunton and the English Book Trade,* p. 315 (Dunton bibliography no. 268). As for exposure in the *Athenian Mercury,* I have checked each number from 19 May 1694 (vol. 14, no. 1) through 4 February 1695/96 (vol. 19, no. 29), in the nearly complete American Philosophical Society copy. Except for a brief revival in May–June 1697, the journal ceased publication with the issue of 8 February 1695/96.

31. I am not sure why, of the seven booksellers who joined in the 1695 composite history project, Temple chose to contact the relatively obscure Bentley. (In 1697, Dunton wrote in his *Life and Errors,* p. 550, Bentley's "principal business is binding . . . He is a very honest man, but has met with misfortunes in the world, by thinking some others as honest as himself . . . .") The list of undertakers is headed by Richard Chiswell, a much more prominent publisher, whom Temple himself had recently used to bring out his *Memoirs of What Past in Christendom* (1691). On the other hand, to spare Temple the imputation of having published his own private memoirs, the *Memoirs* had masqueraded as an unauthorized publication. Temple may accordingly have shied away from a publisher whom he should have pretended not to know. Bentley was part of the history consortium because, with Jacob Tonson, he held the copyright for one of the histories to be used—Camden's *History of the Most Renowned and Victorious Princess Elizabeth* (see Arber, *Term Catalogues,* II, 264–65, Easter Term, 1689; and compare the two 1688 issues in New Wing, one for Tonson alone and one for Bentley alone, nos. C.363 and C.363A). Although Tonson's name does not appear among the undertakers, I suspect that it was through him, or through the Simpsons checking with him, that Temple knew to write to Bentley. Tonson was one bookseller besides the Simpsons whom Temple might have been expected to know openly, and two years later, at least, the Simpsons were cooperating with Tonson in publishing their respective Temple properties. Already well established by 1690, Tonson spent the decade developing contacts among major authors and major Whigs at least partly through the forerunner of his Kit-Kat Club, the origins of which seem to reach back to approximately this time. See Harry M. Geduld, *Prince of Publishers: A Study of the Work and Career of Jacob Tonson* (Bloomington, Ind.: Indiana University Press, 1969), pp. 152–54. By 1689–90, together with Awnsham and John Churchill, Tonson had bought up two of the most important Temple copyrights, those to *Observations upon the United Provinces* (first published 1673) and to the first volume of *Miscellanea* (1679). He continued to expand his holdings. In 1697 he and the Churchills joined with the Simpsons, who owned *Miscellanea, The Second Part,* in bringing out a dual edition with a joint title page reading *Miscellanea, In Two Parts,* "The Fifth Edition." When Temple died in early 1699, Tonson seems to have been recognized as one of Temple's official publishers. It was to him, to the Churchills, and

to the Simpsons, at any rate, that Swift jointly offered Temple's two-volume *Letters* that year. Meanwhile (some time after 1694) Tonson had also acquired an interest with Chiswell in the popular *Memoirs of What Past in Christendom*, and together they published an edition designed to accompany the Temple *Letters* (dated 1700, like the *Letters;* the title page indicates that the memoirs begin "exactly where His *Letters* leave off").

32. The history of Richard II which Temple thought he had seen was probably *The Life and Reign of King Richard The Second. By a Person of Quality* (London: for M.L. and L.C., and sold by Langley Curtis, 1681). Authorship was attributed to Sir Robert Howard, K.B. Howard is now chiefly remembered as Dryden's lightweight brother-in-law but in Temple's day was well known as a would-be poet and dramatist as well as a successful courtier and placeman under Charles II and William III. Despite a certain reputation for valuing himself too highly ("not ill-natured, but insufferably boasting," said Evelyn), Howard was just the sort of person to qualify as "a good hand" in Temple's estimation. Besides his highly visible literary and political activities, Howard belonged to one of England's most distinguished families. The Earl of Berkshire's brother, he was a descendent not only of Edward VI's Duke of Norfolk but also (through his mother) of Elizabeth's Lord Burghley. During the 1680s Howard dabbled in history. Apart from the 1681 book on Richard II (the attribution of which is now sometimes questioned), he produced a study of the period from Edward I through Richard II which was published anonymously in 1689 and reissued in the following year as *The History of the Reigns of Edward I and Richard II, Written in the Year 1685 by Sr Robert Howard.*

33. [John Duncombe, ed.], *Letters, by Several Eminent Persons Deceased. Including the Correspondence of John Hughes, Esq.* (London: for J. Johnson, 1772), I, 1–7. Duncombe prints from the A.L.s., which "with the post-mark on it, is in the editor's hands . . ." (p. 2 n.). Temple's modern champion, Homer Woodbridge, treats the letter only briefly, ignores the curious or damaging parts, garbles the chronology, and generally misses the point (*Temple*, p. 234), while Ehrenpreis, in a footnote, barely acknowledges the letter's existence (*Swift*, I, 169 n. 1). More recently, in " 'So Ancient and Noble a Nation': Sir William Temple's History of England," *Neuphilologische Mitteilungen* 77 (1976), 97–98, Robert C. Steensma draws attention to the letter anew, considers the identity of the publisher whom it addresses, but otherwise adds little to Woodbridge's account.

As for Thomas's reading Dunton's letters to Temple aloud—instead of Temple's reading them for himself—this seems to have been a frequent practice for the secretary at Moor Park, thanks to Temple's bad eyes and indolent disposition. See Temple's letter about Swift in 1690: since Swift arrived a year before, "he has lived in my house, read to mee, writ for mee, and kept all accounts . . ." (*Correspondence*, I, 1).

34. Woodbridge, *Temple*, p. 233 n. 16; for her burial place, see Temple's will (drawn up a month later, and witnessed by Thomas Swift) in Courtenay, *Memoirs of Temple*, II, 485 (cf. codicil, p. 486).

35. The few substitutions occur where Temple had been at his most vague and offhand. In Thomas's letter, for instance, Temple recommends "the lives

of Edward IV. Edward V. and Richard III. written, *as he remembers,* by Sir Thomas More, *if they are still extant"* (*Letters, by Several Eminent Persons Deceased,* I, 5, my emphases; cf. Temple's *Introduction,* sig. A2ᵛ, referring to "Part of Edward the fourth and Richard the third by Sir Thomas Moor"—presumably the portions about which Temple felt surest). Sir Thomas More, however, had not written a separate life of Richard's brother Edward IV, who is at least partly included in the life of Richard, and so Bentley's proposals add Thomas Habington's life of Edward IV to More's of Richard III. (Temple's biographer Courtenay lifts an eyebrow over Temple's uncertainty about the survival of More's history; any questions arising from its differing Latin and English versions do not account for Temple's vagueness, although they may help to explain the fresh translation which Bentley's successors ultimately commissioned, in 1705. See Courtenay, *Memoirs of Temple,* II, 222 n.) Likewise, the Bentley group proposed to commission a new history of Richard II instead of choosing the anonymous but distinguished author's effort which Temple *"thinks he has seen,* many years ago," and about the existence of which it "will be your part to inform yourselves." In other instances, e.g., using Samuel Daniel for the period from William Rufus through Edward III, the Bentley group seems to follow a recommendation present in Thomas's letter but absent from the *Introduction* preface, where Temple says nothing about the period one way or the other. It is possible, though, that the Bentley group had fixed upon Daniel before Thomas wrote, and that Temple's influence upon their choices chiefly stems from the recommendations printed in the *Introduction* rather than the last-minute list sent in Thomas's letter. Certainly some of the commentary in the proposals—e.g., the talk of using Camden's MS. corrections and additions—suggests that the Bentley group had gone into the subject much more thoroughly than Temple ever had. Indeed the influence of Thomas's letter seems to lie more demonstrably in the organization and emphasis of the *Compleat History* broadside, rather than in its specific choices for the histories to be used in the project. It was Thomas's letter, for instance, which had dwelled upon "approved and esteemed authors," "authors of name and estimation," and which felt it necessary to say, of More's supposed histories, that "it will be but justice to his memory" to print them as is. After listing More's one history in the proposals, the Bentley group similarly feels obliged to add a brief explanation, likewise appealing to his memory, that More's work has "met with a general Esteem answerable to the Character of the Author."

36. Richard Chiswell, Brabham Aylmer, Richard Bentley et al., *Proposals for Printing A Compleat History of England: Or, The Lives of all the Kings To His Present Majesty,* broadside, [London: late Feb. 1694/95], quoted from the Harvard copy (revised shelf mark *pEB65. C4487. 695p) by permission of the Houghton Library, Harvard University. On the verso are some MS. annotations listing alternate authors in a manner reminiscent of Temple (e.g., "K. James by Sanderson, an ill stile but very faithful") and in a hand similar to his, though of necessity badly cramped to fit the limited space available in the margin. None of the authors mentioned, however, corresponds to any of Temple's known recommendations, and I know of no similarly compressed example of Temple's

hand from the 1690s with which to compare the autograph. The date of the broadside's publication is suggested by an advertisement in the February number of *The Present State of Europe* (6, no. 2, licensed 6 Mar. 1694/95), verso of t-p. There Dunton and his partners advertise their original proposals for Tyrrell's history together "with a Vindication of the said Work from some Cavils and Exceptions." This "Vindication" seems to correspond with a Dunton broadside which specifically vindicates the Tyrrell project against the insinuations in the *Compleat History* proposals, and attacks that project in turn. That the *Compleat History* proposals were not yet published on 14 February is suggested by Thomas Swift's offer to look at proposals "if you send any abroad," as well as by their use of strategies suggested in Thomas's letter of that date.

37. *The Present State of Europe*, 5, no. 11 (licensed 1 Dec. 1694), verso of t-p. This advertisement seems to reflect the project before Dunton abandoned Temple's scheme and engaged Tyrrell to write a fresh history.

38. Bentley also insinuates that Dunton was running into problems with Tyrrell's history, and that it was likely to be superficial anyway. "But the many Disappointments which have already happen'd," he says, together with the chance of future accidents, give the public "so little Prospect of hoping for a *Compleat History* by any such way," that a composite history makes more sense. Besides, he adds, the individual authors in a composite history "had better Opportunities of informing themselves thorowly, and less Temptation to run it over superficially." On the first count, at least, Bentley may have been right. Years later Dunton noted, with some wryness, that Tyrrell "deserves a better character than I am able to give him," that the history "was ten months longer in the Press than we expected, yet he was so much *disinterested* in the matter [presumably about payment for his work], that we had no reason to complain." See Dunton, *Life and Errors*, p. 178 (original emphasis).

39. Henry Rhodes, John Dunton, et al., *Advertisement, Concerning Some Mistakes in the late Proposals for Printing a Pretended Compleat History of England, &c.*, broadside, [London: late Feb. or early Mar. 1694/95]; see Parks, *John Dunton and the English Book Trade*, p. 293, Dunton bibliography no. 210. I quote from a xerox of the apparently unique copy at Yale, furnished through the kindness of Dr. Parks. This broadside seems to correspond with the "Vindication" of the Dunton proposals "from some Cavils and Exceptions," advertised in the February *Present State of Europe*, 5, no. 2 (licensed 6 Mar. 1694/95), verso of t-p.

40. In July 1701 White Kennett contracted to write a continuation of the history down through the reign of James II; see G. V. Bennett, *White Kennett, 1660–1728, Bishop of Peterborough* (London: S.P.C.K., 1957), p. 168 & n. The completed history was eventually published in 1706 in three volumes, the third of which (Kennett's) drew fire for its strongly whiggish bias. See Arber, *Term Catalogues*, III, 510 (cf. 459, advertisement of 1705). Of the original undertakers in 1695, only three firms had retained an interest—Aylmer, Matthew Wotton, and the partners Samuel Smith and Benjamin Walford. With a few minor adjustments, the first two volumes followed the formula laid down in 1695.

41. *Tale of a Tub*, p. 59. (Guthkelch and Smith find no such collection among the many projects which Dunton undertook or advertised—ibid., n. 1.) As in

Temple's proposed collection of fine historical authors, a project implied in Dunton's earliest advertisements, the authors in Dunton's proposed "Treasury of British Eloquence" have been previously published. Similarly, in Temple's recommendations for the authors to be used, considerations of style figure nearly as highly as those of the authors' public standing. Temple proposed one study because its author is an author "of good judgment, and no ill style," and he recommended the distinguished anonymous author's life of Richard II partly because it is "written well." The diversity of styles in the proposed collection Temple considers a virtue in itself: "And he [Temple] thinks the variety of the several hands and styles may render it yet more agreeable to the readers than if it were all written by the same pen . . ." (Thomas Swift to Bentley, in *Letters, by Several Eminent Persons,* 1, 4–6, repeating the terms of the earlier letter to Dunton).

The placement of Swift's comments on Dunton is equally felicitous—or infelicitous—considering Temple's preoccupation with glorifying his own name through the proposed composite history. The criminals deliver their speeches from the Ladder, one of the three mystic wooden machines available in England to the man who "hath an Ambition to be heard in a Crowd" and who must accordingly exalt himself "to a certain Degree of Altitude above them" (*Tale,* pp. 55–56). Had he ever encountered the Dunton passage in the *Tale,* all the same, Temple should have found no resemblance between Dunton's collection and the one he once proposed to Dunton and Bentley. Between "approved and esteemed authors" like Temple and common criminals at Tyburn there is a great gulf fixed, and Swift's description concludes on a note which sets the mind wandering in new and somewhat safer directions—for instance towards Dryden's gaudily produced translation of the *Aeneid* (1697), which had just appeared, in folio, with its famous complement of copperplates for each of the twelve books (including one plate inscribed to Temple's sister Lady Giffard). Swift praises the published speeches of common criminals,

> which I look upon as the choicest Treasury of our British Eloquence, and whereof I am informed, that worthy Citizen and Bookseller, Mr. John Dunton, hath made a faithful and painful Collection, which he shortly designs to publish *in Twelve Volumes in Folio, illustrated with Copper-Plates.* (my emphasis)

If anything, Temple should have appreciated an attack on a bookseller whom he had come to despise, and he should have appreciated the indirect reflections on the modern English literary scene, for which he had little praise.

42. *Prose Works,* v, 193–94.

43. Simon DuCros, *A Letter from Monsieur de Cros . . . Being an Answer to Sir Wm Temple's Memoirs, Concerning what passed from the Year 1672 until the Year 1679* (London: for Abel Roper, 1693), quotations from p. 4. Woodbridge seems to have known only the other issue of the same printing, with a slightly different title page and the imprint "London, Printed in the Year, 1693." To discredit Du-

Cros's charges, he makes much of the pamphlet's appearing (as he supposes) without any hint of the publisher's identity (*Temple*, p. 225). The date(s) of publication can be guessed by those of the two pamphlet retorts to DuCros, the first recorded in the Hilary *Term Catalogue* for 1692/93 and the second in the Easter (Arber, *Term Catalogues*, II, 442, as the last item listed in its category, and II, 457). There was also a much longer (expanded?) edition of DuCros containing at least 61 pp. in the pamphlet proper, according to page citations given in the first retort. The two copies of DuCros which I have examined (Yale's for the Roper imprint, for the other an imperfect copy offered by A. R. Heath, catalogue 32, Bristol, 1976) belong to a shorter edition containing only 32 pp. in the pamphlet proper, paginated *1*, 2–25, 27–30, 32, 31, 33. By imprints, these two copies seem to correspond to Wing D.2437 and D.2436, but both copies are octavos (in half sheets) whereas Wing D.2436 calls for a quarto.

44. Woodbridge, *Temple*, pp. 224–28. The contemporary observer (quoted in Woodbridge) is Charles Hatton, writing to Viscount Hatton in February 1692/93. The *Answer* actively encouraged the supposition that Temple had written it. To the "Importunities" of Temple's friends "and not to his own Inclinations," the pamphlet begins, "is the Reader obliged for the following *Remarks*" (*An Answer to a Scurrilous Pamphlet*, p. 5).

45. Swift knew all this because Temple eventually used him to copy the "Hints" in 1697 or so, roughly two years after Temple composed them. The young opponent was the scholar William Wotton, then a mere private chaplain who in 1694 (well after the DuCros business) had challenged some of the more extravagant assertions in Temple's essay *Upon Ancient and Modern Learning*. Temple meant the "Hints" to be incorporated into an attack on Wotton by a "Mr. H," the friend (student?) of a friend at Oxford. Mr. H. instead proposed to print the "Hints" separately as an appendix, thus isolating them and increasing the chances that people might identify Temple as their author. Temple promptly withdrew the "Hints" and suppressed the whole undertaking. When Wotton's expanded second edition appeared in 1697, Temple next decided to circulate the "Hints" privately and (it appears) had Swift make the copy which now survives in the Rothschild Collection. Eventually the piece appeared in a revised and expanded form—under Temple's own name, and lacking his open self-praise and most of his sarcastic abuse of Wotton—as *Some Thoughts Upon Reviewing the Essay of Antient and Modern Learning*, in *Miscellanea, The Third Part* (1701). For more particulars, see chapter 3.

46. *Tale of a Tub*, p. xlviii (emphasis as given in the earliest printed, oldest surviving text of the letter, probably by its editor); *An Answer to a Scurrilous Pamphlet*, p. 6. On the common assumption that Temple's 1698 letter refers to the *Battle of the Books*, see below, n. 68 in chapter 5.

47. George Mayhew, "The Early Life and Art of Jonathan Swift," unpublished study. Portions have appeared in the form of articles, but the three chapters on DuCros remain unpublished and (since 1972, I am told) inaccessible to researchers. I had corresponded with the author in 1969–70, but my later attempts to view the transcript proved unsuccessful. A revived project for publication has been reported a possibility, but by the end of 1979 questions of

format and degrees of revision or of incorporation elsewhere remained unsettled.

CHAPTER 3

1. Judging from the frequency of new editions, Temple's works sold briskly through the 1690s and steadily if less spectacularly thereafter. See Woodbridge's useful but incomplete biography of editions (*Temple*, pp. 334–36, the later list in Wing being in places unreliable). The *Letters* themselves did not do so well, despite Swift's mighty claims for them in the preface. They were not reprinted until 1720, in Temple's collected *Works*. I have seen a copy of the rare "Second Edition" of 1716, for Vol. I ("Printed for Ralph Smith at the Bible under the Piazza of the Royal Exchange in Cornhill"), but it turns out to be a reissue of the original sheets with a new title page. After sixteen or seventeen years, in other words, the original printing had not yet been exhausted.

2. For the 1703 volume of *Letters* he received £50; for the *Memoirs, Part III* (1709), £40; see *The Rothschild Library*, no. 2256 and 2259.

3. *Prose Works*, v, 193–94. For the date of composition see ibid., p. xxii, and George Mayhew's review of Ehrenpreis, *Swift*, ii, in *Philological Quarterly* 48 (1969), 399–400. As for Swift's important errands for Temple, Swift served at least once more as some sort of messenger to Court; see Longe, *Lady Giffard*, p. 216.

4. It is especially surprising that Temple's name does not figure in the 1721 letter-essay addressed to Pope (*Correspondence*, ii, 365–74), in which Swift defends himself from charges of Jacobitism, cites his long experience with government, and lays claim to Old Whig principles not too different from Temple's. Both subscribe to the "Gothick" form of government, with the monarch dependent on frequent parliaments representing the owners of land (Ibid., pp. 372–73; Temple, *Miscellanea, The Second Part*, pp. 253–56, 248–49).

5. Prefaces reprinted in *Prose Works*, i, 255–59, 265–66, 261–63, and 267–71, respectively.

6. Temple, *Miscellanea, The Second Part*, p. 61.

7. Only in September 1700, when he took possession of his new Irish living at Laracor, did Swift gain a measure of true security (Landa, *Swift and the Church of Ireland*, pp. 44, 34). Landa cites Swift's surviving account books in estimating the yield at somewhat over £100 a year (Ibid., p. 36 & n. 3), a decent but not princely sum.

8. Ehrenpreis, *Swift*, ii, 34–35.

9. Swift could have inserted the dedication—the easiest piece to change or add—as late as late October or early November 1699, when he was safely in Dublin. The Temple *Letters* were advertised for sale in London on 30 November (Ibid., ii, 34 & n. 4). It is certain that Swift sent at least one textual change back from Dublin: he left England thinking that he had been appointed Berkeley's secretary as well as chaplain, but by the time he reached Dublin he found, much to his chagrin, that the secretary's post was going to someone else (Ibid., pp. 6–8). Accordingly, the *Letters* title page styles Swift merely "Domestick Chaplain to

his Excellency the Earl of Berkeley, one of the Lords Justices of Ireland." As for the preface, which he would have finished before any final determination about the dedication, Swift was definitely working on the rough draft some time between May and mid-July. In the fragment of the rough draft, he speaks of "not knowing how soon I may cross the Seas into Ireland, where some Concerns are like suddenly to call me . . ." (MS. described in *The Rothschild Library*, no. 2254, printed in *Prose Works*, I, xix). The reference dates the fragment to the period between Swift's appointment and Berkeley's announcement of the departure date. Berkeley could not have appointed Swift before May, when he himself received his appointment, and the Earl left London (to be joined by Swift en route) on 18 July; see Swift, *A Discourse of the Contests and Dissentions Between the Nobles and Commons in Athens and Rome*, ed. Frank H. Ellis (Oxford: The Clarendon Press, 1967), p. 22; on the voyage itself see Ehrenpreis, *Swift*, II, 5. As Ehrenpreis notes, the announcement of a competing edition of Temple's letters, on 20 May, probably hastened Swift's decision to publish as soon as possible. His own announcement of his intent to publish appeared on 3 June (Ibid., II, 34 & nn. 2, 3).

10. In 1699 the situation in Ireland was unusually fluid. As a rule power was concentrated in a Lord Lieutenant, but the last such (Lord Capel of Tewkesbury) had died in 1696 and his eventual successor, Laurence Hyde, Earl of Rochester, was not named until December 1700 *(Dictionary of National Biography)*. Between 1699 and 1700, the viceregality was split among three Lords Justices, of whom Berkeley, something of a cipher, was a mere replacement for an earlier triumvir. Even in the funerary inscription which Swift composed for the Earl (at the Berkeley family's request), Swift termed him only "secundus inter tres summos justiciarios" (*Correspondence*, v, 223).

11. According to Swift's autobiographical fragment, Swift petitioned William early in 1699 for "a Prebend of Canterbury or Westminster" which the King had promised Temple for Swift. He blamed his failure on the negligence of his seconder at Court, the Earl of Romney (*Prose Works*, v, 195). In an earlier account—written half bitterly and half banteringly to the Earl of Halifax in 1709, to thank him for favors never conferred—Swift mentions "a Prebend of Westminster" for which he petitioned the King "in Pursuance of a Recommendation I had from Sr William Temple" (*Correspondence*, I, 144; cf. Murry, *Swift*, p. 150). In his letters in the 1690s Swift sometimes hints at hopes of preferment, but seldom with any specificity. The only specific reference to a prebend in the King's gift dates back to 1692, when Temple is said to "promise me the certainty of it" while being "less forward than I could wish" in pursuing it (*Correspondence*, I, 12). Later in this chapter we shall investigate the doubtful strength of Swift's assurances nearly seven years later, in 1699.

12. The Temple *Letters* speak well of William (then a youth) on the few occasions on which they mention him, but the Dutchman they primarily celebrate is William's one-time nemesis, the republican Grand Pensionary De Witt, whom Swift goes out of his way to mention in the preface (I, sig. A3^r). De Witt was not removed from William's path until 1672, when as a result of the temporarily successful French invasion of Holland—itself the upshot of Temple's

Triple Alliance, which isolated Holland from its former French allies—a Williamite mob caught De Witt in the street and tore him to pieces. (William never publicly acknowledged his emnity to De Witt but made no pretense of mourning his death.) Moreover, the *Letters* celebrate De Witt for reversing his traditional pro-French policy in order to oppose the inroads of Louis XIV. In 1699, though somewhat unwillingly, William had temporarily abandoned his aggressively anti-French policy in order to placate Louis instead, by negotiating a second treaty for partitioning the Spanish dominions. For that matter, William was out of England from 31 May to 18 October *(D.N.B.)*, the period in which Swift probably composed the dedication. It is possible that Swift's decision to inscribe the *Letters* to William (or at least do so in 1699) sprang partly from a private sense of mischief or anger. In later years, at least, Swift sang few paeans about "Nassau, who got the name of glorious/ Because he never was victorious" *(Directions for a Birth-Day Song*, lines 251–52, in *Poems*, ii, 468).

13. "It was the general Opinion," reports Boyer in his *Memoirs of Temple* (p. 413), that Temple had published the *Introduction to the History of England* (1694) "both to compliment that Prince, under the *Character* of the Norman Conqueror, which he draws and sets off to great Advantage; and to assert the late *Revolution*, by shewing, that Edgar Atheling, who had an *undoubted Right* of *Succession* to the Crown, was *twice laid aside*" (Boyer's emphases). Woodbridge makes a good case that Temple had similar intentions in his preceding book, the *Memoirs of What Past in Christendom* (1691). In both instances his strategy should also have reminded his readers of the King's confidence and trust in him, similarly celebrated in the *Memoirs*.

14. See the simple dedication text (i, A1r): "These Letters of Sir W. Temple having been left to my Care, they are most humbly presented to Your Majesty by . . ." with Swift's name in large italic type at the bottom of the page.

15. *Prose Works*, i, 268–70.

16. Ehrenpreis, *Swift*, ii, 339.

17. Woodbridge, *Temple*, pp. 222–23, 246–47. This opinion was current at the time. Woodbridge cites a MS. entry of 1692/3 (Ibid., p. 246 n. 9), and Boyer mentions those who believe that Temple concerted publication, an opinion which Boyer himself tends to accept *(Memoirs of Temple*, pp. 381–82).

18. E.g., Temple, *Letters*, i, 166, on the conclusion of the preliminary round of negotiations towards the Triple Alliance: "After this I entered into Detail of my whole Progress to that Time, . . . of His Majesty's Reasons, of the common Interests of *Christendom* [i.e., France's neighbors]; . . . Of our discourses about engaging Sueden in the same Measures . . . for our own mutual Defence, the Safety of Flanders, and thereby of *Christendom*. . . . The [Swedish envoy] professed . . . to be confident that Sueden would be content to go his Pace in all the common affairs of *Christendom* . . ." (my emphases). A rough count suggests that the word occurs at least fifty times through the two volumes.

19. In the preface to the *Letters*, Swift asserts (in phrasing highly reminiscent of Temple's) that the volumes contain "an Account of *all the chief Transactions and Negotiations, which passed in Christendom* during the seven Years, wherein they are dated," adds a list of the negotiations, and later in the preface announces that

"that which will most value them [the letters] to the Publick, both at home and abroad, is, First, that the Matters contained in them, were the Ground and Foundation, *whereon all the Wars and Invasions, as well as all the Negotiations and Treaties of Peace in Christendom,* have since been raised . . ." (i, sig. A2^r, A3^v, my emphases).

20. Ehrenpreis, *Swift,* i, 98; cf. Woodbridge, *Temple,* pp. 169–76, 185–87. Woodbridge feels that the negotiations "deserved to be described by the familiar demon who sometimes wrote with Swift's satiric pen" (p. 169).

21. *Prose Works,* i, 269; first emphasis mine, the second Swift's.

22. Temple, *Memoirs, Part III,* pp. 169–70. For an Englishman bound by laws of *lèse majesté,* Temple is fairly tart in his implications, although he meant them published in a later and different reign.

23. In 1679–81 Charles was confronted with the major crises of his reign, the Popish Plot and the Exclusion Bill. Temple's value lay in his reputation as the proponent of honest and true-blue Protestant alliances, an invaluable asset to a Court under seige for its real and imagined papistry. Temple served Charles by originating a scheme for reviving an enlarged privy council, which he then joined. As Thomas Seccombe observes in the *D.N.B.,* it was "a way [for Charles] to obtain from Temple's reputation whatever fillip of popularity it was able to give to a thoroughly discredited administration." Cf. Woodbridge, *Temple,* pp. 194–95 & n. 4. Unlike Temple, Charles never seems to have intended the council for anything but show. Even in the Triple Alliance negotiations, for which Temple claimed and received such glory in his lifetime, Temple again seems to have been a pawn and a dupe. In "John de Witt and the Triple Alliance," Herbert H. Rowen suggests that the actual instigator was Charles II—and that far from wishing to ally with Holland against France, Charles meant to detach De Witt from his traditional French alliance (which had protected Holland from England) and to compel Louis XIV to buy back English cooperation at a more profitable figure. See *The Journal of Modern History* 26 (1954): 1–14. If Rowen is correct, Temple eagerly negotiated a treaty designed to hurt the Dutch and defeat everything Temple stood for, as in fact it nearly did. Rowen's most impressive witness, incidentally, is the French ambassador Pomponne (pp. 5–6), whom Temple later admiringly called "a Person of great Worth and Learning as well as Observation"; see Temple, *Miscellanea, The Third Part* (London: for Ben. Tooke, 1701), p. 122. Temple never seems to have realized the extent of his mistake, though he later learned a little. He had persevered in his innocence about Charles's intentions well past the stage of renewed Anglo-Dutch unfriendliness, but he later doctored one of his letters to suggest that he had actually possessed a certain amount of foresight about the 'new' policy at Court—more foreknowledge, at least, than almost anyone else claimed. See chapter 1.

24. Temple, *Memoirs, Part III,* pp. 5–6, and especially p. 11: ". . . he told me, he had none left, with whom he could so much as speak of them [foreign affairs] in Confidence, since my Lord Treasurer's [Danby's] being gone. And this gave, I suppose, His Majesty the Occasion of entring into more Confidence with me, than I could deserve or expect."

25. Ibid., pp. 90–92, and especially pp. 130–31: Temple "told the King that I was very sensible how much of his Confidence I formerly had, and how much I had lost, without knowing the Occasion," and told Charles his dislike of *"Swallowing what other People had Chew'd"* (Temple's emphasis).

26. *Prose Works,* I, 270. Swift further notes that Temple "has often assur'd me it was a Thing he never affected," and that, in the new installment of memoirs, Temple accordingly exchanged his gallicisms for English expressions, "tho' perhaps not so significant."

27. Ibid., p. 268.

28. Murry, *Swift,* pp. 149–50.

29. Swift received his money for the *Memoirs, Part III* copy on 14 April 1709 (*The Rothschild Library,* no. 2259), and the book itself appeared on 23 June (Ehrenpreis, *Swift,* II, 339 n. 2).

30. Landa, *Swift and the Church of Ireland,* p. 58; for the account of Swift's lobbying efforts, see pp. 55–59.

31. Notwithstanding this, Murry asserts that Swift was merely "keeping all his irons in the fire" (*Swift,* p. 149), and Ehrenpreis, that in his "half-hearted compliments," Swift is merely "refusing to grant the ministers any excuse for overlooking his ten years' persistence in waiting for a lift" (Ehrenpreis, *Swift,* II, 339).

32. Landa calls the interview, in June 1708, "a turning point in Swift's relationship with the Whigs" (*Swift and the Church of Ireland,* p. 56). For an account of the interview, see also *Correspondence,* I, 84–86. For Swift's probable reaction to Godolphin, see Craik, *Life of Swift,* pp. 149–50. By late March 1709 Swift was also sounding cold about the younger Lord Sunderland, who receives a share of the flattery in the preface (*Correspondence,* I, 132).

33. Sheila Biddle, *Bolingbroke and Harley* (New York: Knopf, 1974), p. 160.

34. As a warning against Godolphin's Church policies, for instance, Swift had already published his *Letter Concerning the Sacramental Test* (Dec. 1708; see *Prose Works,* II, xxi–xxiii), and had written but not yet published his *Argument Against Abolishing Christianity in England,* which Herbert Davis considers an appeal intended for the Whig leadership (Ibid., p. xix).

35. *Journal to Stella,* I, 5–6 (9 Sept. 1710); *Correspondence,* I, 173–74.

36. Temple, *Miscellanea, The Third Part,* p. 231 (hiatus and Swift's note), sig. A2ᵛ (Swift's comment in preface); *Tale of a Tub,* p. 316 (Wotton's commentary on hiatus, reprinted from his *Defense* of the *Reflections Upon Ancient and Modern Learning*), p. 170 (Swift's hiatus in the Digression on Madness). Earlier in his *Defense,* Wotton discussed Swift's unconvincing claim of not knowing the Temple essay's purpose or origins, reproved Swift for hurting Temple's reputation by publishing it, and plausibly concluded by supposing "that Dr. Swift had no mind to defend that Paper, and thought it best by such a Declaration, to insinuate, that he was willing to have it shift for it self"; see Wotton, *Reflections,* 3rd ed. (London: for Tim. Goodwin, 1705), pp. 486–87 (this portion not reprinted in the *Tale of a Tub* appendix).

37. Murry, *Swift,* pp. 26–27, 32–45, 48–51; Ehrenpreis, *Swift,* I, 109–41; Emile Pons, *Swift: les années de jeunesse et le "Conte du Tonneau,"* Publications de la

Faculté des Lettres de l'Université de Strasbourg, Fasc. 26 (Strasbourg: Librairie Istra, 1925), pp. 142–43, 163–64, 177–79; Peter J. Schakel, *The Poetry of Jonathan Swift: Allusion and the Development of a Poetic Style* (Madison, Wisc.: University of Wisconsin Press, 1978), pp. 7–10.

38. Ehrenpreis, *Swift*, I, 120–21.

39. Ibid., pp. 109, 131; Schakel, *The Poetry of Jonathan Swift*, pp. 15, 23; Robert W. Uphaus, "From Panegyric to Satire: Swift's Early Odes and *A Tale of a Tub*," *Texas Studies in Literature and Language* 13 (1971), 55–70; Kathryn Montgomery Harris, " 'Occasions So Few': Satire as a Strategy of Praise in Swift's Early Odes," *Modern Language Quarterly* 31 (1970), 22–37; Donna G. Fricke, "Jonathan Swift's Odes and the Conversion to Satire," *Enlightenment Essays* 5, no. 2 (Summer 1974), 3–17; Martin Price, *Swift's Rhetorical Art* (1953; rpt. Hamden, Conn.: Archon, 1963), pp. 43–45; Herbert Davis, "Swift's View of Poetry," in *Studies in English by Members of University College, Toronto*, ed. Malcolm W. Wallace (Toronto: University of Toronto Press, 1931), pp. 23–29.

40. For the period encompassing Swift's first two sojourns at Moor Park, between 1689 and 1694, Williams prints only seven letters (*Correspondence*, II, 1–18), including one by Temple to Sir Robert Southwell and one written for publication in the *Athenian Mercury*. The remaining five average about one a year.

41. *Correspondence*, I, 7 & n. 4.

42. Ibid., p. 9. So far as I know, Swift had had only one piece published by May 1692, his *Ode to the Athenian Society*, published by John Dunton. A page earlier in the letter, Swift mentions Dunton in terms which suggest that Dunton can hardly be "my Bookseller"; see Mackie L. Jarrell, " 'Ode to the King': Some Contests, Dissensions, and Exchanges among Jonathan Swift, John Dunton, and Henry Jones," *Texas Studies in Literature and Language* 7 (1965), 154.

43. *Correspondence*, I, 10.

44. Ibid., pp. 9–10. Since Swift characterizes himself as an incurable self-admirer, the "likeness of humors" would provide Temple with the same characterization.

45. Johnson suggested that Swift's odes were *practical* in inspiration: "Like other odes of his time Swift's were probably intended as a means to an end, political when they flattered the King or Sir William Temple, religious when they praised Dr. Sancroft"; see *The Sin of Wit: Jonathan Swift as Poet* (Syracuse, N.Y.: Syracuse University Press, 1950), p. 6. The idea deserves further investigation even if the specific implications about the *Ode to the King* and the *Ode to Dr. William Sancroft* seem untenable at first glance. When half the nation seemingly addressed flattering odes to William III in the aftermath of the Glorious Revolution, Swift had little to gain from the King by writing yet another one, especially when he did not publish it and when the King probably never saw it. As for the ode to Sancroft, Swift claimed to be writing it on "half a Promise" to the nonjuring bishop Francis Turner (letter to Thomas Swift, *Correspondence*, I, 9), but though Sancroft and Turner were two of the celebrated Seven Bishops unsuccessfully prosecuted by James II in May and June 1688, they had become worthless from a pragmatic point of view. In the new reign, Sancroft had been deprived of his archbishopric more than two years before Swift wrote and thus

was in no position to forward the career of an aspirant for holy orders. Turner had not only been deprived of his bishopric but had had a warrant out for his arrest since February 1691, more than a year before Swift mentioned him *(D.N.B.)*. On the other hand, an ode to the King could only have pleased his long-time friend and supporter, Sir William Temple. I suspect that the same was true, in a much more private sense, for Swift's praise of the saintly archbishop, whose career presented so many striking parallels with Temple's—and in one important crisis, a standing reproach. Like Temple, Sancroft had sworn allegiance to James II, had disagreed with James's policies (and actively opposed them, unlike Temple in the 1680s), and then declined to serve in any way under the more congenial William of Orange when William insisted on the crown rather than a regency, a step which would have made Sancroft break his oath. Sancroft kept his word faithfully and went into retirement in the country, while Temple faltered once, with tragic results. In 1686 Temple had promised James to live as a good subject and never to accept public office again. He interpreted his promise to include his only surviving son John, forbade him to meet William on his landing in England, but afterwards either relented or changed his mind. In April 1689, at the unusually tender age of thirty-four, John became secretary of war, a post which he tried to resign almost immediately. Within a week he had drowned himself in the Thames. Only a few months later, the events were recorded by Temple's admiring sister, Lady Giffard, who almost always reflects Temple's point of view. Amid the signs of trauma, grief, and even evasion (in her longer draft she cannot mention John's death directly and pretends that Temple refused John his consent), seems to lurk the awareness of the hand of God, whom she invokes sombrely at the end (Temple, *Early Essays,* pp. 23–25, xii; cf. Woodbridge, *Temple,* pp. 216–18, and Courtenay, *Memoirs of Temple,* ii, 122–24, 129–32). It is no coincidence, I think, that Swift celebrates Sancroft for private virtues rather than ecclesiastical merits—and invokes him as one who shows God's way to men: "Thus Sancroft, in the exaltation of retreat,/ Shews lustre that was shaded in his seat . . ." and (invoking Sancroft directly) "Kind Star, still may'st thou shed thy sacred influence here,/ Or from thy private peaceful orb appear;/ For, sure, we want some guide from Heav'n to show/ The way . . ." (lines 211–12, 154–57, in *Poems,* i, 41, 39). Though almost certainly of later composition, the poem was dated May 1689, the month following John's suicide (Ibid., pp. 33–34). In the most recent treatment of the poem—"Swift's *Ode to Sancroft:* Another Look," *Modern Philology* 73, Arthur Friedman festschrift (May 1976), S24–39—Edward W. Rosenheim Jr. helpfully provides much background information about the times but, citing Ehrenpreis, rejects without discussion the possibility of a Moor Park readership (Ibid., p. S32).

The question of Swift's intended readership in the odes has also been raised, in passing, by Nora Crowe Jaffe in *The Poet Swift* (Hanover, N.H.: University Press of New England, 1977). "Swift wrote the poems in part to please Sir William Temple," Jaffe asserts at one point, "and he probably took up some points of view that fit Temple better than himself" (p. 70). Unfortunately she pursues the idea no further, offers no evidence, and instead continues with an orthodox critical synthesis which explains the odes, once again, as largely an earnest botch—the result of Swift's trying to write against his natural talents and instincts (pp. 61–74). On p. 70 she even suggests that, in part because Swift seems to espouse things he later mocked, the odes are "adolescent poems," though in fact Swift was in his middle twenties when he wrote them.

46. The *Ode to the Athenian Society* he sent to the Athenian Society, where it met with approval. It wound up published in a supplement to the *Athenian Mercury*. In addressing the Athenian Society it in fact addresses John Dunton and his two brothers-in-law. Swift was probably aware of the fact. In his covering letter to the Athenians, he mentions hearing an "Account and Opinion" of them, from a learned gentleman whom he consulted at Oxford (*Poems*, I, 15). Within the book trade, at least, "The true composition of the Athenian Society was probably an open secret," as Stephen R. Parks remarks in *John Dunton and the English Book Trade*, pp. 85–86. Swift's request that the poem be published in the *Athenian Mercury* implies a further audience, the wide assortment of 'prentices, citizens and their wives, chambermaids, witty scoffers, and credulous country gentlemen to whom the journal chiefly addressed itself. See *Poems*, I, 13–15, and Gilbert D. McEwen, *The Oracle of the Coffee House: John Dunton's "Athenian Mercury"* (San Marino, Calif.: Huntington Library, 1972), pp. 30–31, 36–37, 45. As for Swift's later poem *To Mr. Congreve*, he once claimed (to his cousin Thomas) that the lines were meant for publication with any of Congreve's plays (*Correspondence*, I, 13–14; *Poems*, I, 43). This would have involved a readership both of Congreve (to authorize publication) and the critics and other purchasers of such printed plays. On the other hand, Williams finds no evidence that Congreve ever received the poem (Ibid.).

47. *Correspondence*, I, 10. Cf. Ehrenpreis, *Swift*, I, 114. Swift's translation has not survived.

48. *Correspondence*, I, 8 (my emphasis). For a brief account of the poem's publication, see McEwen, *Oracle of the Coffee House*, pp. 33–34. Despite Swift's air of innocent enthusiasm, there is some odd equivocation in his words to Thomas. The parenthesis in the phrase "quoted my Poem very Honorably (as the fellow calld it)," with the contemptuous ring in the word "fellow," weakens the sense of the honor done the poem; it seems odd that Swift cannot answer certainly for his pleasure at publication ("so that *perhaps* I was in a good humor"); and the last two clauses make Swift's admiration of the Athenians something less than wholehearted, since it depends on Temple's for inspiration and raises as many questions as it settles about poetic "Honesty," which here depends on secondhand zeal. The passage occurs a page before Swift confesses his wrongheaded love of his own productions (along with Thomas's and Temple's). Neither the poem itself nor the circumstances surrounding it, including Temple's actual involvement with the Athenian project, have yet received thorough inspection or evaluation.

49. *Poems*, I, 14–15.

50. McEwen, *Oracle of the Coffee House*, pp. 33, 46 n. 2.

51. Lines 60 and 188, in *Poems*, I, 17, 21.

52. The Pindaric *Ode to the King*, which is almost certainly Swift's, appeared in an unauthorized collection of 1735 (*Poems*, I, 4–6, xxxvii–xxxviii, xli; Jarrell,

Texas Studies in Literature and Language 7: 145–46, 153), and the *Ode to the Athenian Society* was three times reprinted in Swift's life, but never in an authorized collection (*Poems*, 1, 13–14). The four other poems appeared only after his death (Ibid., pp. 26, 33–34, 43, 51).

53. Ehrenpreis, *Swift*, 1, 109, 113, 116 & n., 117–19, 130, 136, 139.

54. Ibid., p. 110.

55. In his essay *Of Poetry*, for instance, he lavished praise on Sir Philip Sidney for writing romance, gave Spenser's poetry mixed notices, and praised Shakespeare for introducing the drama of humors. In general, he speaks of English verse as something degenerated from its classical antecedents, partly because of the new taste for conceits, and most of all because of the new taste for ridicule (Temple, *Miscellanea, The Second Part*, pp. 335, 349, 356, 349–54, respectively).

56. In the essay *Of Heroick Virtue* (Ibid., p. 147).

57. Temple, *Letters*, 1, 116; to Lord Lisle, August 1667. Cf. Ehrenpreis, *Swift*, 1, 110–11.

58. Temple, *Miscellanea, The Second Part*, p. 316. Temple also calls for careful revision, study, good sense, and judgment (pp. 317–18), but makes clear that they remain secondary to the basic poetic fire, which "can never be produced by any Art or Study, by Pains or by Industry, which cannot be taught by Precepts or Examples; and therefore is agreed by all, to be the pure and free Gift of Heaven or of Nature, and to be a fire kindled out of some hidden spark of the very first Conception" (pp. 316–17). Temple's notions about the inspired poet have always been common enough—witness Shakespeare on the "poet's eye, in a fine frenzy rolling"—and they may help to illuminate Swift's stance in the odd letter to his rhyming cousin Thomas, not only in the breathless and chaotic style, which seems to reflect a "Noble and Vital Heat of Temper, but especially of the Brain," but also in his remarks on the Moor Park Muse (". . . if the fitt comes not immediatly I never heed it but think of something else . . ."). In later years, at least, Swift found such theories laughable. See Davis, "Swift's View of Poetry," *Studies in English*, pp. 14–21.

59. Lines 59–61, in *Poems*, 1, 28.

60. Cf. lines 199–200 (Ibid., p. 32): "Then (Sir,) accept this worthless Verse,/ The Tribute of an humble Muse. . . ."

61. Based closely on French originals; see Temple, *Early Essays*, pp. xvii–xxi, 208–15.

62. Temple, *Miscellanea, The Second Part*, p. 335 (in *Of Poetry*). In the next paragraph, Temple pays the ultimate compliment by classing Sidney with the ancients: "With him I leave the Discourse of ancient Poetry, and to discover the Decays of this Empire, must turn to that of the Modern. . . ."

63. Ibid.

64. Johnson, *Sin of Wit*, pp. 4–5; Davis, *Studies in English*, p. 25.

65. Ehrenpreis, *Swift*, 1, 118–19, 121–26. For a fuller account of parallels, echoes, and other signs of Temple's influence, see Gerald J. Pierre, "The Influence of Sir William Temple upon the Mind and Art of Jonathan Swift," Dissertation, University of Minnesota, 1970, pp. 21–67. Pierre largely shares Ehrenpreis's assumptions and conclusions.

66. Temple, *Miscellanea, The Second Part,* pp. 69–70; *Poems,* i, 27–28. Ehren-preis broadly states that both "the imagery and central ideas of the poem are largely derived from" the essays *Upon Ancient and Modern Learning* and *Upon the Gardens of Epicurus (Swift,* i, 118), but provides no evidence of borrowed imagery.

67. There is some uncertainty about the ode's date of composition. See *Poems,* i, 26. Swift would have done secretarial work on the essay during his first stay with Temple, in 1689–90, and could have read it in print during the second stay, from the end of 1691 onwards.

68. "The rest of the Neighbours began first to rail at Pedants, then to ridicule them; the Learned began to fear the same Fate, and that the Pigeons should be taken for Daws, because they were all in a Flock: *And because the poorest and meanest of the Company were proud,* the best and richest began to be ashamed" (Temple, *Miscellanea, The Second Part,* p. 70, my emphasis). As for Swift's two lines, it is not clear exactly what he means, literally and figuratively, by "fling our Scraps before our Door," although in context the poet's use of "our" is awkward enough, coming as it does one line before Temple reenters the poem as "you." Possibly Swift refers to rejecting knowledge, by flinging one's only scraps of it away; more probably, he refers to a vain and foolish ostentation of knowledge, by showing one's only scraps of it as if they were the unwanted remnants of a great feast. Whatever the case, I suspect that Swift was inspired by Temple's reference to the flock of pigeons and daws: they and other such scavengers usually dispose of unwanted scraps of food thrown outside houses.

69. *Poems,* i, 8, line 62; for Swift's later reflections on romance, see Ibid., i, 223, line 47 (in *Phillis, Or, the Progress of Love*) and ii, 711, line 795 (in *Cadenus and Vanessa*).

70. Ibid., i, 27, line 49, my emphases.

71. Temple, *Early Essays,* pp. 27, 28. Compare Swift's deplorably ungenteel table conversations at a comparable age, when to the shock of his young friend Laetitia Pilkington he baited the servants; *Memoirs of Mrs. Laetitia Pilkington,* i (Dublin printed; rpt. London: for R. Griffiths and G. Woodfall, 1748), pp. 54–56.

72. *Poems,* i, 26, 31–32.

73. Temple, *Miscellanea, The Second Part,* pp. 92–93, 139–41; French, "Swift, Temple, and 'A Digression on Madness,' " *Texas Studies in Literature and Language* 5 (1963), 45.

74. Temple, *Miscellanea, The Second Part,* p. 28.

75. Ibid., pp. 47–50.

76. For the word *Utopia,* for example, almost all of the *Oxford English Dictionary*'s mid- and late seventeenth-century instances are pejorative in tone. For Temple and the Philosopher's Stone, see *Miscellanea, The Third Part,* p. 254, and cf. p. 282, where Temple includes it in his list of the Moderns' scientific absurdities.

77. Uphaus, *Texas Studies in Literature and Language* 13: 55, 60 & n. 4, 57–58. Cf. Mackie Jarrell on Swift's using the same clichés in both the *Ode to the King* and *A Tritical Essay upon the Faculties of the Mind* more than a decade later (Jarrell, *Texas Studies in Literature and Language* 7: 152). Jarrell thinks the later work to be a case of "self-criticism." For imagery, shared by the *Tale* and the odes, see

Ehrenpreis's summation in *Swift*, I, 198 & n. 3, and Pons, *Swift*, pp. 179, 184, 246–47.

78. *Journal to Stella*, I, 98 (18 Nov. 1710).

79. Mrs. Pilkington, *Memoirs*, I, 54.

80. *Poems*, I, 28–29, lines 76–80.

81. Uphaus, *Texas Studies in Literature and Language* 13: 60. In the next two stanzas the poet tries to undo the damage but only makes things worse. "Only the Laurel got by Peace/ No Thunder e'er can blast," he begins in stanza VI— thus shifting attention away from the impermanence of military-political solutions to the permanence of Temple's Jovian glory as a statesman and peace- maker ("About the Head crown'd with these Bays,/ Like Lambent Fire the Lightning plays"). In a stunning mixture of metaphors, the stanza reaches its climax with the observation that the laurel of peace (or is it the lightning which spares it?) "melts the Sword of War, yet keeps it in the Sheath"—a messy and wasteful business, if nothing else. If warfare is bad, at any rate, then statesman- ship must be good—but only until the beginning of the next stanza, which effectively undercuts the notion. "The wily Shafts of State, those Juggler's Tricks," the poet begins, "Which we call deep Design and Politicks," are actu- ally gross and shallow cheats which Temple, to his everlasting glory, has ex- posed:

> Great God! (said I) what have I seen!
>   On what poor Engines move
> The Thoughts of Monarchs, and Designs of States,
>   What petty Motives rule their Fates! (*Poems*, I, 29–30.)

So much for the glories of the statesmanship which determines the fate of nations. (The stanza continues by picturing the proverbial mountain which with mighty rumblings brings forth a mouse—"Out starts the little Beast, and mocks their idle Fears"—but in the next stanza the mouse turns into an evil and monstrous Serpent, corruption in courts, with whom Temple unavailingly does battle.)

82. Temple, *Early Essays*, p. 29. Because of Temple's considerable losses, she reports, he "resolv'd to give it quite over," though seemingly more the high stakes than the gambling itself. Years later, Swift recollected gambling with Temple at cards, with trifling stakes provided by Temple (*Journal to Stella*, II, 561 [9 Oct. 1712]). Temple was gambling for moderate stakes only four months before his death (Longe, *Lady Giffard*, p. 227).

83. Temple, *Miscellanea, The Second Part*, pp. 300–301. A more particular source may occur in *An Introduction to the History of England*, when Temple describes the battle nearly fought between the great hero-kings William the Conqueror and Malcolm Canmore of Scotland. Instead of fighting, the two kings conclude a lasting peace because they both

> considered the Event, in the Uncertainty and the Consequence; the Loss of a Battle might prove the Loss of a Crown, and the Fortune of one Day determine the Fate of a Kingdom, and they knew very well, that whoever

fights a Battle, with what Number and Forces, what Provisions and Orders or Appearances soever of Success, yet at the best runs a Venture, and leaves much at the Mercy of Fortune, from Accidents not to be foreseen by any Prudence, or governed by any Conduct or Skill.

(Temple, *Introduction to the History of England*, pp. 221–22)

Unlike the view advanced in Swift's *Ode to Temple*, however, Temple's praise of the peace is based on the assumption that the battle will provide a lasting outcome to the quarrel. The peace between the two heroes takes place because each is prudent enough to fear that the fortune of battle may affect his crown and kingdom permanently—and also because both heroes have made equally strong preparations for war (Ibid., p. 224). With Swift, it is just the opposite. Fortune's role is to confound the outcome of war, and by extension, to overturn any peace based on the outcome of war: "For though with Loss or Victory awhile/ Fortune the Gamesters does beguile,/ Yet at the last the Box sweeps all away." For Temple there are heroes; for Swift, only fools.

84. Temple, *Miscellanea, The Third Part*, p. 251. (Temple is trying to counter William Wotton's suggestion that Sarpi's history bears comparison with the best ancient histories.) In his late *Defense* (1705) of his *Reflections Upon Ancient and Modern Learning*, Wotton comments on Temple's statement, and appropriately echoes both Temple's requirements for history ("a noble and great Subject" of actions rather than mere negotiations) and Temple's earlier condemnation of war in *Of Heroick Virtue* ("the designs and effects of Conquests, are but the slaughter and ruin of Mankind, the ravaging of Countries, and defacing the world"). After pointing out that the Council of Trent affected almost all Western European affairs, lay and clerical, for at least forty years, Wotton sarcastically concedes Temple's objection. "But there was no Fighting indeed," he says, "no Burning of Towns, and laying Wast whole Countreys, no knocking out of Mens Brains, in order to do them good, in F. Paul's History; all which I suppose are necessary to make up *such a Great and a Noble Subject, as may be worth the Pains of an Historian.*" See Wotton, *Reflections Upon Ancient and Modern Learning*, 3rd ed., p. 498 (Wotton's italics). For Swift's treatment of a similar theme, see chapter 5, on the greatness of Louis XIV, who "amused himself to take and lose Towns; beat Armies, and be beaten; drive Princes out of their Dominions; fright Children from their Bread and Butter; burn, lay waste, plunder, dragoon, massacre Subject and Stranger, Friend and Foe, Male and Female" (*Tale of a Tub*, p. 165).

85. Both Temple and Lady Giffard seem to have retained a special fondness for things Spanish. In her *Life* of Temple she speaks warmly of the Spanish viceregal capital at Brussels, which (she says) Temple especially fancied (Temple, *Early Essays*, pp. 6, 12, 13). Both learned Spanish there and so enjoyed the language that Temple wrote her his hoaxing love-letter in Spanish (see chapter 1). In the 1690s she was still translating poetry from the Spanish. Temple's Spanish tastes probably helped to cement his bond with his admired first patron, the Hispanophile Lord Arlington, a former emissary at Madrid who was later mocked for his Castilian dress and airs (*D.N.B.*; cf. Temple quoting Spanish to him in a letter reprinted in Courtenay, *Memoirs of Temple*, 1, 51).

86. Temple, *Miscellanea, The Second Part*, p. 71.

87. Temple, *Early Essays*, pp. 28, 30: Temple was "a kind Husband, a fond and indulgent Father, & the best friend in the World & the most constant, knowing himselfe to be soe made him impatient of the least suspicion or Jealousy from those he loved." At the same time, "As he never did injuries soe he was very hard to bear them from any man. . . ."

88. Temple, *Miscellanea, The Second Part*, pp. 70–71: the Spaniard "would needs have it," "he said," "this Spaniard would needs have [it] pass for. . . ."

89. Ibid., pp. 71, 61. Temple also praises *Don Quixote* in his essay *Of Poetry* (Ibid., p. 353).

90. Temple, *Early Essays*, p. 27.

91. Temple, *Miscellanea, The Second Part*, p. 72 (my emphasis); cf. *The Complete Poems of John Wilmot, Earl of Rochester*, ed. David Vieth (New Haven: Yale University Press, 1968), p. 134. The borrowing also allows Temple to identify Charles, among the "more than one or two Ministers of State," without risking *lèse majesté* by naming him.

92. Temple, *Miscellanea, The Third Part*, pp. 281–82. Cf. *The Athenian Mercury* for 6 June 1691 (Vol. 2, No. 4, question 2). The querist (who asks about the operation's safety) claims to have witnessed a transfusion of blood from an unspecified *"tame Animal"* into a convicted prisoner, who was much invigorated thereby: "this trial was made on him, when in Years, and yet he returned to the Vigour of his Youth." The Athenians scoff at the report. "The story of the Physician is very pleasant," they note in reply, "who pretended an Experiment of this Nature with a *Transfusion of Calves Blood*, till the Party cry'd *Bah.*" For the idea behind Temple's sarcastic list of anticipated Modern inventions, the inspiration is almost certainly Joseph Glanvill's enthusiastic list of wonders which the future can expect from the New Science, with its empirical methods and Cartesian principles. See Glanvill's *Scepsis Scientifica: Or, Confest Ignorance the way to Science* (London: by E. Cotes for Henry Eversden, 1665), pp. 133–34. Should "those Heroes go on as they have happily begun," Glanvill exclaims, posterity may consider "a voyage to the *Southern* unknown *Tracts,* yea possibly to the *Moon*" to be "no more strange then one to *America,*" while "it may be as ordinary to buy a *pair* of *wings* to fly into remotest *Regions; as* now a *pair* of *Boots* to ride a *Journey.*" In Temple's sarcastic equivalent are listed "The Art of Flying, till a Man happens to fall down and break his Neck," and "Discoveries of new Worlds in the Planets, and Voyages between this and that in the Moon, to be made as frequently as between York and London." (What humor Temple found, Glanvill had helpfully pointed out: "those, that judge by the narrowness of former *Principles* and *Successes,*" Glanvill observed, "will smile at these *Paradoxical* expectations. . . .") It may have been Swift who introduced Temple to Glanvill's book, or perhaps the other way around. Temple composed his essay in stages between 1694 and 1698, while Swift had read Glanvill in Ulster some time between 1694 and 1696—"a fustian piece of abominable curious Virtuoso Stuff," in Swift's opinion (*Correspondence*, I, 30).

93. Temple, *Miscellanea, The Third Part*, p. 209; French epigrams quoted on pp. 209–11.

94. *Poems*, 1, 32–33. The praise which debauches is presumably Temple's encouragement for writing such poetry, but in a certain sense, perhaps inadvertent, the description suits Temple equally well, in his life of indolence at Moor Park and his healthy appetite for praise. As will be seen, Temple once felt obliged to tell the world that his friends assured him he had achieved success in his writings.

95. Temple, *Miscellanea, The Third Part*, pp. 99–100. Publication came in 1701, but in his preface Swift reported that this essay was "written many Years before the Author's Death" (sig. A2ʳ). Woodbridge tentatively dates its composition to the period before 1686 (*Temple*, p. 212).

96. *Poems*, 1, 15 (Swift's emphasis).

97. Ibid. Swift asks that the ode "be Printed before Your *next Volume* (which I think, is soon to be published,) it being so usual before most Books of any great value among Poets. . . ."

98. *Journal to Stella*, 1, xxiv–xxvii; Murry, *Swift*, pp. 19–21; Ehrenpreis, *Swift*, 1, 254–56, especially 256 n. 1. On Temple's fondness for children see Temple, *Early Essays*, p. 29. Stella maintained ties with Lady Giffard, who held £300 or £400 and who still employed her mother (*Journal to Stella*, 1, 74 [26 Oct. 1710], 99 [21 Nov. 1710]). After the quarrel over Temple's *Memoirs, Part III* in 1709, Swift broke off any remaining relations with Lady Giffard, even though his sister Jane still worked for her (Ibid., 1, 26 [21 Sept. 1710], 366 [24 Sept. 1711]).

99. Ibid., 1, 230.

100. Temple, *Early Essays*, p. 27: "cruel fitts of spleen and melancholy."

101. *Journal to Stella*, 1, 231.

102. Ibid., 1, 92 (11 Nov. 1710).

103. Ibid., 11, 401 (3 Nov. 1711). Ehrenpreis notes that Swift frequently mentions Temple in conjunction with St. John, but does not point out the implicit contrasts which Swift's contexts usually provide (*Swift*, 11, 457–59). The passages may, as he suggests, provide an insight into Swift's fondness for St. John, but if so I believe the reason lies more in the temperamental *differences* between the two statesmen than in the various parallels which Ehrenpreis draws.

104. Williams, *Swift's Library*, p. 62.

105. *Prose Works*, v, 276–77; see also Emily H. Patterson, "Swift's Marginalia in Burnet's *History of His Own Time*," *Enlightenment Essays* 3 (1972), 47–54.

106. Burnet, *History of His Own Time*, 1, 378; *Prose Works*, v, 276. Davis indicates (ibid., p. xxxvi) that he did not have access to the original volumes, then privately owned.

107. Cf. Swift's strictures on the word in *The Tatler*, in *Prose Works*, 11, 175–77.

108. Similarly, later in the *History*, Swift rouses himself somewhat when Burnet again reaches the area of baseless scandal (Ibid., v, 291). When the bishop charges Temple with being a dupe or agent of Tyrconnel's Irish rebels (apparently the case not with Temple but with his son John; see Woodbridge, *Temple*, p. 217), Swift calls Burnet a Scots liar and states that Temple did not know Tyrconnel.

109. See Mayhew, *Harvard Library Bulletin* 19: 400 & n. 3, 403–5.

110. Lyon, MS. entry in his annotated copy of Hawkesworth's *Life of Swift*,

on preliminary leaf 7^v as now bound; quoted by courtesy of the Victoria and Albert Museum.

III. It is not clear whether Lyon actually owned the journal after Swift's death, as he did some of the other MS. items later transcribed and sent to Scott, or had only seen and taken notes of it some years before, when he had the run of the Deanery. Scott prints Swift's entry in a different form, with the warmer description "all that was good and amiable" substituted for "all that was great and good" (Scott, ed., *Works*, I, 43). Somewhat earlier, about 1782, Lyon had released many of his remaining papers to a friend of the younger Thomas Sheridan. See John Lyon to the younger Deane Swift, ALs, 8 Mar. 1783, Forster Collection no. 570 (48. G. 6/20), Victoria and Albert Museum. In practice, however, Sheridan seems to have scanted the sources at his disposal and primarily relied upon Lyon's notes in the annotated *Life of Swift* as John Nichols had published them in the 1779 *Supplement* to the Hawkesworth edition of Swift's *Works* (vol. 25; London: for J. Nichols), pp. 364–404. One way or the other, the version which Sheridan printed is clearly derived from Lyon's note in the annotated *Life*. Compare the 1779 *Supplement*, p. 369, with Thomas Sheridan, *The Life of the Rev. Dr. Jonathan Swift* (London: for C. Bathurst et al., 1784), p. 26 n. Scott may have worked from a recent transcription of Swift's journal, but I suspect that his variant reading comes from an error in transcribing Nichols or Sheridan, and that Lyon never owned the journal to begin with. Even if he had, his own transcription would carry greater authority than any made for Scott. As an antiquary, Lyon was unusually sensitive to the need for accuracy.

112. Lyon is also a source (MS. Lyon annotations, p. 27) for the story of Swift's taking lessons in "the right manner of cutting Asparagus, according to ye most approved method used in Holland," from William III himself at Moor Park. The anecdote sounds like a Swiftian hoax. It also makes much of the King's frequent visits to Moor Park, and Swift's frequent attendance on him, and as such seems to echo Swift's approach in the unreliable autobiographical fragment, as discussed earlier in this chapter. Whatever the case, Lyon presents the story in all earnestness. Possibly he had it from the younger Deane Swift, the biographer, who said he "heard [it] from the Doctor's own mouth"; see Deane Swift, *An Essay Upon the Life of Swift*, p. 108. Deane Swift's biography had appeared a decade before Lyon made his annotations. John Nichols had dated them July 1765 (1779 *Supplement*, p. 364), while a more recent commentator dates at least one entry to the period between 1774 and 1778 and others to the period shortly before July 1766. See Phillip S.Y. Sun, "Swift's Eighteenth-Century Biographies," Dissertation, Yale University, 1963, p. 117 & n.

113. For Temple's retiring habits when ill see Temple, *Early Essays*, p. 31. The letter to young Boyle (who at twenty-two was nine years Swift's junior) is preserved in a transcript authorized by Boyle's son John, fifth Earl of Orrery, among the Orrery Papers at Harvard (MS Eng. 218.2, vol. 5, pp. 10–11). Though printed some time ago (with a few inaccuracies) in *The Orrery Papers*, ed. Emily DeBurgh-Canning Boyle, Countess of Cork and Orrery (London: Duckworth, 1903), I, 21, neither the letter nor Temple's intended meeting with Boyle seems to have received attention from Swift scholars. The invitation to Boyle grew out

of the young aristocrat's attack on Temple's opponent, Dr. Richard Bentley, in
Dr. Bentley's Dissertations on Phalaris examin'd, which had appeared that March or
April (Harvard MS Eng. 218.2, vol. 5, p. 8). The text of Temple's letter, reproduced by permission of the Houghton Library, Harvard University, is as follows:

> *For Mr Char. Boyle at / the Countess of Orrery's in Park-Place. London.*
>
>   Moore Park. July 17th 1698.
> Sir,
>   Though I doubt it will not be my Advantage, that you should know
> me better, for Fear you should like me less than I have Reason to think you
> do, yet I shall be very glad to run that Venture, rather than lose the Honour
> of your Acquaintance, and Company here, which I find, by your Letter,
> you intend me. I am sorry you should think there is Need of any Body to
> introduce you, but hope my Lord Berkley [of Stratton, Temple's nephew-
> in-law] will at least make you the Offer of conveying you hither, where he
> intends to come the Beginning of this Week, and which is a Time I should
> like the better, because there will be no other Company that I know of here:
> But either in this, or any other, or alone, you will be always wellcome to,
>   Sir, / Y^r most Humble Servant / Wm Temple

At first glance Temple's assertion that "there will be no other Company that
I know of here" seems to slight Swift, but as a regular employee in Temple's
household, Swift would probably not have qualified as "Company" for a visitor
to meet. Even so, the special distinctions which Temple pays his young correspondent should not have flattered his older and more talented secretary-amanu-
ensis, who had already begun more powerful work against Temple's opponents
in *A Tale of a Tub* and *The Battle of the Books.*

114. For Temple's trip in September, see Longe, *Lady Giffard,* p. 227. Re-
sponding to a letter (now lost) from Lady Giffard of 30 August, her nephew-in-
law William Berkeley, fourth Baron Berkeley of Stratton, mentioned in passing
that he was "sorry to hear the gout troubles him [Temple] again." See the
unpublished A.L.s., dated 6 Sept. 1698, in the Osborn Collection at Yale, Osborn
Gift 70.1.5.

115. *Poems,* 1, 49, original emphasis. Congreve would be "blest" to be in
Swift's situation and know Swift's country muse: "How proudly would he haste
the joy to meet,/ And drop his laurel at *Apollo*'s feet." The poem's first editor,
Nichols, rightly identifies Apollo as Temple (Ibid., n.), the only suitable male
verse-reader at Moor Park. This is a fairly restrained touch considering the
Christ imagery we have seen in the ode to Temple. It is a fitting and graceful
touch from Temple's point of view, considering his belief that divine honors go
to the possessors of heroic virtue in its peaceable aspects. In his essay *Of Poetry,*
Temple himself expounds the view that Apollo inspires the true poetic fire, the
sort claimed by Swift in his ode to Temple. See Temple, *Miscellanea, The Second
Part,* p. 316, and earlier in this chapter; cf. Swift on the source of his inspiration
in the Athenian ode (Temple himself, that is). As for poor Congreve, cut off

from the joys open to Swift, he was in London at the time of writing, suffering a *succès fou* as the town's brightest young wit and Dryden's acknowledged successor. From a Moor Park point of view, Congreve's eminence heightens Swift's compliments to Temple, but any other point of view renders them ludicrous. In 1693, Swift was as obscure as Congreve was famous. Moreover, Swift was aware that Congreve's reputation had a bearing upon the poem's effect. Before deciding whether or not to send Congreve the poem for publication, or so he wrote to his cousin Thomas, Swift wanted to know what success Congreve's most recent play was having (*Correspondence*, 1, 14). It was *The Double Dealer:* the reception was disappointing, and apparently Swift never sent the poem (Ibid., n.).

116. Longe, *Lady Giffard*, pp. 198, 202, 208, 213, 227; in the remaining letter (p. 215) she discusses her decision to dismiss an overly ladylike servant, and reports that Temple agrees to the woman's departure "lest he fall in love with her." During attacks of ill-health, especially gout, a man does not normally think of love.

117. Temple, *Early Essays*, pp. 29, 31 ('A' manuscript), and p. xii ('B' manuscript); echoed in *The Life and Character of Sir William Temple, Bar$^{t.}$ Written by a particular Friend* (London: for B. Motte, 1728), p. 18: "He lived four Years after [i.e. after Lady Temple's death in 1694/5] extreamly afflicted with the Gout, which at last wore out his Life; and with the help of Age and a natural Decay of Strength and Spirits, ended it in January, 1698, in his seventieth Year. . . ." The *Life* was incorporated as a new preface for the second issue of the 1731 *Works* of Temple. It generally follows Lady Giffard's 'A' manuscript of 1690, except for the four final paragraphs, which include the information about Temple's health in the 1690s (drawn from the 'B' manuscript of later years) and which report on Temple's visits to William III at Richmond and Windsor, as well as the King's visit to Moor Park "in his Way from Winchester" (Ibid., p. 17). Swift is not mentioned once. See further in *Early Essays*, pp. xi–xv, although Moore Smith is unaware of the 1731 publication of the *Life*, as is also the case with Woodbridge (*Temple*, p. 223, n. 17).

118. The exceptions are a polite wish for Temple's good health in the 'penitential' letter to him (*Correspondence*, 1, 18), and the title of the Moor Park poem *Occasioned by Sir W—— T——'s Late Illness and Recovery*, dated Dec. 1693 and apparently intended for Temple, his wife ("Mild Dorothea"), and Lady Giffard (the weeping "Dorinda"). Except for the title, the poem does not say anything about Temple's illness, but rather deals with the reactions and mental associations in the two ladies and (most of all) in the poet and his muse.

119. *Correspondence*, 1, 24; the letter of 13 January will be discussed in this chapter.

120. Swift made himself useful as a deputy or assistant to Temple's brother Sir John, in drawing up the final financial accounts for the Moor Park estate. During this period Swift also seems to have continued keeping track of some household expenses at Moor Park (cf. *Correspondence*, 1, 1–2), including the disbursal of sums for the household's mourning clothes and terminal wages. The Osborn Collection at Yale preserves a good deal of both men's work of this sort,

including several receipts written and docketed by Swift. The latest I found was dated 20 Feb., on a receipt itself dated 21 Feb. (fb 182, fol. 63). On 21 February Swift had completed his account work and received a small gratuity for his pains. On a list of monies disbursed by Swift, Sir John Temple noted that Swift still held £5 14s. 5d. together with "the [ten broad] shillings in Miss Bettyes mony which was given him for his care and trouble on the 21 of Febr: 1698" (Ibid., fol. 23). By 9 March he had probably left Moor Park. Swift had regularly drawn up and docketed receipts for wages and legacies paid out in the household, but on 9 March appears a late receipt for a small legacy drawn up in the hand of Ralph Mose, the Moor Park steward, and docketed by Sir John Temple (Ibid., fol. 79).

121. Longe, *Lady Giffard*, p. 242 (checked against A.L.s. at Yale, Osborn Gift 70.1.5). On the same day Henley wrote to Lady Giffard to say as much (Ibid., p. 239). Both he and Danvers also advised her against publishing Temple's *Memoirs, Part III* in 1709, when she sent out her own MS. of it (Ibid., pp. 243–44, 248–49). Born in 1650, Danvers was the son of the regicide Sir John Danvers by his third wife, Lady Temple's mother's sister, and in 1697 he held some sort of government post in London (Ibid., pp. 24, 198; *D.N.B.*, s.v. Sir John Danvers). For Henley, Swift's friend in London a decade later and probably in 1699 as well, see *D.N.B.*; Pat Rogers, "Anthony Henley and Swift," *American Notes & Queries* 8 (1970), 101, 116–20; *Journal to Stella*, I, 54 n. 16; and *The Rothschild Library*, no. 2319. The last describes a book which Henley gave Swift on 12 July 1701, only three months after Swift set foot in England for the first time since 1699.

The visiting clergyman who wrote the sermon, Mr. Savage, is tentatively identified by Williams as the minor author and translator John Savage, a product of Temple's alma mater, Emmanuel College, Cambridge (*Journal to Stella*, II, 423 n. 26). See also John Savage's *Select Collection of Letters of the Antients* (London: for J. Hartley et al., 1703), a book which places him in the ranks of Temple's sympathizers in the Ancient-Modern controversy. The book flaunts Phalaris' name on the title page (heading its list of Greek letter-writers) and though he deprecates the recent dispute about the genuineness of Phalaris' letters, Savage pays homage to their *"Air of Antiquity"* much as Temple had done, and alludes slightingly to Temple's opponents as supercilious critics who might "assert that some few of this *Collection* are not *Genuine*" (sig. A2ᵛ–A3ʳ).

122. Longe, *Lady Giffard*, p. 242. The sermon went unpublished, although Savage received a gratuity through Swift, either for his pains or for his mourning expenses. Sir John Temple drew up an expenditure list entitled "Mourning & funerall," with the entry "To Mʳ. Savage pd by Mʳ Swift – – – 05-10-0" (Osborn Collection, Yale, fb 182, fol. 65ʳ). See also Swift's own list recording the disbursal, dated 4 Feb. 1699 (Ibid., fol. 24ʳ).

123. Longe, *Lady Giffard*, p. 232 (my italics).

124. Ibid. (my italics). The reading is a novel one, but she gives no source for it. Probably she mistranscribed from a published source. Her quotations occur in adjoining paragraphs, and it was a short step from the version then current, "good and amiable among men," to her "good and excellent in Man." See Craik, *Life of Swift*, p. 74; and John Forster, *The Life of Jonathan Swift* (New York: Harper, 1876), p. 115; both follow Scott's text, discussed in note III in this

chapter. On the other hand, because Miss Longe worked from Lady Giffard's MSS. and other Moor Park materials which descended in her family, it is also possible that she transcribes accurately from a transcript or note of Swift's journal preserved by Lady Giffard herself. If so, it becomes certain that Swift intended the entry for Lady Giffard's eyes. On the dispersal of the Longe family's MSS., see the Sotheby auction catalogue for 3 Aug. 1934, pp. 98–103. The sermon was in lot 1081; it went to a buyer named Lampson, whom I have been unable to trace.

125. *Journal to Stella*, II, 423 (28 Nov. 1711). Farnham was the town nearest Moor Park. Swift's words do not necessarily imply that Savage published the sermon, as Williams thinks (Ibid., n. 26), because Swift's parallel is ironic. In quality as in topicality, the sermon was not exactly in a class with the *Conduct of the Allies*, and its fate was that of being espoused by Lady Giffard, sent to London, and then returned with the tactful suggestion that it be spared publication.

126. Mayhew, *Harvard Library Bulletin* 19: 404 n. 7. Mayhew is not as clear about Swift's ownership inscription in the book, and reports some questions about its position on the flyleaf. From the testimony of the man who saw the inscription in 1811, he gives the inscription's date as St. Valentine's Day, 1697. Since Swift often used purely Old-Style dating, long superseded by 1811, the transcriber may have confused an O.S. date reading 1697 but meaning 1698 New Style.

127. Temple, *Miscellanea, The Second Part*, pp. 148–50; cf. *Aeneid*, VI, 660, 663–64.

128. "The Form and Manner of Ordering of Priests," *The Book of Common Prayer*. I quote from the London ed. of 1704 (folio, by Charles Bill and the Executrix of Thomas Newcomb), sig. Ttl^r.

129. [Duncombe, ed.], *Letters, by Several Eminent Persons Deceased*, I, 2 n. ("This letter, the original of which, with the post-mark on it, is in the editor's hands, is indorsed . . ."); title page to Thomas Swift's sermon *Noah's Dove* (published 1710), quoted in *Journal to Stella*, II, 405–6 n. 11.

130. Thomas's basic duties were the same as Jonathan's—not only secretarial work but also bookkeeping (see Longe, *Lady Giffard*, p. 216, where Lady Giffard calls Thomas the "brother" of the current "secretary," Jonathan). For documentation of Temple taking to his bed (in Oct. 1697), see ibid., p. 208 and Temple, *Early Essays*, p. 31 (for the period before 1690, withdrawing from family when in pain). No matter what his private views of religion, Temple probably did his duty as a proper seventeenth-century gentleman, and held family prayers. See the family prayer which he "made in the Fanatic Times," when his servants belonged to odd and clashing sects (printed in Courtenay, *Memoirs of Temple*, II, 373–76).

131. The *Complete Key to the Tale of the Tub* terms both Thomas and Jonathan "Domestick Chaplains to Sir William Temple" (*Prose Works*, I, xxx). For the *Key*'s connections with Thomas Swift, see *A Tale of a Tub*, pp. xiv–xix, and Robert Martin Adams in *Modern Philology* 64: 198–201 & passim. Swift never mentioned any ecclesiastical duties, that I can find, and I doubt that they extended to anything more than household prayers, either on a regular basis or as a stand-in for the ailing Temple. It was the clergyman Savage who composed

Temple's funeral sermon. What is more, Swift had good reason to keep silent about any priestly association with Temple, thanks to Temple's reputation for doubtful orthodoxy (chapter 1; cf. Boyer, *Memoirs of Temple*, pp. 417–18). To the best of my knowledge, Swift never once mentioned Temple's religious views, one way or the other, and in his autobiographical fragment he passes over the period 1696–99 with notable economy ("and continued in Sr W Temple's house till the Death of that great Man"; *Prose Works*, v, 194). Thomas, with his lack of discretion, was no more afraid of claiming a formal religious association with Temple, than of claiming credit for writing the controversial religious allegory in *A Tale of a Tub*.

132. *Prose Works*, I, xxxvii & plate facing; Ehrenpreis, *Swift*, I, 258.

133. Mayhew, *Harvard Library Bulletin* 19: 404 n. 7; "confe[r]ta" emended from "confesta" (cf. Scott, ed., *The Works of Jonathan Swift, D.D.*, 2nd ed. [Edinburgh: for Constable, 1824], I, 467): the snow 'lay dense on the earth, not only in the night but indeed until about noon on the following day; this I have seen near the village called Farnham in the county of Surrey.'

134. See the *Athenian Mercury* for 5 April 1692 (Vol. VII, no. 3), completely devoted to proposals for "A *Scheme of Enquiries* proposed to all *Ingenious Gentlemen*, and other *Inquisitive Persons* . . . in order to Form a Body *of the Natural* Artificial and Civil *History* of *England* . . . ," especially sections I (meteorological wonders) and VII (wonders concerning men and animals, including "Any thing remarkable that attends a *Family* or single person in their *Lives* or *Deaths?*"); as well as the earlier request (1 Dec. 1691, Vol. V, no. 1, announcement on verso) for accounts of people who had *"dy'd suddenly* within these few *Months,"* together "with the most remarkable *Circumstances* relating to their Deaths." From the beginning, a standing invitation for reports of oddities had been in effect, repeated in the Athenians' standing rules and elsewhere: "If any Person whatever will send in any new *Experiment*, or *curious Instance*, which they know to be truth, and matter of fact, circumstantiated with time and place, we will insert it in our Mercury; (but we shan't use the Authors Name without his License) and if it wants a *Demonstration* to the Senders, we will endeavour to find one, for the satisfaction of them as well as of all other Ingenious Enquirers into *Natural Speculations*" (advert. at end of preface, Vol. II; also in adverts. at end of Vol. I, Nos. 14, 17, and Supplement preface; Dunton's emphases).

135. For comets and meteors, see *Miscellanea, The Third Part*, pp. 42–43: " 'tis hard to determine whether some Constellations of Celestial Bodies, or Inflammations of Air from Meteors or Comets, may not have a powerfull Effect upon the Minds, as well as Bodies of Men, upon the Distempers and Diseases of both, and thereby upon Heats and Humors of vulgar Minds, and the Commotions and Seditions of a People who happen to be most Subjected to their Influence." For the ancient sages, see *Miscellanea, The Second Part*, pp. 26, 44. The "strange height" the prognosticators reached was that of being believed demigods, the ultimate reward of heroic virtue.

136. *Athenian Mercury*, 22 Dec. 1691 (Vol. V, no. 7), question 1. In later years Dunton identified the questioner as Temple; see McEwen, *Oracle of the Coffee House*, p. 33 & n. 2, and Dunton, *Life and Errors*, p. 193. Dunton's highly deferen-

tial tone in the issue's prefatory remarks seems to confirm the identification—
as does the nature of the questions themselves, which largely deal with problems
at issue in *Upon Ancient and Modern Learning.* Temple's Athenian contributions
have not yet been fully explored or evaluated.

137. Temple, *Miscellanea, The Third Part,* pp. 246, 255 (ancient priests' cheats
and superstitions), 224 (Empedocles), 218–21 (Delphic oracle). On the date of the
essay's composition, see the manuscript note entitled "A Fragment written
upon the Subject of Ant. & Mod. Learning," which accompanies the surviving
portion of Temple's early draft fragments (composed ca. 1695) preserved in the
Rothschild Collection (Rothschild no. 2253: the fragments themselves are in
Swift's hand under the title "Hints: written at the Desire of Dᴿ F. and of His
Friend"). According to the note, Temple began composing the fragments "some
months" after William Wotton first published his *Reflections upon Ancient and
Modern Learning* late in 1694. The book had exposed some of Temple's false
steps in the essay *Upon Ancient and Modern Learning.* At first Temple meant the
fragments to be incorporated in an answer to Wotton being prepared by one
"Mʳ H" at Oxford, but the project fell through. Now that Wotton has brought
out a second edition (1697), continues the note, Temple has decided to let the
fragments "take their Fortune abroad." (Wotton's 1697 edition contained Richard Bentley's highly damaging appendix, which disproved Temple's claims
about the genuineness and antiquity of Phalaris' letters.) We shall encounter
Temple's "Hints" again later in this chapter.

138. Oxford: E Theatro Sheldoniano, 1679. (Together with two retorts to
objections raised against it, the treatise was reprinted in Vossius' *Variarum
Observationum Liber* [London: apud Robertum Scott, 1685], pp. 209–397.) Vossius
gives special attention to Sibylline texts showing signs of Hellenistic Jewish
forgery, but also concerns himself with the wider pattern of ancient oracles
predicting a Great King's advent. According to the *D.N.B.*, it was *De Sibyllinis*
which apparently inspired Charles II's remark about Vossius, "that he would
believe anything if only it were not in the Bible." The book seems to represent
Temple's interests more directly than Swift's. Swift's library lists record no
other titles by Isaac Vossius, and Swift himself mentions Vossius only once in
his writings—to associate him with Temple. Among the Army of the Ancients,
in the *Battle of the Books,* "The *Allies,* led by *Vossius* and *Temple,* brought up the
Rear" (*Tale of a Tub,* p. 238 & n. 2). Vossius has not yet been inspected for signs
of influence on Temple, but the *D.N.B.*'s list of his works suggests many parallel
interests, and even the possibility of personal contact in Holland or in England,
where he dedicated his *De Poematum cantu et viribus rythmi* (London, 1673) to
Temple's early patron, Lord Arlington. A reading of *De Sibyllinis* may lie behind
comments in Temple's two essays about ancient and modern learning. Though
credulous enough about "Magick" and the Delphic oracle, Temple shows himself aware of the doubts surrounding the authorship of many Sibylline fragments (*Miscellanea, The Second Part,* p. 11; *Miscellanea, The Third Part,* p. 267).

139. See *A Tale of a Tub,* pp. lvi–lvii. The Temple influence is apparent in
the list's healthy proportion of books relating to travel and exotic foreign countries. It is comparable in this way to the list of books bought by Temple in 1698

(Ehrenpreis, *Swift*, 1, 286–87). We have already noted Temple's interest in voyages of discovery. His essays *Of Heroick Virtue* and *Upon Ancient and Modern Learning*, in *Miscellanea, The Second Part*, had devoted considerable attention to far-flung peoples, including the Chinese, the ancient Brahmans, Assyrians, and Ethiopians, the Vikings and Icelanders, the Scythians and Tatars, the Incas of Peru, and the Arabs. For Temple's probable reading in this area, see Woodbridge, *Temple*, pp. 282–88. This is not to say that Swift himself had no interest in the subject, but Swift's interest chiefly manifested itself a good two decades later, in Gulliver's *Travels*, where it appears in a spirit very different from Temple's. The strongest sign of Temple's influence in Swift's reading list, though, is its inclusion of two of Temple's works which Swift had helped the author prepare for the press not long before, the *Memoirs of What Past in Christendom* and the *Introduction to the History of England*, listed next after "Virgil, bis" and "Horace, 9 volumes." It is strange that Swift would want to reread them so soon after transcribing and entering Temple's corrections in them. On the other hand, the inclusion of books (if known) would have been highly gratifying to their author: as Pope later wrote of a gratified gentleman patron, "Horace and he went hand and hand in song."

140. See *The Rothschild Library*, no. 2321, where the book's binding is described as quarter calf. When Lord Rothschild acquired the book in 1938, through A. S. W. Rosenbach, the binding was an earlier one advertised not as contemporary but rather as "full maroon morocco, gilt fillet border on the sides, gilt edges" —from the sound of it, a mid-eighteenth century or even nineteenth century production. See lot 261 in the American Art Association auction catalogue for 13 January 1938 (New York, Anderson Galleries). Dr. Philip Gaskell informs me that the *second* free endpaper, adjacent to the endpaper bearing Swift's inscription, may be old enough to be original, and that it definitely does not represent the same paper as the inscription leaf. This raises the possibility that, to enhance the book's value or interest, some early collector or bookseller may have removed the inscription leaf from another volume and transferred it to the Vossius. It is not quite clear, though, why anyone would have wished to doctor a book as obscure as the Vossius, which brought only $75 in 1938, especially when it *already* contained Swift's signature (written on the dedication page) and when the transfer meant lowering the value and interest of the book from which the inscription leaf originally came. As described in the 1938 A.A.A. catalogue, the Vossius was sold with a letter from the distinguished nineteenth-century Swift scholar, John Forster, "authenticating these signatures." Although Forster's letter now seems to be lost, it would appear that the tipped-in inscription was present in the volume in December 1859, when Forster wrote. Possibly the book had already been grangerized by then (with the results escaping Forster's notice), but I lean towards the alternate explanation—that the inscription leaf originally came with the Vossius, and that the second free endpaper was supplied during the course of rebinding in the eighteenth century (which itself would have necessitated some sort of cutting out and tipping in of the endpaper bearing the inscription). Because of the signature on the dedication page, there seems to be no reason to doubt that the book itself once belonged to Swift. The

title appears in both his 1715 and 1745 library lists. Later in this chapter we shall return to the inscription and others of the same sort. I am grateful to the Rosenbach Foundation, and to Ms. Suzanne Bolan of its staff, for allowing me to inspect Dr. Rosenbach's files, including his annotated copy of the 1938 sale catalogue.

141. *Tale of a Tub*, p. lvii.

142. Temple, *Early Essays*, p. 31. For Lady Giffard's recommending Temple's written self-portrait "to those that care either to know or imitate him," compare Temple, *Miscellanea, The Second Part*, p. 287:

> Who-ever has a mind to trace the Paths of Heroick Virtue, which lead to the Temple of True Honour and Fame, need seek them no further, than in the Stories and Examples of those Illustrious Persons here assembled. And so I leave this Crown of never fading Lawrel, in full view of such great and noble Spirits, as shall deserve it, in this or in succeeding Ages. Let them win it and wear it.

143. Ibid., pp. xi–xii. She and her brother agreed that the *Life* should be prefaced to any eventual collected edition of Temple's works (as eventually happened in 1731). Moore Smith believes that it was Sir John who caused her to rewrite the *Life* in a shorter, less personal form.

144. See chapter 1. Boyer's account of Temple's life deals almost exclusively with the public side, and is largely drawn from Temple's published works, which Boyer quotes for pages at a time.

145. For the descriptions of Temple's appearance, compare Boyer, *Memoirs of Temple*, pp. 418–19, with Temple, *Early Essays*, p. 27. The Lely portrait appears engraved as Boyer's frontispiece. Boyer concludes the paragraph with an awkwardly-introduced reference to Temple's "intirely-beloved Sister, the ingenious Lady Giffard: who, as she shar'd and eas'd the Fatigues of his Voyages and Travels during his publick Employments, so was she the chief Delight and Comfort of his Retirement and Old Age."

146. Boyer, *Memoirs of Temple*, pp. vii–viii, my emphasis. In Temple's farewell letter to her, which he directed "To be opened after my death" and which she carefully preserved until her own, Temple had paid tribute not to the sister but to the friend. He voiced his confidence that "you will never fail of doing me all the good offices I do or can deserve of you, either during my life or after my death, considering the sure Friendship that has soe long existed between us without interruption and perhaps without example, and which I am sure will do soe to the end of our lives . . ." (Courtenay, *Memoirs of Temple*, II, 227; Longe, *Lady Giffard*, p. viii). Appropriately enough, when Lady Giffard's *Life* of Temple eventually appeared, it respected her wish for anonymity and bore the ascription "Written by a particular Friend" (Temple, *Early Essays*, pp. xiv, xi).

147. Boyer, *Memoirs of Temple*, p. iv (Boyer's emphases).

148. Temple, *Miscellanea, The Second Part*, pp. 309 and 239, respectively. Dating as it does from the period before Swift began his *Tale of a Tub*, Temple's

call for "a clear Account of Enthusiasm and Fascination from their natural Causes" has an oddly prophetic ring.

149. Longe, *Lady Giffard*, p. 239 (A.L.s. now at Trinity College, Cambridge, Rothschild no. 1009[ii]).

150. Originally Temple named a third executor, his brother Henry, but Henry had died by the time Temple drew up his codicil in early 1698. See Courtenay, *Memoirs of Temple*, II, 485–86.

151. Sir John's bound executor papers, in the Osborn Collection at Yale (fb 182, fol. 71ʳ). Apparently Lady Giffard was to keep Swift's legacy for the immediate future, in return for paying the interest—a common arrangement in the days before savings banks. For Temple's codicil, see Courtenay, *Memoirs of Temple*, II, 486.

152. Swift received £50 for the third volume of Temple's *Letters* (receipt in the Rothschild Collection, Rothschild no. 2256) and £40 for the *Memoirs, Part III* (Ibid., no. 2259). With the 1699 volumes of *Letters* and the *Miscellanea, The Third Part*, his total receipts should have amounted to about £200 or £250, spread over a decade.

153. Courtenay, *Memoirs of Temple*, II, 484–85.

154. The texts printed or described in Longe, *Lady Giffard*, and in the *Early Essays* remained at Moor Park, and eventually descended in the Longe family. Besides Temple's early essays and romances (not intended for publication) and Lady Giffard's *Life* of Temple (meant for eventual publication with Temple's collected works), Lady Giffard retained some fragmentary early drafts of Temple materials published posthumously by Swift (Sotheby catalogue, 3 Aug. 1934, lots 1070, 1081), the draft translation of Temple's facetious Spanish love letter to her (the translation never published; see chapter 1), and the early but full autograph draft of the *Memoirs, Part III*, which she first considered publishing herself and then (after correspondents persuaded her that it could give offense to mutual friends) tried to use as a lever to forestall or discredit Swift's authorized edition, some months later in 1709. She knew that Temple had appointed Swift, not her, as his literary executor: "You wonder why I should complain of yʳ refusing me those Papers when I was possessed of correct Copyes," Swift wrote her that year. "It was because I could not possibly be secure while there were any Copyes out of my Possession, and those sometimes as your Ladyship owned to me, lent abroad; and besides I knew that they justly belonged to me . . ." (*Correspondence*, I, 157). In addition see Longe, *Lady Giffard*, pp. 243–44, 247–49. Despite Miss Longe's attempts to exonerate her, Lady Giffard seems to have acted arbitrarily and discreditably throughout the affair. In *American Notes & Queries* 8: 99, Pat Rogers publishes an additional letter to Lady Giffard on the subject, from her old friend Anthony Henley, whom she had consulted about publishing her MS. of the *Memoirs*. In 1709 Henley was also on friendly terms with Swift. When Swift published the *Memoirs* from the revised MS.—thus reasserting his rights as Temple's literary executor, ending her own options, and angering her in the process—Henley found himself caught in the crossfire. In his letter he tries to mollify Lady Giffard without joining her attack on Swift. Accordingly he insists that she has nothing to lose, after all, from publication,

that she need not fear "reproaches or resentment" from friends of hers on whom the *Memoirs* may reflect, because she did not publish it herself. Despite Rogers's conjecture, the letter does not support the view that Swift remained ignorant of Lady Giffard's *Memoirs* MS. Swift had worked far too closely with Temple's papers to remain ignorant of it, and even if he had forgotten it by 1709, he would soon have heard when Lady Giffard sent it around for advice about publishing it—that is, even before she herself acknowledged her action (the copies "sometimes as your Ladyship owned to me, lent abroad"). In Stella's mother and (periodically) in his own sister Jane, Swift enjoyed excellent contacts in Lady Giffard's household, and even after he broke off all direct commerce with their mistress in 1709 he continued to receive news from them (*Journal to Stella*, pp. 19, 39, 92–93, 107, 172, 246, 357, 366, 420, 428, 558). Swift already knew that Henley was an old friend of Lady Giffard's, and probably had heard or guessed that she had consulted him about publishing the *Memoirs*, just as she had about publishing Savage's sermon ten years before. If Henley's account is correct, Swift then clarified his position to Henley in the most tactful but knowing terms, without naming Lady Giffard directly or implicating Henley in her designs: "I never heard Dr Swift say one word of it [her deliberations about publishing the *Memoirs*]," Henley writes her, "but that hee heard there were coppys of em in the world and he beleivd they would bee printed . . ." (quoted in Rogers, *American Notes & Queries* 8: 99). As Rogers remarks (p. 100), the explanation also allows Henley to clear himself, in Lady Giffard's eyes, from any suspicion of cooperating with Swift. He begins his letter by professing as much surprise as hers in "seeing an Advertisement of the memoirs beeing printed." All in all, Henley walks his tightrope with considerable skill.

155. In April 1698, when Swift wrote to his friend and successor at Kilroot, the Rev. John Winder, he reported his failure to win advancement through the Earl of Sunderland and hinted at other plans in the offing. Writing to Winder nine months later, on 13 January 1699, he says nothing more about them or his prospects generally. If anything, he sounds almost wistful about his lack of importance in the world. Winder was anxious to have Swift's good opinion, it seems, and Swift remarks that "I wish You could as easily make my Esteem and Friendship for You to be of any Value, as You may be sure to command them" (*Correspondence*, 1, 29).

156. Longe, *Lady Giffard*, pp. 232–33, 235. She bases her argument on a phrase in Savage's sermon, about Temple's trying "to steal silently out of the world," and a note from Sir John's daughter, Lady Berkeley of Stratton, who reproaches herself for not accompanying her father to Moor Park to be present there at the time of Temple's death: "I wish I had gone down now with my Father. . . ." Here and elsewhere in the note, the niece sounds as if Temple's death came as a surprise. Swift's letter to Winder, two weeks before, had not mentioned anything about Temple's health—not that Swift ever did, so far as we can find, except to Temple and Lady Giffard. In September, after reporting a touch of gout in August, Lady Giffard described Temple as healthy and cheerful—with a certain tone of relief, as Miss Longe notes (*Lady Giffard*, pp. 227–28; cf. Lord Berkeley to Lady Giffard, A.L.s. of 6 Sept. 1698, Osborn Gift 70.1.5 at Yale).

157. *Correspondence,* I, 32. Hindsight may color her account a little because by the time she wrote (26 May), Swift had probably given up his suit at Court and shifted his attention instead to the Earl of Berkeley, newly appointed to his Lord Justiceship in Dublin. Jane's report undoubtedly reflects Swift's point of view: I find no mention of her in the Moor Park account books of 1698–99 (the "Mrs Swift" who appears once or twice there seems to be the mother at Leicester), and I conclude she was not yet at Moor Park serving Lady Giffard. Williams thinks she was in Dublin at the time (Ibid., n. 1). She had been at Moor Park for a period in 1692 (Ibid., pp. 11–12). Jane writes to the same cousin Deane Swift whom Jonathan addressed so impressively five years before (see chapter 1), and she may unwittingly exaggerate Temple's great fondness and intended helpfulness to Swift. It is worth noting that, when Swift decided to resign his living at Kilroot early in 1698—a step which, by depriving him of something to fall back upon, threw him even more completely on Temple's good offices—Temple advised him instead to renew his license to be absent from the parish (*Correspondence,* I, 26; cf. Ehrenpreis, *Swift,* I, 171, and Landa, *Swift and the Church of Ireland,* p. 24).

158. Autobiographical fragment, *Prose Works,* V, 195.

159. Longe, *Lady Giffard,* p. 234, corrected by A.L.s. at Yale, Osborn Gift 70.1.5.

160. Ibid., p. 239.

161. Ibid., p. 241. I see no reason to think that Lady Giffard's request involved Swift in any way. Possibly she needed the King's permission for something relating to Temple's interment. The bulk of him had been buried on 31 January in Westminster Abbey, next to his wife and daughter Diana, but in his will he directed that his heart be buried at Moor Park (not consecrated ground). See Courtenay, *Memoirs of Temple,* II, 485–86.

162. Longe, *Lady Giffard,* p. 237, corrected by A.L.s. at Yale.

163. In one of Swift's loose papers in the Moor Park accounts (Osborn Collection, Yale, fb 182, fol. 26^r) appears the entry, "Febr. 10th to Mr Swift for Mourning and his Journy to London &c. 10–13–0." Swift would not be reimbursed for making a trip or buying mourning on his own account, and had he stayed at Moor Park during the few days following Temple's death he would not have needed to lay out money for mourning. As a Moor Park employee, he qualified for receiving his mourning clothes gratis at Moor Park, as did everyone else from the steward down. The wholesale mourning bills for household employees (draper's, tailor's, shoemaker's and hatter's bills, respectively fols. 20, 58, 56, and 57, the earliest dated 27 January and receipted 3 February) indicate that Swift eventually received some of the regular issue at Moor Park but by then did not need a hat, or a coat or anything else belonging to his mourning clothes but "Wastcoat & Breeches," as he entered the correction himself on the tailor's bill. Ralph Mose, the Moor Park steward, had also gone up to London right after Temple died: comparison of his accounts indicates that his business was with the immediate family, and that Swift's lay elsewhere. Mose left for London on 28 January, the day following the night Temple died, and spent only £3 1s. od., including 12s. 9d. to hire a man to accompany him (fols. 25, 48, 49^r, 52). His

trip took three days—the first night spent en route at Kingston-on-Thames, the nearest town to the family houses at Sheen and East Sheen, and the second night in London, where Temple's granddaughters and daughter-in-law were living. He claimed no expenses for mourning—a sure indication that his business lay no further than with the other Temple households—and his departure date indicates that he brought them news of Temple's death. Another messenger was necessary soon afterwards, someone to carry up further instructions, before the family arrived for the funeral, for the family's financial agent in London (Charles Hanbury) and for the various professionals and friends involved in business directly consequent on Temple's death. There was much to do, in little time. Hanbury's later statement of expenditures indicates that Temple's interment took place on 31 January—a private affair in Westminster Abbey—and under the same date it lists such telltale miscellaneous expenses as "Coach Hire to Give notice, &c." and "proveing The will" (fol. 64^r). Almost certainly Swift was the second messenger from Moor Park. His mourning expenses not only suggest that he attended the funeral, but also that his errands in London took him into public. In Sir John Temple's "Mourning & funerall" memorandum, Swift appears among the passengers listed for what seems to be one of three funeral coaches—"Lady Gifford chariott, Cousen Dingley Mr Swift & servant" (fol. 65^r). Similarly, on the same day that Swift reimbursed himself for his London trip, he recorded another business expense he had paid in London—£15 4s. od. for Temple's burial tax, "whereof the Certificate is sent to Mr Hanbury" (fol. 26^r). Of all the people at Lady Giffard's and Sir John's disposal, he was also the most suitable to send to wait on important London friends like Henley and Lord Romney. Whatever he did and whomever he saw, he was back at Moor Park by 3 February. For practically every day between then and the 10th, when he entered his expenses, the Moor Park accounts show something dated in his hand, which would place him there then. Before 3 February there is nothing by Swift. London was forty miles distant, too far in 1699 for a round trip in a single day.

164. *Prose Works*, v, 195. Though the two Berkeley peers were only distantly related (*D.N.B.*, s.v. Berkeley Family), the Earl's notorious sister Lady Henrietta ("Harriette") Berkeley seems to have been living with the family of Lord Berkeley of Stratton, no doubt to the relief of her own family (which included four other living siblings), whom she had disgraced in 1683 by having an affair with her brother-in-law and involving the family in a protracted and comical public trial from which practically no one emerged unscathed. It is unclear when Lady Harriette joined the Stratton family—Miss Longe was unable to find any other reference to her after the period of the trial—but in 1707 (after Lady Berkeley of Stratton died) Lady Harriette had to go elsewhere to live. As head of her own family, her brother became responsible for her on their father's death in October 1698, seven or eight months before Swift received his appointment as the new Earl's chaplain. See Longe, *Lady Giffard*, pp. 274–75, 276–77, 266–73; cf. Frederic Barlow, *The Complete English Peerage . . . To the Year 1772* (London: for the author, 1772), I, 372–73, and II, 227–28. Lord Berkeley of Stratton was doubly related to the Temples, not only through his wife, Sir John Temple's daughter

Frances, but through his brother's widow, Sir John's daughter Martha, who was
Lady Giffard's favorite niece (see family tree in Longe, facing p. 360). Of all Lady
Giffard's correspondents in 1699, he seems to have been the most anxious to
please, judging from the selection of letters printed by Miss Longe.

165. From all appearances, the Earl of Berkeley was not the close friend
that Romney was. Miss Longe's biography of Lady Giffard pays considerable
attention to her and Temple's social acquaintance in the late 1690s, but does
not mention Berkeley in this context. Ehrenpreis supposes that Romney
helped Swift with Berkeley (*Swift*, 1, 261). This seems odd if, as Swift charges,
Romney had done nothing to assist Swift's original application at Court (*Prose
Works*, v, 195). Instead, Lord Berkeley of Stratton seems a likelier candidate for
helping Swift with Berkeley, both from his closer ties to Lady Giffard and his
stronger claims on the Earl's cooperation. This impression is strengthened by
an odd remark which Swift made to Berkeley of Stratton some fourteen years
later, while introducing him to another distant Berkeley kinsman, the young
philosopher George Berkeley, later Bishop of Cloyne. The Bishop's grandson,
George Monck Berkeley, gives the anecdote in the postscript to his "Inquiry
into the Life of Dean Swift," and can only explain it in terms of Swift's eccentricity. "When Swift (who did every thing in his own way) introduced Bishop
Berkeley to Lord Berkeley of Stratton," he writes, "he made use of these
words: 'My Lord, here is a relation of your Lordship's who is *good for something;* and that, as times go, is saying a great deal.' " See George Monck Berkeley, *Literary Relics* (London: for C. Elliot and T. Kay, 1789), p. liv (original
emphasis). Swift jokingly implies that Stratton has relations who are *not* good
for much—and that Stratton knows whom he means. Swift may glance at
Stratton's wife's relations—the Temple family, that is—but when introducing
one Berkeley to another, he seems to imply that the worthless relations are
also Berkeleys. This points directly at the genial but bumbling Earl of Berkeley, who had failed to advance Swift's career as rapidly as Swift had hoped,
and whose natural abilities did not fill Swift with respect. See Swift's marginal comment on him, *Prose Works*, v, 259; cf. Ehrenpreis, *Swift*, II, 5–12, and
Landa, *Swift and the Church of Ireland*, pp. 27–34. Swift's remark to Stratton
sounds like a joking half-reproach. Unless Stratton felt some responsibility for
the Earl—or for Swift's former association with him—Swift's remark seems
pointless, and in fact the two peers were too distantly related for Stratton to
feel any responsibility. (Stratton belonged to a cadet branch of the family,
anyway, while the Earl headed the senior line.) The anecdote itself seems
wholly reliable. The *Journal to Stella* (II, 659) confirms that, on 12 April 1713,
Swift tried to help the young philosopher at Court by introducing him to
Berkeley of Stratton, who was then on the Privy Council. Swift does not record what he said at the meeting, but George Monck Berkeley undoubtedly
had his anecdote from his father, the Rev. Dr. George Berkeley, who had been
the Bishop's favorite son. He draws on him for other Swift anecdotes experienced or heard by the Bishop (*Literary Relics*, pp. xvi, xxxvi).

166. Mayhew, *Harvard Library Bulletin* 19: 405 n. (my emendation for Mayhew's "ominam"; cf. Scott, ed., *Works*, 2nd ed., 1, 467): '. . . there rages a pestilence

among horses, having proceeded not only through the British Isles but almost wholly through Europe.'

167. Mayhew, *Harvard Library Bulletin* 19: 404 n.

168. Scott, ed., *Works*, 1st ed. (1814), 1, 43, followed by almost all succeeding biographers of Swift and Temple.

169. *The Rothschild Library*, no. 2321. I have not seen the book since 1970, when I did not take notes on it, and am accordingly indebted to descriptions furnished by Dr. Gaskell.

170. William Laud, *A Relation of The Conference Betweene William Lawd, Then, L^{rd.} Bishop of St. Davids; Now, Lord Arch-Bishop of Canterbury: And Mr. Fisher the Jesuite . . .* (London: for Richard Badger, 1639). Now in a private collection, it contains marginalia in Swift's hand as well as the crossed-out ownership inscription dated 16 Apr. 1692, shortly before Swift went up to Oxford to collect his M.A. (cf. *Correspondence*, 1, 12 & n. 2). The volume will be fully described in a forthcoming article by the Rev. Prof. C.P. Daw, to whom I am indebted for my information.

171. Cf. Colin L. McKelvie, "Scriblerians' Books in Armagh Public Library," *Scriblerian*, 8, no. 1 (Autumn 1975), 56. I am grateful to the Very Rev. Henry A. Lillie, then Dean of Armagh and Keeper of the Library, for sending me xerox copies of the two inscriptions and of the title page, which also bears Swift's signature, and I acknowledge Mr. McKelvie's help in forwarding further specifics on the book. Someone (not Swift) has recopied the two deleted inscriptions in pencil. The book appeared in Swift's 1715 library list (Le Fanu, *Proceedings of the Royal Irish Academy* 37: 273), but not in the 1745 catalogue.

172. *Correspondence*, 1, 27–30.

173. Temple, *Introduction to the History of England*, pp. 21–22, 24, 25–26, 28–30, 31. Temple's chief targets at the end are apparently the earliest annalists, such as Nennius and Gildas, or perhaps their mediaeval successors, such as Geoffrey of Monmouth. Unfortunately Temple neither mentions any by name nor details any of their fanciful constructions, next to which his own might appear sober and responsible. Here as elsewhere—apart from the craven Buchanan and his peers, who fail to tackle the problem—Temple refrains from mentioning the work of recent historians, and so the reader is left with the impression that Temple alone has faced the obscurities of ancient British history—that, in effect, all was nonsense before he arrived on the scene. "And I have the rather made this Excursion," Temple continues, "because I have met with nothing in Story more Obscure . . ." (pp. 31–32).

Attempting to explain away some of Temple's self-contradictions—after basing one argument on Odin's being a historical personage, Temple pours scorn on the Arthurian legend—Homer Woodbridge suggests that contemporary historians took Teutonic myth somewhat more seriously than British or Celtic tradition. He points to one legitimate history which assumes Odin to be historical, picks apart Arthurian legend, and shows disrespect for fabulous or traditional materials set forth as history by early mediaeval writers (Woodbridge, *Temple*, p. 258 & n. 12). This is John Milton's *History of Britain*, which Woodbridge thinks one of Temple's sources. But however much Temple may have leaned on Milton's conclusions, Milton's history could hardly differ more strongly from Temple's. Simply stated, Milton is a historian here, Temple a historical writer. One deals in evidence tending towards conclusions, the other in conclusions with a little evidence thrown in, occasionally, for plausibility's sake. Where Temple makes Odin part of his argument—endowing him with great military and legal abilities, a people to lead, a destination to lead them to —Milton works in the opposite direction, from evidence to findings. Noting that various Saxon leaders traced their descent back to Woden (Odin), at four or eight or ten removes, Milton simply assumes that Odin was a historical figure (since deified for the fame of unspecified acts) from whom many Saxon leaders were descended. See *The History of Britain, That Part especially now call'd England* (London: by J.M. for John Martyn, 1677), pp. 131, 141, 142, 157. Nowhere does Milton pretend to give Woden's history, much less base an argument on it, and he sets no great store on Saxon genealogical matters anyway. He could easily set forth the claimed lineage linking Woden and the various chiefs, he says, but he thinks this would "encumber the story with a sort of barbarous names, to little purpose." Exit Woden. In similar fashion, Milton's treatment of the early annalists differs sharply from Temple's. Instead of making vague general condemnations, he investigates the various chroniclers' accounts, compares them, isolates the improbable and the asinine, and only then (and only on occasion) allows himself a value judgment, applied to specific figures for specific reasons. Only in his history's first book, dealing with the earliest periods, does Milton proceed without much citation or discussion of individual sources. His reasons are very different from Temple's, though. The book is given over to fanciful traditional accounts of Britain before Caesar—Lear and Cordelia, Gogmagog, Gorbuduc, the Trojan Brutus, and the lot, all set forth with great good humor, "be it for nothing else but in favour of our English Poets, and Rhetoricians, who by thir Art will know, how to use them judiciously." Indeed Milton declines the task of tracing British beginnings from the materials at hand (p. 7). By the same token, he likewise ventures no conjectures about the origins of the Scots, and so Temple may be right in congratulating himself on facing so knotty a problem. It is all Milton can do to evaluate conflicting accounts of the Scots' homeland in the late Roman era, "whoever they be originally" (p. 112). But as a responsible historian of his time, Milton could hardly hope to reach safe conclusions on a question which, by its nature, admitted of no solution. "The Beginning of Nations, those excepted of whom Sacred Books have spok'n, is to this day unknown," he had said on the opening page of his history: "Nor only the Beginning, but the Deeds also of many succeeding Ages, yea, periods of Ages, either wholly unknown, or obscur'd and blemisht with Fables." It was for Temple to rush in where Milton feared to tread.

174. Temple, *Early Essays*, pp. 5, 29.

175. For Swift's reading in 1696/97, see *A Tale of a Tub*, pp. lvi–lvii. The biographer Deane Swift claimed that Swift spent ten hours a day "in hard study," from the time he left Trinity College, Dublin, until Temple's death a decade later (*Essay Upon the Life of Swift*, p. 271).

176. Temple, *Miscellanea, The Second Part*, p. 249 (Regnor and "baro"), pp.

239–40 (Regnor's "Pindarick" verse). On p. 239 Temple cites Olaus Wormius' *"Literatura Runica,"* properly traced and verified in Clara Marburg, *Sir William Temple: A Seventeenth Century "Libertin"* (New Haven: Yale University Press, 1932), pp. 64–65; cf. Frank Edgar Farley, "Scandinavian Influences in the English Romantic Movement," in *Studies and Notes in Philology and Literature* (Harvard) 9 (1903): 62–65. In the 1636 edition of Olaus (citation in text) the lines analyzed by Temple appear on pp. 222–23 and 226. Temple drops the word "brevi" from the line "Bibemus cerevisiam brevi," but otherwise follows Olaus faithfully. For some of Temple's other forays into etymology, see *An Introduction to the History of England* (1694), where after "raking into all the rubbish" of other historians, Temple asserts etymologies for "Britain," "Armorica," "Batavia," "Caledonia," and "Ireland" (as well as "Scots"), derived from various ancient Celtic and Teutonic dialects of which he knew nothing (pp. 2–5, 22–24).

177. Temple, *Miscellanea, The Third Part,* pp. 256–60.

178. Temple, "Hints: written at the Desire of D^r F[ulham] and of His Friend," MS., Rothschild no. 2253, p. 12, Sect. 5 (my emphases). Though from a fair copy originally meant for private circulation, the passage shows signs that Temple later meant to revise it: after Swift had copied it, someone drew a large *X* through the more questionable portions following the first sentence.

179. In his *Alumni Oxonienses,* 1, 538–39, Foster lists a family of seventeenth and eighteenth century Fulhams with ties both to Magdalen College and to Christ Church, whence came Temple's other allies in the Ancient-Modern controversy. The likeliest candidate is Dr. George Fulham (1660–1702), D.D. 1694, praelector of moral philosophy in 1685 as well as rector of Compton, Surrey, about six miles east of Moor Park. By 1693 he had received livings in Hampshire and become a prebendary of Winchester, about 25 miles west of Moor Park. Fulham had matriculated at Christ Church in 1676 but the next year was entered as demy, or scholar, at Magdalen. His father, Dr. Edward Fulham, was a Christ Church man, professor of moral philosophy in 1634–38 and D.D. in 1660; he died at the age of eighty-six on 9 December 1694, the end of the year in which Wotton's *Reflections* first appeared.

I have not yet identified the "M^r H" whose attack on Wotton Temple encouraged and then suppressed. Eventually, in 1698, Charles Boyle stood forth as Temple's champion against the Moderns, chiefly Wotton's ally Dr. Bentley. The following year, in a collection of Latin poems largely composed by Christ Church and Magdalen men (students, dons, alumni distinguished and not so distinguished), appeared a reprint of a joint effort by Boyle and two fellow Christ Church students, including one William Hayes, described as a knight's son. His association with Boyle and Christ Church puts him under suspicion as "M^r H," but may mean nothing in the end. See *Musarum Anglicanarum Analecta: Sive, Poemata quaedam melioris notae, seu hactenus Inedita, seu sparsim Edita . . . ,* vol. II (Oxford: E Theatro Sheldoniano, 1699), 35–43. This book appeared in the auction catalogue for Swift's library (no. 639). The poem by Boyle and Hayes had been reprinted from an Oxford occasional miscellany of 1693 which Temple may have read because it included a short prose oration on the pros and cons of the Ancient-Modern question (by Addison, Richard Smallbrook, and

Edward Taylor, all Magdalen men). See *Theatri Oxoniensis Encaenia, sive Comitia Philologica* (Oxford: E Theatro Sheldoniano, 1693), sig. $\pi2^r$, $B1^r$–$C1^r$ (Boyle et al.), and $L2^v$–$N2^v$ (Addison et al.). The Addison piece was not reprinted in the 1699 collection.

180. Note entitled "A Fragment written upon the Subject of Ant. & Mod. Learning," preserved with Temple's "Hints: written at the Desire of D^r. F. and of His Friend," Rothschild no. 2253. The date of the note itself is sometime in 1697 or possibly early 1698, after Swift had copied over the "Hints" but before Temple decided to work them up as his essay *Some Thoughts Upon Reviewing the Essay of Antient and Modern Learning.* See above, in this chapter. Whether or not Temple began to circulate the "Hints" privately in 1697 (as the note implies), in retaliation for Wotton's expanded second edition of the *Reflections* that year, he must soon afterwards have begun the task of revising them for his essay, which eventually appeared under his name in 1701. In the Harold Williams bequest at the University Library, Cambridge, are two quarto leaves in Temple's hand, foul papers containing three short draft improvements for the "Hints," two for passages marked for revision on the fair copy Swift had made.

181. Temple, *Miscellanea, The Third Part,* pp. 271–77.

182. Wotton's patron was Daniel Finch, 2nd Earl of Nottingham, later celebrated by Swift and others as 'Dismal.' A Tory in the 1690s, he was the son of Temple's old associate Sir Heneage Finch, had helped to bring William of Orange over in 1688, had become privy councillor and secretary of state, but had fallen out of favor by 1694. Wotton's Epistle Dedicatory says nothing about teaching duties. What Temple means about Wotton's teaching "*Mr Finch's* Children" is unclear, although the job is made to sound suitably humble. Perhaps Temple is confused and thinks of the current Lord Nottingham as plain Mr. Finch, as he had been until his father was created earl in 1681 (the year before the father's death). If Wotton had any teaching duties, they would more probably have involved the second Lord Nottingham's children, not those of some untitled brother, uncle or cousin. By his first wife (m. 1674) Nottingham had had a daughter; by his second (m. 1685) he had two daughters and five sons surviving infancy, including his successor Daniel, born in 1689.

As for Temple's broader insinuation—that Wotton wasn't actually Nottingham's chaplain but had merely "assumed this Stile to sett Himself upon a Level" with Temple—Temple seems to be dealing, at best, with a truth told with the intent of deceiving. There is no reason to doubt Wotton's position as Nottingham's chaplain; see *D.N.B.* Temple capitalizes on Wotton's Epistle Dedicatory in the *Reflections,* in which Wotton says that "since I have taken the Freedom . . . to dissent from a Gentleman [Temple], whose Writings have been very kindly received in the World, I am bound to declare, that the chief Reason of this Address was, to let the World see, that I have a Right to subscribe my self" as Nottingham's chaplain (Wotton, *Reflections upon Ancient and Modern Learning,* sig. $A4^{r-v}$; note that Temple borrows Wotton's phrase about "taking the freedom to dissent" from Temple). Temple's essays have been so well received, in other words, that Wotton fears that he will not get a hearing unless his readers realize his connection with the famous statesman Nottingham. His frank avowal implies no admission of fraud in calling himself Nottingham's chaplain, no concession of professional inferiority to Temple, but only a realistic sense of factors which sway the reading public.

183. Temple, *Miscellanea, The Third Part*, p. 335.

184. Ibid., pp. 269–70 (Temple's italics). This section does not survive in the "Hints" fragments. Temple quotes from Wotton, *Reflections upon Ancient and Modern Learning*, p. 310. Temple next applies a couple of proverbial stories to Wotton, and returns to the attack with open contempt. Wotton "will not have his own Perfections and Excellencies owing to any thing else, but the true Force of his own Modern Learning"—as opposed to perfections owing to a great reputation or a great worldly experience, perhaps—"and thereupon he falls into this sweet Extasy of Joy, wherein I shall leave him till he come to Himself." For Wotton's penchant towards self-applause—and for Temple's too, I suspect—see the Preface in Swift's *Tale of a Tub* (p. 47):

> As for the Liberty I have thought fit to take of praising my self, upon some Occasions or none; I am sure it will need no Excuse, if a Multitude of great Examples be allowed sufficient Authority: For it is here to be noted, that *Praise* was originally a Pension paid by the World: but the *Moderns* finding the Trouble and Charge too great in collecting it, have lately bought out the *Fee-Simple;* since which time, the Right of Presentation is wholly in our selves.

Even in the ironic talk of the many "great Examples" (cf. Temple wondering "who this great man [Wotton] should be"), Swift follows Temple's lead in a most gratifying fashion, and in so Modern a context, Temple would never have thought to apply Swift's findings to himself.

185. Temple, *Miscellanea, The Third Part*, pp. 99–100.

186. With several inaccuracies, Temple quotes anew from Wotton's Epistle Dedicatory in *Reflections upon Ancient and Modern Learning*, sig. A3ᵛ. The qualities which Wotton's "Ancient Worthies" seem to have lacked (not that Wotton actually accuses them of lacking anything) are Nottingham's "Exemplary Piety and Concern for the Church of England" and "Zeal for the Rights and Honour of the English Monarchy," as well as the fact "that these Vertues do so constantly descend from Father to Son in Your Lordship's Family, that its Collateral Branches are esteemed Publick Blessings. . . ." Of the three qualities, the heroes of antiquity might have managed the last but would have been hard pressed to be pious towards the English Church or zealous for the English monarchy, neither of which existed in those days. Temple probably means to score some sort of point against Wotton here, much as Swift himself was to do in the *Tale of a Tub*'s Digression in the Modern Kind. There, speaking as a Wottonian Modern, Swift berates Homer for "gross Ignorance" in the English common law and in the doctrine and discipline of the English Church (*Tale of a Tub*, p. 128).

187. I have also been able to eliminate the hand of Swift's friend John Geree junior, son of the Vicar of Farnham, on the basis of his A.L.s. to Swift in the

Public Record Office (24 Apr. 1714; SP 63/370 ff. 245–46). Hands which I have been unable to check include those of the mysterious Mr. Savage, Temple's cousin and legatee William Dingley (young Geree's classmate at Oxford), and Geree's three cousins, the wards of his father at Farnham.

188. The point of view in the note is one which we would expect from Temple. It even reflects Temple's contempt for classical scholarship: in his second edition Wotton has proceeded "like a true Grammarian," in that he thinks two negatives make a positive. The note works hardest to suggest Temple's complete disinterestedness in answering Wotton (a disinterestedness scarcely borne out by Temple's tone in the "Hints" themselves). At first, says the note, Temple dissuaded his friends from answering so feeble a book as Wotton's, which should be permitted to "dye of it self"; only after Fullham approached him with Mr. H's draft ("some months after," or probably in 1695) could Temple be "prevayled with," out of kindness to Mr. H., to write his "Hints" for Mr. H. to incorporate. As in Thomas Swift's letters of 1694–95, Temple has clearly authorized the note, and probably half-dictated it as well.

189. Box 3, Williams Bequest, Cambridge University Library (Add. MS. 7788): Temple's autograph draft of the letter to his brother Sir John, dated 23 May 1672 and described in chapter 1. The unknown secretarial helper has added the word "Sheen" to the dateline and entered at the top, in an almost unintelligible scrawl, "[For] S^r J T[emple]" and [?D^r Br]" (i.e., "Dear Brother," the salutation used in the printed text but not picked up by Swift in copying the text into the Downton transcript, perhaps because of illegibility here). It looks as if Temple had this assistant enter the necessary salutation, heading, and dateline details to be used in his edition of the *Letters*, although it is possible that the man was merely identifying the loose draft and entering the missing details from a later transcript or even from the printed volume.

190. *Prose Works*, 1, xxxvii & facing plate; Ehrenpreis, *Swift*, 1, 258.

191. Ehrenpreis, *Swift*, 1, 258–59; cf. Herbert Davis in *Prose Works*, 1, xviii–xix.

192. Cf. Ehrenpreis, *Swift*, 1, 259.

193. Because Swift seldom if ever used New Style dates, "When I come to be old. 1699" must date from after the O.S. New Year late in March. By this time Swift had left Moor Park for London. By September he was with Lord Berkeley in Dublin. Although it has previously gone unremarked, Swift also seems to have revisited Moor Park some time between May and August, when he sailed from Bristol (Ibid., 1, 261). Swift's rejected draft fragment for the preface to Temple's *Letters*—composed between May and mid-July, as we have noted earlier—remained at Moor Park, with the miscellaneous manuscripts by Temple and Lady Giffard. Possibly Swift also wrote it there. Together with the other Moor Park materials, the fragment descended in the Longe family of Norfolk and appeared in the Longe sale at Sotheby's, 3 August 1934 (lot 1071). Swift did not return from Ireland until April 1701; it is highly unlikely that he would have carried back with him a small rejected scrap of prose, superseded for nearly two years, to deposit for reasons unknown at Moor Park. In the summer of 1699, Moor Park would have been a pleasant place to be. It was especially agreeable

during the growing season, thanks to its gardens and nearby downs, and though it was now Lady Giffard's during her life (by the terms of Temple's will), she was probably elsewhere at the time. Back in mid-February, encouraged by friends and relatives, she had talked of going to her own house at East Sheen, about thirty miles away and not far from Sir John's home (Longe, *Lady Giffard*, pp. 242–43).

194. In the essay "On Being an American," reprinted in H.L. Mencken, *Prejudices: A Selection*, ed. James T. Farrell (New York: Random House pb., 1955), pp. 90, 92.

195. These terms are relative, of course, and Swift did not personally witness Temple's honorable actions at Court or at the negotiating tables abroad. On the other hand, by his own admission (*Correspondence*, I, 155), he had helped transcribe Temple's *Introduction to the History of England* (1694), in which Temple lifts and adapts large blocks of prose from Samuel Daniel's *Collection of the History of England* without once mentioning Daniel's name (Woodbridge, *Temple*, pp. 254–57). Swift was undoubtedly aware of the fact. As Ehrenpreis notes in another context, when Swift turned to English history-writing he used Temple's *Introduction* and "started from Temple's sources," notably Daniel's *Collection*, which he had in his own library (Ehrenpreis, *Swift*, I, 175; cf. *Prose Works*, V, ix–x; Williams, *Swift's Library*, catalogue no. 358). In Swift's day, to be sure, plagiarism was a far less serious matter than today, although in the Apology to the *Tale of a Tub* Swift once professed to "know nothing more contemptible in a Writer than the Character of a Plagiary . . ." (*Tale*, p. 14).

196. Temple, *Early Essays*, pp. 27–31.

197. *Journal to Stella*, II, 561 (9 Oct. 1712).

198. Ehrenpreis, *Swift*, I, 256.

199. *Correspondence*, I, 1–2 (Temple to Sir Robert Southwell, 29 May 1690); Ehrenpreis, *Swift*, I, 107. Then as now, job-seekers tried to be first in line to apply. The letter's signs of obvious haste (it is just "this afternoon" that Temple has heard about Southwell's appointment) suggest that Swift ("the bearer") meant to hurry the recommendation immediately up to London, where Temple's London agent Charles Hanbury has recently spoken with Southwell. Southwell was to accompany the King to Ireland, and at the time of writing the King had just adjourned Parliament and announced his decision to defer his Irish expedition no longer. He left town for Hoylake on June 4, six days after the date of Temple's letter *(D.N.B.)*. Because nothing came of the recommendation to Southwell, wrongly endorsed as a recommendation "for Mʳ Hanbury," we may guess that Swift later travelled to Ireland on his own, to seek his way through his own family contacts in Dublin. Probably this happened some time after mid-July, when the news of victory at the Boyne and the fall of Dublin reached England. It would have been difficult as well as foolish for an obscure, impecunious, and unattached young civilian to accompany the King's military expedition in June.

200. *Correspondence*, I, 21.

201. Landa, *Swift and the Church of Ireland*, pp. 9–10; Ehrenpreis, *Swift*, I, 153 & n. 3.

202. Ehrenpreis, *Swift,* 1, 251–53, 247–50, 261–62. On his hopes of advancement through Temple's friend Sunderland, see chapter 1.

203. In early 1697, even with his sermons, he expressed a strong unwillingness, mingled with contempt, about seeing them in print (*Correspondence,* 1, 31; cf. Landa in *Prose Works,* IX, 97–98).

204. Temple, *Miscellanea, The Second Part,* pp. 62–64 (*Upon Ancient and Modern Learning*). Temple speaks with open distaste of the "endless Disputes and litigious Quarrels upon all these Subjects" of divinity. "Many excellent Spirits," he says, "and the most penetrating Genys, that might have made admirable Progresses and Advances in many other Sciences, were sunk and overwhelmed in the abyss of Disputes, about matters of Religion. . . ." Worse, theological controversy helped to raise the various wars of religion—"almost a perpetual Course or Succession, either of Civil or of Foreign Wars" with which Christendom has been "infested" for the past century—and war itself has damaged the progress of the arts and sciences.

205. Ehrenpreis, *Swift,* 1, 250.

206. *Poems,* 1, 15; McEwen, *Oracle of the Coffee House,* pp. 23, 27. We have already noted the attempts which Swift made to find out who the Athenians were, at least in a general way. Even without making the inquiries he did, Swift might have guessed the essentials of Dunton's operation from his readings in the *Athenian Mercury,* with its eccentric mixture of sensationalism, biblical exegesis, feeble wit, classical scholarship, scientific dabbling, advice about etiquette, and hyper-Protestant Williamite propagandizing.

207. Ehrenpreis, *Swift,* 1, 261–64. Ehrenpreis concedes that, after returning to Temple in 1696, Swift "gave up the power to act without Temple's approval."

208. Ibid., p. 263.

209. Temple, *Early Essays,* p. xiv. Benjamin Motte, Swift's new publisher in England, brought out the *Life*. Although it added material which carried the narrative through the 1690s (the *Life* itself having been composed in 1690), the continuation chiefly dwells on Temple's association with William of Orange as King and never once mentions Swift. It is also worth noting that, in the late 1720s, Swift was again entertaining hopes for a good English benefice, through a rapprochement with Walpole, the influence of Mrs. Howard, the aid of Bolingbroke and Pulteney, or other possibilities opened by the new reign, which had begun in 1727.

210. *Prose Works,* V, plate facing p. 192, and p. xxii. Herbert Davis opposes Denis Johnston's sensible observation that the fragment presents "a valuable account of what JS wished to have said about himself," because of the several signs of carelessness in what Davis himself calls "an unfinished sketch." He also notes that several of Swift's marginal additions have been crossed out, a good sign that Swift was getting bogged down. Swift undoubtedly reached the eventual conclusion that the piece could not be published or circulated—indeed, it reads very unconvincingly at times—but this hardly proves that Swift originally conceived it as a private exercise, existing in a vacuum. Davis also points out that Swift may not have intended to write a full-scale autobiography, but instead only "an introductory sketch to the well-known facts of his public

career." This could well be true (Johnston had in fact suggested it), but it has nothing to do with the question of Swift's original intentions about publication —except by implication, since an introductory sketch must introduce something to someone. Cf. Denis Johnston, *In Search of Swift* (Dublin: Hodges, Figgis, 1959), pp. 10–14.

211. It is conceivable that there was some contact in the spring of 1689, when Temple's son John became secretary at war and, within a week, committed suicide. Blathwayt was John's predecessor in office and apparently stayed on to help break him in, though reportedly for self-interested motives rather than out of friendship for John's father, who at least officially kept an ostentatious distance between himself and his son's appointment. Blathwayt's biographer quotes a contemporary letter saying that, "knowing how well Mr. Temple was at Court," Blathwayt helped initiate him "to gain his friendship." (In the event, Blathwayt was reinstated to his secretaryship.) See Jacobsen, *William Blathwayt*, p. 239. For Blathwayt's and Downton's position under Temple at the Hague, twenty years before, see pp. 68–75. Jacobsen is unable to document any continuing contacts after 1671 and has to admit that Temple's relations with Blathwayt "probably never went beyond the kind concern of a man for a youth who had started out in public office under his direction" (p. 52). Even this may exaggerate the situation.

212. Temple to William Godolphin, 22 January 1666 [N.S.], transcript in the 2nd Viscount Palmerston's hand, Temple Family box, no. 41, in the Palmerston Papers from Broadlands on deposit at the Hampshire Record Office, Winchester; cf. Temple, *Miscellanea, The Second Part*, p. 194 *(Of Heroick Virtue)*. The letter is quoted by permission of the Trustees of the Broadlands Archive. I am grateful to the staff of the Hampshire Record Office, especially D. F. Lamb, for answering questions, drawing up summary lists, and providing photocopies of this and other early Broadlands materials there.

CHAPTER 4

1. In his useful Yale dissertation, "Swift's Eighteenth-Century Biographies" (1963), Phillip S. Y. Sun provides interesting glimpses of the way Swift's earliest biographers battened on each other's work. Sun's chief aim is to evaluate each successive biographer's contributions, in new information and the reliability thereof, but along the way he shows how strongly each new biographer was influenced by his predecessors (both positively and negatively) and how much he depended upon them for materials. Here the most surprising case is the younger Thomas Sheridan, who was Swift's godson and the son of Swift's old friend the schoolmaster. Although Sheridan's biography is easily the longest of the several which Sun considers, Sun shows that apart from miscellaneous anecdotes, Sheridan advanced only a small amount of new information despite his seemingly dazzling opportunities (Sun, pp. 160–66, cf. pp. 149–51, 118 & n. 3).

2. Deane Swift, *Essay*, pp. 32–33, 35, 37, 73–75.

3. Ibid., pp. 39–40, 59–60.

4. For Sheridan's comment on Deane Swift see his Introduction, in the *Life*

of Swift, sig. A7ʳ. For Sheridan's use of Deane Swift, see Sun, "Swift's Eighteenth-Century Biographies," pp. 153 (Sheridan uses Deane Swift more than anyone else), 118 & passim. Apropos Sheridan's romanticization of Swift at Moor Park, see also pp. 158–60 (instances of fictionalization in other contexts) and pp. 154–56 (suppression of negative evidence). Sun's chapters on Sheridan and on John Lyon (whose valuable evidence Sheridan apparently obtained not from inspecting the original but from using the little-known published version in the 1779 *Supplement* of the Hawkesworth edition of Swift's works) serve as a useful corrective to Sir Harold Williams's better-known assessment of Sheridan in the essay "Swift's Early Biographers," in *Pope and His Contemporaries: Essays Presented to George Sherburn,* ed. James L. Clifford and Louis A. Landa (New York: Oxford University Press, 1949), pp. 114–28. It was Williams's ignorance of the earlier publication of Lyon's notations, for instance, which made him suppose that Sheridan first located and published it (Sun, p. 118 & n. 3).

5. Sheridan, *Life of Swift,* sig. A1. For Sheridan on the Whigs, Orrery, and Johnson see ibid., sig. A2ᵛ–8ᵛ. The commentary on Sheridan comes from Sun, "Swift's Eighteenth-Century Biographies," pp. 153–54. Johnson's opinion of Sheridan is quoted, with further commentary ("Sheridan cannot bear me . . ."), under the date 28 July 1763 in Boswell's *Life of Johnson,* ed. George Birkbeck Hill, rev. L. F. Powell (Oxford: The Clarendon Press, 1934), I, 453–54.

6. Sheridan, *Life of Swift,* pp. 8–9, 11–12 (Swift before Moor Park), p. 26 (Providence and Temple), pp. 15, 28 (Temple and Swift).

7. Sun, "Swift's Eighteenth-Century Biographies," chap. 9.

8. Sheridan, *Life of Swift,* p. 30.

9. *The Correspondence of Samuel Richardson . . . Selected from the Original Manuscripts, Bequeathed by Him to His Family,* ed. Anna Laetitia Barbauld (London: for Richard Phillips, 1804), VI, 173–74.

10. T. B. Macaulay, "Sir William Temple," in *Critical and Historical Essays Contributed to the Edinburgh Review* [first published 1843], 13th ed. (London: Longmans, 1870), II, 599, 597–98.

11. W. M. Thackeray, *English Humourists of the Eighteenth Century: A Series of Lectures, Delivered in England, Scotland, and the United States of America* (London: Smith, Elder, 1853), pp. 13, 16–17, 23. Amusingly enough, Thackeray also follows Sheridan in making Temple at least indirectly responsible for the growth of Swift's skills: "His initiation into politics, his knowledge of business, his knowledge of polite life, his acquaintance with literature even, which he could not have pursued very sedulously during that reckless career at Dublin, Swift got under the roof of Sir William Temple" (p. 16). Most of these acquirements, however, Thackeray attributes to observation rather than tutelage. Swift gains an insight into public affairs, for instance, by comparing himself to the powerful politicians who visit Temple: "what small men they must have seemed under those enormous periwigs . . ." (p. 17).

12. Ibid., pp. 31, 33, 40.

13. Macaulay, *Works* (New York: Longmans, Green, 1898), V, 389–90.

14. Woodbridge, *Temple,* p. 238. Despite Woodbridge's implications, Craik actually stops short of suggesting that Swift harbored a secret resentment of Temple. Temperamentally the two were opposites, notes Craik, and "compara-

tively little sympathy could exist" between them. Despite this not very comfortable association, Craik still believes that in such poems as Swift's ode to Temple, Swift shows an "entire and genuine respect for his patron." See Craik, *Life of Swift*, pp. 40–41 (cf. 26) and 33.

15. Arthur H. Scouten, "Swift's Progress from Prose-Man to Poet," 1979 Clark Lecture, William Andrews Clark Memorial Library, Los Angeles (awaiting publication), quoted with the author's kind permission from the typescript, pp. 14–15. Significantly, Scouten singles out Ehrenpreis as an example of "protective silence" maintained in the face of troublesome materials—in this case the documentation unearthed by Denis Johnston (1959) in the course of his attempts to demonstrate that Temple might have been Stella's father and that Swift might have been born too late to be the son of Jonathan Swift senior.

16. Thackeray, *English Humourists*, pp. 13, 32, 7.

17. John Boyle, 5th Earl of Orrery, *Remarks on the Life and Writings of Dr. Jonathan Swift* (London: for A. Millar, 1752), pp. 4, 87, 121–22.

18. For a brief account of Orrery's active acquaintance with Swift, lasting roughly from 1732 to 1738, see Sun, "Swift's Eighteenth-Century Biographies," pp. 26–27. There seems to have been a good deal of mutual cosseting, though of questionable sincerity on Swift's side. Swift's letters to Orrery and about him (to Pope, for instance) are full of friendly praise and ostensible deference, though hard to take at face value. That Orrery had once or twice felt Swift's sting, even so, is suggested by his assertions about Swift in old age: "From the year *thirty nine* to the latter end of the year *forty one*, his friends found his passions so violent and ungovernable, his memory so decayed, and his reason so depraved, that they took the utmost precautions to keep all strangers from approaching him" (Orrery, *Remarks*, p. 264). Again, this may or may not relate something accurate about Swift, but much more surely it reflects Orrery's state of mind. Years later, George Monck Berkeley recounted a story (originating with Swift's friend Bishop Berkeley, the relater's grandfather) that Orrery was once admitted to Swift's study where he found one of his old letters to Swift, unopened and bearing the endorsement "This will keep cold." See George Monck Berkeley, *Literary Relics*, p. xvi, and further in Sun, "Swift's Eighteenth-Century Biographies," p. 45.

19. Scott, ed., *Works*, i, pp. 26–27 n.

20. Forster, *Life of Swift*, pp. 72 (against Richardson's version), 75–76 (against Macaulay's version), 99–100 (against Macaulay's version).

21. Woodbridge, *Temple*, pp. 238–39, cf. pp. 220–21 (Swift's hero worship of Temple—here derived from Stephen Gwynn's popular biography of Swift, 1933 —and the claim that "the formative influence of Temple upon the mind of his young secretary has never been fully recognized").

22. Ehrenpreis, *Swift*, i, ix.

23. Ibid., p. 148.

24. For Swift's 'penitential' letter, see chapter 2. Other entries in Jack Temple's hand occur towards the end of Swift's transcript of Sir Henry Osborne's translations from Juvenal, Rothschild no. 2252, fol. 47^r (Trinity College, Cambridge); on the title-page of Swift's transcript of Lady Giffard's translation from Jorge de Montemayor, Rothschild no. 2251; and at the end of Lady Giffard's

unpublished ms. translation of Temple's Spanish letter (itself published by Swift) sent under the name of Gabriel Postello or Possello, 30 March 1667, in the Osborn Collection, Yale, Box 70, no. 1, fol. 5. For Jack Temple and Moor Park, including his relationship with Lady Giffard, see Longe, *Lady Giffard*, pp. 211, 243, 352, and Swift, *Correspondence*, 1, 52–56 (a business letter of June 1706 to Jack Temple, then settled at Moor Park).

25. The first Lord Palmerston's autograph copy of the 'penitential' letter (very carefully done, even as to Swift's odd use of spacing) is no. 39 in the Temple Family box of the Palmerston Papers from Broadlands, on deposit with the Hampshire Record Office and cited by permission of the Trustees of the Broadlands Archive. Palmerston has docketed his copy in his slightly shaky hand of the 1750s ("J. Swift [now *crossed out*] since Dean's submissive Letter to Sr Wm Temple . . ."), while his autograph in the copy itself suggests an earlier date—perhaps 1725–26, when he and Swift had quarrelled. Besides the Moor Park estate and funeral papers, a large number of which found their way to the Osborn Collection at Yale (at least twenty documents, including most of the upper servants' wage and legacy receipts, having been previously removed), Lord Palmerston owned two contemporary transcripts of Swift's later poem, *Apollo to the Dean*, which Sir Harold Williams calls "Ashley (1)" and "Ashley (2)" in his edition of the *Poems*. They are now respectively in a private American collection and in the Kaufmann Swift Collection at Cornell University.

26. Murry, *Swift*, p. 20 & n. Ignorance allows Murry to speak with less of the bias notable in Forster and his specialist successors in the field. Murry says he is unable to trace the authority for Swift's £20 salary further than Macaulay, and he generally seems unaware that anything deriving from the Richardson anecdote had become, among Swiftians, something of a taboo.

27. Rosalind K. Marshall, *The Days of Duchess Anne: Life in the Household of the Duchess of Hamilton, 1656–1716* (New York: St. Martin's, 1973), p. 74, cf. p. 65. The chaplain, legal helper, and 'governor' (children's tutor) each received £200 Scots plus board. It took £12 Scots to make up £1 sterling. Part of the wage scale at Hamilton Palace can be compared with that known of Moor Park in 1698. Among the more menial employees, the Moor Park rates seem to have been somewhat higher—e.g., about £24 Scots for most of the Hamilton maids, compared to £4–£5 at Moor Park.

28. Moor Park estate papers, Osborn Collection, Yale, fb 182, fols. *2, *12–13, *15–20, *17' (erased), *22–24, *26–30, 79; Temple's deed of settlement, 1–2 July 1697, "abstract" in the hand of his brother and executor Sir John, Temple Family box, no. 35, Palmerston Papers from Broadlands, now on deposit at the Hampshire Record Office and cited by permission of the Trustees of the Broadlands Archive; J. Jean Hecht, *The Domestic Servant in 18th-Century England* (1956; rpt. London: Routledge, 1980), tables pp. 142–49.

Judging from internal evidence and Sir John's "abstract" of Temple's will, which accompanies the settlement "abstract," the settlement "abstract" is in fact a close copy of the original deed of settlement, possibly lacking preamble and an occasional provision dealing with minor ancillary property (not at Moor

Park) with which Sir John did not need to concern himself as trustee, beneficiary, remainderman or near kin thereof.

29. Moor Park estate papers, fols. 13–14 (cloth and notions, Aug.–Nov. 1698), 56–57 (shoes, hats). These do not include the bills for mourning clothes for the household, which Temple's estate would have provided for everyone as a matter of course. The bill for the year's liveries for the six livery servants is on fols. 15–16 (7 Nov. 1698).

30. For the tenants at Moor Park, the only direct record I have found is a brief entry in the Moor Park estate papers at Yale, fol. 23^v, noting the receipt of £5 representing "an Arrear of Rent of the Tenants about More-Park," collected shortly after Temple's death. Nearby, at Farnham, Temple also had a lease on a mill (see Sir John Temple's abstract of his brother's deed of settlement, on deposit at the Hampshire Record Office).

For Bridget Johnson's wage and legacy receipt, see the Moor Park estate papers, fol. *27. A total of £150 is due her upon a bond deposited with Temple (then £120), her special legacy under Temple's will (£20), and her wages plus her regular legacy equal to a half-year's salary (together £10, with the amount of wage arrears unspecified). If Mrs. Johnson were owed for a bare minimum of arrears, a half-quarter, her salary would work out to £16 a year; if for a maximum, 3 1/2 quarters, it would come to £7 6s. od. Of the other surviving wage receipts, all but one were either for 3 1/2 quarters or 1 1/2 quarters. Since £7 6s. od. seems too low a figure, I think the likeliest arrears for her would be 1 1/2 quarters, which would give her an annual salary of £11 8s. 6d. Since all the other known Moor Park salaries are in round numbers, 2 quarters is also a strong possibility: it yields an even £10 per annum, the same as her caretaker salary under Temple's deed of settlement.

31. Hecht, *The Domestic Servant,* pp. 48–49; Temple, *Miscellanea, The Second Part,* p. 141. Temple writes as if his garden had been an international mecca for horticulturists. Among other things, he gives himself credit for introducing four new grape varieties into England (p. 120) as well as the Brussels apricot (p. 123—"one of the best fruits we have"). Frenchmen inspecting his garden find his peaches as good as anything in France "on this side Fountainbleau" and his grapes as good as anything they have eaten in Gascony, while visiting Italians agree that his white figs are as good as any in Italy (p. 111). His orange trees are the biggest he has seen anywhere but at Fontainebleau and in Holland at the Prince of Orange's, they bear more fruit than he can use, and the oranges taste as good as any imported from abroad "except the best sorts of Sevil and Portugal" (pp. 111–12). Temple is describing his first garden at Sheen, in 1685, but prospective visitors would think of him at Moor Park, Surrey, his seat when the essay was published. To compound the confusion, Temple speaks of a garden once at Moor Park, Herts., as "the perfectest Figure of a Garden I ever saw, either at home or abroad" (p. 127).

32. Marshall, *The Days of Duchess Anne,* pp. 74, 63–64. £530 Scots comes to £44 3s. 4d. sterling. The secretary, David Crawford, had built up "a thriving practice" in law in Edinburgh during the time he worked for the Hamiltons. Somewhat like Swift at Kilroot, he was eventually persuaded to give it up and

return to Hamilton Palace full time. By then he had become "a man of substance," with a rich house in the adjoining town. In other words, he had been in an excellent bargaining position.

33. Ibid., p. 77, cf. pp. 63, 66, 69. More than thirty years later, when Dean of Saint Patrick's, Swift could describe a young clergyman sometimes being allowed to sit at the steward's table in terms which suggest some contempt. In almost every respect, though, the case is too different to allow safe inferences about Moor Park and common standards a generation before. In his *Intelligencer* essay on the fates of clergymen, Swift describes the rise of a dull and servile young clergyman named Corusodes, a farmer's son and Oxford graduate who begins his career by reading prayers in the town house of a lecherous nobleman for ten shillings a month, carries himself so obsequiously that he "would shake the Butler by the Hand," and "was sometimes admitted to dine at the Steward's Table" (*Prose Works*, XII, 42). Corusodes is not a regular live-in domestic chaplain, however, but only a part-time employee not belonging to the regular staff (he serves several other noblemen's houses as well). Again, a town house was not quite the same as the family seat in the country, or the duties and standards always identical in each. Most of all, by 1729 Swift had become too much a champion of parsons' rights (and too much a critic of the clergy's low standing in society) to be an objective authority on proper dining arrangements for chaplains, domestic or otherwise. The *Intelligencer* essay suggests that by the 1720s Swift thought that clergymen ought to be estimable enough to sit down with the family at table, that they often were not (and often did not, regardless), that they should show more self-respect than the servile but successful Corusodes, and that their employers should show better breeding and discernment. (Corusodes rises in the Church through the influence of his sister, a waiting-woman in the household who has caught His Lordship's eye.) What Swift thought in the 1690s is harder to determine, though we may be tempted to guess that a seat at the steward's table might not have pleased him even if he *had* considered himself only a chaplain, rather than a secretary.

34. Ibid., pp. 77, 62. For the entire period 1656–1716, Marshall provides a figure varying between "at least thirty" and "as many as fifty." By 1703 the number would have been at the lower end of that range because of increasing economies necessary in the household. In that year twenty-six ate at the Palace and a few others (chiefly among the inferior servants) received food to consume at home. Twenty years before, notes Marshall, the household had been "much larger."

35. See Longe, *Lady Giffard*, pp. 203 and 208 (letters just received from Petworth, 1697), and p. 227 (Temple and Lady Giffard presently visiting Petworth, 1698); see also pp. 19, 210, and chap. xii.

36. [Béat-Louis de Muralt,] *Lettres sur les Anglois et les François* ([Paris]: n.p., 1725), pp. 171–72; cf. Woodbridge, *Temple*, pp. 231–32.

37. An engraving of Loo and its gardens is reproduced in Elizabeth Hamilton, *William's Mary* (New York: Taplinger, 1972), in the section following p. 146, with a brief account of the gardens on pp. 151–52. The landscape architect was Daniel Marot, a refugee Huguenot who was becoming popular in Holland (and

was working for the Prince of Orange) at the time of Temple's last visits there in 1678–79 while serving at Nimeguen (pp. 78–79).

For a good photograph of the drawing of Moor Park (formerly owned by the Bacon family but recently acquired by the Surrey County Council), see the plate for lot 66 in the Christie's catalogue of English drawings and water-colors, 20 July 1976. (I am grateful to David Woolley for sending me an excellent enlargement showing the details.) The drawing has also been reproduced (in its unrepaired state) in W. A. Speck, *Swift* (New York: Arco, 1970), opposite p. 6, and (with some cropping) in Christopher Hussey, *English Gardens and Landscapes, 1700–1750* (New York: Funk & Wagnalls, 1967), following p. 16 (plate 3). In his gardening essay Temple himself held up an English rather than a Dutch model: the gardens laid out by the Countess of Bedford at Moor Park, Herts., where Temple had honeymooned thirty years before (*Miscellanea, The Second Part,* pp. 127–30). From the details he gives it is apparent that it had some influence on the design of his gardens at his own Moor Park, although it apparently lacked a few of the most basic features, including the canal and the central tree-lined perspective. The one odd feature at Temple's Moor Park was an irregularly shaped island with serpentine paths, tucked half out of sight between the little river Wey and the canal at the foot of the main garden and off to the left. It has been proposed as an example of Temple's *Sharawadgi,* the Chinese ideal of asymmetrical beauty in garden design. See *Miscellanea, The Second Part,* pp. 131–32; the Christie catalogue notes for lot 66; and Hussey, "Templum Restauratum, Sir William Temple's House and Garden at Moor Park, Farnham, Reconstructed," *Country Life* 106 (25 Nov. 1949), 1578–81. There is another possible source for Temple's island, which I have not been able to pursue. In 1679 Temple's old friend, Prince Maurice of Nassau, offered to send his own architect to Holland from Cleves (only fifteen miles from Temple's base at Nimeguen) to propose alterations for William of Orange's gardens at Soestdyck. Prince Maurice's architect, one Rust, was apparently a believer in a casual and informal style of garden, not symmetrical, employing many natural waterworks—itself a notable feature at Moor Park, with its canal, fountains, locks, and the use of the little river's channels. See Hamilton, *William's Mary,* p. 90 & n.

38. Mark Girouard, *Life in the English Country House* (New Haven: Yale University Press, 1978), pp. 11, 123, 136, 138–40, 143. Girouard's study centers on establishments which (like Petworth) were measurably larger and grander than Moor Park. Because such houses tended to establish standards of style and politeness in country living, they can offer insights into the establishments of less wealthy or powerful gentlemen who like Temple considered themselves nothing lacking in politeness and gentility.

39. Ibid., p. 136, cf. p. 140. Among the higher-ranking employees at the Duke of Chandos's palatial seat at Cannons, a generation after Temple's death, there were even separate dining arrangements for the upper servants (at the chaplains' table) and the gentleman-retainers (in the gentleman-of-the-horse's room). Such fine distinctions would almost certainly not have been observed at Moor Park, where the staff was much smaller and included no separate chaplain,

gentleman of the horse, or other gentleman retainers. Only Rebecca Dingley had much to boast of from her family connections.

40. For the Moor Park itemized bills, see the Osborn Collection, fb 182, fols. 17–20, 58, 61 (also including the steward's wife, Mrs. Mose, who receives the honorific "M^rs"; she appears so seldom in the accounts that I conclude she did not normally figure in the Moor Park household). Leonard Robinson's occupation is also suggested by fol. 58, a bill drawn up in his autograph. It allows him to be reimbursed for the tailoring expenses incurred by the Moor Park staff (all but himself) for their mourning clothes. With Mose and Temple's secretary at the time (Thomas Swift) he also witnessed Temple's will in 1694, and with Lady Giffard and Stella's mother witnessed the codicil of 1697; see Courtenay, *Memoirs of Temple*, ii, 485–86. For the usual pecking order among female employees (first the lady's maid, next the housekeeper), see Hecht, *The Domestic Servant*, pp. 60–63.

41. Osborn Collection, fb 182, fol. 79. Here I have excepted early downpayments on sums due from wages, legacies, and bonds. We have already noted the one that survives: the receipt for Bridget Johnson, dated 16 Feb. and in Swift's hand, for £19 of the £150 due her on all three accounts (fol. *27).

42. Ibid., fol. 66. For Temple's will see Courtenay, *Memoirs of Temple*, ii, 485: "I leave for a legacy to Bridget Johnson, Ralph Mo[s]e, and Leonard Robinson, twenty pounds a piece, with a half year's wages to them and all my *other* servants . . ." (emphasis added).

43. Only once in the Moor Park account papers can I find an unequivocal instance of a tradesman's supplying merchandise for both family and staff. It is the local shoemaker's bill, dated 3 February 1698/99 (Osborn Collection, fb 182, fol. 56). Besides listing a pair of shoes each to Swift, Ralph Mose, Stella's brother, and the servants proper ("10 pair of Shoes att 4/8 per pair"), it lists a pair each for Temple's young granddaughters and "two pair of Buck-skins for Sr Willm Temple" himself, at 16s. each. On a local drapier's bill covering the period from August through November 1698 (fol. 13–14), Mose later docketed the heading "Mr Garyes Bill for my master and others," but Temple is never named anywhere in the bill itself, which seems to be exclusively concerned with goods ordered for the staff. The drapier himself headed the bill "Sr William Temples bill ffor M^r: Joanes &c:" (Thomas Jones, probably the butler). There is not even anything which can be safely linked to Temple in the local apothecary's bill, covering the period between April 1698 and a couple of days before Temple's death (fol. 41). On 12 August and in September there are unspecified charges "For Ingred^ts for an Emplaister," but they seem to have been for Thomas Jones, under similar treatment from August to November, or possibly for "Jone" (Joan Draper, a maid or other minor servant), mentioned under the July heading.

44. In theory Swift should not have required mourning clothes because he was in holy orders and presumably wore a black gown. As a household retainer, however, he still qualified for and in fact received a fresh set of clothing for the occasion just as the others did (waistcoat and breeches at Moor Park, unspecified other clothing earlier in London).

45. Osborn Collection, fb 182, fols. 17–20, 58, 61 (cf. fol. 26 for Swift's mourn-

ing and other expenses, and fol. 27 for "Mrs Hetty's Mantowoman" or Manteau-woman—see *manteau-maker* in the O.E.D.).

46. For the diminishing authority and dignity of stewards, increasingly drawn from the yeomanly classes, see Girouard, *Life in the English Country House,* pp. 139–40. In the 1699 estate accounts, we have seen that Swift was the chief account-keeper, under Sir John Temple. By comparison, the steward Mose drew up or docketed relatively few documents, generally of lesser importance. As at Hamilton Palace, where the secretary was likewise the ranking retainer, the secretary's position at Moor Park seems to have involved account-keeping from the beginning. As early as 1690 Temple reported that Swift had "kept all accounts as farr as my small occasions required" (*Correspondence,* 1, 1–2).

47. *Prose Works,* v, 227.

48. Ehrenpreis, *Swift,* 1, 256 n. Ehrenpreis has just quoted Lady Giffard writing to her niece that "I make use of my cousin Dingley when ever I am in want, Hettys place being the heigh[t] of her ambition." At Moor Park there would have been nothing surprising in Lady Giffard's preferring Stella, if she were bright, useful, and appealing, to the older and duller Rebecca Dingley, distant cousin though she was. Lady Giffard's comment breathes a certain contempt for Dingley, which may be reflected in Temple's will. Of the six higher-ranking retainers at Moor Park, all but Dingley come in for special legacies there or in the codicil. If she or her family connection figures at all, it is through the £100 legacy which the codicil left to a William Dingley, then a university student. Presumably he was one of her eight siblings.

49. Osborn Collection, fb 182, fol. 20. The other two are Plumridge's wife Mary, the dairymaid, and Thomas Jones, probably the butler.

50. Ibid., fols. 65, 66. There is also a reference to "Cousen Dingley," who sits with Swift and a servant in Lady Giffard's coach at the time of Temple's funeral, but this is more probably the distant cousin William Dingley to whom Temple had left a £100 legacy in his 1697 codicil, just as he had Swift. See Sir John's note on fol. 71 about the "200 l. more that I am to pay out of my store to my Cousen Dingley & Mr Swift. . . ."

51. Ehrenpreis, *Swift,* 1, 103, apropos Temple's friendship with Henry Sidney, Earl of Romney.

52. John Clive, *Macaulay: The Shaping of the Historian* (New York: Knopf, 1973), pp. 105–6, 400, 263.

53. Ibid., p. 262 (quoting Macaulay to his sister Hannah, 6 July 1832); *Journal to Stella,* 1, 112 (Swift to Stella, 3 Dec. 1710). In the nickname "Poor Presto" Clive is aware of the allusion to Swift, but he has not noticed Macaulay's source in the nonsense verses.

CHAPTER 5

1. See chapter 3; passage first noted by Clarence M. Webster, in "Temple, Casaubon, and Swift," *Notes & Queries* 160 (1931), 405.

2. Ehrenpreis, *Swift,* 1, 189, 209; see also pp. 198, 205, 207, 216–17, 219; Pierre, "The Influence of Temple upon Swift," pp. 77–105. In their critical apparatus

for the *Tale*, Guthkelch and Smith had earlier drawn attention to a number of specific parallels, analogues, and echoes of Temple (*Tale of a Tub*, notes on pp. 39, 44, 48 [twice], 80, 93, 94, 113, 127, 128, 129, 157, 161 [cf. 157]). In my own work with the *Tale* and *The Battle of the Books*—by no means exhaustive—I encountered many more echoes, analogues, or rough parallels, and found that single passages in Swift may contain multiple allusions, from two or more different pieces by Temple.

3. For Wotton, see *A Tale of a Tub*, pp. 295, 327, 314 (mentioned in French, *Texas Studies in Literature and Language* 5: 46). For John Traugott's essay "*A Tale of a Tub*," see *Focus: Swift*, ed. C. J. Rawson (London: Sphere, 1971), pp. 83–85.

4. *Tale of a Tub*, pp. xliii–xlvii.

5. Ehrenpreis, *Swift*, 1, 186–87; *Tale of a Tub*, pp. xlvi–xlvii. By contrast, Herbert Davis thought it "quite possible that Temple may also have seen the *Tale*" as well as the *Battle*, but Davis did not argue the point in detail or consider its possible ramifications (*Prose Works*, 1, xviii).

6. Deane Swift, *An Essay Upon the Life of Swift*, p. 60; *Tale of a Tub*, p. xiv, n. 1. Like Lyon, Deane Swift subscribed to the theory that Swift had begun the *Tale* (its chapters of religious allegory, anyway) while an undergraduate at Trinity College, Dublin. Cf. *Tale of a Tub*, pp. xxxiv–xxxvi, xlvii; and Davis in *Prose Works*, 1, ix.

7. *Tale of a Tub*, p. 28. For the evidence bearing on manuscripts of the *Tale*, and for the standard interpretation of them, see pp. xi–xii. In *Modern Philology* 64: 202–6, Robert M. Adams cites a set of Thomas Swift's annotations of the *Tale*, which cross out the words "since dead" in the phrase "lent it to a Person, since dead." Adams argues in favor of Thomas's assertion that he had lent the MS. to Swift, and hence in favor of Thomas's claim to authorship of the *Tale*'s sections of religious allegory. Even if Thomas's central claim deserves much trust—something I doubt from the impression of his vanity, foolishness, competitiveness, and literary ambitiousness conveyed in Swift's 1692 letter to him and from his readiness to cover for Temple and break his word to Dunton, as we have seen in chapter 2—it still appears that Thomas deleted the words "since dead" *not* to deny that Temple ever had (or had seen) a copy, but rather to insist that Swift had a copy (and to insist that it was a copy of something which Thomas had composed). In the "Bookseller" 's view of the matter, as Jonathan presents it, the copy owned by Thomas was not the one left with the "Person, since dead," but was rather the "surreptitious Copy, which a certain great Wit had new polish'd and refin'd, or as our present Writers express themselves, *fitted to the Humor of the Age*" (*Tale of a Tub*, p. 29; cf. p. xi, and *Correspondence*, 1, 166). This in itself looks like a gauntlet thrown down before Thomas—and mockingly thrown, at that. As such it gave Thomas a personal motive for making some sort of counterattack, and to a scholar it provides an additional reason for distrusting Thomas's claims of authorship when they came.

8. Temple, *Miscellanea, The Second Part*, pp. 73, 84, & passim.

9. *Tale of a Tub*, p. 174; French, *Texas Studies in Literature and Language* 5: 50–51.

10. Temple, *Miscellanea, The Second Part*, p. 91.

11. For alchemy and the phrase "Knaves upon Fools," see chapter 3, and

Temple's MS. "Hints: written at the Desire of D.ʳ F[ulham] and of His Friend," Rothschild no. 2253, pp. 15–16 (Wotton a "superficiall Sciolist"), p. 9 (Wotton thinks chemistry means alchemy), and p. 10 (Wotton a crack-brained alchemist). Despite Temple's implication that Wotton is on Borrichius' side, as a believer in alchemy, Wotton had attacked Borrichius' claims for the alchemists of antiquity—and had attacked them much more tellingly than Temple does (Wotton, *Reflections upon Ancient and Modern Learning*, pp. 118–28).

    12. Temple, *Miscellanea, The Second Part*, pp. 83–86.

    13. More charitable than most, Woodbridge paraphrases the passage as if Temple actually made the distinction anyway, despite the evidence of the text. See his summary of Temple's argument, in *Temple*, p. 270. Ricardo Quintana's summary does the same thing: see *The Mind and Art of Jonathan Swift* (London & New York: Oxford University Press, 1936), p. 16. Woodbridge papers over other difficulties as well. While Temple generally remained sceptical about the powers of human reason and generally favored an easygoing approach to life, he has received far too much credit for maintaining a systematic and consistent philosophical position. As with most other mortals, when Temple dips into philosophy it is usually to justify or dignify the course which his own life has taken. If individual statements sometimes seem to contradict each other, they remain consistent in their application.

    14. Compare Temple's later praise of Epicurus, his preferred model for the sort of life he advocates. Epicurus was justly beloved for his "Temperance of Life," among other virtues, and by retiring from public life to his garden he enjoyed improved health and contemplation, chiefly thanks to "the Exemption from Cares and Sollicitude" which such retirement encouraged (*Miscellanea, The Second Part*, pp. 86, 91–92). A few pages before Temple compares Stoics and Epicureans, he discusses the attitude which gives rise to moral philosophy, and discusses it in qualified but generally approving terms:

> Whilst Mankind is thus generally busied or amused [with sensual entertainments], that part of them, who have had either the Justice or the Luck, to pass in common opinion for the wisest and the best part among them, have followed another and very different Scent; and instead of the common designs of satisfying their Appetites and their Passions, and making endless Provisions for both, they have chosen what they thought a nearer and a surer way to the ease and felicity of Life, by endeavouring to subdue, *or at least to temper their Passions, and reduce their Appetites to what Nature seems only to ask and to need.* And this design seems to have brought Philosophy into the world, at least that which is termed Moral, *and appears to have an end, not only desirable by every man, which is the Ease and Happiness of Life, but also in some degree suitable to the force and reach of human Nature* . . . (Ibid., pp. 79–80, my emphases).

The italicized portions suggest how much Temple garbled his later discussion. They indicate that Temple generally felt the better Stoic-Epicurean position to be more or less sensible and suitable to the needs of human nature. In his later discussion of Stoicism and Epicureanism—the "most reasonable" Stoics and the "best" Epicureans, lumped unwittingly with the most extreme Stoics—Temple makes the accusation that their precepts are "against common Nature and common Sense."

15. It is possible that Temple's unaccountable volte-face may ultimately derive from a faulty or faultily-arranged abstract of some source, perhaps Diogenes Laertius (who transmits a few of Epicurus' writings and summarizes others) or Lucretius (whose *De Rerum Natura* closely follows Epicurus' teachings). Temple's problem may also stem directly from his sources. In Diogenes Laertius it is sometimes difficult to separate the author's statements from his quotations, and H.S. Long notes that the long quotations from Epicurus need to be "separated from the inserted marginalia that sometimes interrupt the sense"—see *The Oxford Classical Dictionary*, ed. N. G. L. Hammond and H. H. Scullard, 2nd ed. (Oxford: The Clarendon Press, 1970), s.v. Diogenes Laertius). As for Epicurus' surviving pieces, D. F. Furley notes that they are "needlessly difficult, clumsy, ambiguous, badly organized, and full of jargon," except in the letter to Menoeceus, a summary of his moral philosophy (Ibid., s.v. Epicurus). Temple had read Diogenes Laertius on Epicurus (or said he had): see *Miscellanea, The Second Part*, p. 87.

16. Note the easily overlooked phrase "though it *be made to* proceed from so diverse Causes," which allows Temple some reservations about their efficacy. Judging from Temple's models of tranquil living—chiefly Epicurus himself, in his manner of living—Temple may also mean to distinguish between ignobly or foolishly gained tranquillity and virtuously or wisely gained tranquillity, or perhaps to suggest that only wise and virtuous tranquillity is truly tranquil. Taken as a whole, the essay seems to reflect the belief that virtuous retirement to a quiet life of gardening will produce reasonableness as well as tranquillity, although reasonableness seems to be necessary for the decision to retire in the first place (*Miscellanea, The Second Part*, pp. 90–91).

17. Temple, *Miscellanea, The Second Part*, pp. 53–54. Cf. *Miscellanea, The Third Part*, pp. 283–87; and *Observations upon the United Provinces of the Netherlands*, 5th ed. (London: for J. Tonson and A. Churchill, 1690), sig. A5$^{r/v}$ and p. 193.

18. Temple, *Miscellanea, The Third Part*, pp. 101–2. Here Temple also admits the value of experience, though in a subordinate role. He introduces his statement about men growing wise and happy through their own thoughts, by asserting that "of all sorts of Instructions, the best is gained from our own Thoughts, as well as Experience. . . ." Contrast Swift in the Digression on Madness: "the more he [a man] shapes his Understanding by the Pattern of Human Learning, the less he is inclined to form Parties after his particular Notions; because that instructs him in his private Infirmities, as well as in the stubborn Ignorance of the People" (*Tale of a Tub*, p. 171). Temple firmly believed in "the stubborn Ignorance of the People," and Swift speaks in a context in which Temple could find much to agree with—a definition of sanity which includes a swipe at the Moderns, an attack on fanaticism and system-builders, and an argument for passing life "in the common Forms." Still, Swift's definition of rational behavior (so limited and unsatisfying considered out of a Moor

Park context) makes sense as the reverse of Temple's stated preference for mental self-sufficiency.

19. Temple, *Miscellanea, The Second Part*, p. 29; cf. p. 30 which (considering Temple's short and undistinguished Cambridge career) carries a somewhat autobiographical ring: "Besides, who can tell, whether Learning may not even weaken Invention, in a man that has great Advantages from Nature and Birth; whether the weight and number of so many other mens thoughts and notions, may not suppress his own, or hinder the motion and agitation of them, from which all Invention arises. . . ."

20. Temple, *Miscellanea, The Third Part*, pp. 292, 301–2, and 300, respectively. It is significant that Swift adopts two additional elements from Temple in his own satiric definition of happiness. Temple speaks of his happy fool in a context which discusses the respective importance of a man's "Condition of Fortune" and the "Temper" which enables him to enjoy it. For Swift it is "he, whose *Fortunes* and *Dispositions* have placed him in a convenient Station to enjoy the Fruits of this noble Art," who is the Epicurean follower after films and images (*Tale of a Tub*, p. 174, my emphases). By "this noble Art," Swift means "an Art to sodder and patch up the Flaws and Imperfections of Nature": cf. Temple's discussion of satire and Cowley's heroic verse (see chapter 3) with his recommendation that governments try to make poets improve upon reality—to "turn the Vein of Wits, to raise up the Esteem of some Qualities, above their real Value, rather than bring every Thing to Burlesque. . . ." If it is Temple indeed who fits Swift's theory of happiness, and whose "Fortunes and Dispositions have placed him in a convenient Station to enjoy the *Fruits* of this noble Art" (my emphasis), a weak play on words may also be involved. Temple's gardening essay gave its greatest emphasis to Temple's success in fruit-growing at Moor Park and his belief in the great importance of eating fresh fruit. E.g., *Miscellanea, The Second Part*, pp. 142–45.

21. Temple, *Miscellanea, The Second Part*, pp. 139–41 (my emphases); Temple quotes Horace, Ep., 1, xviii (to Lollius), 96–97 & 101–3. The connection to the passage in Swift's Digression was earlier made by Denis Donoghue in *Jonathan Swift: A Critical Introduction* (Cambridge: Cambridge University Press, 1969), pp. 55–57. I am grateful to A.H. Scouten for directing my attention to Donoghue's brief discussion, and with it the important parallel with which Donoghue deals. Donoghue is chiefly interested (pp. 40–58) in illustrating what he considers Swift's deep psychological need to rid himself of the terror or contamination of "difficult material, difficult because intangible"—"all forms of speculation and subtlety," anything extreme or innovative or hard to grasp—and rid himself of it not in any merely nay-saying way (as F.R. Leavis once charged) but with great verve and gusto, as a positive good in itself. Swift's satire expels or otherwise destroys such alien pretensions by parody in the larger as well as regular sense of the term, Donoghue maintains. One favored technique is the sudden shifting of the terms in an argument (or "idiom," as Donoghue calls it) from the eulogistic to the censorious, thus negating values which the argument had begun by praising. It is this shifting of "idioms" which Donoghue chiefly means to illustrate in Swift's treatment of Epicurean folly, the happiness of the man

truly wise who lives as a fool among knaves. Perhaps because he maintains that
Swift attacks all 'difficult' or speculative positions indiscriminately, Donoghue
fails to pursue the biographical question which his findings raise, much less the
question of Swift's intended readership in the Digression. In fact Donoghue
seems unaware of the heavy matrix of Temple material present elsewhere in the
passage and elsewhere in the Digression. French's earlier work is not mentioned, nor does Donoghue instance any of the valuable parallels which French
found—parallels which help us trace and establish Swift's use of Temple in the
passage far more accurately and persuasively than Donoghue's single discovery
can do in itself. For instance, instead of exploring Temple's illuminating use of
the phrase about the predations of "Knaves upon Fools," Donoghue turns to
Empson on the word 'folly' in *King Lear* and to the "tradition of Stultitia" best
known through Erasmus. Temple may indeed have had some vague notion of
this tradition—I suspect that he did—but it is Temple's particular *use* of it, while
inviting praise, which sheds light on Swift's satire. As a result, Donoghue not
only misses the sharp personal irony of Swift's phrase "a Fool among Knaves,"
but also seems uncertain how to account for Temple's very presence in the
passage, further than as a vehicle for the concept of wise folly in the Erasmian
tradition. Why indeed should Swift bother with Temple at all when he could
choose among more prominent representatives—and when the profundities of
poor Temple's thought were so much less threatening than most? At first
Donoghue asserts that Swift's "whole paragraph is a description of Sir William
Temple," but soon suggests that Swift actually thinks Temple a fool "only in
[the] specially defined sense":

> To be a fool among knaves is consciously and conscientiously to seek the
> life of the garden, rejecting the life of the world which, in this Epicurean
> setting, is the work of knaves. It is Temple's choice, one kind of folly rather
> than another, Moor Park rather than the Court. . . .

Therefore, Donoghue asserts, the sentence cannot be a trap for the reader
(presumably a trap of the kind which Leavis had postulated). Even so, he finds
that the reader is driven "from one idiom to another without warning," that
"the energy at work is critical, sceptical, and subversive," with the object of
driving out the matter under consideration ("The object is good riddance"). But
if Swift subverts the combined Epicurean-Erasmian concept of wise 'folly,' I do
not see how he can avoid subverting Temple the wise 'fool' as well, still assuming that "the whole paragraph is a description of Sir William Temple." How
can Temple remain a fool only in the exalted Epicurean-Erasmian sense, when
the Epicurean-Erasmian concept of folly is itself redefined as folly pure and
simple—and so dismissed? In the final phrase about the "Fool among Knaves,"
the shift in 'idiom' involves something more than a shift in mere value judgment, from eulogistic to dyslogistic, and the only fool in sight is Temple. So far
as Swift and Temple are themselves concerned in the passage, Donoghue's
interpretation offers little more satisfaction than that of French, who thinks that
Swift suffered from a divided consciousness (accepting Temple's position intel-

lectually while rejecting it emotionally).

22. Temple, *Miscellanea, The Third Part,* pp. 34–35, 28.

23. A fuller discussion of Temple's personal motivations as an author must await another occasion, but his conscious or unconscious angling after praise in the gardening essay raises a question which deserves a brief comment here. Just how secure did Temple feel in his own high estimation of himself? We have seen the contempt which brought forth his phrase "a Practise of Knaves upon Fools," apropos Wotton and alchemists, but elsewhere Temple applies the same scornful phrase in a way which sits more uneasily. This is the passage which French identified in the essay *Of Popular Discontents,* the natural companion piece to Temple's gardening essay. (In the first, Temple discusses the public knavery which makes wise and good men retire; in the second, he investigates the retirement which such wise and good men seek.) In both essays Temple habitually opposes knaves to wise and virtuous patriots like himself, but the one time he openly opposes knaves to *fools*—the people whom knaves dupe—his tone towards the fools wavers confusingly between scorn and empathy, between the impatience one feels with others and the understanding one feels for oneself. When factions arise in a state, he says, *"The Practice begins of Knaves upon Fools, of Artificial and Crafty Men, upon the Simple and the Good;* these easily follow, and are caught, while the others lay Trains, and pursue a Game, wherein they design no other Share, than of Toil and Danger to their Country, but the Gain and the Quarry, wholly to themselves" (*Miscellanea, The Third Part,* pp. 32–33, my emphases). For once wisdom (or at least intelligence) is on the side of the knaves, and the fools who are contemptible in one breath partly merge in the next with more empathetic folk, "the Simple and the Good." It is not clear which tone is intended to prevail, the contempt or the appreciation, and both soon give way to Temple's anger over the knaves' knavery. Elsewhere in the essay Temple holds himself fittingly aloof from the impressionable sort of people who are "caught" by knaves—the people who make up "vulgar Opinion" (as he terms it), mere common folk for whose allegiance the wise patriot must battle the knave, and whose restless irrationalities usually condemn the patriot to failure. The empathetic note towards "the Simple and the Good" is therefore something of an anomaly, although not entirely out of place in an author whose public career began with being duped by the Bishop of Munster and ended by being duped (for the second or third time) by Charles II. In a sense, the essay *Of Popular Discontents* may be a response to Temple's public career—both a dissociation of himself from the foolish dupes who support demagogues and foredoom the patriot's efforts, and a demonstration of his own political wisdom, which sees all and understands all as it hovers above the fray. And if, in passing, Temple once mingles empathy with his scorn for dupes, he may be betraying similarly conflicting feelings towards himself. In some secret corner of his mind, Temple may have mocked himself for a fool among knaves long before Swift did, and brilliantly appropriate though Swift's treatment of him is, it may also strike us as somewhat cold and inhumane—a little too brilliant for comfort, in a world which warms more readily to mercy than to justice.

24. *Tale of a Tub,* p. 52; cf. pp. 48, 51. Swift speaks here of general satire.

Particular satire he would never attempt, either, because a man can expect "to be imprisoned for *Scandalum Magnatum:* to have *Challenges* sent him; to be sued for *Defamation;* and to be *brought before the Bar of the House*" (p. 53). Swift also discusses satire in the preface to the *Tale*'s companion piece, *The Battle of the Books*, which elsewhere shows signs of covert mockery of Temple, as we shall see. "Satyr is a sort of *Glass*, wherein Beholders do generally discover every body's Face but their Own," begins Swift, "which is the chief Reason for that kind of Reception it meets in the World, and that so very few are offended with it. But if it should happen otherwise, the Danger is not great; and, I have learned from long Experience, never to apprehend Mischief from those Understandings, I have been able to provoke . . ." (*Tale of a Tub*, p. 215). At the time of writing, Swift had no experience at all in publishing satire, at least as his works are currently identified.

25. Woodbridge, *Temple*, p. 32; cf. pp. 10–11, 14, 87 (giving references from at least one Temple letter which Swift would have known). When Temple felt his first twinge of gout, he wrote a year afterwards in 1677, "I confest I was in pain, and thought it was with some sprain at Tennis" (*Miscellanea, The First Part*, p. 197, also known to Swift).

26. With some success, French attempts to justify a literal reading of the section culminating in Swift's definition of happiness (*Texas Studies in Literature and Language* 5: 49–50): Reason in fact may serve only to uncover faults which spoil our happiness, and happiness may accordingly depend on self-deception. By arguing Temple's supposed point of view—more probably Temple's instinctive feelings, rather than conscious ones—French illustrates the feeling of instinctive acceptance which Swift may have meant Temple to feel. As in a trap, it would have led Temple onwards to increasing discomfort as the ironies grow stronger and harder to ignore. To a lesser extent, the passage should operate this way on other readers as well.

27. *Oxford Classical Dictionary*, s.v. Epicurus, my emphasis. For a different treatment of Epicurean philosophy and the Digression on Madness, see Miriam K. Starkman, *Swift's Satire on Learning in "A Tale of a Tub"* (Princeton: Princeton University Press, 1950), pp. 39–40. Philip Harth also discusses Epicurean sensationalism in the Digression, but mainly in terms of Cudworth and Hobbes; see *Swift and Anglican Rationalism* (Chicago: University of Chicago Press, 1961), pp. 137–41.

28. Temple, *Miscellanea, The Second Part*, pp. 80–83. Similar in many respects to the theories of Democritus, from whom he largely derived them, Epicurus' natural philosophy explained the formation of the world by a fortuitous collision of atoms. Atoms generally move downwards but with individual deviations which introduce the element of randomness or chance. The soul, too, is composed of such atoms, which disperse upon death. See Furley's summation, largely drawn from *De Rerum Natura*, II, 62–332, in the *Oxford Classical Dictionary*, s.v. Epicurus. French briefly draws attention to the distinction which Temple made between Epicurus' ethics and metaphysics (*Texas Studies in Literature and Language* 5: 44, 48). Temple suggests it most succinctly in *Some Thoughts Upon Reviewing the Essay of Antient and Modern Learning*. "Democritus," he says, "was

the Founder of that Sect, which made so much Noise afterwards in the World, under the Name of Epicurus; who owed him both his Atoms and his Vacuum in his Natural Philosophy, and his Tranquility of Mind in his Morals . . ." (*Miscellanea, The Third Part*, pp. 224–25).

29. Temple, *Miscellanea, The Third Part*, pp. 107–9. Temple could afford to sound contemptuous about the "Philosophers" and their gross mistakes, because Epicurus had defended the primacy of sense impressions in a somewhat different way. Where Temple accounts for delusions in terms of weak or unhealthy sense organs, which receive their impressions faultily, Epicurus theorized that delusions occur when objects occasionally give off defective atoms which men fail to judge correctly: "Delusions occur when single or damaged *eidōla* cause an image to form which looks like those formed by continuous streams of *eidōla;* a man is deluded only by judging it to *be* one of the latter" (Furley's summary in the *Oxford Classical Dictionary*, s.v. Epicurus). Temple seems to think he is refuting the Epicurean insistence on the validity of sense impressions, while he is in fact building and improving on it.

30. Temple, *Miscellanea, The Third Part*, pp. 101–2 (on the right use of thinking, to make oneself "Wise and Happy") and p. 196 (on the need for reading, good conversation, etc., in a man in the prime of his life). Immediately before discussing the causes of pleasures, Temple also notes that (among other drawbacks) ill health can affect the pleasures of imagination and hinder "the common Operations both of Body and Mind" (p. 107).

31. By giving his assent to Swift's seeming attack on the implications of Epicurean atomism, Temple would have found himself half-agreeing to its carefully obscured implication, that following Epicurus in matters of happiness (as Temple himself did) leads to self-indulgence and folly. In much the same way, Swift's apparent source in the gardening essay functions to trap a reader. There Temple invites his reader to approve the temperate pleasures of rational self-control, as prescribed by the better Stoics and Epicureans, and then without warning dismisses it scornfully—"pretends to make us wise no other way, than by rendring us insensible," "against common Nature and common Sense," or no better than saying "that a man to be wise, should not be a man." Temple constructs his trap unconsciously, of course, and the chief victim is himself, since he emerges from the section appearing fuzzyminded and self-indulgent. Even so, it is a disagreeable and confusing experience, for a reader, to give his assent to a proposition and then hear it denounced as foolish and unnatural.

32. Temple, *Miscellanea, The Second Part*, pp. 86–87.

33. Neil Schaeffer, " 'Them That Speak, and Them That Hear': The Audience as Target in Swift's *Tale of a Tub*," *Enlightenment Essays* 4 (1973): 33–34.

34. *Tale of a Tub*, p. 166.

35. Cf. Temple, *Miscellanea, The Third Part*, pp. 204–5, where Temple expresses "a just Indignation at the Insolence of the Modern Advocates, in defaming those Heroes among the Antients, whose Memory has been sacred and admired for so many Ages; as Homer, Virgil, Pythagoras, Democritus [whom Temple associated with Epicurus], &c. This I confess, gave me the same kind of Horror I should have had, in seeing some young barbarous Goths or Vandals,

breaking or defacing the admirable Statues of those antient Heroes of Greece or Rome. . . ."

36. Ibid., pp. 205–7 (examples of Moderns who "pretended to exceed or equal the Antients"). Paracelsus and his disciples "introduced new Notions in Physick, and new Methods of Practice," but they were "not able to maintain their Pretence long . . ." (yet see p. 149, where they "brought a mixt use of Chymical Medicines into the present Practice"). Descartes, Temple continues, "was the next that would be thought to excel the Antients, by a new Scheme or Body of Philosophy, which I am apt to think, he had a Mind to impose upon the World, as Nostradamus did his Prophesies, only for their own Amusement. . . ." After discussing the systematizers, Swift himself takes up the question of how they attracted followers (*Tale of a Tub*, pp. 167–68).

37. Swift again seems to borrow from Temple here, but applies the borrowing uncomfortably. In his essay *Upon Ancient and Modern Learning*, Temple had spoken in similar terms about man's ignorance and pride. Like Swift, who speaks of reducing "the Notions of all Mankind, exactly to the same Length, and Breadth, and Height of his own," Temple employs metaphors of measurement:

> But God be thanked, his [man's] Pride is greater than his Ignorance; and what he wants in Knowledge, he supplies by Sufficiency. *When he has looked about him as far as he can, he concludes there is no more to be seen; when he is at the end of his Line, he is at the bottom of the Ocean;* when he has shot his best, he is sure, none ever did nor ever can shoot better or beyond it. *His own Reason is the certain measure of truth, his own Knowledge, of what is possible in Nature. . . .*
> (*Miscellanea, The Second Part*, pp. 53–54, my emphases. Cf. *Miscellanea, The Third Part*, p. 306: one of "The two greatest Mistakes among Mankind" is "to measure Truth by every Man's single Reason.")

Temple has been speaking of the Moderns, who pretend to equal the ancients yet fall far short, and his observation about human nature is meant to put them in their place. To be sure, Temple does not seem aware that what holds true for the Moderns will also hold true for the ancients, if both groups are human. Swift applies the idea more indiscriminately, not just to accuse the Moderns of pride and ignorance, but also to relegate Temple's beloved Epicurus and Lucretius, among others, to the ranks of the frankly insane.

38. *Tale of a Tub*, p. 167 and n. 1 (citing Lucretius for the technical term 'clinamen'). Compare Swift's phrase "a certain Fortuitous Concourse of all Mens Opinions" with Temple's phrase "the fortuitous Concourse of Atoms," cited above in the text.

39. Swift even seems to borrow his terms of condemnation from Temple. Temple may have believed Epicurus modest and virtuous, but in one of his sweeping statements about natural philosophers he suggested that when they did not busy their brains to no purpose (half suggesting a form of irrationality), they wrote out of personal vanity: "For as to that part of Philosophy, which is called Natural, I know no end it can have, but that of either busying a man's

Brains to no purpose, or satisfying the Vanity, so natural to most men, of distinguishing themselves by some way or other, from those that seem their Equals in Birth, and the common advantages of it . . ." (*Miscellanea, The Second Part, Upon the Gardens of Epicurus,* p. 80).

40. French, *Texas Studies in Literature and Language* 5: 52.

41. *Tale of a Tub,* p. 165.

42. E.g., Temple, *Letters,* 1, 396–97, where Temple plays ironically upon Louis's pretense of being 'the first gentleman of Europe' and upon Louis's official style as king, 'His Most Christian Majesty'. Even so, Temple fully expects him to break his promises made in the Alternative and that the Franche-Comté will accordingly be returned to Spain in a damaged condition—"dans un estat si peu convenable a la promesse du Roy tres Chretien."

43. Temple, *Miscellanea, The First Part,* 5th ed. (for J. Tonson and A. & J. Churchill, 1697), p. 32 (*A Survey of the Constitutions and Interests of the Empire, Sweden, Denmark, Spain, Holland, France and Flanders; with their Relation to England, in the Year 1671*). Temple originally submitted the essay to Arlington's ministry, to persuade it to retain an anti-French foreign policy.

44. In his essay *Of Health and Long Life,* Temple registers his amusement over "the various and fantastical Changes of the Diseases generally complained of." First the vogue was rickets, then consumption, "the Spleen," scurvy, and "the Ferment of the Blood," while most recently, "to all these, succeeded Vapours; which serve the same Turn, and furnish Occasion of Complaint among Persons, whose Bodies or Minds ail something, but they know not what: And among the Chineses would pass for Mists of the Mind, or Fumes of the Brain, rather than Indispositions of any other Parts" (*Miscellanea, The Third Part,* pp. 163–64; cf. French, *Texas Studies in Literature and Language* 5: 47–48). In the process of laughing "Vapours" out of serious consideration, Temple unwittingly accepts a theory of vapors—the "Mists of the Mind, or Fumes of the Brain" which the wiser Chinese would supposedly diagnose. Here he makes a distinction between diseases of the mind (psychosomatic ailments) and of the body, although the English "Vapours" was supposed to include depression of the spirits, as Temple himself concedes in passing ("whose Bodies *or Minds* ail something"). In *An Essay Upon the Cure of the Gout by Moxa,* Temple is apt to believe that "a malignant Vapour" may cause gout—the explanation offered by the sage "Indians" of Java, whose prescriptions for burning moxa have helped in his own case—and he states that we owe the psychosomatic malady "the Spleen" to fumes or winds in the body, much as we do the colic (*Miscellanea, The First Part,* pp. 207, 227). Early in the essay *Of Health and Long Life,* Temple likewise betrays a belief in vapors which link the physical and mental, when he talks of "Meat, swallowed down for Pleasure or Greediness, which only charges the Stomach, *or fumes into the Brain,* if it be not well digested . . ." (*Miscellanea, The Third Part,* p. 102, my italics; cf. *Observations upon the United Provinces,* 5th ed., sig. A6^v–A7^r, pp. 125–26, and p. 186, the last on the spleen and "fumes of Indigestion"). In his definition of Epicurean tranquillity, he had called for "Tranquility of Mind, and Indolence [i.e., freedom from pain] of Body; for while we are composed of both, I doubt both must have a share in the good or ill we feel." Since

happiness lies in the mind ("the good or ill we feel"), mental conditions again seem dependent on the physical.

Into the 1690s Temple seems to have retained a certain curiosity about the cause and working of vapors. Along with his questions relating to problems in his first essay on the Ancients and Moderns, Temple asked the Athenian Society to explain "What Wind in our Body is, whence it proceeds, and what are the true remedies for it?" (*Athenian Mercury*, 5, no. 7 [22 Dec. 1691], q. 2; see chapter 3). The Athenians return an answer (acceptable, I suspect) which concentrates upon belching and farting and explains such "offensive Wind" by a theory of what they call "Vapours." Among other things, it appears, "steams are always reaking in our Bodies . . . these steams are humidities rarifi'd, and inoffensively pervade all parts." In Swift's early satire, the theory of vapors enters in other places besides the description of Louis XIV, and they may be worth examining in light of Temple's confused attitudes and beliefs about vapors and other factors affecting human health and behavior. But in the particular passage about Louis, I think, Temple should have found Swift's jargon about the circulation of vapors especially appealing (at first) for another reason. In its solemn use of scientific and medical terminology ("this *Phaenomenon,*" "in perpetual Circulation," "the *Zibeta Occidentalis,*" "gathering there into a Tumour," "*Anus,*" "*Fistula*"), it seems to parody Temple's detested opponent Wotton, who had waxed both solemn and technological about the circulation and interaction of the various human bodily fluids. See Wotton, *Reflections upon Ancient and Modern Learning*, pp. 206–38 (chapters 18 and 19, "Of the Circulation of the Blood" and "Further Reflections upon Ancient and Modern Anatomy"), and especially pp. 197–98 (chapter 17, "Of Ancient and Modern Anatomy"), with its discussion of that Modern discovery, "the *Animal Spirit* in the Brain," which is separated from the blood and carried from the upper brain into the *medulla oblongata* "through little Pipes," and which contrary to ancient belief is not found in the "Ventricles of the Brain" ("those Cavities are only Sinks to carry off excrementitious Humours, and not Store-Houses of the Animal Spirit").

45. Ehrenpreis, *Swift*, 1, 123; Temple, *Miscellanea, The Third Part*, p. 36; Temple, *Memoirs of what past in Christendom, From the War Begun 1672. To the Peace Concluded 1679*, 2nd ed. (London: by R. R. for Ric. Chiswell, 1692), p. 334; Temple, *Letters*, 1, 11. As an admirer of heroes, all the same, Temple could maintain a position diametrically opposed to the one he urged as an historian. In the essay *Of Heroick Virtue*, for instance, we have seen him arguing that history waits to be made by great heroes, who lead their people to glory in the arts of peace and in military conquests. In his *Introduction to the History of England*—apropos that great hero, William the Conqueror—Temple asserted that "all great Actions in the World, and Revolutions of States may be truly derived, from the Genius of the Persons, that conduct and govern them," and that "to attribute such great Events to Time or to Chance, were to destroy the Examples, and confound the Consequences of all Virtues and Vices among Men" (*Introduction to the History of England*, pp. 301–2). It is interesting that Temple now argues from moral imperatives rather than historical truths. In effect, he seems to maintain that we should exempt a hero's actions from the historical process he has described

elsewhere, and that we should interpret them in light of what we need to believe —in this case, the reality and transcendent worth of heroic virtue. From Temple's position it is not too far to that of Swift's narrator in the Digression, who a few pages later argues for surface over substance, fiction over truth, and explains that "Imagination can build nobler Scenes, and produce more wonderful Revolutions than Fortune or Nature will be at Expence to furnish" (*Tale of a Tub*, p. 172).

46. Temple, *Miscellanea, The Third Part*, p. 99 (cf. pp. 94–95). Compare the *Tale*'s title-page ("Written for the Universal Improvement of Mankind") and the end of the Digression on Madness:

> That even, I my self, the Author of these momentous Truths, am a Person, whose Imaginations are hard-mouth'd, and exceedingly disposed to run away with his *Reason*, which I have observed from long Experience, to be a very light Rider, and easily shook off; upon which Account, my Friends will never trust me alone, without a solemn Promise, to vent my Speculations in this, or the like manner, for the universal Benefit of Human kind; which, perhaps, the gentle, courteous, and candid Reader, brimful of that *Modern* Charity and Tenderness, usually annexed to his *Office*, will be very hardly persuaded to believe.
>
> (*Tale of a Tub*, p. 180)

Of course Swift's speaker presents himself as a rank Modern, while Temple despised the Moderns and counted himself the staunchest sort of Ancient. Many of Temple's speculations still seem decidedly Modern in spirit: for instance, his conjecture that the ancient priests of Delphi may have invented gunpowder to scare off invaders (see chapter 3), or that trained parrots may discourse intelligently in human speech (*Miscellanea, The Third Part*, pp. 4–5; for his evidence see *Memoirs of What Past in Christendom*, pp. 57–59).

47. Kathleen Williams, *Jonathan Swift and the Age of Compromise* (Lawrence, Kans.: University of Kansas Press, 1958), p. 13; Traugott, in *Focus: Swift*, pp. 83–93, 108, 77–79, 117.

48. Traugott in *Focus: Swift*, pp. 116–17, 90.

49. *Tale of a Tub*, pp. 172–74; Temple, *Miscellanea, The Third Part*, pp. 258–59. For Wotton's place in the passage as first written (before considerable expansion) see Temple, "Hints," MS., Rothschild no. 2253, pp. 11–12; for Temple on heroic virtue see his *Miscellanea, The Second Part*, p. 150; and for Temple on Harvey, see ibid., pp. 42–43.

50. Temple, *Miscellanea, The Second Part*, pp. 356–61 *(Of Poetry)*. (Presumably the laundress was an Epicurean only in natural philosophy, but in an author as self-contradictory as Temple, it is hard to be sure.) For his treatment of heroic virtue and education, see ibid., p. 150; and for his ambivalent treatment of Mohammed, see ibid., pp. 257–63.

51. *Tale of a Tub*, p. 162 (Swift's emphases).

52. Temple, *Miscellanea, The Third Part*, pp. 30–31, 67. Compare Temple's "Heads" for an essay on conversation (ibid., pp. 319–20): "Sometimes in one Age,

Great Men are without Great Occasions; in another, Great Occasions [are] without Great Men; and in both, one lost, for want of the other."

53. *Tale of a Tub*, pp. 166, 175. For one such failed hero, unfairly reputed mad, the narrator names Empedocles. Temple likewise thought Empedocles a great hero, called him "the Glory and the Boast of Sicily," and apparently identified with him as a great inventor, patriot, reformer of the privy council, and refuser of high public office. See Temple, *Miscellanea, The Third Part*, pp. 223–24. Greatness will also depend upon the differences in men's particular understandings, according to Swift's narrator—upon the angle at which the vapor strikes the understanding and "upon what *Species* of Brain it ascends" (*Tale*, p. 169). Indeed Temple had argued that the same objects affect men in different ways because of differences in their sense organs, sometimes caused by distempers. Hence he concluded

> that our Perceptions are formed, and our Imaginations raised upon them, in a very great measure, by the Disposition of the Organs, thro' which the several Objects make their Impressions; and that these vary according to the different Frame and Temper of the others; as the Sound of the same Breath passing through an Oaten Pipe, a Flute, or a Trumpet.
>
> (*Miscellanea, The Third Part*, pp. 108–9)

Where Temple resorts to a comparison with wind instruments to explain different perceptions and imaginations in men, Swift employs a metaphor of stringed instruments, to explain how a man may capitalize upon such differences. Madmen can find ready disciples, it seems, because

> there is a peculiar *String* in the Harmony of Human Understanding, which in several individuals is exactly of the same Tuning. This, if you can dexterously screw up to its right Key, and then strike gently upon it; Whenever you have the Good Fortune to light among those of the same Pitch, they will by a secret necessary Sympathy, strike exactly at the same time.

Here good fortune is important (as it was for Temple's heroic virtue) because "if you chance to jar the String among those who are either above or below your own Height, instead of subscribing to your Doctrine, they will tie you fast, call you Mad, and feed you with Bread and Water" (*Tale of a Tub*, pp. 167–68).

54. *Tale of a Tub*, p. 179; Temple, *Miscellanea, The Third Part*, pp. 62–65. Temple suggests that robbers be sent "either to Slavery in our Plantations abroad, or Labour in Work-Houses at home," and appends the suggestion that they have their noses slit or cheeks branded as well. How all this is supposed to accord "with the Mildness and Clemency of our Government" which he appeals to, Temple never explains. Instead he observes that such punishment would be harder for Englishmen to bear than the "short and easy Deaths" dealt out under the current dispensation. For an ironical glance at the *"great Lenity and Tenderness"* of a similar sentence (execution commuted to blinding and

forced labor) under very different circumstances, see *Prose Works*, XI, 70, 72–73 (Gulliver in Lilliput).

55. Pinkus, *University of Toronto Quarterly* 29: 55–56; *Tale of a Tub*, pp. 127–29 (Swift's emphases).

56. Pinkus omits another strongly ambivalent reference, early in the passage. Homer is guilty of many omissions and imperfections, Swift's speaker asserts, because "first of all, *as eminent a Cabbalist as his Disciples would represent Him*, his Account of the *Opus magnum* is extreamly poor and deficient; he seems to have read but very superficially, either Sendivogius, Behmen, or *Anthroposophia Theomagica*" (*Tale of a Tub*, p. 127, first emphasis mine). The ancients' advocates, in other words, praise Homer for understanding occultism, a foolish Modernism not to be found in Homer. While Swift pokes fun at the Moderns most of the time, for seeking anachronistic rubbish in Homer and blaming him for its absence (itself a backhanded compliment to Homer, to whom the Moderns concede everything else), the speaker's search for "a compleat Body of all Knowledge" in Homer itself parallels the work of Ancient advocates like Temple, and taints the whole enterprise with a touch of absurdity.

57. Temple, *Miscellanea, The Second Part*, p. 42; cf. p. 43 ("sense can very hardly allow" Harvey's theory). Even after Wotton took Temple to task on the point (Wotton, *Reflections*, pp. 217–18—"Sense therefore here allows it . . ."), Temple could not quite bring himself to believe either in a Modern discovery of the circulation of the blood, or in its actual existence. Note his careful qualifications in *Miscellanea, The Third Part:* "Doctor Harvey gave the first *Credit*, if not *Rise*, to the *Opinion* about the Circulation of the Blood . . ." (p. 149, my emphases). Even before Wotton's *Reflections* challenged him, Temple was bothered by the problem enough to include a question to the *Athenian Mercury* asking "How the Blood circulates in a Body whose Leggs are cut off?" (vol. 5, no. 7, 22 Dec. 1691, q. 5, referred back for an answer to vol. 2, no. 19, Aug. 1691, q. 2). The Athenians had already dealt with the question, somewhat confusingly, after the initial observation that, "When the *Inquisitive Doctor* Harvey first asserted the Circulation, this was one of the Objections raised against it by them, who could not presently admit it then."

58. Temple, *Miscellanea, The Third Part*, pp. 280, 281, and see chapter 3. Temple had also sent the *Athenian Mercury* a question about the invention of the compass—"Whether the Ancients knew the Mariners Compass? and who first invented it?"—but received a generally negative answer giving credit to a fifteenth-century Italian. At most the Athenians were willing to concede that Europeans did not know the compass "till two or three Centuries last past," but "for the Chineses 'tis at least very probable, they had it long enough before us, as well as Guns and Printing . . ." (*Athenian Mercury*, 5, no. 7, 22 Dec. 1691, q. 13).

59. Temple, *Miscellanea, The Second Part*, pp. 320–21 *(Of Poetry)*.

60. Temple, *Miscellanea, The Third Part*, pp. 212–14. Temple indicates that the "Storm" which Perrault finally escaped by recanting had resulted from the translation and publication in France of Temple's earlier essay on ancient and Modern learning (Ibid., pp. 208–9).

61. See chapter 3.

62. The reference to flies and spittle is especially apt, not only for mocking Wotton but also for pleasing Temple. For Wotton's solemn scientific discursus on both subjects, see *Reflections,* pp. 266–67 (flies, in chapter 22) and pp. 204–5, 291–92 (spittle, in chapters 17 and 25). What Temple thought of Wotton's treatment of flies has not survived—his rebuttal of Wotton's chapter 22, on animals, belongs to the essay's great hiatus with its note by Swift (*Miscellanea, The Third Part,* p. 231; cf. the hiatus in *Tale of a Tub,* p. 170, as previously noted in chapter 3). The discursus on spittle, however, seems to have made an impression which survives. In his scornful list of Modern inventions and discoveries which we may expect from the coming age, Temple includes "The admirable Virtues of that noble and necessary Juice called Spittle, which will come to be sold, and very cheap in the Apothecarys Shops" (*Miscellanea, The Third Part,* pp. 282–83). In chapter 17, Wotton had called spittle "that necessary and noble Juice," while tracing the discovery of the various ducts which carry it to the mouth, and in chapter 25 he emphasized its importance as one of "the main Instruments of Digestion," which a physician should consider in cases of poor digestion. Temple has merely taken Wotton a step further, in burlesque. Swift himself returns to spittle a few lines later in the *Tale,* and seems both to borrow and to improve on Temple's version. Temple had imagined spittle sold at the apothecary's; Swift imagines taking or producing enough of it to cure the clap. "What can be more defective and unsatisfactory than his [Homer's] long Dissertation upon *Tea?*" asks Swift's Wottonian speaker, "and as to his Method of *Salivation without Mercury,* so much celebrated of late, it is to my own Knowledge and Experience, a Thing very little to be relied on" (*Tale of a Tub,* p. 129; treatment with mercury, usual for venereal disease in Swift's day, causes excessive salivation—see *Oxford English Dictionary,* s.v. *salivation*). No admirer of Wotton or Wotton's profession (divinity), Temple should have enjoyed seeing his own attack so improved upon. To be sure, satire can be a two-edged sword, whether wielded consciously or unconsciously. As a young clergyman living in a nobleman's family in the country, Wotton was an unlikely candidate for venereal disorders, while Temple was a seasoned man of the world who had bored Laurence Hyde, years before, with "some stories of his amours, and extraordinary abilities that way, which had once upon a time very nearly killed him" (quoted in Woodbridge, *Temple,* p. 190). Still, it was gout from which Temple acknowledged suffering, and being a systemic disorder, it seemed to affect him in different organs at different times (see Longe, *Lady Giffard,* pp. 198, 202; and chapter 3). Besides the gout, "the spleen," troublesome eyesight, and (probably) the effects of old age, not much is known of Temple's health, or of the ailment or ailments which finally carried him off in 1699. In late January 1699, an obscure French surgeon ("The Surgeon Monsieur Triquel") had been called down to Moor Park from London, but it is not clear whether he was summoned to treat the dying Temple (who usually served as his own doctor) or to cut the heart out of the corpse for separate burial at Moor Park, according to the provisions of Temple's will. See the Moor Park account books, Osborn Collection, fb 182, fol. 64^r, 65^r. Dr. G. C. R. Morris, of the Royal College of Surgeons, has found no entry for Triquel, either in R. R. James's extensive notes of the Barber-Surgeons Company's rec-

ords, or in other standard compendia. At least in law, the company of barber-surgeons enjoyed an exclusive right to heart-burials and embalming, and as late as the eighteenth century, surgeons used to prepare the bodies of the wealthy for burial; see Mary Nash, *The Provoked Wife: The Life and Times of Susannah Cibber* (London: Hutchinson, 1977), pp. 10–11. Temple's health is of particular interest because it may have something to do with the anomalies in his writings and in the mental processes which they reveal during Swift's most important years at Moor Park. Temple's proceedings against Dunton in 1694/95 and against Wotton in the period 1695–98, as well as his various arguments in his "Hints" and in the *Introduction to the History of England* themselves, raise questions about Temple's mental condition during his last five or six years of life. His tendency towards illogical reasoning and angry contempt for his own position as manifested in others seems more strongly marked than in earlier works. Was he merely acting like himself, only more so, or was he beginning to show signs of mild senility or some other form of mental deterioration? Beyond the hints in Swift's 1699 *jeu d'esprit*, "When I come to be old" (see chapter 3), we do not know the answers.

63. The reminder of Wotton comes in the phrase "such wonderful Acquirements [in knowledge] since his [Homer's] Age, especially within these last three Years, or thereabouts"—i.e., since Wotton's *Reflections* first appeared in 1694 (*Tale of a Tub*, p. 129 n. 2). For Wotton's critique of the Dutch scholar Vander Linden, who "has taken a great deal of Pains to prove that Hippocrates knew the *Circulation of the Blood*, and that Dr. Harvey only revived it," see *Reflections*, pp. 207–8. (In Wotton's 'Second Edition, with Large Additions' of 1697, pp. xxv–xxxiii, 229–30, he also considered the claims of the sixteenth-century physician and heretic Michael Servetus.) Temple himself had not troubled to present any evidence or any references. In a Wottonian context, an Ancient advocate's proclaiming an ancient's discovery of the circulation of the blood should have put Temple in mind of Vander Linden, not himself. In a Modern context generally, Temple found the circulation of the blood a subject rich with comic potential; see chapter 3.

64. For Wotton on the spleen, see *Reflections*, pp. 226–27. For Temple on "the Spleen" as a malady, see n. 44 earlier in this chapter; *Observations Upon the United Provinces*, 5th ed., pp. 186–87; and *Miscellanea, The Third Part*, pp. 191–93 (*Of Health and Long Life*). In the essay, Temple rejects "the Spleen" along with "the Vapours," as an amusing fashion in diseases which probably have no physical base. When he later returns to the subject, however, he notes that "whatever the Spleen is; whether a Disease of the Part so called, or of People that ail something, but they know not what; It is certainly a very ill Ingredient into any other Disease, and very often dangerous." He mentions the sorry case of "most vigorous Youths, most beautiful Virgins in the Strength or Flower of their Age," and other seemingly fortunate and healthy types who "sink under common Distempers, by the Force of such Weights [of spleen or melancholy], and the cruel Damps and Disturbances thereby given their Spirits and their Blood." In Temple himself Lady Giffard diagnosed "cruell fitts of spleen and melancholy, often upon great damps in the weather . . ." (Temple, *Early Essays*, p. 27). In his essay

Of Poetry, published in the year in which Lady Giffard wrote her "Character" of her brother, Temple emphasizes the tremendous effects which the weather can have on the finest temperaments, and hints that he has had some experience of it personally. England, he confesses, is

> what a great Foreign Physician called it, The Region of Spleen, which may arise a good deal from the great uncertainty and many suddain Changes of our Weather in all Seasons of the Year. And how much these affect the Heads and Hearts, especially of the finest Tempers, is hard to be believed by Men, whose Thoughts are not turned to such Speculations.
>
> (*Miscellanea, The Second Part*, pp. 359–60)

In the longer account of "the Spleen" in the *Observations*, written years before, at a busier and more vigorous stage in his life, Temple had traced its effects upon the thoughtful mind but took a less sympathetic view of its causes. He concedes that "the Spleen" (whatever it really is) may partly arise from slight alterations in ordinary health or vigor, from "the fumes of Indigestion," or from sudden changes in the weather ("which affect the finer Spirits of the Brain"), but he suggests that the root cause is idleness. The Dutch, an industrious people, do not suffer from anything like "the Spleen," although visitors do. Indeed, Temple reflects with a touch of contempt, "the Spleen" itself "seems to be the Disease of People that are idle, or think themselves but ill entertain'd, and attribute every fit of dull Humour, or Imagination, to a formal Disease, which they have found this Name for. . . ." The older, idler, and more splenetic Temple grew, the more sympathetic a view he took of such ailments and their effects on fine sensibilities like his own, but he never abandoned his contempt for the coarser and duller folk who complained of "the Spleen."

65. Temple's appetite for praise and deference seems to have been substantial, but he may have preferred them served up with a modicum of finesse. This at least is the conclusion I draw from a remarkable section of his "Heads" for an essay on conversation. In itself it seems calculated to reflect well on the speaker:

> Flattery like Poyson, requires of all others the finest Infusion.
> Of all Things the most nauseous, the most shocking, and hardest to bear.
> K. James the first used to say, Nay, by my Soul, that's too hard.
> Pride and Roughness may turn ones Humour, but Flattery turns
>   ones Stomach.
>
> (*Miscellanea, The Third Part*, pp. 326–27)

Swift's direct praise of Temple in the *Battle* and the *Ode to Temple* may in itself have sat uneasily with him, apart from any additional discomfort from Swift's manner of presentation.

66. *Tale of a Tub*, pp. 255–56. Apollo and Boyle step in on the unconscious leader's behalf. In the *Tale*, he scarcely figures in his own right. Years after Temple died, Swift mentioned him briefly in the "Apology" written for the fifth edition of 1710 (pp. 11–12). The only direct reference from Temple's time is a

slightly more veiled one, in the dedication to Prince Posterity: ". . . I have beheld the Person of William W–tt–n, B.D. who has written a good sizeable volume against a *Friend of Your Governor,* (from whom, alas! he must therefore look for little Favour) in a most gentlemanly Style, adorned with utmost Politeness and Civility . . ." (p. 37, Swift's emphasis). Grammatically speaking, there is a certain confusion of antecedents here (in "from *whom,* alas! *he* must look"), but the sense of the passage demands that it be Wotton whom the Prince's Governor (Time, that is) will not favor, because of the unforgivable attack on Temple. Otherwise it is the "Friend"—Temple, that is—who can expect little favor from Time.

67. Temple had "no mind to Enter the List, with such a Mean, Dull, Unmannerly Pedant" as Bentley and his friend Wotton (whom Temple lumped with Bentley); see his letter of 1698, reprinted in *A Tale of a Tub,* p. xlviii. Compare the headnote to his MS. "Hints: written at the Desire of D^r. F[ulham] and of His Friend," itself dated about a year before (Rothschild no. 2253, discussed in chapter 3): "After the Reflections upon A[ncient] & M[odern] Learning were publisht [by Wotton], S^r W T being asked by some of his Friends whether He would take notice of them or no; & being answered he would not, They desired that He would give them leave to Answer th^t book; but He dissuaded them from it. . . ."

68. *Tale of a Tub,* p. xlix & n. 2 (striking resemblances), p. xlviii; see also Davis in *Prose Works,* 1, xviii, and Pierre, "The Influence of Temple upon Swift," pp. 111–28 (especially 111–16). Both Davis and his opposite numbers cite the 1698 letter in which Temple speaks of a "Mr ———," who gave Temple's correspondent the occasion of writing to Temple: "What he saw," says Temple, "was written to a Friend—who had undertaken—without my Knowledge: Which I afterwards diverted, having no mind to Enter the List" with Bentley or Wotton. What Mr. ——— saw, I suspect, was not the *Battle of the Books* but rather Temple's fragments for *Some Thoughts Upon Reviewing the Essay of Antient and Modern Learning,* which Temple then called "Hints: written at the Desire of D^r. F[ulham] and of His Friend" (a "M^r H"), and which appeared in its published form only after Temple's death. See chapter 3. This is the version in which Temple compares himself very favorably with Wotton and which he meant for Dr. Fulham's Oxford friend to incorporate in his own attack on Wotton. After Temple first urged his own friends to make no reply to Wotton (preceding note), the manuscript's headnote explains, he was eventually persuaded to compose his fragments for Fulham's friend to use. When Temple learned that the man wanted to print them separately as an appendix (thus risking exposure for Temple), Temple "absolutely refused" the request and "thereupon desired the Doctor to prevayl with his Friend to suppress the whole Thing; which was accordingly done." This all seems to tally fairly well with Temple's 1698 statement, that what his correspondent's friend had seen "was written *to* a Friend —who had undertaken—without my Knowledge; Which I afterwards diverted . . ." (my emphasis). Once Wotton rudely embarked on a second edition in 1697, continues the headnote, "the Author of these careless Papers has been at last content that they should take their Fortune abroad, as well as the others upon th^t Subject have done." The statement not only accounts for Swift's publication

of the expanded version in 1701, but it also suggests that Temple may have been privately circulating an earlier MS. version.

69. Pinkus, *University of Toronto Quarterly* 29: 49–51; cf. Pinkus, *Swift's Vision of Evil: A Comparative Study of 'A Tale of a Tub' and 'Gulliver's Travels,'* 1, ELS Monograph Series, no. 3 (Victoria, B.C.: University of Victoria, 1975), pp. 118–19, 124. See also Ronald Paulson's comments on the *Battle*, in *Theme and Structure in Swift's 'Tale of a Tub'* (New Haven: Yale University Press, 1960), p. 92 & n. 6. Paulson finds that Temple appears in the *Battle* "rather embarrassingly," and that Swift "pays lip service to the greatness of Phalaris and the other points upon which Temple was incontrovertibly proved wrong." Swift's defense of Temple on specific points "seems to me perfunctory at best" yet "carries echoes of Temple himself." Like Ehrenpreis, however, Paulson believes that Temple exerted a great positive influence upon Swift (p. 93), and his explanation proceeds accordingly.

70. *Tale of a Tub*, pp. 217–19.

71. Temple, *Miscellanea, The Second Part*, p. 289 (*Of Heroick Virtue;* cf. p. 293); *Miscellanea, The First Part*, p. 61 (*An Essay Upon the Original and Nature of Government);* and *Miscellanea, The Second Part*, p. 357 (*Of Poetry),* cf. *An Introduction to the History of England*, p. 60, on the Saxon civil wars (". . . War ended in Peace, Peace in Plenty and Luxury, these in Pride; and Pride in Contention, till the Circle ended in new Wars"). The first notice of the parallel passage about north-to-south invasions was taken by Pierre in "The Influence of Temple upon Swift," p. 112 n.

72. Temple, *Miscellanea, The First Part*, pp. 61–62 (*An Essay Upon the Original and Nature of Government);* for identification of Hobbes and Hooker as the theorists at whom Temple glances, see Woodbridge, *Temple*, pp. 141–44, especially p. 143 n. 10. Although Woodbridge praises Temple for rejecting theoretical political philosophy, he attributes to him a patriarchal theory (largely theoretical) similar to Filmer's.

73. Temple, *Miscellanea, The Second Part*, pp. 293–94 (*Of Heroick Virtue*). Though fewer in number, the conquering northern peoples possessed more health and vigor in their bodies and greater fearlessness and patriotism in their minds. In other contexts Temple could splutter about the Moderns being barbarous Goths who shockingly deface the statues of ancient heroes, but he could also find plentiful heroic virtue in the same Goths and other northern barbarians. Considering that Swift himself eventually equates the Moderns with the northern invaders, he chooses an unusually awkward phrase to echo in Temple. It only draws attention to Temple's implicit self-contradiction.

74. *Tale of a Tub*, p. 217, with Swift's learned note, *"Vid. Ephem. de Mary Clarke; opt. Edit."* (which may have been added after Temple died; the source given in the text itself is the vague and dignified *"Annual Records of Time,"* which could in itself be some subdepartment of Truth's or of Clio's). On Temple's aphoristic genealogy of Pride, Plenty, and Wantonness, see *Miscellanea, The Second Part*, p. 357. As the ultimate result of the Pride family's interrelations, says Temple, "we come to have more Originals [among Englishmen], and more that appear what they are, we have more Humour because every Man follows his

own, and takes a Pleasure, perhaps a Pride to shew it." Accordingly, the English stage abounds with characters of diverse humors, whereas the drama of other peoples seems deficient in them.

75. Temple, *Miscellanea, The Third Part,* pp. 1–16. (On the material and political inequalities which fan envy and discontent, a major theme shared with Swift, see pp. 15–16 especially.) With an air of mild contempt, Temple begins by attributing claims of similarities between men and animals to "the Comtrollers of vulgar opinion" (p. 2)—apparently those who help form popular opinion, since he contrasts them with the "curious and busie" men who seek differences instead (p. 1)—but soon he takes up their theme in his own right. Even for the faculty of "Reason," he notes, the examples "of Brutes, as Dogs, Horses, Owls, Foxes, but especially Elephants," are too well known to need further illustration (p. 5). Men and animals seem to differ only in two respects—men possess the faculty of laughter (pp. 5–6) and "a certain Restlessness of Mind and Thought, which seems universally and inseparably annexed to our very Natures and Constitutions, unsatisfied with what we are, or what we at present possess and enjoy, still raving after something past or to come . . ." (p. 7). Somewhat confusingly, Temple associates this last faculty with man's greatest supposed "Prerogative," which is reason again ("a great Debasement of the greatest Prerogative Mankind can pretend to, which is that of Reason"). This use or abuse of reason is "the true natural and common Source of such Personal Dissatisfactions, such Domestick Complaints, and such Popular Discontents, as aflict not only our private Lives, Conditions and Fortunes, but even our Civil States and Governments . . ." (p. 8). I think that Temple meant to make a clear distinction between the possession of reason (which animals share with men) and the use of reason to stir up the passions (an exclusively human trait), but his digressiveness and vague diction work against clarity. In essence, Temple implies that only animals do not misuse reason. (Thus horses—animals instanced by Temple—will be reasonable enough, as they are in Gulliver's *Travels,* while only men will exhibit a debased and perverted use of reason.) If my reading is correct, the *Battle*'s sketch of the republic of dogs also differs from Temple's position by making "such Personal Dissatisfactions, such Domestick Complaints, and such Popular Discontents" no longer exclusively human. Somewhat paradoxically, Temple's treatment tends to glorify man, who achieves a certain eminence of restless misery which animals cannot pretend to, while Swift's treatment diminishes him, by denying that his restlessness is unique and by lumping him with animals which complain out of balked lust and hunger.

76. Ibid., pp. 10–12. The best ancient philosophers accordingly spent all their time trying "to improve Mens Reasons, to temper their Affections, to allay their Passions," and so on, but naturally failed because they ran up against human nature—to which they themselves, it appears, were not subject (p. 14). Although Temple's theory traces civil discontent primarily to conditions under good government, much of the rest of his essay seems to discuss the difficulty if not impossibility of good government—followed by a long section of proposed reforms which will bring good government to England.

77. See chapter 1 *(Of Heroick Virtue).* Compare Temple's *Essay Upon the*

Original and Nature of Government: "Authority arises from the opinion [among the people] of Wisdom, Goodness, and Valour in the Persons who possess it," and formerly, at least, from "the opinion of Divine Favour." In the ancient sense, heroes are "Persons issued from the mixture of Divine and Human Race, and of a middle nature between Gods and Men . . ." (*Miscellanea, The First Part,* pp. 55, 57). One major distinction sets the two formulations apart. In the later essay, *Of Heroick Virtue,* the leader is a hero and actually possesses wisdom, valor, etc. In the earlier essay, the leader is only *thought* to possess heroic virtue, whether or not he actually does. Although Temple suggests that the genuine article will most easily turn the trick, he also allows for success through an outward appearance of heroic virtue and through the authority of custom (Ibid., pp. 55–59).

It is Temple's later distinction from *Of Heroick Virtue,* between the born hero and the race of common mortals, which explains Swift's uncomfortable flattery of Temple in the *Ode to the Hon*[ble] *Sir William Temple (Poems,* 1, 32):

> Shall I believe a Spirit so divine
>   Was cast in the same Mold with mine?
> Why then does Nature so unjustly share
> Among her Elder Sons the whole Estate?
>   And all her Jewels and her Plate,
> Poor we *Cadets* of Heav'n, not worth her Care,
> Take up at best with Lumber and the Leavings of a Fate. . . .

These lines follow Swift's triumphant comparison of Temple with the Second Adam, through whom, in the paradise of the Moor Park garden, man "must rise again" (see chapter 3). As elsewhere in the *Ode,* Swift's applause for Temple is undercut in the telling. The better to exalt Temple at his own expense, the poet inadvertently shifts his imagery. Having begun with Temple the godlike redeemer, who will help man rise again, he continues by hinting a parallel with the Egyptian pharaoh, who ruled as god while his Hebrew slaves made bricks. "Poor we *Cadets* of Heav'n" must "take up at best with Lumber and the Leavings of a Fate," Swift says in self-abasement:

> Some she binds 'Prentice to the Spade,
> Some to the Drudgery of a Trade,
> Some she does to *Egyptian* Bondage draw,
> Bids us make Bricks, yet sends us to look out for Straw. . . .

Here the villain is ostensibly "Nature," whom Swift substitutes for the real ruler of Egypt, but the metaphor is singularly ill chosen. The Hebrews were not slaves for want of natural abilities or primogeniture, any more than it was "Nature" who set them to wandering throughout Egypt after straw while still requiring them to make bricks as before (*Exodus,* 5:6–13). "Egyptian Bondage" most often denotes injustice and oppression from which God will redeem his people. Although Swift eventually shifts his metaphors into a safer channel (he himself is a slave in the Muse's galleys), he speaks here as one of the common brickmakers ("Bids *us . . .* yet sends *us*"). Considering his circumstances at the time of the poem's composition—now listed under 1692, it was probably completed in 1691 (*Poems*, 1, 26), although Swift dated it back to June 1689, a few weeks after the suicide of Temple's son—the story in *Exodus* offers curious parallels, though to all appearances inadvertent and coincidental. At least by 1692, Swift wished to serve the Church but instead had to work for Temple, just as the Hebrews wished to serve God but had to labor for Pharaoh, who worried about their growing power. Not yet ordained, Swift was waiting for Temple to get him a church living through the King, and was complaining that Temple "is less forward than I could wish" because, Swift supposes, Temple finds Swift "a little necessary to him" (*Correspondence*, 1, 12; 29 Nov. 1692). In the Biblical story Swift refers to, the Hebrews gather straw after Moses' return from his Midianite sojourn (Swift had been off in Ireland from mid-1690 to mid-1691) and after Moses had asked permission for them to journey into the desert to sacrifice to God. The instructions which God had given Moses are especially telling in light of the *Ode*'s talk of "Elder Sons" and "Cadets of Heav'n", a position which God reverses, and in light of Swift's identifying himself with the common mortal cadets, the Hebrews in bondage. "And thou shalt say unto Pharaoh," God commands Moses, "Thus saith the Lord, Israel is my son, even my firstborn: And I say unto thee, Let my son go, that he may serve me: and if thou refuse to let him go, behold, I will slay thy son, even thy firstborn" (*Exodus*, 4:22–23). In 1691–92 Temple had no son to lose, but as predated to June 1689, the *Ode* acquires a peculiar force in the parallels which its imagery suggests. If they are only coincidental, the coincidence is remarkably extensive and apt.

78. *Poems*, 1, 30. In the tradition of Hercules, the evil Serpent has some Hydra-like characteristics. The Hydra's heads multiplied as Hercules cut them off, and Temple's Serpent has her regenerative powers too: "(In pieces cut, the Viper still did reunite)." There may also be a hint of the evil Serpent of Eden here: two stanzas later (pp. 31–32), Swift indicates that Temple is the Second Adam.

79. *Tale of a Tub*, pp. 94–95. For the divine attributes of a successful hero, see Temple, *Miscellanea, The Second Part*, pp. 147–48. As in the other passages we have seen, Swift's imagery, structure, and phrasing seem tailor-made for Temple. Temple had treated Hercules with some dignity, for instance, but had allowed Swift an opening for making fun of him. The true historical Hercules one should take seriously, but it seems there are false Herculeses whom one should not. The true Theban Hercules, says Temple, freed Greece "from Fierce Wild Beasts, or from fiercer and wilder Men" including "Robbers and Spoilers," but earlier Temple indicates that there must have been two or more Herculeses and that the story of one of them (the Hercules said to have conquered India) "is grown too obscure" or is "disguised by the mask of Fables, and Fiction of Poets" (Ibid., pp. 156, 154). Swift loyally presents his Hercules in the terms of fiction or fable, but unfortunately it is the Hercules whom Temple took seriously—the standard Hercules, whom Swift presents "Combating so many Giants, and Dragons, and Robbers."

At the end of the hero-critic passage, Swift likewise introduces an ostensibly flattering figure with whom Temple could identify, in opposition to the Modern critics who hunt monster-faults, multiply them "like Hydra's Heads; and rake them together like Augeas's Dung." This is the Stymphalian fowl. A Modern critic's duty is also to "drive away a sort of *Dangerous Fowl,*" who perversely seek to "plunder the best Branches of the *Tree of Knowledge.*" In other words, Modern critics are enemies to true lovers of learning like Temple, who seek the best rather than the worst. But even here the image could not have been wholly pleasing. The Stymphalian fowl (to whom Swift openly likens the "Dangerous" birds) were dirty creatures who voided dung on their attacker (an awkward parallel for the Temple who denigrated his attacker Wotton in the "Hints"); the original Tree of Knowledge was protected by a divine prohibition; and for that matter, the Augean dung which critics like Wotton rake together is treated as if real enough, even if multiplied by critical attention. If Swift's attack on Wottonian criticism has its uncomfortable undertones from Temple's point of view, so does Swift's implied praise of a Temple-like search for only the best in learning.

80. So far, at least, I have noticed relatively few oddities in the *Discourse Concerning the Mechanical Operation of the Spirit* and in the *Tale*'s Introduction, with few if any in the *Tale*'s sections of religious allegory.

81. Temple, MS. "Hints: written at the Desire of D.ʳ F[ulham] and of His Friend," Rothschild no. 2253, pp. 9–10, 12, 15–16; see chapter 3.

82. *Tale of a Tub,* pp. 230–31 (Swift's italics); Temple, *Miscellanea, The Third Part,* pp. 256–57. As Guthkelch and Smith point out, in a note to the Bee's rejoinder (*Tale,* p. 231 n. 4), Temple admired the untrammeled ways of bees— in this case, used as a metaphor for the free genius of poetry, which cannot be constrained by rules or ever "learnt, even of the best Masters" (*Miscellanea, The Second Part,* pp. 322–23). By using the approved bee to represent the true lover of learning, Swift should have guaranteed that any resemblance between Temple and the Spider would go unremarked by Temple.

83. Both Wotton and Bentley had 'urged on their reasons' by publishing expanded second editions after retorts by the young Charles Boyle and his backers at Christ Church, Oxford. Following Boyle's edition of Phalaris (1695) appeared Wotton's second edition of the *Reflections* with Bentley's *Dissertations upon the Epistles of Phalaris . . . And the Fables of Aesop* (1697), and following Boyle's retort (in *Dr. Bentley's Dissertations . . . Examin'd,* 1698) Bentley published his greatly expanded *Dissertation upon the Epistles of Phalaris, With an Answer to the Objections of the Honourable Charles Boyle . . .* (1699).

84. Woodbridge, *Temple,* pp. 315–16. All Temple's other essays receive summaries. This one, Woodbridge claims, would "certainly" never have been published by Temple in its present form—wishful thinking, in light of Temple's earlier decision to circulate the even more fragmentary MS. "Hints" for the essay.

85. *Tale of a Tub,* pp. 229 & n. 2, 231 & n. 1.

86. Temple, *Miscellanea, The Second Part,* pp. 45–46.

87. Temple, *Miscellanea, The Third Part,* pp. 227–30.

88. *Tale of a Tub,* p. 232. Working without any special knowledge of Temple

or the parallels which Swift's Spider shows with him, Roberta Borkat has sensibly pointed out the fable's "complexity of effect" and "ambiguity of implicit attitude" towards the Ancient-Modern controversy. Rather than continue arguing with the Spider, she notes, the Bee grows impatient with the loss of time and flies away, implying that "the English 'Ancients,' whatever the merits of their case, waste time by debating such a trivial matter at length." The observation has clear applications to Temple, as does the partial reversal of traditional associations which Borkat charts in her article—the bee being most often associated with the followers of Bacon, the spider most often with the medieval rationalist philosophers whom they opposed. She also notes that Wotton himself had used spider imagery to denigrate Epicurus, whom we recall as one of Temple's favorite ancients. (Epicurus "gloried in this, that he spun all his Thoughts out of his own Brain. . . .") See Roberta F. Sarfatt Borkat, "The Spider and the Bee: Jonathan Swift's Reversal of Tradition in *The Battle of the Books,*" *Eighteenth-Century Life,* 3, no. 2 (1976), 44–46; and Wotton, *Reflections upon Ancient and Modern Learning,* p. 302.

89. *Tale of a Tub,* pp. 37–38. With the apparent inadvertence so common in the earlier *Ode to the Hon*^{ble} *Sir William Temple,* Swift winds up saying the reverse of what he so obviously seems to mean—in this case, that Wotton is "a worthy Yokemate" to Temple, rather than to Bentley. After some ironic praise of Bentley's "infinite Wit and Humour," Swift turns to Wotton and praises him (predictably) for faults which Temple had complained of:

> Farther, I avow to *Your Highness* [Prince Posterity], that with these Eyes I have beheld the Person of *William W–tt–n,* B.D. who has written a good sizeable volume against a *Friend of Your Governor,* (from whom, alas ! he must therefore look for little Favour) in a most gentlemanly Style, adorned with utmost Politeness and Civility; replete with Discoveries equally valuable for their Novelty and Use: and embellish'd with *Traits* of wit so poignant and so apposite, that he is a worthy Yokemate to his forementtion'd *Friend.* (Swift's italics)

Obviously Swift must mean that Wotton is a worthy yokemate to the equally witty Bentley. Anyone familiar with the second edition of Wotton's *Reflections* (London: by J. Leake for Peter Buck, 1697) would remember Bentley's long appendix there on Phalaris, and from Wotton's talk of "my most Learned and Worthy Friend, Dr. Bentley" (2nd ed., Preface, p. xviii), conclude Bentley Wotton's friend—just as Temple himself did when yoking the two in 1698 (*Tale,* p. xlviii). But nowhere in the Dedication does Swift actually say that Wotton is Bentley's friend. The only "forementioned *Friend*" in the passage is Temple, whom Swift has just mentioned (in matching italics) as the *"Friend of Your Governor."* Any casual reader noticing the anomaly would see only an unfortunate blunder—a poor choice of words which invokes the wrong antecedent and so reverses the meaning—and would therefore conclude that the poor author had tangled himself up in the difficulties of English syntax. On the other hand, when closely considered, Temple appears at least as worthy a yokemate for

Wotton as the professional scholar Bentley was. As we have seen, Temple was in many ways more "Modern" in spirit (as Swift uses the word) than Wotton at his worst. Wotton at his worst was foolish and literal-minded enough to take Temple's pronouncements on ancient and modern learning as a learned disquisition deserving a book's worth of comment, rather than a genteel meandering essay to be read in an hour and then put aside, its absurdities forgotten but its grace remembered.

90. *Tale of a Tub*, pp. 11–12. Swift's superlatives achieve a mildly negative effect. He seems to strain too hard: Temple is *"universally* reverenced for *every* good Quality that could *possibly* enter into the Composition of the *most* accomplish'd Person." At the same time, Swift never actually says that Temple *was* an accomplished person or that he possessed any one of an accomplished person's good qualities. Instead, Temple was "universally reverenced" as such—that is, everyone believed him to be so. Compared to Swift's warm and enjoyable praise of Lord Somers, in the Bookseller's Dedication, the panegyric of Temple seems surprisingly feeble, as if Swift had never known Temple personally, to judge him for himself. Oddly enough, Swift's characterization also fits one of Temple's observations about the heroic virtues—not his definition of heroic virtue itself, but of the authority which naturally stems from heroic appearances (*"the opinion of* Wisdom, Goodness, and Valour" in a leader—see *Miscellanea, The First Part*, p. 55). Considering Temple's long campaign to appear great in the world's eyes, Swift's characterization is doubly appropriate. He pays homage to Temple's preferred public image, but without endorsing Temple himself, and in doing so he adopts the distinction which Temple had made while discussing the benefits of an exalted public image.

91. *Tale of a Tub*, pp. 43–44. Temple felt that, for writers of very different times and places, a reader should try to bridge the gap. Regnor Ladbrog's Viking ode is truly poetical "and in its kind Pindarick," so long as one takes it "with the allowance of the different Climats, Fashions, Opinions, and Languages of such distant Countries" (*Miscellanea, The Second Part*, p. 240). In more general terms, he castigates men who bring narrow mental horizons into their investigations. The Dutch who miscalculated England's actions under the Triple Alliance, for example, not only failed to acquaint themselves with the English constitution and political situation in the late 1660s, but also made the mistake of judging English actions by their own Dutch standards, by thinking that the English would only act from motives of self-interest (*Observations upon the United Provinces*, p. 266). Cf. *Miscellanea, The First Part*, pp. 1–2 (a statesman's need to know the situation in neighboring nations) and pp. 46–47 (human nature a constant which is nevertheless affected by geography, climate, etc.), and *Miscellanea, The Second Part*, pp. 53–54 (the folly of mental self-sufficiency, in judging truth purely from one's personal point of view). Even wit, learning, and human greatness ultimately depend upon circumstance. Just as Swift argues that wit depends on its walks and purlieux, so we have seen Temple arguing that greatness depends on the age and the openings provided thereby: some ages produce many worthy men but few opportunities for greatness, others many opportunities but few worthy men; some ages nurture only fools; and Temple's own age

and country are so degenerate that his public-spirited suggestions for reform will earn him men's mockery rather than thanks (*Miscellanea, The Third Part*, pp. 30–31, 67). In the essay *Upon Ancient and Modern Learning* Temple applied a similar principle to the productions of wit and learning. In the wrong times and places, he implies, they will never manifest themselves. Because of the interest in various theological disputations attendant upon the Reformation in "almost all the *North-West* Parts" of Europe, he argues,

> The endless Disputes and litigious Quarrels upon all these Subjects . . . either took up wholly, or generally imployed the Thoughts, the Studies, the Applications, the endeavours of all or most of the finest Wits, the deepest Scholars, and the most Learned Writers that the Age produced. Many excellent Spirits, and the most penetrating Genys, that might have made admirable Progresses and Advances in many other Sciences, were sunk and overwhelmed in the abyss of Disputes, about matters of Religion, without ever turning their Looks or Thoughts any other way. (*Miscellanea, The Second Part*, pp. 63–64)

But if the era's theological disputation is the deadening "abyss" which Temple claims, it can hardly exhibit the fine wit or penetrating genius which he thinks the disputants would have shown in other fields, had they only entered them. From here it is not far to the position of Swift's narrator, who claims fine wit and penetrating genius in productions which, by the time we see them, are notably lacking in both. In each case we must disbelieve the evidence before us, and take the wit and genius on faith.

92. *Tale of a Tub*, pp. 44–45.

93. Another safeguard should have kept the passage from grating too actively on Temple. In context, Swift is arguing a larger point which reflects Temple's own point of view: that Modern wit is so dependent upon externals like fashion that to be successful it must occur within absurdly narrow "Walks and Purlieus" of time, place, and persons (Ibid., p. 43). Temple had observed much the same phenomenon. "Changes in Veins of Wit, [are] like those of Habits [i.e. clothing], or other Modes," he remarked in his "Heads" for an essay on conversation. "Upon K. Charles the Second's Return, none more out of Fashion among the New Courtiers, than the old Earl of Norwich, that was esteemed the greatest Wit in his Father's time, among the old" (*Miscellanea, The Third Part*, p. 329). The most modern kinds of wit, especially coarse railing, Temple especially disapproved of (Ibid., pp. 335–36).

94. On Temple's reaction to Wotton's second edition in 1697, see chapter 3. Together with its appendix by Bentley disproving Temple's claims about Phalaris, the book had been announced (as the second item in its category, a long one) in June 1697 in the Trinity *Term Catalogue* (Arber, *Term Catalogues*, III, 28).

95. Ehrenpreis, *Swift*, I, 189: "My only postulate is that behind the book [the *Tale*] stands not a list of philosophical propositions but the idea of a good man" —Temple. Even so, Ehrenpreis next says that this model-following places Swift in "the tradition usually called Christian humanism and descending to Swift from the great line of Spenser, Sidney, and Milton" (p. 190).

96. Ibid., p. 207.

97. Rawson, *Gulliver and the Gentle Reader* (London: Routledge, 1973), pp. 3, 5–6; cf. p. 33. In his preface Rawson also says that "Some of the 'unofficial' energies of Swift's writing move further still, beyond satire to some kind of indulgence of the things mimicked or satirized" (p. viii).

98. Sams, "Swift's Satire of the Second Person," *ELH* 26 (1959): 37–40.

99. Sams speaks interchangeably of "a twentieth-century reader of Swift," "the critic," and "the modern reader" (Ibid., p. 37). Rawson, who regularly uses the first person plural (thus embracing the readers of his book), seems to set up no distinction between his own readers and Swift's. Much of his criticism involves comparisons with the work of Antonin Artaud, Norman Mailer, and other modern writers who have exerted an intellectual appeal.

100. Swift's preface to Temple, *Letters*, I, sig. A2^v.

101. *Tale of a Tub*, pp. 47 (Preface), 131 (Digression in the Modern Kind), and 167 (Digression on Madness). There is no way, of course, that Temple could have imagined himself in any of the passages. He scorned the Moderns, wrote prefaces as short as Dryden's were long, and knew he was no madman.

102. Hugh Blair, *Lectures on Rhetoric and Belles Lettres* (London: for W. Strahan et al., 1783), I, 394.

103. *Prose Works*, XI, 295.

104. Ibid., IV, 99–100, for Wagstaff in *Polite Conversation*. The other treatise is Temple's essay *Of Health and Long Life*, included in *Miscellanea, The Third Part*, pp. 99–100. Temple's unfinished "Heads" for an essay on conversation occurs on pp. 319–36.

105. See for example the Clark Memorial Library set, 10 vols. in 6, 1693–1703, described in the *National Union Catalogue*, and the T. A. Hollick set, 11 vols. in 7, 1699–1709, lot 347 at Sotheby's, London, 19 May 1980, though inaccurately described in the catalogue. The first six volumes of the latter set were bound up all together, seemingly ca. 1705–8, and the seventh volume (including the first ed. of *Memoirs, Part III*, 1709) was bound up to match shortly afterwards.

106. In varying degrees a similar approach has been taken in the two more derivative biographies which have appeared since Woodbridge's, Pierre Marambaud, *Sir William Temple, sa vie, son oeuvre* (n.p. [Paris]: Publications de la Faculté des Lettres et Sciences Humaines de Nice, 1968), and Robert C. Steensma, *Sir William Temple* (New York: Twayne, 1970).

107. Murry, *Swift*, p. 35; Boswell, *Life of Johnson*, I, 218–19; Lyman H. Butterfield, Marc Friedlaender, et al., eds., *Adams Family Correspondence* (Cambridge: Belknap Press, 1963–73), IV, 129, 324, 325. Abigail says she has been reading Temple's "memoirs" about his negotiations with De Witt. She must mean the *Letters* instead: Temple had destroyed his memoirs of this period and adapted the *Letters* to serve in their place. John had been negotiating the first American treaty with Holland (1782), and to do him justice he was canny enough to recognize that Temple was one of those who "had more masterly Pens to celebrate their own Negotiations" and more leisure to do so.

Appendices

Autographs and Dates of the Downton Transcript of Temple's *Letters*
(Rothschild 2255)

In his preface to the Temple *Letters* of 1699 (I, sig. A2^r), Swift notes that the transcript was originally copied by Thomas Downton, one of Temple's chief secretaries during his first embassy at the Hague (1668–70). The largest part of the transcript, some 197 pages out of the 326 bearing copy, appears in Downton's hand and is identifiable by comparison with his signed letters preserved in the Public Record Office—State Papers Foreign, Flanders, vol. 36 (1668) and State Pap. For., Holland, vols. 184–86 (1668–70). Downton absented himself from the Hague for some months between the summer of 1669 and spring of 1670; see Jacobsen, *William Blathwayt*, p. 68. Only after his return in 1670 does his P.R.O. handwriting match the script in the Rothschild transcript. Though still nominally ambassador, Temple returned to England for good in late September 1670, and Downton must have accompanied him. The secretary was on hand in England to copy two letters of a later date: Temple's to the Grand Duke of Tuscany, dated from London more than a month after Temple's return (II, 285–87; T, p. 343), and Temple's to Jan de Witt, dated the following July from Surrey (II, 229–301; T, p. 346). It was almost certainly during this period in England—while Temple was waiting for the King to end his embassy officially and was meanwhile composing his effectively pro-Dutch *Observations upon the United Provinces* (1672/3)—that Temple selected and Downton copied the bulk of the transcript letters.

Downton's work was only a beginning, though. In the same transcript volume there are signs of activity dating from as late as 1696–98. This is the period usually assigned to Swift's work in preparing the *Letters* for publication (Ehrenpreis, *Swift*, I, 172). Swift returned to Moor Park around June 1696, and Temple died in late January 1698/9. Before his death, Temple had authorized some further textual changes not present in the Downton transcript. Swift later reported that the third or companion volume of letters (*Letters to the King,* published in 1703) had been "the last of this, or indeed of any kind, about which the Author ever gave me his particular Commands" (*Prose Works*, I, 266), and the work on the first two volumes probably preceded it, perhaps directly. This would narrow the range from mid-1696 to some time in 1698. The impression is borne out by Swift's autograph in the Downton transcript. He uses his formal copy hand, in a version noticeably closer to his autograph in the Fountaine MS. of *The Discovery*, dated 1699 and now in the Pierpont Morgan Library, than to the rounder, more boyish-looking version in his copy of White's *Institutionum Ethicarum*, dated April 1692, during his second sojourn at Moor Park between 1691 and 1694 (see chapter 3). The Fountaine MS., however, uses the standard 'Italian' form of lower-case *e*, while the other two gravitate towards the more formal 'English' or inverted form, which Swift seems to have used only in the 1690s. (In Swift's sole copy of a *French* letter in the Downton transcript, however, he uses the 'Italian' *e* exclusively; see T, p. 359). I have also identified one of the autographs in the transcript as young Stella's: T, pp. 194–204, a hand hitherto thought to be Swift's, copying the letter to Temple's father dated 10 Oct. 1666 and printed in the Temple *Letters*, 1, 52–66; see my note in *Scriblerian*, 9, no. 2, 134–39. In March 1696 Stella reached the age of fifteen, old enough to be trusted as an amanuensis.

To save other investigators the trouble of too much duplicated effort, I append a tentative list of the Downton transcript's secretarial hands ranged in the chronological order determined from my research in the Rothschild Collection, the Public Record Office, and the (then) British Museum in 1969–70. Besides 1670–72 and 1696–98, the late 1670s seem to have been a time of concerted activity, whether of addition or revision:

    1. Thomas Downton, ca. 1670–72. Transcript pages 39–40, 43–54, 57–60, 99–114, 117–26, 147–84, 211–36, 241–302, 329–55.

    2. Scribe A, probably between Downton's and Scribe C's time, though possibly later. Transcript pages 41–42, 55–56, 115–16 (all cancel leaves preserving original pagination; texts dovetail into the surrounding pages copied by Downton).

    3. Scribe B, between Downton's and Scribe C's time. Transcript pages 185–86 (a cancel leaf).

    4. Scribe C, between 1677 and Swift's time, most likely ca. 1677–79. (Paper used elsewhere by this scribe, in the Longe bequest, British Library, Ad. MS. 9801, is the same as paper once used by Downton earlier in the decade, in Ad. MS. 9797, fol. 66–67.) Transcript pages 1–16, 61–88 (pp. 62–64 blank), 127–43, 186–92 (on p. 186, a cancel, Scribe C begins a letter after Scribe B leaves off), 209–10, 237–40 (cancel leaves), 303–13, 356–58. The same scribe copied a letterbook containing Temple's diplomatic correspondence between 12 July 1676 and 5 July 1677 (apparently a full record for the period), in the Longe bequest, Ad. MS. 9801. Bound into Ad. MS. 9802, as a late addition, is Scribe C's chronological index or table of contents for all Downton transcript letters dating from 1665 through July 1668, the exact period of volume I of the *Letters* as eventually printed. The index includes the scribe's new contributions to the transcript, and bears a few corrections in Temple's hand. Comparison with the Downton transcript as it now survives indicates that, in Scribe C's time, the transcript lacked the additions made by Scribe D, Stella, and Swift.

5. Scribe D, between Scribe C's and Swift's time. Transcript pages 88–91, beginning on the same page on which Scribe C ends one of his sections.

6. Esther Johnson (Stella) working under Swift's direction, ca. 1696–98. Transcript pages 194–204. Swift's chronological index or table of contents lists the letter which Stella copied, an earlier and much shorter transcript of the same letter copied by someone else (pages since removed), and all surviving transcript entries by the first five scribes.

7. Swift, ca. 1696–98. Transcript pages 92–97, 144–46, 205–7, 314–19, 359–60. These letters (six in all) are *not* listed in Swift's chronological index to the transcript.

Thomas Swift's Letter to John Dunton—The Nature of the Draft in the
Osborn Collection (Box 67, no. 18)

In Temple's project for a composite history of England, first negotiated with
Dunton and later proposed to the competing bookseller Richard Bentley, the
draft in the Osborn Collection appears to have played a central role. Not only
does it preserve the text of Thomas Swift's letter to Dunton (9 Nov. 1694), but
it also seems to have served, in part, as a working draft for Thomas's later letter
for Temple to Bentley (14 Feb. 1694/5). It may even be the copy which Thomas
claimed that he made at Dunton's shop and promised Dunton never to divulge
to Bentley (see chapter 2).

Provenance and incidentals suggest that the Osborn Collection document
is a fair copy from Temple's files rather than the original actually sent to
Dunton. When Courtenay saw the document in the 1830s, it was still in the
possession of the Longe family of Norfolk, through whom most of Temple's
Moor Park MSS. have descended to us. (See Courtenay, *Memoirs of Temple*, II, 221
n., Coddenham being the home of the Rev. Robert Longe, to whom Courtenay
was indebted for access to the Moor Park MSS., as he indicates in I, vi.) The
document duly appeared as item 1073 in the Longe sale at Sotheby's on 3 August
1934. (According to A.S.W. Rosenbach's annotated copy of the catalogue, it went
to Maggs for £2 10s. od.) When I inspected the document in New Haven, I noted
no endorsement, postmark, or other obvious sign of a letter actually sent and
received. But although a copy, it is an unusually complete and formal copy—
neatly if rapidly penned (though with many standard abbreviations), without
any alterations or additions except Temple's, and with the salutation, signature,
and dateline fully supplied. In other words, it shows every sign of being the
careful record of a letter already completed—of a letter either sent to its recipient and there copied, or of a letter on the point of being sent—rather than an
intermediate draft to be recopied for posting. For an intermediate draft,
Thomas would hardly have bothered to copy the signature and dateline.

In three places, Temple has entered alterations in the document. Under the
circumstances, these alterations would seem to belong to the period after
Thomas posted the original letter to Dunton. It appears that Temple used the
text of the Dunton draft in drawing up part of the letter to Bentley. In all three
cases, the Bentley letter follows the altered reading as Temple entered it on the
copy. In the Dunton letter, Thomas had originally said that, in Temple's view,

writing a complete new general history of England "would perhaps be a greater undertaking than any man thinks of before He engages in such an attempt." Temple has crossed out the words "thinks of" and substituted "beleeves." Apropos Samuel Daniel's history of the Norman and Angevin kings, Thomas gives Temple's opinion that Daniel "is an author of good Judgment & no Ill Style *& may be a better abridgment of those raigns than a new* [word obscured] *would prove.*" Here Temple has crossed out the second (italicized) part of the statement. Finally, Thomas reports that the life of Bloody Mary should be "follow'd by Camden's Elizabeth." Temple indicates an insertion: the life of Mary should be "follow'd by *an Abridgment of* Camden's Elizabeth." The later letter to Bentley preserves all three altered readings (Duncombe, ed., *Letters, by Several Eminent Persons Deceased*, 1, 4–6).

Conceivably, instead of being a late copy of the letter sent to Dunton, the Osborn Collection document might represent a letter which Thomas was on the point of sending to Dunton but then retained for Temple as a copy after Temple looked it over and made his alterations. Although this would account for the signature, dateline, and alterations, it is a less probable hypothesis. Thomas's many abbreviations suggest a copy rather than a would-be original. If his cousin Jonathan's work is any guide, Temple expected his secretaries to eschew abbreviation when writing for the master. Swift's work for Temple is notably free from it, although he was not always so fastidious when writing on his own account (e.g., *Correspondence*, 1, 13 and 27, from personal letters of 1693 and 1698). All told, the document in the Osborn Collection corresponds to what we would expect of a copy taken from the original in Dunton's shop, just as Thomas implied that he had done. There is rapidity because Thomas was there on an awkward errand, and on sufferance, but there is fullness (and care) because of the original letter's importance to Temple. Not only did it contain an outline for the proposed composite history (which Temple could have reconstituted from his notes, if necessary), but it also represented a hostage which Temple had left with Dunton, whom he was now trying to thwart. Without the reassurance of a complete record of text, dateline, and signature, Thomas could not have safely pretended to Bentley that "it was I [who] writ" to Dunton, rather than Temple who did. Although Thomas's letter to Bentley is full of disingenuousness, I suspect he spoke truth when he indicated that he copied the Dunton letter in London.

It is less certain, though, that Dunton actually made Thomas promise not to show the text to Bentley. The account which Thomas later gave Bentley is an obvious attempt to puff Temple's proposals by illustrating the value which the competition put on them. Yet if Dunton did not recognize the intrinsic value of Temple's directions for the history, he surely realized the tactical value of the letter which contained them, even apart from the advertising points that he had already scored with it. Thomas's request for a copy would have alerted him to the possibility that it might somehow be used against him. If Thomas did not need to give Dunton his word outright, he might still have needed to make some less formal assurance about the use to which the copy would be put.

Apart from the long outline for the proposed history, the two letters by

Thomas are different compositions, to be sure. An intermediate draft or drafts would have been needed before Thomas could have sent out the finished letter to Bentley. That Temple kept up his supervision is indicated by one substantive change in the outline section, not entered in the Dunton draft but present in the letter received by Bentley. To Bentley Thomas reported Temple's recommendation that Holinshed be used for the reign of Mary, while to Dunton he had indicated that Temple thought the reign must be "new written." I cannot account for this change except by supposing that Temple took a look at Holinshed and decided that Holinshed's account of Mary would suffice. Any such review by Temple would have taken place at approximately the time of his wife's last illness and death.

Swift's *Abstract of the History of England* and his *Reigns* of William Rufus, Henry i, Stephen, and Henry ii

Simple notes on some of the chief English historical events down to 1066, Swift's *Abstract of the History of England* (printed in *Prose Works*, v, 3–7) has received little attention over the years. In "Swift's History of England," *Journal of English and Germanic Philology* 51 (1952): 177–78, Irvin Ehrenpreis briefly notes that Temple's *Introduction to the History of England* appeared on Swift's 1697 reading list, that Swift was fairly active at this time in making abstracts of his reading, and that the strong Temple element in the *Abstract* probably indicates a date of composition prior to Temple's death in January 1698/99. Thus far Ehrenpreis seems on solid ground, but it is somewhat less certain that Swift sought in the abstract "a simple way of studying English history, perhaps under Temple's instructions." That Temple might condescend to coach an admiring humble secretary in the rudiments of the subject is credible enough, but that Swift should have felt a genuine need for such assistance is hard to believe. He should already have known the rudiments. By his own account, Temple's *Introduction* was one of the books which Temple had him prepare for the press—copying, reading aloud, entering corrections (*Correspondence*, i, 155). This would have been in early 1694. Had Swift's memory in his late twenties degenerated so badly that, three or four years later, he should have felt a need to reread the book—solemnly entering it after Virgil and Horace on his list—much less compose an abstract based on it? And even if Swift felt a genuine need to abstract the *Introduction*, why did he choose the vaguest and feeblest parts of the book? In the preface to the composite history of England which appeared more than a decade after Temple approached Bentley, the editors tactfully explain that, for the period up to the Norman Conquest, "Sir William Temple, tho' he has very ingeniously treated the same Subject, is not particular enough" for them to use, "and seems so much in haste to come to his Favourite Character of William the Norman, that the rest of his Book is indeed but *an Introduction*"—an opinion echoed by Temple's modern champion Homer Woodbridge, who concedes some of the weaknesses in Temple's account of the period to 1066 but argues that Temple was less interested in writing a proper history than in glorifying William of Orange through the figure of William the Conqueror, to whose reign Temple accordingly gives the lion's share of his attention. See White Kennett et al., *A Complete*

History of England: With the Lives of All the Kings and Queens thereof, 2nd ed. corr. (London: for R. Bonwicke, Tim. Goodwin et al., 1719), I, sig. aI^r; and Woodbridge, *Temple*, pp. 254, 258–59.

The *Abstract*'s construction and contents add to the difficulty. By bulk, at least three quarters of the piece follow the appropriate passages in the *Introduction*, though methodized and purged of Temple's more embarrassing hypothetical digressions (e.g., the long mythico-etymological discursus on the Scythians, Odin, and the origins of the Scots, *Introduction*, pp. 22–33), and with its chronology and various repetitions reduced to better order (e.g., Temple's repeated accounts, some apparently unintentional, of the migrations into the Saxons' now-deserted homeland on the Continent, ibid., pp. 62 and 70–71; of Egbert's becoming the first sole king of England, pp. 61–62 and 69; of the Romans' wall in Scotland, pp. 21 and 37–38; and of the Conquest itself, pp. 84–85 and III–19). Apart from a few isolated statements (Swift's own or interpolated from a third source), the remainder of the *Abstract* represents ancillary details or corrections brought in from Samuel Daniel's *Collection of the History of England*, which had been Temple's chief if unacknowledged source for the *Introduction*. Swift draws from Daniel only when the *Introduction* first raises a topic. Where Temple neglects important developments treated in Daniel, Swift loyally ignores them too, even though some clear verbal echoes indicate that he worked with Daniel's book close at hand. Daniel, for instance, gives full attention to Alfred the Great, "the mirrour of Princes," whose important legal, educational, and administrative innovations are duly chronicled—subjects which we might think normally of interest to Swift (see Ehrenpreis on Swift's own history of England, *Journal of English and Germanic Philology* 51: 181). Temple had barely mentioned Alfred, as a minor ship-building precursor of the great King Edgar, that "Prince of great Wisdom and Felicity" who *(inter alia)* first built up a navy able to defend the coasts from Danes. Swift reduces the passage to a bare minimum excluding Alfred altogether ("After many invasions from the Danes, Edgar king of England sets forth the first navy") and then fleshes out Edgar's glory with details, some very minor, paraphrased from Daniel. See Daniel, *The Collection Of the History of England* (London: for Simon Waterson, 1626), p. II (Alfred) and pp. 12–13 (Edgar); Temple, *Introduction to the History of England*, p. 75; and Swift, *Prose Works*, v, 5. All in all Swift's method suggests that he aimed less at a proper abstract of early English history than at an abstract acceptable to Temple.

To compound the *Abstract*'s oddity, there is also an extreme simplicity, even childishness, in much of Swift's diction and in the substance of many entries, as if he were trying to demonstrate his naiveté, or alternatively, as if he meant the *Abstract* as an aid for teaching the young. (Young Stella comes to mind.) Extremely compressed notes can sometimes give an effect of simplemindedness, but Swift's give the effect more often than necessary. When discussing the ancient Britons before Caesar's time, for instance, Swift interpolates a sentence (present in neither Temple nor Daniel) gravely informing the reader that "In their religion they were Heathens, *as all the world was before Christ, except the Jews*" (*Prose Works*, v, 3, my emphasis). As a further help, the note "Heathens" appears in the margin opposite. Swift's statement is all very true, but apart from the very young and the very simple, how many people would find the observation worth recording for themselves, or deem it a valuable addition to their fellows' understanding? The same question might well be asked of several other solemn notes, seemingly Swift's own interpolations, revealing (for instance) that a millennium earlier the English language was "extremely different from what it is now," or that Albion is "an old name of this island" (ibid., p. 5). Along with useful if sometimes simpleminded marginal glosses, this childish element rules out Herbert Davis's confident guess, that the *Abstract* represents notes for a preliminary chapter for Swift's own history of England, a genuinely adult effort which Davis otherwise considers a continuation of Temple's *Introduction*. Never published in Swift's lifetime, the *Abstract* and the history in fact first appeared in print separately, in volumes issued three years apart. (See ibid., pp. ix and 349, and cf. Ehrenpreis, *Swift*, II, 61, which halfheartedly picks up Davis's idea, in what is otherwise a recapitulation of his own earlier findings.)

Something of the same grave foolishness appears in Swift's paragraph on the Druids, wise but unlettered priests to whom Temple had granted a certain astronomical sophistication and whom he had celebrated both for their high moral standards and their temperate lives, passed "in Woods, Caves, and hollow Trees" (*Introduction*, pp. 12–13). In the *Abstract*, Temple's treatment is reduced to two short clauses. "Their priests were called Druids," Swift writes: "These lived in hollow trees . . ." (*Prose Works*, v, 3)—thanks to the one ill-chosen detail, an absurd compression of Temple's rather romanticized portrait. As if to atone, the *Abstract* next adds a romantic touch, somewhat lame in context, but borrows it from Daniel rather than Temple, who had good reason not to use it himself. Besides living in hollow trees, it seems, the Druids "committed not their mysteries to writing, but delivered them down by tradition, whereby they were in time wholly lost" (cf. Daniel, *Collection*, p. 3: the Druids "committed not their mysteries to writing, but delivered them by tradition, whereby the memorie of them after their suppression . . . came wholly to perish with them").

In his essays on ancient and modern learning, Temple had maintained much the same thing of the colleges of prehistoric sages whom he conjectures to have existed far to the East, whence all knowledge comes, among the most ancient Brahmans and Egyptians. From these great unknowns, Temple had argued, the most ancient Greek philosophers (lesser than their teachers but greater than anyone since, including the later Greeks whose works have actually survived) had borrowed all their knowledge, and it was upon the absence of written records of these Eastern illuminati, as much as upon fable or ancient hearsay, that Temple finally based his claim for their preeminence. (See Temple, *Miscellanea, The Second Part*, pp. 3–26, e.g., pp. 14–15, on the Brahmans' reputed learning and institutions, which "were unwritten and only traditional among themselves, by a perpetual succession"; and Temple, *Miscellanea, The Third Part*, pp. 232–34, with its bitter complaint that the Moderns reject the prehistoric ancients' preeminence "because we know none of the Records or Histories of those Nations remaining, but what was left us by the Greeks; and conclude the Infancy of the Aegyptians in other Sciences, because they left no

Account of their own History. . . .") Because no Druid records survive, to be sure, the same claim of preeminent wisdom could with equal logic be advanced for the Druids—though not half so comfortably, because not even Temple (for all his praise of the Britons' virtues and love of liberty) was ready to claim that ancient British learning surpassed that of their Roman conquerors. Actually Swift says nothing of British learning, but by applying the keystone of Temple's argument about the ancient sages to a set of rough heathens living in hollow trees, he doubles the implicit absurdity of mentioning their lost "mysteries" so solemnly. Admittedly, in Swift's dry and serious recital of facts, there is nothing to hint a satiric impulse. From Temple's point of view, at least, Swift's treatment would have seemed as admirable in intention as it would have seemed inept in execution. What Swift intended by his *Abstract* remains uncertain, but unless he was a genuine booby, it is doubtful that he wrote for self-instruction. At the moment the simplest hypothesis would be that the *Abstract* was a teaching aid for Stella or some other young person— perhaps one of Temple's young granddaughters, Elizabeth and Dorothy Temple, born some time between 1685 and 1689—and that Swift composed it with Temple's knowledge or at Temple's suggestion.

Swift's Reigns *of William Rufus, Henry* I, *Stephen, and Henry* II

Like the *Abstract,* Swift's unfinished history of England (the *Reigns* of William Rufus, Henry I, and Stephen, together with fragments on Henry II) may reflect an emergent interest in English history during his last years at Moor Park, although the date usually assigned to the work is a little later (Ehrenpreis, *Journal of English and Germanic Philology* 51: 181, and Herbert Davis in *Prose Works,* v, ix–x). Swift's history begins where Temple's *Introduction* left off, with the death of William the Conqueror, and Davis accordingly assumes that Swift was engaged in a "projected continuation of Temple's history." Davis may be right. Not only does the *Reign* of William Rufus begin abruptly enough to suggest some sort of continuation ("At the time of the Conqueror's death, his eldest son Robert . . . being absent . . ."), but it also refers back, in specific terms, to one of Temple's characterizations in the *Introduction.* There the Conqueror's half brother Odo, Bishop of Bayeux, appears three or four times in unflattering terms—"This ambitious Prelate" at one point, "a Man of incurable Ambition" at another (Temple, *Introduction,* pp. 233, 307). In his first reference to Odo, Swift calls him the bishop "of whom frequent mention is made in the preceding reign, *a prelate of incurable ambition*" (*Prose Works,* v, 13, my emphasis).

Making acknowledgments to Myrddin Jones's unpublished B.Litt. thesis, Ehrenpreis points out another feature shared by the *Introduction* and Swift's history. Just as Temple used the Conqueror to defend and glorify William III, so Swift's history uses King Stephen for an attempt to defend William III. In the early part of the *Reign of Stephen,* for instance, Swift draws obvious parallels between Stephen's difficulties and William's, especially with an unappealing Pretender hovering in the wings (the Empress Maud). Later in the *Reign,* as Stephen's actions grow harder to defend, Swift hints at less obvious analogies with James II's reign—this time with Stephen as James, and Maud's son Henry as William of Orange (Ehrenpreis, *The Personality of Jonathan Swift* [1958; rpt. New York: Barnes & Noble, 1969], pp. 61–62 and 62 n. 1). But if Swift was following Temple's lead, he was following it with much the same loyal ineptitude he showed in the *Abstract*. A capable monarch if technically an usurper, William the Conqueror was a worthy vehicle for shadowing forth his later namesake's praise, but in Stephen, usually remembered as a weak usurper whose reign marked a low point in English history, Swift applies Temple's aims and methods to singularly intractable material. He makes the most of Stephen's strengths and tries to account for some of Stephen's blunders by claiming him too virtuous for his age (e.g., his "unseasonable mercy" to traitors, p. 51) or by shifting the blame to his unruly subjects (the reason why even good governments fail, according to Temple) who exacted too many privileges in return for placing him on the throne. Even here Swift runs into difficulties. As Stephen's reign draws to its sorry close, we see the shadow of William III, in Stephen, opposing his earlier self, in Henry Fitz-Empress. Swift's two divergent analogical schemes overlap. One of the traits by which we identify William in Stephen is their shared taste for strenuous but inconclusive military exercise, especially sieges. As Swift says at the outset, Stephen's reign "was entirely spent in sieges, revolts, surprizes, and surrenders, with very few battles, but no decisive action" (p. 49). When Henry invades towards the end of the reign, it is an amusingly Williamite Stephen who awaits him: "The king was employed in his usual exercise of besieging castles when the news was brought of Henry's arrival" (p. 68). Yet the Henry who invades is also William and the Stephen who awaits him, James II. On the Continent, Henry has been delayed by countering an attack from the French king, now in league with Stephen, who meanwhile tries to have his son crowned as heir and jails his bishops when they refuse to acquiesce—actions reminiscent of James II in 1688 (pp. 67–68). At best this is all very confusing. At worst it is maddeningly so. Because Swift fails to make his new set of analogies register as crisply as the original set, we may also see the admirable William III paying the price for his blunders—being forced to recognize his rival's equally admirable son, the young prince James Francis Edward, as his successor. To all appearances Swift tries his hardest, but in his hands Temple's method produces a hodgepodge which his master, had he seen it, could hardly have relished, despite the apparent sincerity of Swift's *hommage*. The odd phenomenon marks a number of works, especially his Pindaric odes, which we know that Swift composed at Moor Park.

Other considerations suggest that Swift's *Reigns* began at Moor Park. Briefly citing Temple's known wish for a good history of England, and pointing out his two approaches to publishers, Ehrenpreis concludes that "Every extant sign points to Temple as the instigator of these 'Reigns' " (*Journal of English and Germanic Philology* 51: 181–82). Although Ehrenpreis gets a few facts wrong—Temple approached the two publishers after the *Introduction* was published, not before, and his wish for a composite history grew rather than dwindled—his conclusions may yet prove correct. The draft of Thomas Swift's letter to Dunton reveals that, at least in 1694, Temple was not entirely decided about the

portion of English history which includes Swift's *Reigns*. Apparently Temple
had been wondering if any extant history of the period was good enough to
incorporate, and weighing the possibility that the reigns immediately following
the Conqueror's might be new written. Originally, Temple had Thomas Swift
inform Dunton that the reigns of William Rufus through Edward III "may be
inserted as they are written by Daniell, who is an author of good Judgment &
no Ill Style *& may be a better abridgment of those raigns than a new* [word obscured]
would prove" (my emphasis). Later on, with the same rolling stroke he used in
a substitution six lines earlier, Temple himself crossed out the italicized clause
and to the competing bookseller Bentley, mentioned Daniel as the only recommended option rather than the better one of two. Had Daniel's history been
unavailable for use, in other words, we have reason to believe that Temple
would have recommended commissioning a new account. By "abridgment"
Temple means a relatively short account like Daniel's, rather than an abridgment in the modern sense: unlike a modern abridger, both Swift and Daniel
draw on a full range of sources and produce original compositions. It may be
no coincidence that, in both length and format, Swift's three completed *Reigns*
are comparable with Daniel's versions. Like Swift, Daniel had divided his *Collection of the History of England* not into modern chapters but into consecutive but
self-contained 'Reigns,' each introduced by the appropriate headline. (Swift
used the formula "The Reign of . . ."; Daniel, "The Life and Reigne of . . .").
Both sets of 'Reigns' are on the same approximate scale. Reprinted in the same
format as Davis's edition of Swift, Daniel's 'Reign' of William Rufus would run
about twelve pages, compared to Swift's fourteen and one half; his Stephen
would go to seventeen pages, to Swift's twenty-six.

In themselves, such similarities prove little, but when Swift returned
from Ireland in 1696, it is doubtful that he found his employer wholly at peace
about the general history of England which he had proposed two years before.
In 1696 appeared the first volume of Tyrrell's *General History of England*—the
same work which Dunton had substituted for Temple's composite scheme, the
same work which the Bentley group's proposals had failed to halt. Tyrrell's
volume was just the sort of history which Temple had damned in his preface
to the *Introduction*—pedestrian in style, often pedantic in substance, a collection of materials as much as a relation of history, and by an author of
markedly less public stature than Sir William Temple. What is more, it bore
no resemblance to the 'abridged' history which Temple had proposed,
whether individual or composite. A thick folio affair, Tyrrell's volume carried
English history only up to 1066. What Temple had seen fit to cover in 86
octavo pages, Tyrrell covered in 471 folio pages set in smaller type, excluding
the two indices, the addenda and errata, and the 136 pages of General Introduction and other prefatory materials. Here was a book unlikely to circulate
widely, unlikely to meet the broad public need which Temple had theorized.
(John Dunton, in fact, sold his share of the copyright shortly before the book
was entered with the Stationers Company in early 1697; see Parks, *John Dunton
and the English Book Trade*, p. 315.) Here, in short, was an occasion to revive or
at least to think about the plan for a proper history of England, headed by

Temple's *Introduction* and followed (as practicable) by sections taken from other great works, or by a continuation newly written for the occasion. (In 1719, at least, Swift said that he had meant to carry his work through the reign of Elizabeth—the full term of Temple's proposed history—but this may refer to a later stage in his planning.) We do not know what Temple said or what Swift did, but the convergence of circumstances in the period 1696–1697 suggests that the secretary began composing his *Reigns* about this time.

That he did so with a realistic hope of publication is much less likely. Temple had twice failed to get his *Introduction* published at the head of a composite history, and hazarding a third attempt may not have appealed. Copyrights might still have posed a problem. The eventual resuscitation of Bentley's proposals in 1701, backed by some of the original undertakers, suggests a lack of maneuvring room in that direction. The Bentley group had declined to include Temple's *Introduction,* although it controlled the Samuel Daniel copyright and those of Temple's other recommended authors. Practically speaking, it would seem that Temple's one hope lay in commissioning a continuation of the *Introduction.* On the other hand, it is difficult to believe that Temple—with his insistence on "authors of name and estimation," and his wish to see himself in company with such peers as More and Bacon—would have wanted his *Introduction* to introduce a history by an obscure Irish-born parson, unknown to the world except perhaps as the author of a turgid ode to the rascal Dunton's Athenian Society. True, Swift was also the secretary of a great man, had learned something of the world by conversing with Temple and working with his MSS., and about this time was proving himself capable of translating Temple's French under close supervision. Temple may even have recognized his secretary's ability to write stylish and well-organized prose, the other chief qualification which Temple looked for in a historian. Past failure may have made him desperate as well, but with all Swift's merits taken into account, it is almost impossible to believe that Temple could have proposed appearing in print as the harbinger for his own employee, especially when the preface to Temple's *Introduction* had spoken of the "abler hand" who will continue Temple's great work and whose coming Temple so devoutly wishes. Saint Simeon's *Nunc dimittis* was not for a man like Temple. Swift was to publish Temple's posthumous *Letters* with every sign of faithfulness to the master's wishes and every sign of humility in himself, a mere transcriber and translator. If Swift began his history at Moor Park— whether as a full continuation of Temple's *Introduction* or as a stopgap for Daniel in a composite history scheme—it is likeliest that he did so merely as a private exercise, with encouragement and possibly guidance from the great historian himself.

But when in fact was Swift's history composed? If there is evidence which suggests that Swift began the *Reigns* at Moor Park, there is also evidence for a later date, the period 1700–1703. With his wretched memory for dates, Swift himself thought in 1719 that he had begun work about sixteen years before (*Prose Works,* v, 11). Ehrenpreis reports a close parallel between a passage in the *Reigns* and an argument in Swift's *Contests and Dissensions,* published in 1701 (*Journal of English and Germanic Philology* 51: 181 and n. 16). In fact, the moral which Swift gives the *Reign of Stephen* better suits those times than the late 1690s. Increasingly after 1699, William's Junto ministers and Dutch favorites faced angry charges of grabbing too much wealth and power; the King found his prerogative under attack; and new divisions appeared between Lords and Commons, Court and Parliament and people. Even the "warmest advocates for liberty," Swift says in the *Reign of Stephen*, "cannot but allow, from those examples here produced, that it is very possible for people to run upon great extremes in this matter, that a monarch may be too much limited, and a subject too little; whereof the consequences have been fully as pernicious for the time, as the worst that can be apprehended from arbitrary power in all its heights . . ." (*Prose Works*, v, 63). Clearly Swift must have worked on the *Reigns* after he left Moor Park, despite the strong signs pointing back. Possibly he began the history as an exercise under Temple and then began to adapt it for publication in the altered times of 1700–1703. Whatever the case, the subject deserves further study.

Temple's Fragmentary MS. Revisions for His "Hints: written at the Desire
of D.ᵣ F and of His Friend"

Temple's fragmentary revisions for his earlier "Hints" are now in the Sir
Harold Williams Bequest, University Library, Cambridge (Add. MS. 7788—
Williams Collection). They and other Temple materials there are quoted by
permission of the Syndics of Cambridge University Library. When I visited in
1970, the Williams papers had not been individually catalogued, and the draft
in question was in Box 3 together with four other documents from Moor Park.

The "Hints" revisions are in Temple's script with frequent corrections,
insertions, and added headings in the hand of an unknown scribe. Soon after
William Wotton had published the second edition of his *Reflections upon Ancient
and Modern Learning* in mid-1697, the same scribe had drawn up the explanatory
notes which preface Swift's draft of the original "Hints" (Rothschild no. 2253).
The "Hints" revisions accordingly date from some time afterwards—late 1697
or more probably 1698. In a memo preserved with the revisions, Sir Harold
Williams mistakenly asserts that they represent preliminary notes or first drafts
towards Temple's second Ancient-Modern essay, published in 1701 as *Some
Thoughts Upon Reviewing the Essay of Antient and Modern Learning.* Similarly Williams claims that the hand responsible for the various insertions and corrections
is Swift's. Apparently he did not know of the existence of the original "Hints"
and had not seen the contemporary scribal notes which accompany them. In fact
the resemblance to Swift's hand is not particularly close, except perhaps for one
carefully penned tag phrase ("For Divinity &c.") which indicates which paragraph in the "Hints"/essay is to follow. Here the upper-case *F* differs in formation from Swift's but is identical to the *F* in the carefully penned title of the
"Hints" notes ("A *F*ragment written . . ."). In the word "Divinity," Williams's
scribe drops a minim, making the word look like "Duinity"—a characteristic
typical of the scribe in the "Hints" notes, but not at all of Swift at this time.

The "Hints" revisions represent part of a working draft and contain fragments of three passages in all (one scored through)—most notably, part of the
passage on classical criticism quoted in chapter 3, and part of the section on
chemistry originally attacking Wotton for being an alchemist. These draft revisions are closer to the text printed in 1701 than the "Hints" text is, but they still
have a distance to go. In the chemistry passage (crossed out in the Williams
draft) Temple is still trying to call Wotton an alchemist—a slur made less direct

(and more effective) in the published essay, by removing the name-calling but retaining a misleading quotation from Wotton. Here Temple quotes Wotton to the effect that many men tend to think there could not be so much smoke without a fire: i.e., that there must be something to alchemy. Closely considered, by itself, the quotation merely suggests that Wotton is aware of people's credulity; read in context at essay speed, it suggests that Wotton himself thinks there must be something to alchemy. This is highly unfair: Wotton in fact shows himself extremely sceptical about alchemy both ancient and modern, especially about the remarkable achievements attributed to the Egyptian magi, whom Temple considered great masters of natural magic. In the true scientific spirit, however, Wotton concludes his treatment by conceding that, even though he thinks alchemy a fraud, it is impossible all the same to reject the *possibility* of transmutation of metals until men learn "the seminal Principles from which Metals are compounded." See Temple, *Miscellanea, The Third Part*, pp. 252–53, and Wotton, *Reflections Upon Ancient and Modern Learning*, pp. 118–30.

In the third and shortest of the three draft passages, Temple tries to justify himself for having called the site of the Delphic oracle "Delphos" rather than Delphi. This is hardly the "desperate" fault which Wotton finds it, Temple notes sarcastically, but instead represents common usage of the most polished writers—an odd excuse from someone who held contemporary literature in such low esteem. Temple's justification never appeared in the essay published in 1701, where Temple stubbornly continues to call Delphi "Delphos." See Temple, *Miscellanea, The Second Part*, pp. 11, 13 (references to "Delphos"); Wotton, *Reflections*, p. 94 (on Temple's "small Mistake"); Temple, *Miscellanea, The Third Part*, pp. 218–21 (continued use of "Delphos"). An earlier (uncorrected) version of the "Delphos" passage does not actually appear in the surviving "Hints" fragments copied by Swift, but I am reasonably sure that it was there originally. At the beginning of the second fragment of Section 6 in the "Hints"—that is, in the comparison of the "Persons" (Temple and Wotton) by whom Ancients and Moderns may be judged—appear some sarcastic concluding lines to a passage now missing. They are about Wotton's name and how he should call it in England—not by the standard English form, but by a foreign version:

> . . . when He was in Italy, was called Wottoni, therefore, He should be called so in England; And I advise Him, that it should be Wottoni in His next Edition.
> ("Hints," p. 15, preceding rest of Temple-Wotton comparison)

This is a retort to Wotton's reasoning on "Delphos" and Delphi—that in English one should invariably use the standard nominative form of a foreign-language place name, rather than a form with the inflection (accusative, dative, or whatever) proper to the original language. (In Latin, *Delphos* is the accusative of *Delphi*.) In his first essay *Upon Ancient and Modern Learning* Temple had said that Thales and Pythagoras travelled "to Delphos." "He might as well have said, that they travelled to *Aegyptum*, and *Phoeniciam*, and *Cretam*," remarked Wotton: "It should be printed therefore, in his next Edition, to *Phoenicia*, and *Delphi*: For the English use the Nominative Case of old Names, when they express them in their Mother Tongue." Wotton's dry comment on "Delphos" clearly accounts for Temple's on "Wottoni," but what are they doing in the midst of Temple's comparison of himself and Wotton as Ancient and Modern? I suspect that Temple had been contrasting his own good judgment and taste in learning, which help the reader savor the best in the ancients, with Wotton's tasteless quibbling pedantry, which only knows how to tear down. Compare Temple's comments on the Moderns' classical criticism, quoted in chapter 3.

Temple may have found Wotton's comments especially galling because the substitution of "Delphos" for Delphi looks less like a case of following English usage (then variable) than like a simple blunder, produced by analogy from other Greek place names (Naxos, Argos, Lemnos, etc.) and by a limited background in Greek language and literature. As one of his original references to "Delphos" makes clear (the wise Greeks went "to Aegypt, *Phoenicia,* Crete, and *Delphos*") Temple was not trying to use the Latin accusative of *Delphi,* but instead was trying to reproduce what he imagined to be the proper nominative singular—for a place which, like Athens *(Athenae,* Ἀθηναι*),* actually takes a plural noun *(Delphi,* Δελφοι*).* Temple may also have confused Apollo's shrine at Delphi, on the mainland, with Apollo's shrine at Delos, the holy isle of the god's birth, much as Shakespeare apparently had when speaking of the "isle" of "Delphos" in *The Winter's Tale,* iii, i, 1–3 & ii, iii, 192–96. Whatever the case, the politest way of dealing with blunders is to ignore them, not single them out as Wotton did, under the solemn pretense that they are errors proceeding from an excess of learning. Some such reflection, in Temple, may partly account for his peevishness in comparing the celebrated Sir William Temple, denizen of the great world, with that poor, rude, and obscure "Sciolist," Wotton.

Probably thanks to Temple, the question of "Delphos" was not allowed to die. Temple suppressed the "Delphos" passage in the essay expanded from his "Hints," but after 1698 he had no reason to retain it. Young Charles Boyle conveniently made the point for him, in a digression in *Dr. Bentley's Dissertations on the Epistles of Phalaris, And the Fables of Aesop, Examin'd . . .* (London: for Tho. Bennet, 1698), pp. 96–97. Where Temple cites "the force and authority of common use in all languages," Boyle likewise argues that "what was according to Propriety, and the receiv'd Use of a Tongue, could not be against Grammar," and where Temple speaks ironically of "the desperate fault" which Wotton charges him with, Boyle ironically calls it "A Capital Mistake, and worthy to be chastis'd by the Acute Pen of Mr. Wotton." Their basic argument is the same: that in English "the most polisht writers" (says Temple), or "all the finest Writers" and "best Judges" (says Boyle), use "Delphos" rather than Delphi. Very likely Boyle saw Temple's full draft "Hints" sometime before he published his book in early 1698, and so was able to expand and incorporate the point (much as Mr. H. was earlier supposed to incorporate Temple's "Hints") in his own book against Bentley. (For the publication date of Boyle's book, and for Boyle's ties with Temple, see Arber, *Term Catalogues,* iii, 60, and chapter 3).

There is also a hint of Temple in Boyle's misleading quotation (practically a misquotation) from Wotton's *Reflections.* According to Boyle, the pedantic and ill-mannered Wotton wrote "that *He* [Temple], *of all men, ought not to have arraign'd the Modern Ignorance in Grammar, who puts* Delphos *for* Delphi, *every where in his Essays.*" Wotton actually said nothing of the kind, though some such inference may reasonably be made there. At any event Boyle was ill advised to take up the cudgels for Temple. In the preface to his expanded *Dissertation Upon the Epistles of Phalaris. With An Answer to the Objections of the Honourable Charles Boyle, Esquire* (London: by J.H. for Henry Mortlock and John Hartley, 1699), pp. xc–xciii, Bentley made a crushing retort to Boyle's argument for "Delphos"— "an absurd usage," he says, and indefensible even if "Delphos" were the standard form used in English, as several equally garbled place names had been in Elizabethan times. In Wotton's *Defense* of his *Reflections upon Ancient and Modern Learning,* published in the *Reflections'* 3rd edition, pp. 482–83, Wotton in turn attacks Boyle's argument and adds to Bentley's case. Boyle had found five genteel writers, including Dryden, who had called Delphi "Delphos," and Wotton cites a number of equally genteel writers who used the correct form, including the reverend gentleman (Thomas Gale, Dean of York) to whom Boyle had paid public tribute for teaching him everything he knew. Once in the *Tale* Swift loyally calls Delphi "Delphos" (p. 161 & n.) but elsewhere, instead of associating the Delphic rites with the ancients' admirable scientific expertise (as Temple had), he associates them with the frenzies of the Modern Aeolists (pp. 156–57 & nn.).

Index

Individual works by Swift and Temple are indexed under their titles, or in the case of letters under the correspondent addressed.